Structure and Direction in Thinking

Structure and Direction in Thinking

D. E. Berlyne

Professor of Psychology
University of Toronto

John Wiley & Sons, Inc., New York · London · Sydney

Library of Congress Catalog Card Number: 65-12720
Printed in the United States of America

Preface

THE KIND OF BOOK that every psychologist worth his salt would most like to write is the kind that introduces new theoretical concepts, formulates rigorous hypotheses using these concepts, describes crucial experiments designed to test these hypotheses, and tabulates findings that confirm the hypotheses beyond reasonable doubt. This is not that kind of book. All these steps are needed if science is to advance. But there must often be a sizable lapse of time before each can be followed by the next, and excessive haste may be dangerous.

This book concentrates on the first of these steps, the introduction of a theoretical language—a system of concepts—that may enable the similarities and differences between thought processes and other forms of behavior to come into view. Hypotheses formulated in terms of these concepts are considered, and relevant experimental evidence is cited when available. There are, however, points at which a great deal of further work will have to be done before the conceptualization can engender fruitful hypotheses and before ways of collecting fruitful data can be devised.

The history of science suggests, first, that what promotes progress more effectively than anything else is not actually the discovery of the right answers but rather the discovery of the right questions. Once the right questions have been raised, the right answers are generally found before long. Second, scientists have usually come to raise the right questions through noting similarities or differences between phenomena that others had up till then either overlooked or thought nothing of. Third, there is plenty of evidence that what similarities and differences among phenomena are taken into account in our overt behavior and in our thinking depends chiefly on the linguistic devices that we use in talking about the phenomena. These are the considerations that justify a high priority for the task of fashioning an integrative conceptualization.

Some psychologists will sympathize with the primary aims of this book and will find an attempt to contribute to them of interest. They are the ones to whom the book is addressed, in the hope that they will

v

devote some attention to the problems discussed in it and be led to improve on the solutions suggested here. There will be other psychologists who can see no point in the enterprise at all and who have no use for a book of this nature. They may care to listen in, but it would be as unseemly for them to kibitz as it would be for a wire tapper or an eavesdropper.

The book is designed to have some usefulness as a text for advanced students. Its primary objectives can appropriately be combined with that of introducing the problems of thinking to those who are being confronted with them for the first time. Nevertheless, the book is not intended as the sort of text in which an effort is made to cover all the literature that might possibly be considered pertinent. It reviews an extensive body of research, including some that is not widely known among Anglo-American psychologists. Yet much of the literature on "cognition," "verbal behavior," "problem solving," and "concept formation" that is commonly cited when thinking is discussed is deliberately omitted. This is because it seems to have little bearing on the problems with which the book is concerned and which are, I submit, the ones that need to be taken up at this juncture if we are to make progress in the investigation of thinking.

The book grew, in the first place, out of a year spent at the Centre International d'Epistémologie Génétique, University of Geneva, in 1958–1959. I had for a number of years been interested in the relations between intellectual processes and the simpler psychological processes that behavior theorists had been investigating intensively. Piaget's writings seemed to be a storehouse of suggestive but elusive hints. The year spent in Geneva provided an opportunity to try to work out what Piaget is telling us in terms to which English-speaking psychologists are accustomed and, above all, what he is telling us that we ought to listen to—what modifications in the prevailing behavior-theoretic conceptions of thinking are called for in the light of his work. Frequent discussions with Piaget and with other participants in the work of the Center, especially with Dr. S. Papert, proved extremely helpful. A preliminary version of the conclusions to which I was led, with special reference to the mathematical operations that formed the Center's principal focus of concentration for that year, was published in the *Etudes d'Epistémologie Génétique* (Berlyne, 1960b).

The next year, 1959–1960, was spent as a visiting scientist in the Laboratory of Psychology, National Institute of Mental Health, in Bethesda, Maryland. There, I was one of a small group, whose other active members were Dr. Morris B. Parloff and Dr. Albert J. Caron, that met weekly to discuss "creativity." The group decided quite early that, before creative thinking could be understood, the mechanisms of thought processes in general needed to be examined. So the ideas that had begun to take shape in Geneva were further crystallized at these meetings.

A study of Russian literature on thinking and cognate matters revealed a remarkable convergence with some of Piaget's ideas, on the one hand, and some additional new directions of inquiry, on the other. Efforts to become acquainted with Soviet work on this and other topics were greatly aided by a visit to the U.S.S.R. that I made in 1961 with the help of a research grant from the National Institute of Mental Health. I benefited also from becoming acquainted with another powerful new approach to thinking, namely that of computer simulation, when I attended the Social Science Research Council's Summer Institute on "Simulation of Cognitive Processes" in Santa Monica, California, in 1958.

This book was written while I was a member of the Psychology Departments of Boston University and the University of Toronto. Its preparation and some of the research reported in it were facilitated by a grant-in-aid for research in the behavioral sciences from the Ford Foundation and by research grants M-4495 and MH-06324 from the National Institute of Mental Health, U.S. Public Health Service.

As well as to the persons mentioned above, with whom invaluable discussions were held, I am indebted to Mrs. J. Witting, to Mrs. E. Winch, and to Mrs. M. Lions, who coped with the arduous task of transcribing the manuscript, to Miss I. Koenig and Mr. T. Hirota, who assisted in the compilation of the bibliography, and to Mrs. R. Niedra, who prepared the figures. Finally, thanks are due to the authors and publishers who gave permission for quotations and figures to be reproduced.

D. E. BERLYNE

Toronto, 1964

Contents

Contrary statements, opinions or appearances, operate on the mind as a pain-
ful jar, and stimulate a corresponding desire for a reconciliation. . . . The
above, however, is not the only way that contradiction wounds our sensibili-
ties. A far more operative evil is that bound up with practical consequences.
. . . The obligation to act, with the inability to decide, causes a torment of
opposing volitions, than which in extreme cases no agony can be more acute
or heart-rending.

A. Bain: *The Emotions and the Will*

Das Denken selbst, das frei sich dünkt vor allen,
Ist eigner Nötigung zu Dienst verfallen.
Hat sich der Grund gestellt, so folgt die Folge,
Und zwei zu zwei ist minder nicht noch mehr
Als vier, ob fünf dir auch willkommner wär'.

F. Grillparzer: *Libussa*

. . . instruction, then, in subject-matter that does not fit into any problem
already stirring in the subject's own experience, or that is not presented in
such a way as to arouse a problem is worse than useless for educational pur-
poses.

J. Dewey: *Democracy and Education*

Chapter 1

Introduction: a neoassociationist
approach

INTEREST IN INTELLECTUAL PROCESSES, including thinking, is currently
on the rise in all three of the psychologically most productive parts
of the world. There appear, however, to be somewhat different reasons for this trend in different groups of countries.

English-Language Psychology

In English-speaking countries, four factors seem to be at work.

1. The efforts to build up systematic behavior theories that grew
out of the behaviorist and neobehaviorist movements in psychology
and out of the logical-empiricist movement in philosophy of science
have now been going on for several decades. It is widely (although
certainly not universally) felt that these efforts have now advanced
to a point where the most complex and uniquely human kinds of
behavior can profitably be brought within their scope.

2. The advent of electronic computers, capable of replicating, and
even of surpassing, many of the products of the human intellect, has
made it necessary to consider the engineering and information-processing aspects of thinking. This not only provides instructive new
ways of analyzing human thinking; it also provides a new research
tool, since the implications of any new conceptualization of thinking
that is proposed can be checked by programming computers to carry
out the corresponding operations and then noting the outcome.

3. The current social, economic, and even political importance of
technological progress has focused attention on the need to identify,
and make the most efficient use of, creative talent. This aim can
hardly be realized without intensive research on how human intellectual processes work and, in particular, on the conditions in which
they give rise to the achievements that we evaluate as creative.

4. The science of linguistics, having come of age, has joined with psychology to produce the borderline discipline of psycholinguistics. While most attention has naturally been paid to the communicative functions of language, through which human beings influence one another's behavior, there is a growing recognition that these should be related to its representational functions, through which human beings regulate their own behavior.

French-Language Psychology

In French-speaking countries, the outstanding innovator, as far as psychology is concerned, has been Piaget. In the 1930's, he embarked on a chronological study of the perceptual and intellectual development of the human child from birth on. The project was completed in the middle 1950's, when it reached the early adolescent period. This, according to Piaget, is when the logical structures that make the most advanced intellectual accomplishments possible are acquired. Piaget's work has been a treasury of information for the pure and applied child psychologist, but its guiding aim was to promote the understanding of adult psychological functions by showing the course of development out of which they have grown. Having now charted this course of development from beginning to end, Piaget and those influenced by him feel in a position to survey perception and thinking as a whole and to consider the general problems of knowledge-gathering processes—"genetic epistemology," to use a term that Piaget has taken over from J. M. Baldwin—with the confidence that comes from having an abundant stock of pertinent data.

Russian-Language Psychology

In the U.S.S.R., intellectual and linguistic functions, including thinking, have long formed a major subject matter for research. This research is, however, being pursued with more zeal than ever at the present time. There seem to be two principal reasons for this concentration.

1. In Soviet psychology, pure research is, under the influence of Marxist philosophy, generally carried out, as a matter of principle, in close conjunction with applied research. The most prominent individuals in pure psychology have, in fact, also done important work on practical psychological problems, especially on those relating to educational practice and to organic deficiencies, such as brain damage and mental retardation. These interests have necessitated in-

tensive study, on the one hand, of the processes by which school children absorb, retain, and understand what they are taught and, on the other hand, of the nature of the intellectual impairments that result from organic disorders and of ways in which they can be remedied or compensated (see Simon and Simon, 1963).

2. Soviet psychologists and "physiologists of higher nervous activity" (whose province would be counted as part of psychology in the West) regard the continuation and extension of Pavlov's (1927, 1928) work on conditioned reflexes as one of their prime responsibilities. In the 1920's, an active group headed by Ivanov-Smolenski (1934, 1951, 1956, 1963) began to investigate conditioning in children, with particular emphasis on the relations between the phenomena that Pavlov had demonstrated in the dog and human intellectual functions, dependent on language and reasoning.

Toward the end of his life, Pavlov became impressed with the vital role of what he called the "second signal system" in human behavior. This consists of those "temporary connections" (that is, associations or habits) that involve speech and response to words. Verbal stimuli were described as "signals of signals," since they stand for nonverbal conditioned stimuli, which signal events of biological importance and participate in the conditioned reflexes belonging to the "first signal system."

Without doubting that the principles derived from the study of conditioned reflexes in dogs hold for human behavior also (as indeed countless experiments before and since have abundantly shown), Pavlov felt that the interaction between these principles and those that govern the second signal system must make for some sharp differences between human beings and infrahuman animals. His successors have therefore given a high priority to the investigation of intellectual, and especially linguistic, processes as the key to the ways in which conditioned responses are acquired and utilized by human beings.

Shortcomings of English-Language Work on Thinking

These three bodies of work on thinking, carried out in widely separated countries and guided by different traditions, have shown some remarkable parallels and convergences. Owing to defective communication, these have not been exploited as fully as they might have been, but this is gradually being rectified.

The English-language current has surpassed the other two in sheer volume as well as in methodological sophistication.   It has, nevertheless, had a number of serious limitations.   The value of what it has achieved is not to be denied or belittled, but a look at some of the ideas and data to be found in the writings of Piaget and the Russians may provide some fresh slants that will eventually help us to overcome these limitations.

Three deficiencies in particular are worth mentioning.

1. Insufficient attention has been paid to the motivational factors in thinking.   This is largely because of the ease with which artificial motives can be induced in human subjects with sufficient strength for purposes of an experiment.   To present a human subject with a problem and to ask him to attempt a solution is often all that is required, although the procedure may be more effective if praise or heightened self-esteem or some token of merit is made to depend on a successful outcome.

A high proportion of everyday thinking is, no doubt, prompted by comparable social pressures.   But we need to know what factors determine when thinking will occur spontaneously and at what targets it will be aimed.   Little or no research has been devoted directly and intensively to these factors, but some hints may be found among the data and theoretical ideas that come out of work on human and animal exploratory behavior.

2. There has been an almost exclusive concentration on difficult and creative intellectual exploits to the neglect of more humdrum and prosaic forms of thinking.   To use a distinction introduced by Selz (1922), which will be examined more closely in Chapter 12, "productive thinking," which generates genuinely new knowledge and solutions to problems, has overshadowed "reproductive thinking" or thinking that simply applies established knowledge and sets established routines in motion.

There have, of course, been plenty of studies of meaningful remembering, but studies of reproductive processes that are a few degrees less mechanical than straightforward recall have been extremely scanty.   We may consider, for example, the procedures by which an engineer works out the strains in a structure of a kind that he has frequently had to deal with and those by which a person who is thoroughly conversant with the layout of a city works out the quickest route to a certain point.   Provided that they have undergone the requisite learning processes, they are not doing anything that would be considered hard or inventive.   Nevertheless, the engineer may never have had occasion to appraise that particular structure before, and the city dweller may never have had to travel to that particular point from his present location. So they cannot solve their problems by merely calling to mind what they did to solve identical problems in the past.

We must surely understand these kinds of thinking and those that a waitress uses to tot up a bill or that a lawyer uses to decide whether a certain statute applies to a case presenting no unusual difficulties, before we can understand the thinking that produces technological inventions, mathematical discoveries, or works of art. Creative thinking usually begins by rehearsing familiar thought sequences, and it has to draw on them continually throughout its course. Furthermore, once productive thinking has achieved its goals, its products often form the content of reproductive thinking in future.

Piaget's monumental studies of the development of thinking have focused almost entirely on the reproductive processes that form the staples of logic, mathematics, and science. He has documented the ways in which every normal child builds up his knowledge structures and abandons earlier and less effective ways of thinking for more mature ones. But he has had very little to say about the ways in which knowledge structures are reorganized in the face of unprecedented problems and in which new insights are generated. A confrontation of theoretical ideas and empirical data supplied by Piaget with those supplied by the English-language tradition (and the earlier German-language tradition with which it has merged) should be a step toward a more balanced theory of thinking in all its aspects. This will, in fact, be one of the major objectives of this book.

3. Most treatments of thinking have been unduly isolated from the study of simpler forms of behavior. Quite a high proportion of the studies that are relevant have been contributed by psychologists studying intelligence testing and, more generally, individual differences in intellectual abilities. There has certainly not been nearly so much contact as there should be between their work and the experimental psychology of thinking or of simpler behavior.

The sharp differences between human thinking and any other process that occur in the animal kingdom are undeniable, but at the same time we must remember that thinking is carried out with the same nervous system that is used for humbler adaptive functions. And the processes that make up thinking must have grown out of more primitive capacities, both in the history of the species and in the history of the individual. There must therefore be some common principles and continuities tying together all behavior from the most automatic reflexes to the subtlest intellectual feats, and we can hardly claim to understand thinking until these links have been laid bare. This does not mean slurring over differences and exaggerating similarities; it means, in fact, discovering how differences result from similarities.

What this means can, in fact, be seen most clearly by considering familiar illustrations from the natural sciences. The heavier elements, such as uranium, have certain properties that distinguish them markedly from the normal forms of the lighter elements, such as hydrogen. The heavier elements are, for example, radioactive and fissionable. Twentieth-century physics has shown, however, that the atoms of all elements have structures that are alike in many essential respects and are subject to the same laws of quantum mechanics, etc. The atoms of the heaviest elements differ from others in containing many more particles in their nuclei and many more planetary electrons. Once this had become clear, it was understood that the peculiarities of uranium occur not because the uranium atom obeys different laws but precisely because it obeys the same general laws as the hydrogen atom. These laws imply that an atom that exceeds a certain size and complexity must necessarily have the kind of instability that gives rise to radioactivity and fissionability and that an atom like the commonest kind of hydrogen atom, consisting simply of one proton and one electron, will not behave in the same way.

Similarly, the chemical structure and behavior of the proteins and nucleic acids that make up a large part of living tissue are being unraveled. The molecules of these substances are vastly more complex than those of simple inorganic compounds, consisting as they do of long chains of thousands or even millions of atoms. Yet they possess many characteristics that are shared by all chemical compounds and obey the same basic laws of chemistry. The rapid progress that is currently taking place in biochemistry is progressively corroborating the view that the laws of chemistry governing the interactions of organic matter must necessarily produce the unique attributes of animals and plants when applied to compounds of sufficient intricacy.

So, to return to thinking, there must be psychological, physiological, and ultimately physicochemical laws whose action is manifest throughout the spectrum of behavior from the crudest to the loftiest. We shall, no doubt, eventually understand how a nervous system evolving in certain directions must sooner or later reach a level at which symbolic capacities come into existence and how symbolic capacities, having advanced to a particular stage, must give rise to thinking. But thinking must be, at least in part, a product of laws that apply equally well to nonsymbolic behavior. It is inconceivable that physicists would know what they now know about the uranium atom or that biochemists would know what they now know about protein molecules if they had, from the start, confined their attention to uranium and to proteins.

With regard to the desirability of relating thinking to what is known about simpler kinds of behavior, Soviet work will repay a periodic glance. Soviet investigators of intellectual processes are wont to couch their theoretical discussions in a language that maintains close touch with studies of elementary conditioning phenomena. Their experimental techniques are often designed to bring out the convergences and divergences between the higher and lower reaches of behavior. Herein lies a source of strengths and of weaknesses. If we try to put together what Soviet and Western work with relevance to thinking have yielded, we may be able to benefit from the former while steering clear of the latter.

Integrative Neoassociationism

The approach adopted in this book is of the kind usually identified with the term "stimulus-response (S-R) behavior theory." This term is, however, unfortunate in many respects. It is doubtful whether the particular words "stimulus" and "response" are of more importance to this approach than to others with which it is contrasted or even whether they are indispensable to it at all. A better term, it would seem, is "neoassociationist" behavior theory.

"S-R theory" has both its fervent opponents and its staunch devotees, but there is no unanimity on what it comprises. It is generally agreed that the term covers the well-authenticated principles that have emerged from Pavlov's experiments on classical conditioning and Skinner's experiments on instrumental conditioning, as well as the higher-level, and thus more precarious, generalizations about learning put forward by Hull and those who came under his influence. In the absence of a coherent body of doctrine that would unite all S-R or neoassociationist psychologists, it is better to think of the approach as one characterized rather by the kinds of questions it asks than by the kinds of answers that it gives.

Since misgivings about "S-R psychology" are so widespread (although they seem often to be directed at earlier phases of this current rather than at a true picture of what its present-day exponents believe and actually do), it seems best to point out some of the things that are not entailed by our neoassociationist approach before proceeding to a positive characterization of it.

Criticisms of S-R Psychology

1. STIMULI AND RESPONSES. The dominant characteristic of "S-R psychology," and the one from which this name derives, is its analysis of behavior in terms of "bonds," "connections," or "associations" between stimuli and responses. This kind of analysis has been under continual attack for many years and from three principal directions.

First, the essential ambiguity of the words "stimulus" and "response" and the numerous discrepant senses in which they are used have often been pointed out. Contemporary S-R psychology concerns itself with associations not between single stimuli and single responses (whatever those would be!) but between classes of stimulus situations and classes of behavior. A stimulus situation consists of the totality of excitation received by an organism's receptors simultaneously, and the members of a class of stimulus situations may be held together by any feature that distinguishes them from nonmembers. Such a feature may be the presence of a stimulus object with specifiable properties, the existence of a particular pattern or network of relations somewhere within it, or the excitation of a particular receptor.

Furthermore, there is now plenty of evidence that the effects on behavior of a stimulus situation belonging to a certain class depend on what other kinds of stimulus situation might have occurred instead and how probable each of them was. This means that each distinguishable feature of a stimulus situation is a selection from a set of alternatives (Bresson, 1958; Broadbent, 1958) and thus bears a certain charge of information. (See Chapter 2.) A stimulus situation may, in fact, be thought of as a collection of items of information, any single one of which, or any combination of which, may be associated with a particular type of behavior. Contemporary S-R psychology must therefore make full use of the resources of information theory.

Nevertheless, it is often convenient to speak of associations between "responses" (that is, kinds of responses) and "stimulus conditions" or "stimuli," and we shall occasionally adopt this practice. These are, however, merely abbreviations. By a "stimulus condition," we mean a class of stimulus situations with some distinguishable property in common. We shall, on the other hand, distinguish "responses" or "response classes" in accordance with what are often called "topographical" criteria, that is, in terms of physically definable changes in the organism's state. It is frequently recommended that all bodily

movements that exert a common effect on the external environment
should be regarded as instances of one "response." This usage seems
inadvisable, however, since we shall need to be able to distinguish
alternative ways of achieving a particular effect.

A second objection is that S-R psychology gives a misleading picture of learning since, when a certain response pattern has been reinforced in a certain stimulus situation, what results is not merely an association between stimulus features that were then present and features of the response that was then performed. This learning experience will cause many different kinds of behavior to be performed
in many different kinds of stimulus situation. S-R psychology has,
however, never implied otherwise since, even in its early days, it recognized various forms of association by similarity or "generalization,"
thanks to which a particular learning experience can give rise to a
variety of behavior patterns in a variety of contexts.

Third, it has long been objected, but with particular force of late,
that only a small number of the features or elements of a stimulus
situation actually affect behavior, namely those that receive attention.
Behavior is therefore not just an outcome of stimuli passively received but the sequel to an active process that selectively focuses on
portions of the stimulation coming in from the environment and ex-
tracts the information that they contain.

This failure to take account of attentive and stimulus-seeking activities has long been a shortcoming of S-R psychology, encouraged
by the simplified experimental situations from which it has drawn
most of its data. They have, however, been equally overlooked by
psychology in general, and several lines of recent research are hastening to make up this deficiency (see Berlyne, 1960a) and show promise of doing so without undermining the whole S-R edifice.

2. REFLEX-ARC THEORY. In its early days, S-R psychology was
closely connected with a certain kind of neurophysiological theory,
namely that based on the notion of a reflex arc. Once it was established that most innate reflexes depend on the conduction of excitation from a set of receptors to a set of effectors through a chain of
neurons, it was only natural to suppose that the higher forms of behavior work in the same way, except that the higher levels of the
central nervous system, including the cerebral cortex, are involved
and that the reflex arcs that produce them must comprise many more
neurons than the three that make up the typical spinal reflex arc. It
was thus assumed that all stimulus-response associations correspond
to reflex arcs.

By now, it is clear that the neural structures that underlie complex behavior do not consist of extra-long one-way strings of neurons. They evidently take on infinitely more varied and intricate forms, including two-way connections, reverberating loops, convergences and divergences. Nevertheless, the function of neural tissue seems still, at all levels, to consist in transmitting excitation from one point to another and ultimately from receptor to effector.

In the 1930's and 1940's, it was customary for S-R psychologists to dissociate themselves entirely from the reflex arc and from any other neurophysiological view. They were anxious to escape involvement in the obloquy that reflex-arc conceptions of brain functioning have often suffered and, in any case, they felt that intimacy with neurophysiology had little positive to offer in exchange for this guilt by association. More recently, neurophysiology has started to make great strides, which no psychologist can afford to leave out of account, but it remains true that the neoassociationist approach implies no prior commitment to any neurophysiological theory.

The notion of an S-R association is, at bottom, a statistical one. It means simply that a particular class of behavior is more likely to occur in the presence of a stimulus situation of a particular class than in the presence of a stimulus situation selected at random.* Statisticians have, in fact, long used the word "association" in precisely this sense (cf. Yule and Kendall, 1947, Ch. 3).

That stimulus-response associations in this sense exist can hardly be denied. If they did not, there would be no point in having sense organs, as information received from the environment would then have no influence over behavior.

To illustrate current disparagement of S-R psychology, let us consider a question put a little belligerently by Miller, Galanter, and Pribram (1960, p. 22): "Has the reflex concept been so tremendously helpful that behaviorists could not afford to give it up, even if its

---

* The notion of a "stimulus-response association" is commonly extended to include subliminal associations. Sometimes, a certain response is not actually evoked by a stimulus situation of a particular class more frequently than by a randomly selected stimulus selection. Nevertheless, if fewer learning trials are needed to establish a manifest association between the response and the stimulus situation than to establish one between the response and a randomly selected stimulus situation, we say that a weak association must already have existed. We assume that the neural processes that are responsible for stimulus-response association have to reach a "behavioral threshold" before associations become manifest and that they may exist with below-threshold intensities.

biological basis were demolished?" The answer surely depends on what, of all the possible things that might be meant, is meant by "the reflex concept."

The word "reflex" is now virtually never used by Western psychologists except to denote the rigid, unlearned behavior patterns that make up a relatively small part of higher mammalian behavior (although there are some hundreds of them in man). Even Skinner who, as these authors note, used to advocate its application to all behavior (cf. 1931, 1938, pp. 20–21) came later (for example, 1953) to exclude most human behavior from its denotation. Russian psychologists use the word "reflex" extensively, but they insist on distinguishing their "reflexive (*reflektorny*)" point of view from "stimulus-response psychology," having a no less astigmatic and obsolete view of the latter than many of their Western colleagues. For them, however, a "reflex" is a stimulus-response association that is highly susceptible to modification by central processes, in accordance with the tradition launched by Sechenov and Pavlov.

If by "the reflex concept" is meant the belief that behavior consists of one-to-one correspondences between stimuli and responses or the belief that the nervous system works entirely through isolated one-way reflex arcs, it would be extremely difficult to find a contemporary defender of either of these beliefs.

If, on the other hand, the "reflex concept" means the concept of a stimulus-response association in the sense that we have outlined, then it must be pointed out (*a*) that the oldest and best established law in psychology is that responses vary with stimulus conditions, and (*b*) that stimulus-response associations constitute a large part of the phenomena that psychology has to explain. A scientific discipline might, one would imagine, be worse off if it threw out its best established law and disowned a large part of its subject matter.

3. THE "EMPTY" ORGANISM. S-R psychology adopts what has come to be called the "black-box" view of the behaving organism. We can observe what goes into the organism and what comes out of it at the other end, but we are unable to observe the processes within the organism that cause particular outputs to follow particular inputs. The only knowledge we can have of how the "black box" works must come from noting the kinds of inputs and the kinds of outputs that occur and the associations between them.

Now, S-R psychologists are often belabored from both sides at once for the manner in which they approach the black-box problem.

On the one side, there are those who cannot content themselves with a psychology that confines itself to input-output relations. They claim either that this kind of conceptualization is far too simple to have any prospect of accomplishing the major tasks of psychology or that they will not be understanding behavior until they have been told what internal "mechanisms" or "structures" are responsible for it. For whatever reason, they object to the "fiction" of an "empty organism."

Those who take this position often feel that it is possible and desirable to gain access to the inner workings of the black box. Some favor calling upon the human subject to describe processes that happen within his awareness between the registering of the stimulus situation and the performance of the response. Others point to the possibility of recording physiological processes that are not detectable without special instrumentation, for example, muscular action potentials, electrical activity in the brain, and processes dependent on the autonomic nervous system.

Nevertheless, it is a misunderstanding to regard either of these procedures as a means of looking inside the black box. By definition, what is inside the black box is unobservable. Verbal reports and psychophysiological measurements simply add to the outputs that must be taken into account. This can, of course, be an important advantage, since the more numerous the input and output events that we aim to represent in a theoretical model, the narrower the range of models that merit consideration and the greater the probable validity of a model that seems to fulfill the requirements.

Most S-R behavior theorists make considerable reference to "intervening variables" and "states" of the organism. The "state" of a system (for example, an organism) is defined by specifying the values of the variables that make up the system (Ashby, 1952). The values to be assigned to some variables can be directly determined by observing changes in the organism's outward appearance or in some recording device with which the organism is connected. At other times, the appearance of the organism remains unaltered, but there is a change in some variable that cannot be observed from without. Such a variable is called an "intervening variable" or "latent variable." A class of states having a particular value of a particular intervening variable in common corresponds to what, in philosophy-of-science terminology, is called a "disposition" or "dispositional concept" (Carnap, 1936–1937). Since the special usage that the word "disposition" has had in the psychology of personality may lead to confusion, we shall instead use the term "condition." * We shall, where necessary, use the word "internal" to differentiate conditions characterized by values of intervening variables from "external" conditions, characterized by particular values of directly observable variables and representing properties either of the organism or of objects in the external environment.

It is generally impossible to tell from outward view whether an organism is in a certain internal condition (for example, in a certain mood, having a certain degree of hunger, possessing a certain skill, or entertaining a certain thought). Nevertheless, an organism in such a condition differs from one not in it because there are circumstances in which the two would behave differently. The only way to detect an internal condition is to apply an appropriate (external) "test condition" and see whether a corresponding (external) "truth condition" is realized.

Intervening variables are thus convenient and abbreviated ways of referring to input-output relations that could, in principle, be expressed without them, although at the cost of considerable, and often prohibitive, awkwardness. Their use is, however, quite legitimate and consistent with the aims of experimental science, provided that their connections with directly observable stimulus and response variables are adequately defined.

Although they do not go far enough to suit some adversaries of the "empty organism," S-R psychologists who make use of intervening variables frequently come in for censure on the other side from advocates of a more radical and ascetic conception of the black box. These critics (for example, Skinner, 1950) decry intervening variables on the grounds that they are not observable entities and that they mean a surrender to the weak-mindedness that goes together with a partiality for "explanatory fictions."

Nevertheless, other branches of science have not been able to refrain from using concepts equivalent to intervening variables or from referring to entities whose existence and nature are not open to immediate inspection but must be inferred from experimental data. Physicists, for example, carry out experimental procedures that produce trails in spark chambers or bubble chambers or cloud chambers, and they attribute the form taken by these to movements and colli-

---

* Technically, a "state" is represented by a *vector* or *n-tuple*, that is, a string of numbers denoting the values assumed by a succession of variables. A "condition" corresponds to a *cylinder set*, that is, a set of vectors or n-tuples having the same number in a particular location.

sions of particles. It would be theoretically possible for them to frame laws predicting what trails will follow from what experimental treatments without mention of atoms and subatomic particles, but it would clearly be impracticable and preposterous to insist on doing so. To try to relate, say, the writing behavior of a mathematician to the printed form of a problem presented to him, without referring to unobservable events within him, would be an equally patent absurdity.

Characteristics of a Neoassociationist Approach

We can now come to the positive characteristics that distinguish a neoassociationist approach.

1. PRIMACY OF S-R ASSOCIATIONS. The S-R psychologist keeps the elucidation of input-output relations or S-R associations constantly in view as his primary aim. He may make copious use of intervening variables and refer to hypothetical processes within the organism, but he regards these as devices for handling networks of input-output relations that would otherwise be intractable. When he makes statements that do not refer explicitly to S-R associations, he is prepared to specify their implications in terms of observable behavior. In the early stages of his research, he may not be able to make these implications very precise, but he works toward the gradual elimination of the imprecision.

It is true that most psychologists today would accept the study of behavior and its relations to stimulus conditions, among other variables, as their primary function. Few are preponderantly concerned with analyzing consciousness, like the introspective experimental psychologists of fifty years ago, and virtually none would subscribe to the view of Descartes and of the contemporary man in the street that physical stimuli bring about physical responses through the mediation of conscious mental events. Despite this, many psychologists, including some who specialize in thinking, fail to make clear to what extent they are endeavoring to explain behavior and how far they are endeavoring to explain conscious experience. Both of these may be legitimate pursuits, but it is important not to confuse the two.

2. INSISTENCE ON GENETIC EXPLANATIONS. The neoassociationist is unable to feel content with a description of an organism's present behavior or characteristics, no matter how full the description may be and how successful in generating valid predictions. He does not regard his understanding of behavior as complete until he knows how the organism came to behave as it does.

This means adopting what is often called a "genetic" point of view, using the term in a sense that is not specifically connected with the science of heredity. It means tracing the course of development from which present behavior sprang, both phylogenetically and ontogenetically. It means relating present processes, in so far as they depend on inherited features of bodily structure, to evolution, analyzing the biological advantages that caused the relevant hereditary factors to become established as part of the common endowment of the species. It means tracing the development of the process through the life history of the individual, which necessitates studying the ways in which maturation and, above all, learning have contributed to its present character.

Of late, it has often been asserted that to explain behavior means to have something in the nature of a computer program or a mathematical model, enabling one to predict with completeness and exactitude the behavior that would result from any conceivable configuration of antecedent conditions. It seems at times to be felt that, if the input-output relations of behavior were adequately mirrored by such a program or model, there would be nothing further in the way of explanation or understanding that could be sought. The neoassociationist dissents emphatically from this position. He would still want to know why and through what course of development the organism came to behave in conformity with this particular program or this particular model.

3. RELATION OF COMPLEX TO SIMPLE. S-R behavior theory was characterized from the start by a dual ambition, most clearly expressed in the work of Hull. The aim was to construct theories generating predictions that would be (a) maximally precise and (b) applicable to as wide a range of behavior as possible. However, if we examine the record of this current, and especially if we consider the life work of Hull, a certain degree of incompatibility between these two aspirations is revealed, at least at the present stage in the history of psychology.

So later theoreticians of behavior (see Berlyne, 1964) have been faced with a choice. Some of them, for example, those who have devoted themselves to mathematical models or to computer-simulation programs, have pursued precision above all else. They have contrived deductive systems that reflect properties of behavior with spectacular accuracy, but this success has been achieved at the cost of confinement to severely circumscribed sets of situations. Others, including those who have been most closely in touch with developments in neurophysiology and those who have been most concerned with motivational problems, have given precedence to seeking principles and concepts that will have the widest possible range of applicability and thus be capable of revealing the interrelations of the most diverse psychological phenomena.

The latter order of priority will characterize this book, whose approach can thus be described as an integrative neoassociationism. Those who concur with it will not be satisfied with a theory that deals with thinking alone, however complete and accurate it may be. They will not consider that the psychology of thinking has fulfilled its task until it has shown how thinking resembles, and how it contrasts with, simpler psychological processes. These will include the spinal-reflex phenomena demonstrated by Sherrington, the classical-conditioned-response phenomena demonstrated by Pavlov, the instrumental-conditioned-response phenomena demonstrated by Skinner, and the instinctive forms of behavior studied by the ethologists.

In aiming at this goal, we must inevitably put up with a great deal of imprecision for a while. It is, however, important not to confuse the imprecision that integrative behavior theory must tolerate with vagueness. The distinction is best understood in terms of information theory. Information, in its technical sense (to be discussed further in Chapter 2), is conveyed by a symbol or a statement that helps to determine which of a number of possible alternative possibilities has been, or will be, realized. From this point of view, imprecision means partial transmission of information, leaving some residual uncertainty. In other words, a theoretical statement that is imprecise leaves us with a number of possibilities from which the actual event is still to be selected. The statement will, however, provide us with some information, so that it will not be worthless, if it either rules out some of the possibilities that had initially to be reckoned with while leaving others still open or if it indicates that some of the possibilities are more probable than others.

The statement "Object A does not cost the same as object B" is thus a highly imprecise statement, although its information content is not nil. It rules out pairs of prices for A and B that are equal, but there are still many pairs of unequal prices that are compatible with it. The statement "A costs more than B" is less imprecise, since it rules out, in addition, pairs of prices in which A costs as much as, or less than, B. The statement "A costs $11.35 and B costs $6.42" is not imprecise at all, since it removes uncertainty completely by excluding all prices except those specified. So, in psychology, we often have to begin by asserting that certain factors will influence certain dependent variables, without being in a position to say what difference they will make. At a later stage, we can state which factors will increase the values of these variables and which will decrease them. Finally, we hope to be able to specify the exact values that the variables will assume when the factors are present. We shall then have arrived at a mathematical model.

A statement such as "Behavior is an expression of ongoing dynamic patterns embedded in the matrix of the total personality" is, on the other hand, vague. It is difficult to see what experimental findings, if any, will be inconsistent with it. In the technical sense, which is the only sense with any relevance for science, it conveys no information at all. So as far as the purposes of science are concerned, it is entirely useless.

4. RECOGNITION OF INTERNAL STIMULI AND RESPONSES. Most present-day psychologists feel obliged to refer, in their theoretical discussions, to processes that are supposed to be going on within the organism. These processes cannot be observed directly, and so their properties must be inferred from outwardly observable events. The different stages that such a process goes through represent different internal conditions; how the subject would react to a particular kind of stimulus situation will vary with the stage that a particular internal process has reached.

The neoassociationist has the idiosyncrasy of referring to the changes that constitute these inferred mediating processes as "responses" and as "stimuli." This is perhaps the most distinctive peculiarity of S-R psychology, responsible for most of the disagreements that have divided it from its competitors.

It is not an empty terminological preference. It carries with it a massive load of working hypotheses. We cannot regard an internal event as a response or as a response-produced stimulus or as both, without provisionally hypothesizing that the principles that govern stimuli (in the strict sense of physical events exciting sense organs) and responses (in the strict sense of muscular and glandular activities) apply also to it. Such hypotheses are, of course, not dogmatic assertions but merely guidelines to direct research and to be retained until shown by experimental data to be untenable.

This is admittedly a debatable feature of neoassociationism, with arguments for and against it. It distinguishes this approach from those of cognitivist theorists (for example, Tolman, 1932; Lewin, 1935; and Miller, Galanter, and Pribram, 1960) who recognize central mediating processes in the form of "cognitions," "expectations," or "images" and assume them to depend on laws that differ from those that determine the occurrence of overt responses. It distinguishes it also from the approaches of those who describe central mediating processes entirely in neurophysiological terms (for example, Hebb, 1949; and many East Europeans) and from those who describe them in ways that emphasize their analogies with computer operations (for example, Newell, Shaw, and Simon, 1958).

How far the concepts introduced by these other approaches are reconcilable with our neoassociationist approach will receive consideration in later chapters. Our approach is, however, characterized by an eagerness (not unconnected with points discussed earlier) to find similarities between the ways in which central mediating processes work and the ways in which observable peripheral stimuli and responses work and to try out hypotheses about central mediating processes suggested by the principles that have been found to govern overt behavior.

The hazards of this predilection are obvious. Some psychologists (for example, Broadbent, 1958) feel uneasy when terms that were introduced to refer to observable events are applied to inferred, inaccessible entities. It may even be considered implausible from the outset that central processes behave just like external stimuli and motor responses. But the guiding assumption is, of course, not that central and peripheral processes conform to identical laws in all respects but that there must be some laws common to them all and that these should be sought at an early stage.

The defense of the practice of classing central events as stimuli and as responses must ultimately rest on how fruitful it is in advancing knowledge. Later chapters will give the reader ample opportunity to pass judgment on its past and future productivity. This productivity is, of course, not simply a matter of how often similarities between central and peripheral processes can be demonstrated. The approach is, if anything, even more productive when it leads us to discover contrasts.

In this book, we shall refer to any change in internal condition, that is, any change in the value of an intervening variable, as an "implicit response" if there is reason to believe that this change can become associated with, and thus subject to evocation by, stimuli in accordance with principles that are known to govern learning. Likewise, we shall refer to such a change as an "internal stimulus" if it can apparently acquire the power to elicit responses, overt or implicit, in accordance with learning principles. If we have no reasons for or against the belief that these conditions are satisfied, we shall feel free to postulate, as a provisional working hypothesis, that they are. Some commentators (cf. Smedslund, quoted by Piaget, 1959) feel that contemporary S-R psychologists give the terms "stimulus" and "response" such broad senses that they mean nothing more than "cause" and "effect"! This is, however, not so. A stimulus is a cause that can acquire causal power, and a response is an effect that can be brought about, through a recognizable learning process.

Thinking, Reasoning, and Symbolic Responses

We must now take some steps toward demarcating the phenomena with which we are going to concern ourselves under the name of "thinking."

Thinking

First, we must note that we are not going to take the whole of thinking as our province. What we are going to examine is *directed thinking*. By thinking, we mean any process that involves a chain (that is, a sequence of two or more members) of symbolic responses. Chains of symbolic responses can take various forms and have various functions. They can, for example, constitute autistic thinking. This is exemplified by daydreaming or by the free association that is demanded in the psychoanalyst's office. It appears to have the function of providing substitute satisfactions through reward value that is transferred from desired situations to representations of these situations. There are also chains of symbolic responses that occur when we recall, for one reason or another, a sequence of past events— "thinking of the days that are no more." Directed thinking is thinking whose function is to convey us to solutions of problems. It consists of the region of overlap between thinking and reasoning.

We are thus obliged to give some account of what we are going to mean by "reasoning" and then of what we are going to mean by "symbolic responses."

Reasoning

For the purposes of present-day psychology, reasoning must be defined as something manifested in behavior rather than as a kind of conscious process: its distinguishing criterion is generally taken to be the formation of an association between a certain class of stimulus situations and a certain class of responses through the joint influence of two or more prior learning experiences.

Hull (1935) spoke of "the assembly of behavior segments in new combinations suitable for problem solution" and Maier and Schneirla (1935) of "combining isolated experiences." Both Hull and Boiko (1959, 1961) have stressed that the emergence of a novel response through reasoning results from the performance and interaction of responses dependent on existing habits. Nevertheless, reasoning may be classed as a form of learning, since it gives rise to new S-R associations. Once a reasoning process has brought about the emergence of a response pattern that solves a problem, the probability of such a response whenever a similar situation is encountered will generally be high.

We must, however, be a little more explicit about what is meant when we say that reasoning makes use of two or more distinct learning experiences or habits. The conditions that must be fulfilled are as follows.

1. An animal organism is exposed to a stimulus situation of a particular class, S_x, and by the end of its encounter with that situation, the association between S_x and a class of responses, R_y, is strengthened (or weakened). R_y may be, and often is, the first member of a whole sequence of responses.

2. The strengthening (or weakening) of the S_x-R_y association is attributable to the organism's possession, in consequence of prior learning, of at least two associations, S_1-R_1 and S_2-R_2. To be more precise, the strengthening (or weakening) is greater than would have resulted from possession of S_1-R_1 or S_2-R_2 alone.

3. Both S_1-R_1 and S_2-R_2 must be distinct from S_x-R_y, by which we mean that the stimulus classes that figure in these associations or the response classes or both must be distinct. Furthermore, S_1-R_1 must be distinct from S_2-R_2. This condition is necessary in order that reasoning shall not include cases classifiable as simple utilization of a previously acquired habit or as generalization or transfer.

Cases in which human thinking leads to a solution of a problem clearly fit this definition. The response pattern that corresponds to R_y is often a long chain of responses, which may be overt or covert and symbolic. The prior learning experiences on which a human reasoning process feeds are, more often than not, extremely numerous.

Experiments on "insightful problem solving" in the chimpanzee (to be discussed more fully in Chapter 12) appear to demonstrate satisfactorily enough that reasoning occurs in infrahuman primates.

According to Piaget's observations, the human child becomes capable of feats of reasoning closely resembling those found in apes during his second year. Maier (1929) and Tolman and Honzik (1930) claimed to have established that reasoning or "insight" may occur in the rat. However, extensions of their work by Dove and Thompson (1943) and by Wolfe and Spragg (1934) show that their experiments did not control adequately for other possibilities.

Nevertheless, behavior that must be conceded to fit our conception of reasoning has been demonstrated in animals by other experiments carried on under different captions.

For example, there is the "sensory preconditioning" that has been found in several mammalian species by both American and Russian experimenters. Kimble's (1961, p. 215) description of the procedure cannot be bettered:

(1) two neutral stimuli, S_1 and S_2 (for example, a light and a tone) are presented together, usually for a large number of trials;

(2) a response is conditioned to one of these stimuli, say, S_1;

(3) the other stimulus, S_2, is presented to determine whether the response transfers automatically to it.[*]

If it does, sensory preconditioning is said to have occurred, and the response in the third stage is recognizable as a joint product of the two previous stages.

Other cases in point are some of the experiments that are placed under the heading of "latent learning." If, for example, a rat is allowed to explore a maze and then, in a later stage, allowed to see food in a goal box while hungry, he will, in a third (test) phase, probably go from the starting box to the goal box (for example, Seward, 1949). Analogously, there is a "latent extinction." Animals that have been accustomed to run to the goal box of a maze and to find food there are, in a test phase, put directly into the goal box, which they find empty. They are immediately thereafter put into the starting box, but the habit of running to the goal box is found to be weakened (for example, Seward and Levy, 1949). In such experiments, the strengthening or weakening of the association that appears during the test phase depends on the combination of an earlier opportunity to learn how to get from the starting box to the goal box and a later opportunity to see that food is or is not available in the goal box.

[*] Reprinted with permission from G. A. Kimble, *Hilgard and Marquis' Conditioning and Learning*, 2nd ed. Copyright 1961 by Appleton-Century-Crofts.

Symbolic Responses

In order to clarify the notion of a "symbolic response," we must first consider the notions of a "sign" and a "symbol." The common view is that a sign or symbol is something that "stands for," or "means," something apart from itself. A person who creates or uses one has a conscious experience constituting its meaning, and he uses the sign or a symbol communicatively to evoke a similar experience in the mind of somebody else.

This is the essence of the influential theory of meaning advanced by Ogden and Richards (1923). It is also the sort of view from which most discussions of aesthetics and most literary, music, and art criticism start out. It cannot, however, be acceptable to a modern psychologist, to whom signs and symbols are important because of their unique role in behavior.

From a behavioristic point of view, signs and symbols have a dual aspect: they are products of responses made by organisms, and they are stimuli or sources of stimuli with profound effects on behavior. When used communicatively, they originate in one organism and affect the behavior of another organism. When used representationally (which covers the cases belonging to the subject matter of this book), they are used by an organism to influence its own behavior. There have thus been two kinds of behavioristic approach to characterizing signs and symbols, one defining them as a special kind of response and the other as a special kind of stimulus.

The most noted exponent of the former approach has been Skinner (1957). Instead of using the terms "sign" and "symbol," he develops the closely related concept of "verbal behavior," defined as "behavior reinforced through the mediation of other persons." The concept covers not only behavior that would be considered verbal in the usual sense, that is, behavior involving words, but also such responses as ringing a doorbell or pointing to something. Skinner recognizes that, once such responses have been learned as a consequence of their making other people behave in some way that their originator finds rewarding, they can come to be used for the regulation of one's own behavior.

Skinner analyzes in great detail the peculiarities that responses whose reinforcement depends on the intervention of another organism will have. The intervention of another organism will, however, not always make a difference, so that Skinner's classification of behavior into verbal and nonverbal does not always coincide with distinctions of psychological importance. For example, in the kind of

Skinner box that is commonly used nowadays, a rat presses a bar or a pigeon pecks at a panel, and this response causes an automatic mechanism to deliver a food pellet. Sometimes in the past, much cruder arrangements have had to be used, such that the experimenter watches the performance of the response and throws a pellet into the box or else presses a button that causes a mechanism to deliver a pellet. In the modern apparatus, the animal's response is nonverbal according to Skinner's definition, but we have a clear case of verbal behavior when the manually operated apparatus is in use. Yet, as far as the psychology of the rat is concerned, there can surely be no difference between the two situations.

We shall adhere to the view of signs and symbols that stresses their stimulus functions. Some of the accounts in this tradition have been virtually all-encompassing. Watson (1924) held that the "meaning" of an object is identifiable with the way a subject reacts to it. Pavlov (1928) spoke of stimuli reaching the distance receptors as "signals," since they give notice of objects with biologically beneficial or noxious effects that are about to come in contact with the surface of the body.

These treatments have encouraged acceptance of virtually any stimulus or stimulus-object as a "signal," "sign," or "symbol" or at least of virtually any stimulus that has acquired, as a result of classical conditioning, the power to evoke some response that was originally associated with a different stimulus. In the latter case, the conditioned stimulus is said to "stand for" or "mean" the stimulus that originally evoked the response.

There is, however, a more recent trend, receiving its impetus from the work of Morris (1946) and of Osgood (1952), toward reserving terms like sign and symbol for restricted classes of stimuli and stimulus-objects having special properties. We shall conform to this trend and, in line with it, we shall examine the preliminary concepts that lead, by a progressive narrowing down, to the concept of a "symbolic response."

1. SIGNS. Morris sets out with the following definition.

If anything, A, is preparatory-stimulus which in the absence of stimulus-objects initiating response-sequences of a certain behavior-family causes a disposition in some organism to respond under certain conditions by response-sequences of this behavior-family, then A is a sign.

This definition, despite the careful thought from which its cumbersome phrasing arises, has some drawbacks. Chief of them is the fact that it ends up being too broad. It includes any stimulus that induces any kind of "set" that some other stimulus could have induced, and this means including many things that we should not want to regard as signs. Osgood has also objected to Morris's failure to confine his definition to learned behavior although, just about the time that Osgood was writing, the ethologists were introducing their findings to the English-speaking world (Tinbergen, 1951), and some of the "sign-stimuli" that they identified as "releasers" for unlearned or instinctive behavior might reasonably be regarded as signs.

Osgood has come up with an alternative definition, which has won wide assent, including apparently that of Morris himself. It is stated as follows.

A pattern of stimulation which is not the object is a sign of the object if it evokes in an organism a mediating reaction, this (a) being some fractional part of the total behavior instituted by the object and (b) producing distinctive self-stimulation that mediates responses which would not occur without the previous association of non object and object patterns of stimulation.

Figure 1-1 depicts the mechanism involved. $\boxed{S}$ is the sign, which stands for the referent or significate, $\dot{S}$. R_T is the total behavior usually evoked by $\dot{S}$, and r_m is the "mediating response" or "meaning," consisting of the portion of R_T that is evoked by $\boxed{S}$. r_m gives rise to internal stimulation, s_m, which in its turn evokes some overt pattern of behavior, R_x, jointly with $\dot{S}$ and other stimuli that may be present.

Osgood's definition is fully in the spirit of Morris's (1946, p. 7) original preliminary definition.

If something, A, controls behavior towards a goal in a way similar to (but not necessarily identical with) the way something else, B, would control behavior with respect to that goal in a situation in which it were observed, then A is a sign.

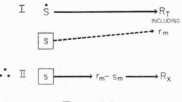

Figure 1-1

We may, however, modify this statement by insisting that the behavior evoked by A should not be identical with that evoked by B. In other words, there should be at least one respect in which A and B evoke different behavior. This is to take account of a point that Piaget (1945) has repeatedly made, namely that the adaptive functioning of symbolic processes demands that the subject be able to distinguish between a sign and what it stands for. He points out that when children begin to play symbolic games, such as pretending to be asleep or pretending that a doll is a baby, they show themselves to be fully cognizant of the differences between make-believe sleep and real sleep and between dolls and real babies. Similarly, when we hear somebody shout "Fire!", we behave in some respects as we should behave if we saw a fire. We may, for example, become terrified or sound a fire alarm or see a fire (in imagination). We should not, however, do all the things that we should do if we saw a real fire. We should not, for example, douse the speaker with a fire extinguisher. There have, on the other hand, often been reports from child behavior or psychotic behavior or primitive magic and religion of failures to distinguish between signs and what they stand for, with maladaptive results.

2. SYMBOLS. Morris defines "symbol" as follows.

When an organism provides itself with a sign which is a substitute in the control of its behavior for another sign, signifying what the sign for which it is a substitute signifies, then this sign is a symbol.

If a sign is not a symbol, it is designated a "signal."

This usage can be adopted, even if we follow Osgood's definition of a sign. A symbol can, of course, influence the behavior of other organisms besides the one that produces the symbol. The usage implies, however, that the symbol must have the same "meaning" for its producer as for others. It thus excludes processes that accidentally provide signs for other organisms while leaving their originator unaffected, for example, a boxer "telegraphing" his punches.

A symbol may be produced by its originator in the form of a concrete object, like a flag or a crucifix or a work of art. It may, on the other hand, take the transient form of the sight or sound of an action performed by the originator. When a response is performed for the sake of symbolic stimuli resulting from it, we shall speak of it as a symbolic response. Speech, gestures, and acts of ritual are clear examples. They all evoke meaning-processes (in Osgood's sense) in the person from whom they issue, and they are likely to have similar effects on others belonging to the same social group.

3. THOUGHTS. In Figure 1-1, Osgood depicts the elementary case where a sign evokes a single-stage mediating or meaning process before the execution of the overt response, R_X, although r_m is likely to be a complex of several component responses of widely varying kinds. In human behavior, there will commonly be quite long strings of such mediators, as depicted in Figure 1-2. Each mediator in the string will have its response aspect, r_m, and its stimulus aspect, s_m. In other words, each mediator can be evoked either by an external sign stimulus or by the stimulus aspect of a preceding mediator, and each mediator can, in its turn, evoke, through its stimulus aspect, either a succeeding mediator or an overt response. Each r_m but the last is a symbolic response according to Osgood's definition. It is, however, strictly speaking not a symbolic response because it is a mediator; it is a symbolic response in so far as it evokes a succeeding mediator.

At this point, it may be useful to recall two ways in which responses can be dichotomized. The first division, introduced by Watson, is that between overt and covert (implicit) responses. Overt responses are responses, like moving a limb or speaking out loud, that can be perceived directly by an external observer. Implicit responses are responses that cannot be directly observed, although they can often be detected with the help of special instrumentation. They may be inaccessible to direct observation for a number of reasons. They may take place in the interior of the body, like visceral changes or electrochemical processes in the brain. Alternatively, they may consist of responses that would be overt were it not for their low intensity; they may take the form of what Washburn (1926) called "incipient" responses, that is, weak skeletal muscular innervations which are not strong enough to produce a bodily movement but suffice to produce kinaesthetic stimulation and action potentials that may be registered by an electromyograph (EMG).

The second distinction appears in the writings of Hull (1930) and Guthrie (1935), although it has often reappeared in different guises. It is a division between instrumental acts, which are acts whose function is to change the external or internal environment into one that is more beneficial, and pure stimulus acts (Hull, 1930) or cue-produc-

$$S \longrightarrow r_{m_1^-}\, s_{m_1^-} \longrightarrow r_{m_2^-}\, s_{m_2^-} \longrightarrow \cdots\cdots \longrightarrow r_{m_n^-}\, s_{m_n^-} \longrightarrow R_X$$

Figure 1-2

ing responses (Miller and Dollard, 1941), whose function is to provide stimuli (exteroceptive, proprioceptive, or interoceptive) for the guidance of subsequent behavior. A good example of a pure stimulus act is pinching oneself to keep awake. Another example is counting, since, whenever we are counting more than eight objects, the only reason for saying "eight" is to make oneself say "nine" on contemplating the next object.

Many, possibly most, responses have both an instrumental and a cue-producing function, but one or the other will usually predominate. As for implicit responses, those that are visceral may be instrumental as far as the internal environment is concerned, but they may also have a cue-producing function at times. Cerebral or incipient muscular responses can have only cue-producing functions. They are incapable in themselves of making the environment more congenial or less noxious, but they are fully capable of providing valuable stimulation to control later behavior.

Whenever a symbolic response is implicit and has a preponderantly cue-producing function, we shall call it a *thought*. We shall refer to a string of such cue-producing symbolic responses as a *train of thought*.

Criteria for Symbolic Responses and Reasoning

In the past century, psychologists attempting to understand the relations between the so-called higher and lower functions have been pulled in two opposite directions. On the one hand, Darwin's theory of evolution has encouraged them to look for continuities, and to distrust the appearance of unbridgeable gulfs, between uniquely human intellectual processes and the simpler activities that human beings share with animals. This trend has been most consistently followed by the Gestalt psychologists and those influenced by them, who have maintained that even the most primitive kinds of animal learning involve "cognitions," "expectations," or "changed perceptions"—in other words, implicit representational events akin to those that support human knowledge and thinking.

On the other hand, there has been the tendency to maximize the gap between the human intellect and behavior of which animals are capable. It can be traced back to the philosophies of Plato and Aristotle, proclaiming a deep separation between the rational and the irrational parts of the mind or soul. This tradition received a massive impetus from theological influences in the Middle Ages and culminated in the philosophy of Descartes at the beginning of the 17th century. The once-powerful ascendancy of theology and Cartesianism over psychology has shriveled to virtual insignificance during the 20th century, but the tendency to contrast intellectual with simpler functions has received new fillips from quite different sources. In Eastern Europe, the peculiarity of man as the sole animal capable of social organization or economic activity is insisted on in accordance with Marxist philosophy. In Western countries, there has been widespread assent to Lloyd Morgan's (1894) canon:

In no case may we interpret an action as the outcome of the exercise of a higher physical faculty, if it can be interpreted as the outcome of the exercise of one which stands lower in the psychological scale.

This has encouraged a tendency to attribute animal behavior whenever possible to elementary functions, which means emphasizing the distance between animal and human activities.

Of late, there have been clear signs in both East and West of a more balanced view which, while recognizing that the advent of the human nervous system introduced some great leaps forward, endeavors to analyze the differences between higher and lower functions naturalistically and with reference to principles that they obey in common. If one accepts this view while agreeing with Lloyd Morgan's plea for parsimony, one will be prepared to find rudiments of human intellectual processes in lower animals but will refuse to infer implicit mediating processes unless simpler alternatives are excluded.

Now, three ways are known in which an association between a stimulus class, S_x, and a response class, R_y, can come into existence: (1) there may be an inherited, unlearned association between S_x and R_y, as in the many innate reflexes and instinctive (species-specific) behavior patterns that are known; (2) R_y may have become associated with S_x through learning, that is, as a result of prior performance in the presence of a situation belonging to S_x and a reinforcing condition; and (3) S_x may have become associated with a mediating response, R_m (which may be overt or covert), and the feedback stimulus, S_m, resulting from R_m, may have become associated with R_x. The dependence of a response on a representational symbolic mediator clearly belongs to the third of these cases.

When we have a process that fits our conception of reasoning, we have an association, S_x-R_y, which would not have existed at all, or would not have existed in such strength, were it not for the prior existence of two distinct associations, S_1-R_1 and S_2-R_2. The possibility that S_x-R_y is an unlearned association is therefore excluded. Since the two associations that give rise to S_x-R_y are distinct, in their stimulus members, their response members or both, from S_x-R_y and from each other, S_x-R_y cannot be attributed to the previous performance of R_y in the presence of S_x together with a reinforcing condition. We are thus left with the third case, and it will generally be found that the mediating response whose existence and operation can then legitimately be inferred conforms to the additional criteria of a symbolic response.

Thus, in sensory preconditioning, it can be inferred that the first phase causes some covert response originally associated with S_1 to become associated with S_2 and that, in the third phase, S_2 evokes the overt response through the mediation of this covert response and its feedback stimulus. Since the covert response is part of the behavior that would be evoked by S_1, it qualifies as a symbol representing S_1.

In general, the occurrence of a covert symbolic response means a change in an animal's internal condition; there must be some external stimulus situations to which his overt response differs according to whether the symbolic response has or has not been evoked. Since covert responses are inaccessible to direct observation, we must be circumspect about assuming their intervention. A sound practice is to invoke them only as a last resort. If, however, neither an unlearned association nor a specific learning experience can account for a piece of overt behavior, if the behavior is part of what the subject would have done if some kind of external stimulus pattern, S_1, had been present, and if we can discern some mechanism that could have produced a covert symbolic response to stand for S_1 in its absence, then we are on firm ground in inferring that a covert symbolic response is at work.

S-Thinking and R-Thinking

To conclude this survey of basic concepts, we must introduce a distinction that will be found useful in later chapters.

One outcome of all kinds of directed thinking, as of all kinds of reasoning, is that responses are evoked by stimulus situations in which they would otherwise have been unlikely to occur. Sometimes, these responses have been performed in other stimulus situations, and the result of the thinking process amounts to a transfer to one class of stimulus situations of a response pattern that is already associated with another class of situations. In such cases, we shall speak of S-thinking. At other times, directed thinking causes a subject to perform a response, or a combination or sequence of responses, that he has never before performed in any stimulus situation and that he would, in all likelihood, never would have performed in any stimulus situation, were it not for the thinking process. We shall refer to such cases, in which thinking gives rise to response patterns that are unprecedented for the subject, as R-thinking.

When a general gives the order to attack or a surveyor writes down a trigonometrically calculated distance, these responses will usually have been preceded by thinking, but they are identical with responses that have already been made on numerous other occasions. On the other hand, when Einstein wrote his paper on special relativity theory and Marconi constructed his first wireless transmitter, they were carrying out response sequences that neither they nor anybody else had ever put together before.

It may be noted that the relation between S-thinking and R-thinking resembles the rather oversimplified way in which classical and instrumental conditioning have often been differentiated, that is, as a matter of attaching old responses to new stimuli and as a matter of coming into possession of new responses to be attached to old or new stimuli, respectively.

Chapter 2

Information and adaptation

ALTHOUGH MUCH OF OUR THINKING has no immediate connection with survival or physical well-being, we may suppose that the capacities used in thinking have evolved in consequence of their contribution to biological adaptation.

We must therefore begin by attempting to see directed thinking in biological perspective. There are many languages in which we can do this, but one that offers many advantages is the language of information theory (Shannon and Weaver, 1949). Since thinking is a matter of handling and processing information, information theory should have something enlightening to say about it. We must, however, beware, since the "information" with which information theory is concerned comes near in some respects to what goes by the same name in everyday life but is, in other respects, quite different.

Elementary accounts of the principal concepts of information theory with special reference to psychology can be found elsewhere (Attneave, 1959; Luce, 1960; and G. A. Miller, 1953). For our present purposes, some general notions will suffice.

The central concept of information theory is known as "uncertainty" or "entropy." A certain degree of uncertainty is said to exist when (1) any of a number of alternative events can occur, (2) there is no knowing in advance which will occur at a particular time, and (3) each alternative occurs with a specifiable relative frequency or probability. Uncertainty is defined by the formula: $-\Sigma p_i \log_2 p_i$, p_i being the probability of alternative i. Two important properties follow from this defining formula: there is more uncertainty the greater the number of alternatives, and there is more uncertainty the nearer the alternatives come to being equally probable. Uncertainty and information which reduces uncertainty are measured in "bits," one bit being the uncertainty that obtains where there are two equally probable alternatives.

Whenever we have two systems of events with some degree of

correspondence or correlation between them, we can speak of "transmission of information." If we find out what is occurring at a particular time in one of the systems, we are in a position to guess which event is occurring at the corresponding time in the other system. In other words, when what is happening in one system is known, uncertainty regarding the other system is reduced.

Before we consider the relations linking uncertainty, information, and directed thinking, we must draw attention to some properties of information transmission, as conceived by information theory, which jar with our everyday conception of the process.

1. INFORMATION TRANSMISSION CAN BE INCOMPLETE. The prototype of an information channel is a perfect telephone line, which leaves the listener in no doubt about what the speaker is saying. When he receives the output signals, the listener's uncertainty about the speaker's input is reduced to zero, so that the transmission of information is complete.

Many information channels, such as a faulty telephone line or an animal organism, are, however, imperfect. Not all of the information delivered at the input end will reach the output. A person stationed at the output will be left with some residual uncertainty about what went into the input. His original uncertainty will be reduced somewhat, and he will be able to make better-than-chance predictions or wagers concerning the input, but he will be unable to deduce the nature of the input signals with absolute assurance.

2. INFORMATION TRANSMISSION IS SYMMETRICAL. When we think of a communication channel, we generally regard one end as the input and the other end as the output. The events regarded as input generally occur before those regarded as output, but this need not be so, and these designations can be quite arbitrary.

It is, for example, most natural to think of the speaker's end of the telephone line as the input and the listener's end as output and to conceive of information as flowing from the former to the latter. But we could equally well conceive of information flowing in the reverse direction. Anybody who knows what comes out of a telephone receiver can make deductions, or in other words has his uncertainty reduced, about what words were spoken into the microphone at the other end. But, as long as the two sets of events are correlated with each other, it is equally true that anybody who knows what words were spoken into the microphone will be less uncertain about what will come out at the listener's end than anybody who does not know.

Information is thus invariably transmitted in both directions at once.

If uncertainty with respect to a set of alternative events, X, is diminished by acquaintance with another set of alternative events, Y, it must follow that a knowledge of Y diminishes uncertainty regarding X. It does not matter which event occurs first or whether the events are simultaneous.

3. INFORMATION TRANSMISSION DOES NOT IMPLY A CAUSAL RELATION BETWEEN INPUT AND OUTPUT. This property follows from the preceding one. If we can regard what happens at either end of the channel as the input, so that what happens at the other end becomes the output, they cannot both determine each other causally. They may, of course, both exert some partial causal influence on each other, as in many mechanical or biological systems with feedback. The existence of information transmission between X and Y, like the demonstration of a significant degree of correlation between X and Y by any other statistical technique, indicates that there is some causality somewhere. But X may cause Y, Y may cause X, or both X and Y may be subject to causal influence from some third source.

An example is provided by the conclave that elects the Pope. The cardinals who are responsible for the election are literally immured within the Vatican, and (except for smoke signals and limited passage of notes) all physical links between them and the outside world are severed. Nevertheless, a person in the outside world can consult an expert on the Roman Catholic Church and derive information from him about what is likely to be going on in the conclave. Uncertainty about developments in the Sistine Chapel will be reduced because there will be an above-chance degree of correspondence between these events and what the expert prognosticates. This is because both the actions of the cardinals and the commentaries of the expert are under the influence of recent and remote events in the history of the church. There is, in other words, an information channel proceeding from the conclave through these events to the expert and, because of property 2, there is also one following the same route in the opposite direction.

4. A CHANNEL CAN TRANSMIT INFORMATION FROM SEVERAL INPUTS TO ONE OUTPUT. When this happens, several different consequences may ensue (McGill, 1954). If events in the various sources possess some correlation with one another, the information coming from them will overlap. If they are all independent, their total information content may reach the output as long as the limits of channel capacity are not overstepped. If they are independent and their total information content exceeds the channel capacity, some of the information

coming from them will be lost. In this case, a portion of the information from all the inputs may be preserved, so that there will then be some residual uncertainty about all of them. Alternatively, there may be complete transmission of information from some of the inputs, while what the other inputs feed in will fail to get through at all.

Transmission between Optimal Response and Actual Response

Most applications of information theory to psychology have pictured an animal as a channel receiving an influx of information through his sense organs and passing on this information through his nervous system to his effector equipment, where it emerges embodied in behavior. They have thus concentrated on the transmission of information between the external stimulus situation and the overt response pattern.

It is obvious that an organism cannot remain alive and healthy unless its reactions vary in concomitance with environmental conditions. Some writers have even written as if the effectiveness of adaptation could be judged by the degree of fidelity with which behavior reflects external events, so that the more information transmitted from sense organs to effectors the better. But this view has limitations that deflect attention from essential aspects of behavior and especially of thinking. The first point to be made in opposition to it is that biological adaptation is not a matter of maximum information transmission between external environment and response but of *maximum information transmission between optimal response and actual response.*

The Optimal Response

At any moment, there are a large number of responses that lie within an animal's capability and that he could thus be performing. Each of these responses would have certain consequences, and to these consequences a "value" or "utility" could be assigned. At present, we need not concern ourselves with the problem of how value is to be determined (for example, whether in terms of biological effects, pleasantness and unpleasantness, or drive and drive-reduction), as long as we recognize that the consequences of some responses that could be performed have a higher value than those of other responses.

We shall call the response whose consequences have the highest value of all the responses that could be performed the "optimal" response. Strictly speaking, we should speak of a class of optimal responses, since there may be several distinguishable responses that would have identical consequences or distinct but equally valuable consequences. We shall, however, speak of the optimal response in the singular for convenience.

Which response is the optimal response at any time depends on two things, namely (1) facts about the external world and (2) the state of the organism. For example, whether or not running to the south is the optimal response for a particular animal at a particular time will depend on such questions as whether there is a potential predator approaching from the north and whether there is a potential source of food located to the south. Many internal variables can make a difference: for example, fatigue and physical ill health. The most important ones will be those that can be classed as "motivational" (see Chapter 9). Optimal responses will vary, although the state of the external world be held constant, if the organism's motivational condition varies. For example, when food is located to the south, the optimal response will in all likelihood not be running to the south if the organism is more thirsty than hungry.

The optimal response thus fluctuates from moment to moment, as external factors and internal variables fluctuate, and every kind of response has its relative frequency or probability of being optimal over the organism's lifetime. This means that we can speak of uncertainty with regard to the optimal response. On the other hand, what the organism is in fact doing—the actual response—is likewise fluctuating from moment to moment, and actual responses also have their relative frequencies or probabilities. So there is a certain quantity of uncertainty with regard to the actual response also.

Biological adaptation can be regarded then as a matter of approximating the actual response to the optimal response or bringing what the organism does as near as possible to what it would be well advised to do. This implies a maximum degree of correspondence between the optimal response and the actual response or, in other words, a maximum transmission of information between the two.

Now, the two most important channels of information transmission between the optimal response and the actual response pass through the external stimulus situation and the organism's state respectively. The optimal response, as we have noted, depends on facts in the external universe, some of which will relate to events in the organism's vicinity that cause sense organs to be excited. These stimuli, in their turn, influence the actual response. There is therefore transmission of information between the optimal response and the external

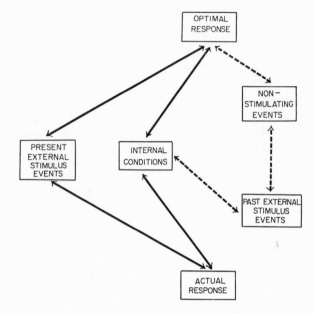

Figure 2-1

stimulus situation and between the external stimulus situation and the actual response. This forms one of the channels represented by the solid lines in Figure 2-1. Lines representing information channels in this figure have arrowheads at both ends because of the symmetry of information transmission that has already been mentioned.

The second major channel is analogous, except that the organism's internal condition takes the place of the external stimulus situation. Since the internal condition, including values of motivational variables, plays a part in determining which response is optimal and also plays a part in determining which response is actually performed, information can reach the actual response from the optimal response by the second channel represented by solid lines in Figure 2-1.

Limitations of Information Transmission through the External Stimulus Situation

The information channel going from the external stimulus situation to the actual response serves adaptation merely as the concluding sector of a longer channel reaching back to the optimal response (see Figure

2-1). In this capacity, it suffers from two significant deficiencies. The first is that it does not convey all of the information from the optimal response that is required. The second is that only a small part of the information passing between the external stimulus situation and the actual response is information that originated in the optimal response and that therefore should reach the effector organs producing the actual response.

The reason for both these limitations is that the external facts affecting the nature of the optimal response and the external facts corresponding to the present external stimulus field overlap without being coextensive; each of these sets of facts contains many items of information that are not found in the other. The situation with regard to the internal facts is similar without being nearly so serious most of the time. There can be internal factors (for example, irrational moods) that are apt to influence behavior but bear no relation to the nature of the optimal response. There can also be internal factors that have a great bearing on the nature of the optimal response but are not represented among internal stimuli, for example, malignant tumors that ought to be surgically removed but give rise to no pain or other sensation until they are inoperable.

Insufficiency of Information from the External Stimulus Situation

On the whole, submammalian animals seem to be largely confined, as far as the control of behavior is concerned, to the information channel between the external stimulus situation and the actual response. They have a specific invariant response pattern available for each of a number of biologically significant classes of stimulus situations and, whenever a stimulus situation belonging to one of these classes confronts them, they perform the appropriate response uniformly with few exceptions. The channel between the internal condition and the actual response also plays some part, apparently increasing in importance as we ascend the scale of evolution. In fishes and in birds, as the rich documentation supplied by the ethologists (Tinbergen, 1951) shows, the likelihood of a particular response in a particular kind of environment often varies with motivational variables, depending on such factors as the time since the animal last had an opportunity to indulge in that kind of behavior and seasonal changes in glandular activity. These associations between external and internal conditions, on the one hand, and behavior, on the other, depend on inherited neural structures. All major groups of animals appear capable of using the mechanisms of learning, which bring additional information to bear on the selection of behavior, but these mechanisms have minor scope until they dominate behavior in the higher mammals.

Learning exploits the redundancies that exist between configurations of external events at different points in time. There is a tendency for events to occur in similar combinations repeatedly. This means that if two (or more) events have given rise to stimuli simultaneously or in close succession in the past, the combination is likely to be repeated whenever one of its components is experienced thereafter.

Thus arises the biological utility of familiar learning processes. If a tone has preceded an electric shock in the past, a dog will perform a classically conditioned leg retraction on hearing the tone alone, which is valuable because leaving the paw where it is is likely, once again, to be dangerous. If a pigeon has previously found that pecking at a red square is followed by the delivery of food, its rate of pecking in the presence of a visible red square will rise, which is useful because the sequence, red square → food, having appeared before, is likely to recur.

The more direct channels going from optimal response through the present external stimulus situation and through the present state of the organism to the actual response are thus supplemented by another channel, represented by a broken line in Figure 2-1. This additional channel has four sectors. The first goes from the optimal response to events (mostly external but occasionally internal) that are not represented in the present stimulus situation; information is transmitted (in both directions) along this channel, since the nature of the optimal response is determined by, and thus corresponds to, such events. There is then a channel going from these nonstimulating events to stimulus events belonging to the past, and what we have said about the redundancies or repetitions between past and present combinations of events implies that information flows along this channel also. The next sector goes from past stimulus events to the internal condition, which contains traces or habit structures generated by, and thus corresponding to, combinations of stimuli experienced in the past. Finally, the channel going from the state of the organism to the actual response conveys information embodied in these habit structures as well as information coming from other internal conditions.

The simplest forms of learning are, however, far from sufficient to fill in the informational gaps in the present external stimulus situation. They are of avail only when a clue to the optimal response can be derived from the combination formed by an external stimulus pattern acting here and now and traces left in the nervous system by a similar stimulus pattern conjoined with other stimuli in the past. Put differently, the simplest forms of learning couple information about present stimuli with information derived from the past about their probable accompaniments.

It must often happen, however, that events with a vital bearing on the optimal response are simply not accessible at all through the present stimulus situation, so that the stimuli to which receptors are being exposed do not suffice for the guidance of behavior, no matter what the organism has learned from encounters with comparable stimuli in its earlier history. Nevertheless, most animals, and especially the higher animals, possess means of gaining access to stimuli other than those constituting the present stimulus field and in this way some of the information that is lacking may be secured. We are thus obliged to recognize the importance of information-gathering (exploratory and epistemic) processes, and these will be of great concern to us in what follows.

Necessity for Information Rejection

Not only is the information contained in the present external stimulus situation insufficient. Most of it is also superfluous, whence arises the other major limitation of the channel going from the external stimulus situation to the actual response.

First, most of the information that comes from external stimuli bears no relation to the optimal response. It reflects events that are totally unconnected with the consequences of the various responses that the organism could perform. Therefore, as far as the channel between the optimal response and the actual response is concerned, the information they contribute is what information theorists call "noise," that is, events (like those that produce background crackles in a faulty telephone circuit) affecting the output but not reducing uncertainty with regard to the input.

Second, most of the information received by sense organs must be discarded in any case, because of the limited channel capacity of the animal organism. Sherrington (1906) compared the central nervous system to a funnel, pointing out that afferent pathways are about five times as numerous as efferent pathways, so that incoming sensory messages have to compete for control over the "final common path." More recently, calculations made with the help of information theory (for example, Luce, 1960) have shown the bottleneck to be much more severe. The variety of combinations of stimuli to which sense organs can be exposed is clearly far in excess of the variety of responses of which motor equipment is capable. This means that response patterns cannot reflect more than a minute proportion of the properties of the stimulus field, with the consequence that only a minute part of the information received by sense organs can be transmitted through the organism and reflected in its responses.

This being so, "noise," or information unrelated to the optimal response, constitutes most of the information content of the external stimulus situation. In any information channel that is being used to the full, noise takes up valuable channel capacity and thus cuts down the amount of information of consequence that can be transmitted, as experience with a "noisy" telephone circuit or radio frequency vividly illustrates.

The rejection of information is therefore no less vital to biological adaptation than the transmission of information, and this necessitates the employment of devices for the proper selection of information to transmit and information to reject. It is made even more vital by the elaborate symbolic capacities possessed by human beings. These add potentially immense hoards of stored information to what is entering through sensory inlets, and these greatly increase the proportion of available information that will have to be left unused. Posner (1962) has studied performance on several tasks that can be assumed to necessitate thinking, such as adding numbers and classifying numbers in two or four categories. He found that time taken, liability to error, and subjective rating of difficulty all varied directly with the extent to which information had to be discarded.

We must therefore review the means that higher animals have at their disposal for information gathering and information rejection, so that we can see where directed thinking fits in.

Mechanisms for Information Gathering

Trial and Error

The most primitive way to obtain missing information about the optimal response and about concealed external conditions determining which response will be optimal is trial-and-error behavior. One overt response is performed after another until one with satisfactory consequences is found. The order in which they occur may be random, but heredity or results of previous learning are likely to make those with a higher initial probability of success come earlier.

This procedure has the obvious drawbacks that a great expenditure of time and effort may be needed before the conclusion of the search is reached and that some of the responses that are tried may have consequences of distinctly negative value.

Nevertheless, the simplest animal organisms have no other recourse. The paramecium that finds its forward progression blocked has no means of freeing itself other than repeatedly reversing a short distance and then advancing in a slightly altered direction, until it finds its way clear (Jennings, 1906). In higher animals, blind groping occurs either as a last resort or in conjunction with other specialized information-gathering activities. The rat placed in strange experimental apparatus invariably inspects its environment first, and the human being who finds himself locked in a room will not only examine doors and windows but also do some directed thinking before he is reduced to aimless movements.

A further advantage enjoyed by higher animals is the possibility of using attenuated versions of overt responses, which are safer, less time-consuming and less fatiguing than the corresponding full-scale actions, but no less informative. Sometimes, a response that is somewhat similar to the response whose consequences are to be evaluated, or a response that constitutes one of its usual preliminaries, can yield the required information without the dangers of a direct trial. In many animal species, a threatening gesture establishes whether an intruder will accept a subordinate status, without the need for a set battle. A human swimmer inserts his big toe into the water before deciding whether to jump in. A diplomat ascertains the probable reaction to a proposal that his government might make to a foreign power by means of unofficial feelers and deliberate "leaks." There is a strong tendency for animals to reduce a response to the minimum vigor that is compatible with its reinforcement (Skinner, 1938; Logan, 1960), and we can suppose that the implicit or internalized responses that make up thinking originate in this tendency.

Exploratory Behavior

Responses whose principal function is either to intensify stimulation from specific portions of the stimulus field or to establish contact with sources of stimulation that were previously outside the stimulus field are called exploratory responses (Berlyne, 1960a). This term covers a highly diversified assortment of phenomena, which can be classified in several different ways. The most obvious and convenient way is by manner of working.

Some of them are *receptor-adjusting responses*. These consist of changes in the physicochemical states of sense organs or movements of certain parts of the body in relation to others, determining the parts of the environment on which sense organs will be focused. The former are exemplified by the retinal processes that underlie dark adaptation and the latter by eye movements, sniffing, and running the fingers over a surface.

When the location of the whole body is altered and an organism receives more information from a stimulus object by moving nearer to it or by moving to a vantage point affording a better view of it, we speak of *locomotor exploration*.

Finally, there is the residual category of *investigatory responses*. These consist principally of manipulatory activities (which may have the effect of bringing the object nearer to the sense organs), performing an operation on the object to make it yield additional stimulation (for example, knocking it or shaking it to make it sound), or eliminating some condition that impedes the receipt of stimulation from the object (for example, pushing aside a screen or turning the focusing button on a pair of binoculars).

Epistemic Behavior

Other responses are aimed at the acquisition of knowledge or, in other words, of information that, once acquired, is retained in the nervous system to be revivified in the form of symbolic processes on future occasions when it can be helpful. Epistemic responses, as we shall call responses with this function, are often exploratory at the same time, that is, the information that they secure can provide immediate satisfaction or guidance for the actual response of the moment, as well as nourishing the symbolic structures that constitute knowledge.

In attempting to classify epistemic responses, we find once again three major categories. There is *epistemic observation*, in which all the resources of exploratory behavior can be employed for the sake of symbolic representation of the stimulus patterns that result from them. *Consultation* is behavior that seeks out verbal material with the required information content, as when one asks a question of an expert or looks up an item of information in a reference book. Finally, knowledge can be acquired through *directed thinking*. Directed thinking has, however, a special status, since other epistemic activities are invariably accompanied by directed thinking and, moreover, the knowledge that accrues from them is usually utilized through directed thinking after it has been assimilated.

Mechanisms for Information Rejection

The processes whose principal function is to gather information must at the same time be contributing to information rejection. Because of the organism's limited channel capacity and because of its limited number of receptors, they will generally afford access to information from certain sources at the cost of diminishing or excluding information from other sources. The only exceptions to this will be processes that heighten the over-all level of "arousal," "attentiveness," or "vigilance" (see Chapter 9) and thus increase the total influx of information.

There are, however, two kinds of mechanism devoted entirely to information rejection.

Attention

First, there are mechanisms of attention. The word "attention" has been used to mean various things in the history of psychology, as in everyday speech. We shall, however, reserve it for processes that block or suppress information coming from particular receptor cells.

A number of processes of this nature have been brought to light by the neurophysiological research of recent years (see Berlyne, 1960a, Ch. 3; Broadbent, 1958). The transmission of nerve impulses representing external stimuli can apparently be obstructed at a variety of levels between sense organs and motor pathways. There are known to be fibers conveying inhibitory influences downward from the cerebral cortex to the first nerve junctions encountered by sensory pathways after leaving receptor cells, for example, those in the cochlear nucleus and immediately behind the retina. Afferent processes that are not barred or attenuated at these points can evidently suffer inhibition from similar corticifugal fibers in the sensory relay stations of the brain stem. Finally, there are good reasons for believing that the cerebral cortex can function properly only if the processes that give rise to clear-cut coordinated motor activity are accompanied by widespread inhibition of processes that would otherwise be occurring at the same time in neighboring areas, including those resulting from external stimuli that do not concern the activity in question (Beritov, 1961; Milner, 1957).

The filtering processes that occur at lower levels of the nervous system can determine which sensory modality will dominate behavior, keeping information from other sensory channels in abeyance. It is possible that they may also make some gross selection among portions of the sensory surfaces belonging to one modality. The final and most subtle selection of items of information from any one modality must, however, be effected in the cortex. This selection must account for the kind of attention that we can transfer from one portion of the peripheral visual field to another without changing our fixation point (cf. Fraisse, Ehrlich, and Vurpillot, 1956). It must also account for the attention that singles out what one voice is saying when many people are speaking at once or concentrates on the theme played by one instrument in an orchestra (Broadbent, 1958).

Attention is often depicted as a matter of intensifying the sensory processes corresponding to the stimuli on which it focuses as well as of weakening of those corresponding to other stimuli. There is, of course, a relative strengthening of the former and weakening of the latter. We must not forget, however, that, while the inhibitory mechanisms of attention can reduce the amount of information reaching the motor apparatus from most parts of the stimulus field, attention (as distinct from receptor-adjusting responses that aid attention) can do no more than allow all the information coming from the stimuli on which it focuses to pass through. It cannot in any way increase the yield of information from any source above what is entering through receptors.

Abstraction

The second group of devices for information rejection comprises mechanisms of abstraction. Information is a matter of selecting among alternatives, making distinctions, reflecting variety. Whenever distinctions are ignored, whenever things that are not identical are treated as equivalent, whenever variety is cut down, information is lost.

It has already been mentioned that, whenever information from a number of input sources is feeding into a channel at once and the total information emanating from all of them exceeds the capacity of the channel, there are two possibilities, each of which means that only part of the incoming information reaches the output. There can be complete passage of the information originating in one input and blockage of information from other inputs or there can be passage of part of the information coming from all inputs. Attention tends toward the first of these solutions. Information from most receptors is blocked, and the bulk of the information from one group of favored receptors is retained, although attention can vary widely in its degree of concentration or dispersion. An organism can respond "single-mindedly" to one portion of the stimulus field and remain completely oblivious to the rest, or it can attend predominantly to one part while taking some account of what is happening elsewhere. A schoolchild may hang on the teacher's every word and resist distractions, or he may follow the general drift of what she is saying while keeping an eye on what is visible through the window.

Abstraction, on the other hand, consists of making overt behavior depend on certain properties of a stimulus pattern while disregarding other properties. It means forming what logicians and mathematicians call an "equivalence class" of stimulus situations, which share some characteristics but are distinct in other respects, and performing the same response to all members of the class.

So, while attention determines how the incoming information that is to be processed will be distributed among sectors of the stimulus field, abstraction determines how it will be distributed among items of information coming from the same sectors.

A stimulus pattern can, in fact, be thought of as a message built up of a number of signals, each specifying one of its properties (Bresson, 1958). In the case of a visual pattern, for example, the first signal might specify its shape, the second its size, the third its color, etc. Abstraction, then, means making behavior take account of some of the signals in the message and disregarding the remainder. As far as behavior is concerned, all stimulus patterns whose corresponding messages have the same signal in certain positions are thus rendered equivalent, even though their signals in other positions are quite different.

Some cases of abstraction appear to occur hereditarily in lower animals. Several instructive cases have been documented by the ethologists. When an adult herring gull alights on its nest, carrying food in its beak, the chick pecks at the adult's beak, which is yellow apart from a vivid red spot across the tip (Tinbergen and Perdeck, 1950). Experiments with models embodying different attributes of the herring-gull beak show that the probability of pecking on the part of the chick depends on the redness of the spot. The color of the background, the size of the spot, and the shape of the head evidently make no difference.

In the higher animals, abstraction generally results from learning processes of the kinds exemplified by experiments on "discrimination learning," "concept formation," and "selective perception."

Frequently, the word "attention" is used in such a way as to include what we are calling "abstraction." For instance, an animal that has been trained to approach a card bearing a triangle, no matter whether the triangle is black or white, large or small, upright or inverted, is said to be "attending" to the shape and "not attending" to the color, size, or spatial orientation. However, in view of the psychological differences between processes that select among stimuli impinging on different receptors and processes that select among attributes of a stimulus pattern impinging on the same group of receptors, and in view especially of the profound differences that must exist between the physiological mechanisms that underlie these processes, it seems advisable to adopt a terminology that differentiates between them.

Another term sometimes used for what we are calling "abstraction" is "coding." For example, an elephant is said to be "coded" as a gray object if the response depends solely on color and takes no account of size, shape, and other properties. Now, it is perfectly clear that abstraction depends on how the information contained in the stimulus pattern is coded or, to use a more technical word, transduced in the nervous system. Nevertheless, "coding" does not seem to be so good a term to use, as it covers all the changes that can intervene between one set of signals and a second set bearing information transmitted from the first set. Abstraction, that is, elimination of information about particular properties of the input, is only one of the kinds of change that can occur.

Directed Thinking as a Means to Information Gathering and Information Rejection

We must now attempt to locate directed thinking in this framework.

It is, first, clear that directed thinking can serve as a means of obtaining information that would not have been available without it. It supplies patterns of internal response-produced stimuli which, since they are charged with some of the information about the optimal response that external stimuli lack, can govern the selection of the actual response in conjunction with them. The implicit responses that produce these internal stimuli are fruits of learning. They thus belong to the channel represented by the broken lines in Figure 2-1. Furthermore, directed thinking is a variety of epistemic behavior. It not only furnishes internal stimuli that steer the subject in the direction of the optimal response as soon as they become available; it also furnishes information that can be stored for future utilization.

Yet the information-discarding functions of directed thinking are no less important, although they have rarely received the emphasis that they warrant.

One has only to consider the operations that lead to the solution of an arithmetical problem. The outcome of these operations will be a single number. But every number can be the solution to innumerable different problems. The amount of possible variety, and hence of information, that the subject takes in when he commences his calculations must therefore exceed by far the amount of variety, and hence of information, contained in what he gives out at the end. The calculations have thus served to transmit some information but to throw away much more. The resulting reduction in information will, however, generate something much more manageable, and therefore more useful, than the original mass of numerical material would have been.

Criminal proceedings offer an even more striking illustration. A jury may have to sit through, and take cognizance of, a spate of evidence and legal arguments occupying several weeks. The alternative sequences of events that might occur during a long trial must be large enough to encompass many millions of bits of information. Yet the objective of the whole process is a verdict for which only two alternatives, "guilty" and "not guilty," are usually open. If the verdict were equally likely to take either form, it would have one bit of uncertainty. Since people are normally brought to trial only when there is a strong *prima facie* case against them, a verdict of "guilty" is actually more frequent, so that the mean informational yield of the jury's deliberations will fall short of one bit. The verdict must transmit information from the evidence and arguments: it must be appropriate to them and take account of them. But the replacement of many millions of bits of information by less than one bit speaks eloquently for the necessity of information rejection in thinking.

More particularly, directed thinking, although it might occasionally aid attention, accomplishes information rejection mainly through abstraction. This can be seen in various ways.

For one thing, the outcome of thinking is usually a description, a pattern of symbols attributing some property or set of properties to something. Descriptions rarely express all the distinguishable features of what is described. They indicate one distinguishable feature or a limited number of them while ignoring others. A description, that is to say, puts entities that fit the description (even though they may differ in other respects) into an "equivalence class."

Most bouts of thinking confer the ability to recognize certain stimulus situations as equivalent with respect to the behavior that is appropriate to them. The effects of thinking on overt behavior may not be apparent within a short space of time, especially when thinking is engaged in "for its own sake," as so often happens. Nevertheless, thinking invariably changes the behavioral significance of certain stimulus situations, grouping them together with others that are superficially different from them. The histories of science, philosophy, and art are replete with illustrations.

One final point, which may be mystifying to anybody who fails to bear in mind the precise technical meaning of "information," is that information collection and information rejection, considered as functions of directed thinking, cannot be separated altogether. Information means selection from alternative possibilities. But the selection of information to discard means selecting from an assortment of items of information that could be discarded. A system of equivalence classes composed of distinguishable stimulus situations is one of many alternative systems of equivalence classes that could be formed out of the same elements.

Chapter 3

Stimulus equivalences

WE NOTED (in Chapter 1) that one type of directed thinking, S-thinking, serves to extend response patterns that are already associated with certain stimulus situations to additional stimulus situations. This means forming equivalences between stimulus situations that were not previously treated as equivalent. R-thinking, which gives rise to new response patterns, invariably works in collaboration with S-thinking and makes use of the equivalences that result from it. We saw in Chapter 2 that a major function of directed thinking in general is to put particular stimulus properties in control of behavior, so that distinguishable stimulus situations possessing these properties become equivalent, while information reflecting other properties is suppressed and denied any influence. We must therefore examine the notion of "stimulus equivalence" more closely.

First, we must distinguish sharply between *ecological equivalence* and *behavioral equivalence*. Roughly speaking, stimulus situations that are ecologically equivalent are ones that *ought to be* responded to alike, while stimulus situations that are behaviorally equivalent *will* be responded to alike. Another way of putting it is to say that ecological and behavioral equivalences are equivalences with regard to the optimal response and the actual response respectively.

Ecological Equivalences

We shall say that two stimulus situations are "ecologically equivalent," relative to particular motivational conditions, if the optimal responses in the two situations are identical when those motivational conditions occur. We shall say that two stimuli or stimulus patterns, S_A and S_B, are "ecologically equivalent" when there is an ecological equivalence, relative to some motivational condition, between any stimulus situation that contains S_A and the same situation with S_B in place of S_A.

49

So we may say that the sight of a blue strip of wood, two inches long, is ecologically equivalent to the sight of a red strip of metal, two inches long. This is because there are motivational conditions in which the optimal response will be the same regardless of which of the two objects is present, for example, when a person is looking for something that will just fill a two-inch gap or when he is asked to state the length of the object in front of him. There are, that is to say, motivational conditions in which the value of the consequences of the subject's response depends solely on length. But there will be other motivational conditions in which the presence of the one or the other object will make different responses optimal, for example, when a person is looking for something that will stand out clearly on a red surface, for something that can be nailed to a wall, or for something that cannot be easily broken, when he is asked to specify the color of the object in front of him, or when he is asked to place red objects to his right and blue ones to his left.

Behavioral Equivalences

Two stimulus situations are behaviorally equivalent, relative to particular motivational conditions, if, when these motivational conditions occur, the most probable response in the one situation is the same as the most probable response in the other. We shall say that two stimuli or stimulus patterns, S_A and S_B, are behaviorally equivalent whenever there is a behavioral equivalence, relative to some motivational condition, between any stimulus situation including S_A and the corresponding situation with S_B in place of S_A.

Adaptation demands that, as far as possible, stimulus situations that are ecologically equivalent shall be behaviorally equivalent and vice versa. This is, in fact, another way of expressing the requirement of maximum information transmission between optimal response and actual response. The burden of ensuring this approximation between ecological and behavioral stimulus equivalences must, of course, devolve upon the mechanisms of natural selection and learning, including directed thinking.

Sources of Behavioral Stimulus Equivalence

We must now review the ways in which two stimulus patterns can become behaviorally equivalent. They must be considered generally, so that the behavioral equivalences established by directed thinking can be seen in perspective as special cases.

In general, the existence of a behavioral equivalence between two stimulus conditions implies that a common response is associated with both. But the converse will not hold, since a response can be associated with both stimulus conditions without being the most probable response to either of them. The only exceptions to the rule that behavioral equivalence means association with a common response will involve stimulus situations that are not associated with any response, that is, ones in which all responses occur with the probabilities that they have over a random sample of stimulus situations. It is possible that these exceptions may be realized in newborn infants, who appear to react to a wide variety of environments with a sequence of diffuse, uncoordinated movements. They may also be found, perhaps, when adult infrahuman animals are confronted with unprecedented situations that fail to call out any prepotent response. But in the human being after early infancy, there can scarcely be any stimulus patterns that do not possess associations with at least naming and describing responses.

If we ask how two classes of stimulus situations can become associated with a common response, behavior theory is familiar with three ways in which this can come about (see Seward, 1948).

1. Independent Association

Two classes of stimulus situations may have independently acquired an association with a common response, whether through inherited neural connections or through separate learning processes.

Thus, flexion of the forearm can be evoked either by applying an electric shock to the fingers or by tapping the shoulder. This is because both of these stimuli are associated with the same response through different innate reflexes, namely, the flexion and the acromial reflexes. If an electric shock to the fingers has frequently been preceded by the sound of a buzzer, the shock and the sound will have a common association with the withdrawal of the forearm, the former innately and the latter as a conditioned response. If, at different times, the sound of a buzzer and the flash of a light have heralded electric shock to the fingers, both of these stimuli will have acquired a learned association with the flexion response.

The case of independent association is of little value for our inquiry, since thinking establishes equivalences between stimuli without the difficulties and drawbacks of associating each of them separately with a response. We must, however, bear independent association in mind as a possibility to be excluded before we can asume that other processes, such as those dependent on thinking, are operative.

2. Primary Stimulus Generalization

The principle of primary stimulus generalization emerged from Pavlov's experiments on classical conditioning (Pavlov, 1927) and has been found equally applicable to instrumental conditioning (for example, Guttman and Kalish, 1956). According to this principle, a learning process that builds up an association between S_1 and R_A will, without further training, produce an association between R_A and any stimulus, S_2, that resembles S_1. The closer the resemblance between S_1 and S_2, the stronger the generalized association will be.

An attempt to specify what we mean by stimuli "resembling" S_1 is apt to entail some circularity, since measuring the degree of generalization is often the only way of telling how similar two stimuli are for a particular organism. All we can say ultimately is that we and many other animal species are so made that certain pairs of stimuli possess a degree of "natural similarity": they evidently affect the nervous system in ways that are sufficiently alike to have similar consequences.

We use the term "natural similarity" rather than "innate similarity" because several writers (for example, Hebb, 1949; Rosenblatt, 1958; Taylor, 1962; and Uttley, 1956) have recently been suggesting that the recognition of certain similarities, for example, similarity in shape, stems from early learning of a sort that all normal members of a species undergo. It would seem, however, that at least some cases of primary stimulus generalization depend on resemblances whose recognition is inborn, as witness an experiment by Ganz and Riesen (1962). These investigators trained monkeys that had spent all their previous lives in total darkness to press a key to obtain sucrose solution during the appearance of light of a particular hue. It turned out that the monkeys would also press the key on seeing different hues. The new hues evoked fewer key-pressing responses than the original hue, but the number of responses increased with their nearness to the latter.

3. Secondary Stimulus Generalization

The third mechanism, secondary stimulus generalization, is usually difficult to demonstrate directly. We are, therefore, entitled to assume its occurrence only when the other two mechanisms can be excluded. We exclude independent association by ascertaining that the response, R_A, has acquired an increment of association with S_2 as a consequence of a learning process that associated R_A with S_1. The best way to rule out primary stimulus generalization is to apply stimuli that are intermediate between S_1 and S_2 along physical dimensions that are used to classify stimuli and to see whether these stimuli evoke R_A more strongly than S_2 but less strongly than S_1 (as they should if primary generalization is at work).

Secondary stimulus generalization occurs whenever a response, R_A, having become associated with S_1, becomes associated with S_2 through the intervention of a second, mediating response.

There are two ways in which this could happen. One involves *stimulus chaining* (Horton and Kjeldergaard, 1961): (*a*) S_1 possesses an association with R_A, either innately or through learning, and (*b*) S_2 acquires an association with a response, R_{S1}, which brings about S_1. Consequently the development depicted in Figure 3-1 takes place. S_2 evokes R_{S1}, which produces S_1, and S_1 in its turn evokes R_A. R_A is thus likely to occur whenever S_1 is encountered and, through the intermediary of S_1, whenever S_2 is encountered.

The clearest examples of the chaining kind of secondary stimulus generalization come from studies of verbal learning. We can take an example from an experiment by Sacks and Russell (cited by Jenkins, 1963). Previous free-association experiments had shown there to be a strong tendency for American students to say "chair" (R_A) on hearing the word "table" (S_1). Subjects belonging to this population were taught to respond "table" (R_{S1}) to the nonsense syllable "ZUG" (S_2). It was then found possible to establish an association between "ZUG" and "chair" with one or two training trials, indicating that a fairly strong association between this stimulus and this response had been produced by the combined action of the two previously established associations.

A further example can be found in a psychotherapeutic technique used by Wolpe (1958). The patient receives an electric shock and is

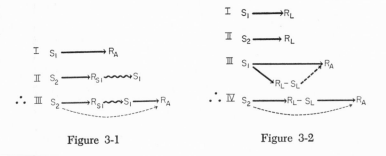

Figure 3-1   Figure 3-2

instructed to utter the word "calm" (R_{S1}), whereupon the shock is terminated. This procedure attaches a fear-reducing response (R_A) to the auditory and proprioceptive stimulation (S_1) produced by saying "calm." The patient is then encouraged to say "calm" to himself (R_{S1}) whenever he feels anxious in his everyday life (S_2), and many patients report that this occasions an immediate feeling of relief (R_A).

The second, and much more important, case of secondary stimulus generalization is *mediated stimulus generalization,* depicted in Figure 3-2. We begin with two stimulus conditions, S_1 and S_2, that have independently, whether innately or through learning, come to evoke a common response (known as the mediating or labeling response, R_L). A learned association is then formed between S_1 and a new response, R_A. S_2 is then found to possess an association with R_A, and the conditions are such that primary stimulus generalization can be ruled out.

The phenomenon is explicable as follows. R_L, like all other responses, produces a characteristic feedback stimulus pattern, S_L (the labeling stimulus). During the learning that associates S_1 with R_A, R_L also occurs, and S_L, as well as S_1, acquires an association with R_A. When S_2 is subsequently reintroduced, R_L occurs once again, and R_A is then instigated by S_L.

Chaining and mediated generalization are ordinarily coupled with each other and hard to separate entirely, because (see Figure 3-2) chaining can produce an equivalence between S_1 and S_L, while mediated generalization can make S_1 and S_2 equivalent.

Various responses can serve as R_L. They include manual responses, as demonstrated by Jeffrey (1953). In this experiment, the external stimulus objects were white, gray, and black patches, and the test responses, which were different for black and white stimuli and which were rewarded with marbles that could later be exchanged for candy, consisted of pushing or pulling a handle. After being trained to perform the appropriate test responses to black and white stimuli, one group of children was taught to perform labeling responses, consisting of turning the handle to the right or to the left. Black and white had different labeling responses, but gray had the same one as black for some subjects and the same one as white for other subjects. During the final test period, in which black, gray, and white stimuli were presented and the labeling responses had to be performed before the test responses, there was a strong tendency for the gray stimuli to evoke the test response associated with the color, black or white, with which it shared a labeling response.

Another group of subjects in Jeffrey's experiment made use of verbal labeling responses. The procedure was the same as that undergone by the group discussed earlier except that, in place of the handle-turning labeling responses, subjects had to say "black" on seeing a black patch, "white" on seeing a white patch, and either "white" or "black" on seeing a gray patch. With this group, there was an even more pronounced tendency for the gray patch to evoke the test response associated with the black patch when it was named "black" and that associated with the white patch when it was named "white."

Symbolic responses, including words, are ideally suited to a labeling function and, as Jeffrey's findings illustrate, can do so with particular effectiveness. They evidently furnish richer and more distinct cues. They, and the combinations that can be built out of them, form an inexhaustible stock of unique labels to draw on. They require little expenditure of effort. Finally, and this is a point to which we shall return, they are organized in systems.

Labeling responses, whether verbal or not, are apt to become reduced to a covert form in accordance with the general principle that responses come to be performed with the least intensity compatible with their function (Mowrer, 1954; Logan, 1960; Skinner, 1938; and Zipf, 1949). Implicit labeling responses may be too feeble or fragmentary to affect the external world or to be observable from without, but they can still furnish feedback stimulation to influence the subject's subsequent behavior. This is all that is needed for them to play their part, with the added advantages of privacy and relative lack of effort. In Jeffrey's experiment, a third group of subjects learned the manual labeling responses but were not instructed to perform them at the same time as the test responses. Nevertheless, there was still some generalization of the test response to the gray color from whichever of the other colors shared a labeling response with it, although it was not so marked as with the other groups. The presumption is that the labeling responses occurred in a covert form while the test response was being performed.

There seems, in fact, to be a general psychological principle, which may be called the *principle of secondary generalization*, to the effect that whenever two stimuli, S_1 and S_2, are both associated with a response, R_A, and one of the stimuli, S_1, later acquires an association with a second response, R_B, an association between S_2 and R_B will result. R_A, even when it is not reformed overtly, is likely to occur covertly and thus to act as a labeling response.

It will be recognized that secondary stimulus generalization must be classed as reasoning, since the association between R_A and S_2 depends on the prior formation of at least three distinct associations, namely S_1-R_A, S_1-R_L, S_2-R_L. This can often be accomplished in two learning processes, the first two associations being established simultaneously.

Mediated generalization has, it is true, become a rather contentious topic of late (see Cofer, 1961; Cofer and Musgrave, 1963). The controversy appears, however, to revolve around such issues as whether mediated generalization will occur in particular circumstances, how far mediators are verbal in nature, and how far mediators obey the laws of learning applicable to overt responses (see our discussion in Chapter 1). Nobody has been able to dispute that mediational processes, whether one refers to them as "responses" or not, must exist or to find a radically different way of explaining stimulus equivalences that are not attributable to independent association or to primary stimulus generalization.

Bases of Behavioral Equivalence

The three mechanisms that we have reviewed cause a response to become associated with two stimuli. These associations need not, however, be retained once they have been set up.

In the case of independent association, a learned stimulus-response bond can be dissolved by extinction, and even unlearned bonds may succumb to habituation if repeatedly activated in the absence of events of biological importance (Dodge, 1927; Harris, 1943). Discrimination learning can undo the effects of primary stimulus generalization when a response is reinforced with S_1 present and not reinforced in the presence of S_2. Secondary stimulus generalization will break down when either the association between S_L and the overt response R_A or the association between S_1 or S_2 and R_L is extinguished.

Labeling responses can even counteract primary stimulus generalization by producing secondary discrimination, which occurs when two stimuli possessing a natural similarity, S_1 and S_2, have different labeling responses, R_{L1} and R_{L2} attached to them. The combinations $S_1 + R_{L1}$ and $S_2 + R_{L2}$ may then be sufficiently distinct to call forth different overt responses without detectable generalization. Mushrooms and toadstools may look alike to the point of disastrous confusion between them, until we learn to name them correctly and attach different behavior to the names.

Even if associations of R_A with S_1 and S_2 continue to exist, this will not necessarily mean that S_1 and S_2 are behaviorally equivalent. R_A may be associated with both of them and yet not be the most probable response to either of them. Moreover, we must remember that the most probable response to a particular class of stimulus situations varies with motivational conditions and that a behavioral stimulus equivalence generally holds only when a particular motivational condition obtains.

Because of these qualifications, we shall refer to a state of affairs in which two or more stimuli have a common association with a response as a *basis for behavioral equivalence*. It will be a necessary but not a sufficient condition for a behavioral equivalence.

Secondary Stimulus Generalization and Directed Thinking

The behavioral equivalences that result from directed thinking can hardly be attributed to independent association or to primary stimulus generalization. They must clearly fall within the category of secondary stimulus generalization.

The labeling responses that are derived from directed thinking come into our possession only after long and laborious sequences of symbolic behavior. In standard experiments on secondary stimulus generalization, the subject receives ready-made labeling responses, which are imparted to him by the experimenter through verbal instruction or demonstration and reinforced when he uses them as intended. In everyday life also, we are often presented with labeling responses whose subsequent use will be rewarded. Posters or mass media tell which candidates represent which parties. A mother introduces a person to her child as "Uncle X" and from then on X is to receive the treatment considered appropriate to a moderately close adult male relative. These are cases where thinking is not necessary.

At other times, the labeling responses that will bring behavioral equivalences into line with ecological equivalences are not supplied from without but must be found by the subject himself. They cannot usually be selected or pieced together until intensive and protracted epistemic activity (comprising or including thinking) has taken place. Directed thinking thus not only identifies classes of stimulus situations that should be made behaviorally equivalent and associated with a common labeling response; it is essentially a means of identifying or constructing appropriate patterns of mediators, including labeling responses, and some of the most crucial problems of thinking are concerned with how this is done.

Systems of Labeling Responses

One of the reasons for the primacy of symbolic, and especially verbal, patterns among labeling responses is that they are organized in systems. What this means will be considered at length in later chapters, since many of the essential properties of directed thinking depend on it. There is, however, one implication that concerns the end product of directed thinking (which is all that we are considering at present), that is, that there can be secondary generalization not only between stimulus situations associated with one and the same labeling response but also between stimulus situations associated with different labeling responses.

We should expect secondary generalization to occur when there is a physical resemblance between the labeling responses attached to distinct stimuli. There would then be a natural similarity between their response-produced stimuli, with consequent transfer of overt responses from one to another through primary stimulus generalization. This expectation is confirmed by an experiment that Phillips (1958) has conducted. Turkish words were associated with different shades of gray and thus presumably made to evoke covert symbolic responses (for example, images, verbal descriptions) representing them. The more similar the shades associated with two words, the greater the stimulus generalization between them as revealed by the magnitude of the galvanic skin response (GSR).

A great deal of evidence shows, however, that physical resemblances between labeling responses are much less important and much less effective in giving rise to secondary generalization than semantic or logical connections.

Most of the experiments in question have not followed the secondary-stimulus-generalization paradigm. They have generally used words as conditioned stimuli and studied the degree of stimulus generalization between them as a function of ways in which they are related. It may be assumed, however, that, if there is a certain degree of stimulus generalization between two words or combinations of words functioning as conditioned stimuli, there will be a comparable degree of secondary stimulus situation whenever the same words or combinations of words are attached as labeling responses to other stimuli.

Semantic Generalization

Razran (1939b) carried out experiments on salivary conditioning in human subjects, using printed words like "urn" and "freeze" as conditioned stimuli. He later presented other words to test for stimulus generalization and found markedly more response to synonyms of the original conditioned stimuli, for example, "vase" and "chill," than to homonyms, for example, "earn" and "frieze."

In a later series of experiments (1949), using the same technique, he investigated generalization between words that were not identical but related in meaning. He found differing amounts of generalization with different kinds of relation, the most effective being with grammatical derivatives of the original word (for example, "sign"—"signal") and words representing subordinate concepts (for example, "flower"—"pansy"). Experiments by Diven (1937) and by Lacey and Smith (1954) have shown that, when a human subject experiences an electric shock during exposure to a word like "barn" or "cow," a fear reaction, evidenced by the GSR, will thereafter be evoked by other words connected with farming.

Semantic generalization has long been a favorite matter for experimental investigation in the U.S.S.R. The most active investigator of this topic has been Ivanov-Smolenski (1951, 1956, 1963), using his technique of "motor conditioning." His subjects were usually schoolchildren, and the response consisted of pressing a rubber bulb with the hand. Various conditioned stimuli, such as colored lights or sounds, were presented, and the experimenter trained the subject to respond to certain of them by saying "Press!" shortly after their appearance, and to refrain from responding to others by saying "Don't press!" instead.

Ivanov-Smolenski's group discovered quite early what they called "elective irradiation." When a response has become associated with a verbal conditioned stimulus, for example, "bell," it generalizes to the corresponding nonverbal stimulus, for example, the sound of a bell, and the reverse holds also. They found that both positive conditioned responses and inhibition generalize from the word "bird" to the word "flies" and to names of species of birds such as "sparrow," "magpie," and "swan." There was generalization from the word "bird" to pictures of particular kinds of birds and vice versa, as well as from the name of one bird species to the name of another.

Analogous phenomena have been demonstrated with other sorts of conditioned responses that must be less susceptible to voluntary control. Some of the most dramatic illustrations come from the work of Volkova (1953, 1957). She used the modification of Pavlov's salivary-conditioning method that Krasnogorski (1907) introduced for the first studies of conditioning in children. The unconditioned stimulus consists of cranberry puree coming down a chute and entering the subject's mouth, and records are made of salivation and masticatory movements. Volkova found that, when the excitatory conditioned stimulus was the word "good," pronounced out loud, and the inhibitory conditioned stimulus was the word "bad," sentences like "The pioneer helps his comrade" and "Leningrad is a wonderful city" evoked conditioned responses, but "The pupil was rude to the teacher" and "My friend is seriously ill" did not. When the positive conditioned stimulus was "Correct!" and the negative conditioned stimulus was "Error!", true statements such as "We live in Leningrad" and "In the week there are seven days" evoked conditioned responses, but untrue statements like "Cats and mice are great friends" and "Apples grow on the fir tree" did not. "Today is January 2nd" evokes a response on January 2nd, but proved to be an inhibitory stimulus on the following day. To mention one final experiment, which is particularly interesting in view of the questions about mathematical equivalences that will be raised later, when "ten" was the positive conditioned stimulus and "eight" the negative conditioned stimulus, conditioned responses were elicited by "8 + 2" and by "5 × 2" but not by "909 − 901" or "4 + 4."

In order to explain all these forms of generalization, we must assume that symbolic stimulus patterns with related meanings evoke implicit mediating responses that either resemble one another or possess common components. When two logically connected verbal formulas are associated as labeling responses with two different external stimuli, we can expect each of them to be accompanied or followed by its corresponding mediator (Osgood's r_m), resulting in secondary stimulus generalization between the external stimuli. Secondary generalization should likewise occur if the mediators become associated with the external stimulus situations in the absence of the verbal responses.

Classes, Relations, and Numbers

The systems of labeling responses that must be of greatest concern to us are those that are both utilized and produced in logical thinking. This consists of a thought process whose starting point and final product correspond to those of a logical argument, although the intermediate steps in the argument need not correspond to the stages through which the thought process passes. It is now generally recognized that logic need not necessarily depict the course of thinking. In certain circumstances, it may, especially in persons trained in logic. This is, however, more likely to be when they are checking the validity of their conclusions than when they are first arriving at them. Two characteristics of logical thinking are that (1) both its input and output can be expressed in propositions, that is, either in sentences of everyday language or in acceptable formulas of specialized mathematical or logical notation, and (2) the derivation of the output from the input must conform to specifiable rules.

Logical thinking (which includes mathematical thinking) is dominated by systems built up of three kinds of elements: classes, relations, and numbers. Piaget and his collaborators (Piaget, 1947; Inhelder and Piaget, 1955; and Piaget and Inhelder, 1959) have traced the development of the kinds of thinking that make use of them. Although elementary forms of logical inference occur earlier, the general finding is that the child achieves a full understanding of classes, relations, and numbers at about the age of seven, when he is entering the "stage of concrete operations." He then becomes capable of the types of reasoning that correspond to simple arithmetic and to the branches of logic known as the "algebra of classes" and the "algebra of relations."

So we must here attempt some preliminary examination of the psychological processes that pertain to classes, relations, and numbers, although many of the problems that arise from them must be postponed until later.

Classes

The words "classify" and "classification" are often applied loosely to all kinds of stimulus equivalence. Psychologists interested in perception sometimes state that perception involves "classifying" or "categorizing" incoming stimulus patterns. By this they usually mean no more than that the subject responds to the pattern in accordance with one rather than another of its properties and in much the same way as he would respond to other patterns that share that property.

The generalizations and discriminations of animals are likewise described by some writers as processes of "classification." If an animal is rewarded for approaching a red triangle when it is presented next to a blue circle and if, thereafter, he approaches a red circle paired with a blue triangle, he may be said to "classify" the stimuli by color rather than by shape.

The kinds of classification that are used in logical thinking involve, however, much more than that, and the word is best reserved for systems of stimulus equivalences that fulfill special conditions. What these conditions are is best seen from the course of development that leads up to them in the child.

Piaget (1945, 1947) describes the "preconceptual stage," occupying roughly the third and fourth year, during which the child has stimulus equivalences but does not understand the relation between a class of objects and the members that belong to it. When he is taken for a walk through the woods and sees a succession of snails, it is not clear to him whether they are distinct but similar snails or whether the same snail keeps on reappearing. The question has, in fact, no meaning for him since, as far as he is concerned, they are all "snail," just as, if a pigeon has been taught to peck at a panel whenever a red spot appears on it, there is no point in asking whether the pigeon believes that different red spots are appearing in turn or that the same red spot is appearing intermittently. He simply pecks whenever he sees "red."

Sometimes, however, it is meaningful to say that a pigeon can tell the difference between members of a stimulus class. An experiment by Reynolds (1961) can serve as an illustration. He used four stimulus patterns that appeared one at a time on a panel: a white triangle on a red background, a white circle on a red background, a white triangle on a blue background, and a white circle on a blue background. When a green lamp was lit, pecking secured food reward only in the presence of a triangle. When a yellow lamp was lit, pecking was rewarded only in the presence of red. The pigeons learned to respond appropriately. The green lamp must thus have generated some kind of internal condition that made stimulus patterns containing triangles behaviorally equivalent. The yellow lamp on the other hand generated an internal condition in which this equivalence was dissolved, since patterns containing triangles on differently colored backgrounds now evoked dissimilar behavior.

In everyday language, to understand the relation of class membership means to recognize the similarity between all members of a class while at the same time being able to distinguish one member of a class from another. Apostel (1959) has suggested that, in S-R language, this means that each stimulus object belonging to the class is associated both with some response common to all members of the class and with some other response that is peculiar to it. In the terminology proposed by Shepard, Hovland, and Jenkins (1961), there must be both "classification learning" (learning which associates one response with each of several stimuli) and "identity learning" (learning that associates one response with one stimulus only).

In order to cover the case of Reynolds's pigeons and equivalent behavior in human beings, we may reformulate Apostel's criterion a little and state that an understanding of class membership exists when there are some motivational conditions in which all members of a class will be behaviorally equivalent and other motivational conditions in which they will not be. To go back to Piaget's example of the snails, this means that there will be times when all snails evoke identical behavior in the child (for example, when he has been offered a reward for collecting as many snails as he can find) but, at other times, the most probable response to one snail will differ from the most probable response to another snail (for example, when he has been offered a reward for picking up the largest snail or the fifth snail that he encounters).

The relation of class inclusion can be handled in much the same way. A subject can be said to recognize that all birds are animals (that is, that the class of birds is included in the class of animals) if, given certain motivational conditions, the most probable response to the sight of any bird is the same as the most probable response to the sight of any animal while, given other motivational conditions, stimulus situations that include the sight of a bird will evoke a different response from stimulus situations in which no bird is visible, even though an animal of some other class may be.

What has been said about classes thus far is, however, vulnerable to the criticism made by Piaget (1959) of Apostel's analysis, namely that it concerns merely sensorimotor classification. Classification on this level, fulfilling both Apostel's criteria and the similar criteria that we have just discussed, appear in early infancy. Many visually perceived objects, for example, evoke the response of looking and can therefore be said to form a class of "objects to be looked at." Some but not all of the objects that can be looked at are also objects that can be grasped. "Objects to be grasped" thus form a class included in the wider class of objects to be looked at. So, in this way, a complicated system of class inclusions grows up, which becomes crystallized as the child learns which actions will be successful and which will be unavailing in various situations.

On the other hand, the ability to make valid inferences about class membership and class inclusion clearly requires additional conditions, which gradually approach fulfillment as the child comes nearer to the stage of concrete operations. For one thing, when the child thinks about class membership and class inclusion, his thinking relates to objects and classes of objects that are not present in front of him. They must be represented by symbolic responses of some sort, and the problem of what sort will be taken up in Chapter 6.

Some of the processes that prepare the ground for classificatory thinking can be recognized from data reported by Piaget and from everyday experience, once it has been considered from this point of view. After he has learned to speak, the child has not merely a common motor response but, in addition, a common verbal response to link all members of the class together. In the case of some classifications, imposed on him by the influence of adults, there may be only verbal labeling responses. Then the child acquires the ability to respond appropriately to verbal labeling responses (for example, by pointing to, or gathering together, objects within his field of vision that possess a common label) and to use them (for example, by naming the class, or the defining property of the class, to which several specified objects all belong).

A little later, he can frame and understand sentences using words like "all" or "some," but it takes time before such sentences mean the same to him as they mean to adults, as Piaget's observations show. He goes through stages where he is apt to make inferences that ordinary adults would regard as wrong and logicians would regard as invalid.

He is particularly susceptible to errors that show his grasp of class inclusion to be incomplete (Piaget and Inhelder, 1959). Suppose that we show the child a row of blue circular tokens with a few red squares dispersed among them. During the "preconceptual stage" (2 to 4 years), if we ask him whether all the squares are red, he is apt to answer "No, because there are some blue tokens." Piaget's protocols indicate that he cannot distinguish between the class of squares and the perceptual figure formed by the squares. He denies that all the squares are red because the figure made up of squares contains some blue circles within its boundaries. A little later, during the "stage of intuitive thinking" (4 to 7 years), he is shown a row made up of blue circles, blue squares, and red squares. When asked whether all of the circles are blue he answers "No, because there are also some blue squares." This time, he evidently confuses the question that is put to him, meaning "Do all the circles comprise some of the blue tokens?", with the question "Do all the circles comprise all the blue tokens?"

To take another illustrative experiment (Piaget and Szeminska, 1941), a child in the intuitive stage is shown a string of wooden beads, most of which are brown but a few of which are white. When asked whether there are more wooden beads or more brown beads, he usually answers that there are more brown beads, "because there are only a few white ones." Questioning makes it clear that he is fully capable of recognizing that all the beads are wooden, just as, in the previous experiment, he was able to draw the tokens accurately from memory. But, in comparing the number of brown beads with the number of wooden beads, he does not understand that a bead that is being counted as brown must also be counted among the wooden beads.

By the age of 7, when the stage of concrete operations has been reached, the child no longer makes errors like these, and he becomes capable of valid inferences in the algebra of classes. His classificatory responses form a structure, which Piaget (1945, 1947) calls the "grouping (*groupement*)," characterized by judgments of the following kind.

1. *Combinativity.* $A + B = C$, for example, all men and all women are equivalent to all adults.
2. *Reversibility.* $C - A = B$, for example, all adults who are not men are women.
3. *Associativity.* $(A + B) + C = A + (B + C)$, for example, all men and all women are equivalent to all fathers and all adults who are not fathers.
4. *General identity.* $A - A = 0$, for example, all women except those that are women are equivalent to nobody.
5. *Special identity.* $A + A = A$, for example, all women and all women are equivalent to all women.

Relations

It is often said that thinking serves to make us "see new relations" between things that formerly seemed unrelated. Perception, likewise, is sometimes described as a matter of apprehending relations rather than particular stimulus properties. Yet, although it is easy to give examples of the kind of relation referred to, it has not always been found easy to specify what is meant by "relations" in general. This way of speaking or writing has, at times, been used as a means of obscuring issues and as an excuse for shirking the quest for precision.

Yet a relatively simple way of clarifying relations is at hand and fits in well with the concepts that we are in process of using (Berlyne, 1960b). It consists of utilizing a definition of "relation" that is current among mathematicians, namely that a relation is a set of ordered pairs. An ordered pair is a pair of elements mentioned in a particular order, for example, $\langle a, b \rangle$. If the same two elements are mentioned in the other order, the result is a different ordered pair, so that $\langle a, b \rangle \neq \langle b, a \rangle$.

Thus, when we talk about the relation "parent of," we are, according to this definition, talking about all the pairs of people that we could name, such that the first-named individual is a parent of the second. It can be seen from this example that, if we reversed the order of the individuals in each pair, we should not be dealing with the relation "parent of" but with the converse relation, "child of." Similarly, the relation "greater than" applied to natural numbers is the set of all pairs of numbers, $<x, y>$, such that $x > y$. The relation "three times as great as" would be all pairs of numbers, $<x, y>$, such that $x = 3y$. The members of this latter relation, including $<6, 2>$, $<27, 9>$, $<396, 132>$, etc., will form a subset of the relation "greater than." It is customary to use the notation "aRb" to denote that "a stands in the relation R to b" or that $<a, b>$ is a member of the class of ordered pairs, R.

In psychology, we can accordingly say that a relation is recognized whenever there is a behavioral equivalence between the ordered pairs of stimulus objects that exemplify the relation. The two stimulus objects in question must appear at different spatial locations or at different times or both, so that they will be ordered spatially or temporally or both.

An animal will, then, be said to recognize the relation "larger than" if, given certain internal conditions, he tends to make a particular response whenever he encounters a larger stimulus object to the left of (or above or before) a smaller stimulus object. The response in question could, for example, be that of approaching the left-hand object in any standard discrimination-learning situation.

Just as equivalences between individual stimulus objects may be attributed either to natural similarities, making for primary stimulus generalization, or to mediated similarities, dependent on labeling responses and making for secondary stimulus generalization, there can be "natural" and "mediated" relations.

Natural Relations

We can demonstrate the existence of a natural relation in the following way. We take a set of spatially or temporally ordered pairs of stimuli and carry out tests to make sure that these pairs do not initially have a most probable response in common. We then train the subject to perform a certain response (which might be button pressing, a movement in a certain direction, or a verbal utterance) to one ordered pair, say, $<S_1, S_2>$, and we ascertain that this response is transferred automatically to the other pairs in the set. The evidence suggests that natural relations include "more intense than," "less intense than," "equal in intensity to," "larger than," "smaller than," "equal in size to," "resembling . . . in a particular characteristic," and "differing from . . . in a particular characteristic."

An experiment that precisely fulfills these conditions for demonstrating a natural relation was performed by Uznadze (1927). He trained a dog to flex a paw in response to a sequence of two tones of equal pitch, of which the second was louder than the first, by applying an electric shock to the paw after the tones were presented. The actual intensities varied from trial to trial but, as long as the second tone was louder than the first, the dog responded. Then, pairs consisting of a louder tone preceding a fainter one or of two tones of equal intensity were presented without shock, and the dog built up a discrimination, responding to only 29% of these inhibitory combinations. Finally, when fainter-louder sequences of tones of a new pitch or of sounds of an electric bell were tested, the dog generalized with the response to these and differentiated them from the same stimuli occurring in the reverse order.

There are several other relevant animal experiments in the literature. Chorazyna (1959) taught dogs to place a paw on a food tray, as a means of obtaining food, on hearing two successive tones of the same pitch. They learned to inhibit the response on hearing the same tone followed by a lower tone. After further training, all sequences of two identical tones evoked the response while all higher-lower sequences did not. The response appeared, however, when a lower-higher sequence was tried. This implies that "lower-higher" represented a different relation from "higher-lower" for these dogs. Lawrence and De Rivera (1954) were able to teach rats to jump to the right when they saw a lighter card above a darker card and to jump to the left when the upper card was darker than the lower one.

Mediated Relations

A mediated relation may be based on a natural relation. For example, a diamond weighing 50 carats would hardly be recognized as heavier than one weighing 49 carats if the two were inspected visually side by side or held in the palm successively. But if they are placed in the pans of a jeweler's balance, the sight of one pan depressed may well induce a verbal pattern, such as "The one on the right is heavier," that can serve as a labeling response. Consequently, we are likely to generalize to this new situation the responses that we have learned to make to ordered pairs of desirable objects, the right-hand one of which is perceptibly heavier than the other, for example, selecting the right-hand one when both are offered at the same price.

To turn to a case of a wholly unnatural relation (in our specialized sense of the term), appearance does not usually enable us to tell married couples from other man-woman pairs seen together. But we learn to refer to a particular woman as "Mrs. X" or "Y's wife," etc., and this labeling response enables appropriate behavior to come to the fore and inappropriate behavior to be withheld.

There are, in fact, two ways in which mediated relations can be produced. One way, illustrated by the examples just considered, consists of attaching a common labeling response, descriptive of the relation, to all ordered pairs that are instances of the relation.

The other way is to attach different labeling responses, between which a natural relation exists, to the two stimulus objects. The president of a certain university is reputed to have delivered an address in which he alluded to "the faculty" (with his right hand on a level with his chest), "the deans" (with his hand on a level with his neck), and "the president" (with his hand far above his head).

Relational Thinking

An infant, like a lower animal, can, of course, respond quite early to natural relations such as "larger than" or "to the left of." But, once again, additional problems arise when we think about relations between objects that are not present or infer relations that are not readily perceptible between objects that are present. In both cases, there is a need for symbolic processes to represent relations which are not manifest in the external stimulus field, and the child becomes capable of them in consequence of a gradual development that comes to fruition at the beginning of the "stage of concrete operations."

Piaget has not coupled his studies of the use and understanding of classificatory language with comparable studies pertaining to relations. He claims, in fact, that ordinary language is much better equipped to express interconnections between classes than interconnections between relations, a claim that could do with more amplification and justification than he gives.

There are, however, studies to show the relatively late appearance of the ability to make inferences regarding relations. Smedslund's (1963) carefully controlled experiments show, for example, that, before the age of 8, a child who has seen that rod A is perceptibly longer than rod B and that rod B is perceptibly longer than rod C cannot be relied on to conclude that A is longer than C in conditions where perception of the relative lengths of A and C is impeded.

A situation that Piaget and his associates have studied intensively (Piaget and Szeminska, 1941; Piaget and Inhelder, 1959) is one in which a child is confronted with a pile of differently colored rods and told to arrange them in order of increasing length. During the preconceptual stage, this task is generally beyond him. During the stage of intuitive thinking, he can succeed at the cost of a great deal of fumbling and false moves that have to be corrected. Only during the stage of concrete operations does he begin to carry out the task methodically, by placing the shortest rod, then the next shortest, etc. Interestingly enough, a child in the intuitive stage can often produce a correct black-and-white drawing of what the series of rods will look like when the arrangement has been completed, although he cannot yet form such a series out of actual rods without considerable difficulty. Piaget explains this paradoxical finding by pointing out that the drawing task involves the equivalent of only half of the arranging task. In both cases, the child has to put next to each element an element that is slightly longer than it. When he is arranging actual rods, however, he has to pick out from the pile of rods that are still unplaced the rod that should be placed next. This requires him to realize that the rod that should come next after those that have already been placed is the shortest of those that are left, and this means making use of the double inference that, when a rod is in its proper place in the series, it is longer than all those that come before it and shorter than all those that come after it. The ability to produce a colored drawing of the series is, significantly enough, not in advance of the ability to arrange the series, since it necessitates the ability to identify the rod that is to come next.

Counting

Children normally learn to count up to four objects by the age of five (Descoeudres, 1914). But a true understanding of the concept of number, which is necessary for coherent thinking about numbers, first appears, according to Piaget's data (Piaget and Szeminska, 1941), at the beginning of the stage of concrete operations, simultaneously with understanding of classes and relations. The crucial test is whether a child realizes that the number of objects in a collection must remain unchanged as long as the membership remains unchanged, no matter what other properties of the collection may be altered.

Suppose, for example, that a child is shown a row of seven white tokens and a row of seven red tokens, aligned so that each white token has a red token opposite it. A child in the stage of intuitive thinking will generally acknowledge that there must be just as many white tokens as red tokens. If the row of red tokens is now spread out so as to take up more space than the row of white tokens and red and white tokens are no longer visibly paired off, he is apt to say either that there are now more red than white tokens (because the row of red tokens is longer) or that there are fewer red tokens (because the row of red tokens is less dense). His ability to count does not protect him against this error. If he is required to count the tokens of each color, he is apt to say that "the number of red tokens is the same as the number of white tokens, but there are still more red ones than white ones" (Gréco, 1962).

From the age of about 7, the child recognizes that, if the two collections are initially equal in number, they must remain equal in number, no matter how their spatial arrangement changes, provided that no token is added or removed. He realizes, moreover, that if collection A is equal in number to collection B and collection B to collection C, then A must contain the same number of elements as C. This is also the age when he is able to carry out and make use of simple arithmetical reasoning, which means putting statements about numbers together to generate new knowledge and is analogous to what he is beginning to do with class and relations.

Piaget, in fact, describes number as a "synthesis" of classification and ordering, and it is clear that both of these must play their part in an understanding of number. On the one hand, the use of cardinal numbers implies the ability to think of objects grouped together in a class, since cardinality is an attribute not of each object singly but of the class. Furthermore, there is a behavioral equivalence between classes with the same number of objects in them. All collections of six objects make up a "class of classes," as Frege (1879) and Russell (1919) recognized when they defined a cardinal number as a set of sets such that the members of any one set can be placed in correspondence with the members of any other set. On the other hand, number implies ordering, both because classes are ordered according to cardinality—classes containing seven objects are "larger than" classes containing six objects, etc.—and because ordinal numbers are used to distinguish and order objects within a class—the seventh object "comes after" the sixth object, etc.

Although numerical responses (that is, pronouncing numbers overtly or subvocally) have great usefulness as labeling responses, they have to work in conjunction with labeling responses of other kinds. When we count the objects in a set, the objects have to be treated as both equivalent and distinct. They are equivalent in the sense that their individual properties make no difference to the ordinal numbers that are attached to them or to the number that is attached to the set as a whole. They could, in fact, be permuted freely or replaced by other objects as long as there were a one-to-one replacement. This equivalence, which masks their distinctions and makes them all simply elements of the set, must depend on the association of each of them with a common classifying response.

On the other hand, even if the objects in the set are identical in their physical properties, they must be kept separate and given an order; we must make sure that each is counted once and once only. When we are counting objects that appear one at a time, the numerical responses can act as distinguishing labels, although there is evidence that other internal responses, taking on different forms as we go through a sequence, help us to recognize temporal order (Berlyne, 1960c). When the objects appear all together, we have to rely on receptor-adjusting responses (eye movements, head movements), finger-pointing responses, or manipulations of the objects (for example, moving each to one side as it is counted), etc. The ordering relation is thus a mediated relation. Once counting has been accomplished, these transient distinguishing responses have completed their task. From now on, the numerical responses can serve as a basis for ordering relations and enable us to distinguish or compare the objects in thought when they are not physically present.

The ability to attach a number to a classificatory label (that is, a stimulus that is produced by a labeling response common to members of a class) takes some some time to appear. Before the age of 5 or 6, children have difficulty in applying a cardinal number to a set of heterogeneous objects, even though they may readily state how many there are when faced with identical objects. Asked how many blocks are in front of them, they are likely to say "one big one and two little ones" (Gast, 1957). Faced with two red and three green tokens and asked to hand over three tokens, they pick out three green ones (Brushlinski, 1960). They evidently find it easier to associate the numerical response with a combination of external stimulus properties common to members of the numbered set. There is also some confusion in 5-year-olds between cardinal and ordinal numbers; a child asked to show four tokens is apt to point to the fourth token, that is, the one with which the number "four" was associated in the course of counting (Brushlinski, 1960).

Measurement

The use of numbers as labeling responses and labeling stimuli constitutes what we call "measurement," of which the specification of cardinal and ordinal numbers by counting is a special case.

Measurement is potentially the most valuable of all forms of secondary stimulus generalization. Numbers can express distinctions that are as broad or as fine, as numerous or as few, as may be needed, so that they can be adapted to any requirements of information transmission.

Numbers are not only unparalleled as vehicles for the transmission of any desired flux of information; they are also supremely suited to the requirements of information rejection. When a number is associated with something as a measure, it reflects one property and is unaffected by other properties that are independent of this one. A measure can thus place in one equivalence class a multitude of entities that are widely different—perhaps so widely different that what they have in common is not readily visible and not ascertainable at all without elaborate computational procedures.

Furthermore, a large part of directed thinking with numbers is aimed at the evaluation of mathematical functions. A function offers a procedure for replacing a number or a collection of numbers (the "argument" or "arguments") with another number (the "value"). Many familiar arithmetical and algebraic operations provide examples. Since several alternative arguments or sets of arguments can yield the same value, whereas the reverse is excluded by the definition of a "function," the number of input possibilities is in excess of the number of output possibilities, which implies that information is generally lost in the process of determining the value of a function.

In 1946, Stevens introduced a fourfold classification of scales that has left its imprint on all later discussion of measurement amongst psychologists. Later writers (for example, Coombs 1950; Coombs, Raiffa, and Thrall, 1954; and Suppes and Zinnes, 1963) have drawn further distinctions and added to the four types of scale described by Stevens.

Some types of scale are more powerful than others, in the sense that they convey more information. For example, the "ratio scale" used to measure length is more powerful than an "interval scale" with an arbitrary zero point (for example, the centigrade scale of temperature), and this in its turn is more powerful than an "ordinal scale" (for example, numbering of houses along a street).

The question arises of how we can determine the type to which a particular scale belongs or the type of scale that is applicable to a particular set of phenomena. Suppes and Zinnes (1963) suggest that scales of measurement can be regarded as mathematical models. Each type of scale, they claim, implies an isomorphism, or similarity of structure, between the model corresponding to it and "empirical operations and relations" bearing on the phenomena to which the scale is applied. It is, however, possible to distinguish the types of scale in terms of behavioral and ecological equivalences. From this point of view, each type of scale sets up certain behavioral equivalences between entities that are being measured. Whether a set of entities (stimulus objects) is *measurable* by a particular type of scale depends on whether the corresponding *ecological* equivalences exist among its elements. What type of scale they are *measured* by depends similarly on what *behavioral* equivalences exist. Specification of the equivalences implied by each type of scale is offered elsewhere (Berlyne, 1960c).

Chapter 4

Response equivalences and habit-family hierarchies

THE LAST CHAPTER discussed directed thinking, and S-thinking in particular, as a means of seeking or assembling advantageous labeling response patterns and attaching them to stimulus situations. Through the behavioral equivalences that arise in this way, overt responses are made to depend on stimulus properties that indicate which response is optimal, and worthless information relating to other stimulus properties is blocked. A common labeling response links two objects that belong to the same class, two classes of objects that are included in the same supraordinate class, two ordered pairs of objects that instance the same relation, two sets of objects that are equally numerous, and two objects that are assigned the same value by a particular measure. Similar links will exist between the symbolic processes that represent these entities in thought.

There are, however, other kinds of equivalence engendered by directed thinking (including thinking that makes use of classification, ordering, and mathematical notions) that do not fit into this framework so neatly or so obviously. Since these raise problems that bring some additional facets of thinking into view, we must devote some attention to them.

Equations

Some of the equivalences that call for examination are ones denoted by "equals" (=) or "identical" (≡) signs when arithmetical or algebraic notation is used. In logical notation, they may be denoted by "implies" (⊃, ⇒) or "equivalent to" (≡, ⇔) signs.

Thinking may, for example, make use of statements, belonging to the algebra of classes, such as "Fungi are the only plants without

74

chlorophyll." If A represents the class of plants, B the class of plants possessing chlorophyll, and C the class of fungi, this statement would be represented by logicians in such a form as $A - B = C$ or $(x \epsilon A) \cdot (x \sim \epsilon B) \equiv (x \epsilon C)$. The algebra of relations provides statements like "x is the uncle of y, and y is the father of z means that x is the great-uncle of z" $(xRy \cdot yR'z \supset xR''z)$. In mathematics, we have equations such as $2 + 2 = 4$ or $(x + y)^2 = x^2 + 2xy + y^2$.

Let us concentrate on this last algebraic equation as a representative of the kinds of equivalence with which we are now concerned. All forms of mathematical reasoning make copious use of equations like this, and a large part of the efforts of creative mathematicians is devoted to the establishment of equations that are comparable except for being less banal.

The symbols that figure in these equations can undoubtedly be interpreted in several ways. They can be regarded as marks that a mathematician writes on a piece of paper or they can be taken to stand for entities, or relations between entities, in a physical world. We, however, are interested in the psychological processes that they represent. These are evidently symbolic processes that have both stimulus and response aspects. The senses in which expressions $(x + y)^2$ and $x^2 + 2xy + y^2$ are mathematically equivalent are reasonably well established. The precise nature of the psychological equivalence that must underlie this mathematical equivalence is not so straightforward.

For one thing, the importance of the equation evidently resides in the fact that there are motivational conditions in which the stimulus patterns $(x + y)^2$ and $x^2 + 2xy + y^2$ are not equivalent! The equation is useful precisely because each of these stimulus patterns is associated with responses that would not be evoked by the other! The replacement of one of these expressions by the other in the course of a piece of algebraic thinking opens up new lines of deduction that could not branch out from the other expression. For example, a student who has to solve the equation $x^2 + 6x + 9 = 0$ may be baffled until it occurs to him that $(x + y)^2 = x^2 + 2xy + y^2$, whereupon he sees that the left-hand side of this equation can be rewritten as $(x + 3)^2$, and it is then easy to see that $x = -3$ is the solution.

The fact that it is permissible to write down the two expressions interchangeably is not the whole answer either. There may be circumstances in which a subject is as likely to write down one as the other. Usually, however, the circumstances in which $(x + y)^2$ will be written and those in which $x^2 + 2xy + y^2$ will be written are distinct.

Finally, the essential point cannot be simply the existence of habits that make a subject replace one of the expressions with the other in the course of his work on algebraic problems. There are circumstances in which he might well have the habit of replacing $(x + y)^2$ with $(x + y)^3$, for example, when he passes from considering the area of a cube's face to considering the cube's volume, or when he finds that he has mistaken one exponent for another. But the expressions $(x + y)^2$ and $(x + y)^3$ are not related in the same way as $(x + y)^2$ and $x^2 + 2xy + y^2$.

Analogous problems arise in connection with logical implications and equivalences such as those cited earlier. The fact of being able to substitute one expression for another must come into it. But the nature and conditions of the substitutability are crucial.

Our only concern at this point is to show that what has been said so far about stimulus equivalences does not suffice to dispose of the problems raised by equations. We shall come back to these problems later in this chapter but, before we do so, we shall have to present some further concepts and arguments.

Quantitative Invariants

A second kind of equivalence that we must examine is, according to Piaget's data, not solidly entrenched until the beginning of the stage of concrete operations. It raises questions of a somewhat different nature, but they are even more pertinent to the essence of directed thinking.

One example has already been mentioned. In the course of the discussion of number in Chapter 3, we had occasion to note the observation on which Piaget bases his contention that a number is not understood before the age of 7. Younger children, it will be remembered, assert that the number of objects in a collection either increases or diminishes when the objects are spread out over a wider area. From the age of 7 on, the normal child appreciates that number depends solely on the membership of a collection and is not affected by its spatial distribution.

Judgments bearing on other quantitative properties undergo a similar development. There is, for example, an experiment (Piaget and Inhelder, 1941) in which the child is shown two rods of equal length placed parallel to each other with their ends aligned. If the upper rod is then moved an inch or two to the right, the younger child will deny that they are still of equal length; he will believe either that the upper rod is longer (because its right-hand end sticks out beyond that of the lower rod) or that it is shorter (because its left-hand end is indented). When he reaches the stage of concrete operations, he realizes that the lengths of rigid bodies are not changed by displacements and that two rods can be of equal length even when their ends are not aligned.

In another experiment, the child is shown two identical balls of plasticine (Piaget and Inhelder, 1941). One of them is elongated into a sausagelike shape, and the child is asked whether the two masses of plasticine are equal in amount. During the stage of concrete operations and later, he answers affirmatively; earlier, he says either that the elongated mass contains more plasticine (because it is longer) or that it contains less (because it is thinner).

As an example on which to concentrate, let us take the case (Piaget and Szeminska, 1941) of conservation of quantity of liquid with changes in shape. The subject is first shown two identical glass vessels, A1 and A2, containing equal quantities of colored water. The experimenter pours the contents of A2 into a narrower vessel, B. The subject is then asked whether the quantity of water in B is greater than, less than, or equal to the quantity in A1.

At the age of 4 or 5, most children will say that B now contains more water than A1 (because the level is higher), although some will assert that B contains less than A1 (because the column in B is narrower). From the age of about 7, a normal subject will, of course, insist that the quantities in B and A1 must be equal.

Piaget has interested himself mainly in what can be learned from the errors that young children make in these situations and in the nature of the transition from the forms of thinking characteristic of the stage of intuitive thought to those characteristic of the older child and adult. For our purposes, we can concentrate on the question of how judgments of equality are reliably made by adults.

Quantitative Invariants vs. Perceptual Constancies

If we ask why the normal adult is immune to the mistaken judgments that young children make in these circumstances, the first factor to come to mind is the following: the child bases his judgment either on the increase in height of the column of liquid in B or on its decrease in width, whereas the adult takes both of these changes into consideration and understands that they compensate for each other.

Experiments on quantitative invariants are, in some ways, reminiscent of experiments on perceptual constancies. When two surfaces in different illuminations are perceived as alike in brightness or in color, despite the different intensities or wavelengths of the light that they reflect, and when two objects seen from different angles or distances appear to have the same shape or size, despite the different shapes or sizes of their retinal images, the subject's response does not depend solely on the stimulation coming from the surface or object that is being judged. It is affected also by cues from the background that supply information about illumination, angle of vision, distance, etc.

Similarly, the adult's judgment of invariant quantity in the experiment with the colored water pays heed to at least two features of the stimulus situation, namely the increase in height and the decrease in width. The two compensate for each other, just as cues indicative of increasing distance compensate for decreasing retinal size when an object recedes and cause the judged size of the object to remain constant.

Nevertheless, the quantitative-invariant judgment is not a perceptual matter. Suppose that one showed an adult the equal quantities of liquid in A1 and A2 and then performed the pouring from A2 to B behind a screen. And suppose that one then confronted the adult subject with a series of glasses resembling B, all containing slightly different quantities of liquid, and asked him to select the one that contained just as much as A1. It is obvious that this would be quite a difficult task. The subject's guesses would, no doubt, have a central tendency approximating the correct answer. But they would have great variability, and the confidence with which they were proffered would hardly compare with that shown by a subject who had witnessed the pouring.

Furthermore, an adult realizes that, if one column of liquid is simultaneously taller and narrower than a second one, the two are not necessarily equal in volume. There has to be just the right excess of height to make up for the deficit in width, and it is extremely difficult to decide by looking at two columns of water whether this condition is realized.

Quantitative Invariants vs. Concept Formation

A second factor that obviously affects the adult's judgment, in contradistinction to the young child's, is his deeply rooted readiness to accept the testimony of knowledge (that is, inference and symbolic processes generally) rather than that of perception, when there is a discrepancy between them. However convincingly a stage conjurer makes a rabbit seem to have disappeared into thin air, the adult spectator does not really believe that the rabbit has disappeared, because he knows that material objects cannot go out of existence in this way and that stage magic depends on illusion. When an adult looks at his watch, the hands appear to be stationary, but he believes nevertheless that they are moving, because he remembers having seen them in a different position ten minutes ago and because he knows that watch hands move at an imperceptible speed.

So the responses of an adult subject in the quantitative-invariant experiment do not depend solely on the external stimuli that are there when he is questioned. They are determined also by his knowledge or memory (that is, his internal symbolic representation) of the fact that the column of liquid now in B was formed out of a column resembling the one now in A1 by the operation of pouring.

Piaget's quantitative-invariant experiments are often mentioned in text books under the heading of "concept formation." But this practice helps to obscure what is most significant and instructive about them.

In the typical concept-formation experiment, the subject is confronted with a series of stimulus patterns and has to identify those patterns that are instances of the concept, that is, those that are "correct" or those to which a certain name is applicable. The patterns usually vary in several properties, for example, in shape, size, and color, and the subject's task is to ascertain and learn which properties define the concept and which properties are irrelevant and therefore to be ignored. The correct patterns may thus consist of those that are triangular, regardless of color or size. Sometimes the concept may be a disjunctive or conjunctive one, so that, for example, any pattern that is triangular or square, or any pattern that is triangular and red, may be correct. But in the typical concept-formation experiment, the information that is necessary for distinguishing instances of the concept from noninstances is derivable from external stimulation. It is a matter of finding out which perceptible properties to use as a basis for the judgment and which to leave out of account.

The quantitative-invariant experiment is essentially different. The subject does not judge the columns of colored water to be instances of the same quantity on the basis of their stimulus properties alone. The information in the perceptual field is, as we have shown above, insufficient to guide the response reliably. It has to be supplemented by information that has been deposited in the subject by previous perceptions and relates to the past history of the stimulus objects that are now present.

Books, chapters, and articles with headings like "Cognitive Processes," "Intellectual Processes," or even "Thinking" are often largely devoted to discussions of concept-formation experiments (for example, Bruner, Goodnow, and Austin, 1955; Leeper, 1951; and Vygotski, 1956). Yet the process of concept formation in itself is not a form of thinking but a form of discrimination learning. It may, of course, be accompanied or aided by thinking. Instead of proceeding by trial and error until differential reinforcement has caused him to respond correctly, the subject may attempt to deduce what the defining attributes must be from the positive and negative instances that he has already been allowed to see. If he is invited to select the patterns that will be sampled, he will, no doubt, use thinking to guide his selection (Bruner, Goodnow, and Austin, 1955). For the reasons that have been given and for others that will become apparent as our discussion advances, the typical concept-formation experiment is actually not a good prototype for directed thinking. The quantitative-invariant experiment is, in many ways, a better one, which is why it is worthwhile to dwell on it.

Behavior Dependent on Combinations of External and Internal Stimuli

There is clearly a behavioral equivalence involved in the quantitative-invariant experiment. There are motivational conditions in which one would behave alike in relation to the columns of water in vessels A1 and B. For instance, if one were thirsty and if satisfaction depended solely on the quantity of water consumed, one would choose indifferently to drink the column of water in A1 or the column in B. If one has six guests for dinner and a bottle containing just enough wine to fill six glasses, one can fill the guests' glasses directly from the bottle or from a decanter into which the contents of the bottle have been poured.

Once more, we are reminded by this last illustration that stimulus equivalences are always equivalences with respect to particular motivational conditions. If one were motivated not merely to see that the guests each received a glassful of wine but also to satisfy their sensitive palates, one would not serve certain wines without decanting them first.

Having agreed that there is a behavioral stimulus equivalence involved, we may go further and consider which of the mechanisms listed in the last chapter is responsible for it. It is not a case of independent association, since the subject has not learned separately to make a common response to the sight of the column A1, the sight of the column in B, and the sights of other columns that could be formed by transferring the same water to other vessels. It is not primary stimulus generalization since, if it were, a column of water with the height of that in B and the width of that in A1 would also be judged equal in quantity to the columns in A1 and B, being intermediate between them in appearance. But this would obviously not happen.

So we are left with the conclusion that this quantitative invariant is a case of secondary stimulus generalization. But what precisely are the stimulus patterns between which this secondary generalization holds? Our previous arguments force us to recognize that, if we use S_{A1} to denote the sight of the column in A_1 and S_B to denote the sight of the column in B, it is not generalization between S_{A1} and S_B. The generalization is rather between S_{A1}, on the one hand, and $S_B +$ $tr(S_{A2}) + tr(P)$, on the other, where tr represents a memory trace or symbolic representation and P represents the process of pouring. In other words, the patterns that are behaviorally equivalent are not S_{A1} and S_B, but S_{A1} and the combination of S_B plus the knowledge or memory that B was formed from a column identical with the one now in A1 by a process of pouring.

To possess or understand a concept like "quantity" means to recognize the changes that something can undergo and still preserve its quantity and to distinguish these from other changes that would alter quantity. In the case of a liquid, one recognizes that alterations of location or shape, including those that occur when a mass of liquid is poured in its entirety from one container to another, leave quantity unaltered, whereas adding to, or substracting from, a mass of liquid does not. Thus we come to recognize a column of liquid as equal in quantity to a second column when the second column differs from the first only in having undergone a kind of change that leaves quantity invariant.

This psychological analysis of quantitative concepts parallels a way in which mathematical concepts are frequently defined, namely by specifying a class of transformations over which the concept in question is invariant. Since Klein put forward his Erlangen Program in 1872, it has been seen that the various geometries, for example, can be ordered in a hierarchy reflecting their differing degrees of inclusiveness. Euclidean geometry, familiar to secondary-school students all over the world, studies properties such as shape, length, parallelism, and curvature, which are preserved only by rotations and translations. Topology, on the other hand, studies the much more general and abstract properties that are unaffected by the distortions to which figures drawn on a sheet of rubber are subject. Other geometries, like projective and affine geometry, occupy intermediate positions.

So the older child or adult can recognize changes that leave quantity constant and distinguish them from other changes that cause an increase or a decrease in quantity. Thanks to this distinction, he can make judgments of equality that are determined jointly by information coming from the present external stimulus situation and information embodied in traces of past experiences that he carries within his nervous system. The quantitative-invariant experiments thus form a simple paradigm for directed thinking in so far as all behavior guided by thinking depends jointly on the external stimuli of the moment and on stored information embodied in self-stimulation resulting from symbolic responses. The stored information commonly takes the form of information about transformations that the objects of our thinking have undergone.

In scientific thinking, we aim to explain, predict, and control natural events. To explain an event means to reconstruct a succession of transformations that connect it, link by link, with some state of affairs that we take as our starting-point. To predict means to anticipate the outcome of a projected series of transformations, while to control means to select transformations that will bring about the desired state of affairs in the future. A large part of science is thus a matter of considering a phenomenon simultaneously as a stimulus pattern and as a link in a chain of transformations. This, in its turn, means recognizing the behavioral equivalences that are preserved unchanged by a particular sequence of transformations and the equivalences that are destroyed. Finally, it means treating the outcomes of several different sequences of transformations as behaviorally equivalent.

Similarly, let us recall that a large proportion of the efforts of mathematicians is directed toward proving theorems. A proof is a sequence of transformations that will lead from the axioms of a system to the proposition to be proved. More generally, mathematicians and logicians are interested in how a system of operations will "behave" (as they frequently put it) when subjected to transformations of particular sorts.

In historical and philosophical thinking, there is not such a clear consensus on aims and methods, but here transformations are clearly just as important, whether they be ones that bridge the gulf between the present and the past or ones that lead from the present to the future. And even in the thinking that underlies artistic creation, equivalences and nonequivalences resulting from transformations are of importance. A sector of physical reality is frequently presented in an altered form, which retains the characteristics of reality that are of concern to the artist and perhaps draws the attention of the audience to them more peremptorily.

Response Equivalences and Stimulus Equivalences

These, then, are some of the problems concerning equivalences created by directed thinking that remain to be considered. They are related to the broader problem of how the chains of symbolic responses that constitute S-thinking can create behavioral equivalences that did not exist before. As a step toward elucidating these problems, we must now examine response equivalences and ways in which response equivalences can give rise to stimulus equivalences.

Response Generalization

We use the term "behavioral stimulus equivalence" whenever two stimulus situations or two stimulus patterns defining classes of stimulus situations possess a common most probable response, given specifiable internal conditions. This generally means that the behaviorally equivalent stimulus situations must be associated with a common response, although the converse is not necessarily true.

We shall say that two responses or response patterns or response sequences are equivalent whenever, given specifiable internal conditions, both are associated with a common class of stimulus situations. Since two different response patterns will, more often than not, be incompatible, this does not mean that both will be *performed* whenever a stimulus situation of the class in question occurs. Generally, such a stimulus situation will sometimes evoke one of them and sometimes the other. Either response pattern will, however, be more probable when such a situation occurs than it would have been otherwise. According to the terminology we are adopting, both response patterns will be *instigated* whenever a stimulus situation associated with both of these is encountered. This presumably means that at least fractional versions or internal correlates of both will be produced in the central nervous system.

Response equivalences can arise in any of three ways, paralleling the three ways in which behavioral stimulus equivalences can arise. Two responses could have become independently associated with a common class of stimulus situations through separate learning processes or through inherited connections. Then, forms of response generalization analogous to primary and secondary stimulus generalization evidently exist in higher animals, although they have received relatively little experimental study and are not easy to handle experimentally.

Response generalization is said to occur when the establishment of an association between R_A and S_1 produces an association between S_1 and another response, R_B. In other words, R_B becomes more likely to occur in the presence of S_1 than in the presence of a randomly chosen stimulus, even though the performance of the original response, R_A, may be more likely still.

Response equivalences, like both ecological and behavioral stimulus equivalences, vary with internal and, particularly, motivational conditions. When two response patterns are equivalent, they must both be associated with a common class of stimulus situations. This does not mean, however, that they are both equally likely to be performed.

Primary Response Generalization

One of the oldest criticisms of attempts to analyze behavior in terms of S-R associations is based on the observation that a particular kind of stimulus situation does not always give rise to exactly the same response. An animal will vary the actual form of its behavior from trial to trial. Thus, a rat that has to move a bar as a means of securing some reward may press the bar sometimes with one paw, sometimes with another paw, sometimes with its nose, and sometimes with its hindquarters. It is likely to approach the bar on different trials from different angles, requiring quite distinct motor patterns. Similarly, a rat that has learned to run to the goal box of a maze will oscillate between alternative paths, if there are several of equal length (Dashiell, 1925). Even when one path is followed repeatedly, the actual course followed by the rat within the walls of the alleys will never be quite the same on any two trials.

From facts like these, it is recognized that learning rarely, if ever, associates a stimulus pattern with a specific pattern of movement. It is much more a matter of associating the stimulus patterns with a probability distribution of motor patterns, so that any of a set of responses may occur on any particular occasion, although some of them occur more frequently than others.

The responses between which primary response generalization holds are ones that we should be inclined to describe as "similar" to one another, just as primary stimulus generalization links a stimulus with "similar" stimuli. But similarities among responses are, on the whole, more difficult to assess than similarities among stimuli, if only because the relevant dimensions are not so clear. There is, however, one easily measurable property in which responses can possess different degrees of resemblance, and that is the degree of force exerted. Skinner (1938) discovered that the force with which a rat pressed a bar for food would vary widely from occasion to occasion about a mean value. The mean could be pushed upward by arranging for no food to be delivered unless a certain minimum pressure was exceeded. Likewise, Arnold (1945) found the degree of force with which rats press a bar to fluctuate according to something resembling a normal, bell-shaped distribution. But once again, differential reinforcement could sharply reduce the variability.

Responses can also be measurably similar or different in spatial direction. Anybody who has attempted to acquire a skill requiring accuracy of aim, from typing to archery, knows how widely responses are scattered about the intended target in the early stages. Unless there is a source of bias to cause a constant error, the responses will be fairly symmetrically distributed about the target, and differential reinforcement will gradually narrow down the range of unreliability as practice proceeds.

Secondary Response Generalization

Like secondary stimulus generalization, secondary response generalization results from the intervention of mediating responses, overt or implicit, symbolic or nonsymbolic, and we have to consider two forms of secondary response generalization, namely response chaining and mediated response generalization, corresponding to the two forms of secondary stimulus generalization.

RESPONSE CHAINING. Response chaining (see Figure 4-1) occurs when a stimulus, S_1, is associated with a response, R_A, and R_A produces some kind of stimulation (internal or external), S_A, which, in its turn, evokes the second response R_B. If this sequence ends with

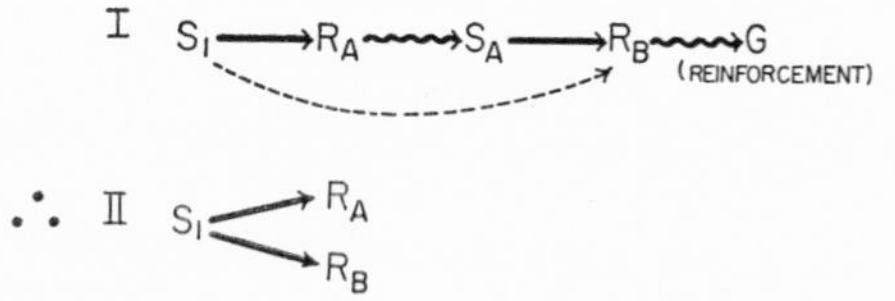

Figure 4-1

reinforcement, S_1 will become associated with both R_A and R_B, so that R_A and R_B will be linked by a response equivalence.

In such circumstances, R_A and R_B might be expected to occur in succession. The principle of the reinforcement gradient, expounded by Hull (1932), explains, however, why R_B may occur in place of R_A. This principle, which is supported by experimental evidence, states that, all other things equal, responses that are more quickly followed by reward are more strongly reinforced. So whenever a sequence of responses leads to a reward, a later response will be separated from the reward by a shorter delay than an earlier response. A later response will thus be instigated more strongly than an earlier response, which will give the later response a tendency to become anticipatory, that is, to be performed before responses that originally preceded it in the sequence. If it does so and if, as is likely, it is incompatible with these other responses, they may be eliminated from the sequence.

SHORT-CIRCUITING. Thus arises the phenomenon of short-circuiting or serial-segment elimination whose importance was continually stressed by Hull. It is a factor that constantly pushes behavior toward maximum efficiency by causing superfluous acts to be ousted. Thanks to its influence, organisms abandon errors and utilize ways of saving time and energy that changed circumstances make available. If a rat has gone down a blind alley in a maze and then returns to the choice-point to follow the correct path, he will soon learn to pass by the entrance of the blind alley and go in the correct direction as soon as that choice-point is reached. If a door that was closed during previous trials in a maze is now open and offers a short cut, a rat will pass through it and give up the detour to which he has been accustomed (Valentine, 1928).

In reasoning, short-circuiting has an especially vital role, since it generally ensures that, once the exertions of the reasoning process have reached a successful termination, the subject does not have to go through them again. In future, the solution—the pattern of responses that came at the end of the process and immediately preceded reward—will be at his disposal immediately. When Köhler's (1921) ape Nueva was first faced with food placed beyond her reach outside her cage, it took her seven minutes to discover how to draw the food toward her with the help of a stick. With the test repeated an hour later, "the animal has recourse to the stick much sooner, and uses it with more skill; and, at a third repetition, the stick is used immediately, as on all subsequent occasions." A man who may have taken an hour to compute his total income for the last year before filling in his income-tax return is able from then on to state, or think of, the total as soon as any authorized person asks him or as soon as he asks himself. An inventor takes less time to construct the second specimen of his invention than he took to construct the original prototype. Even when a thinker needs to run through a symbolic process from beginning to end, and a contemplation of the end point alone will not suffice, there is a strong tendency to abbreviate as much as possible, as Vygotski (1956) showed. The "inner speech" that is used in thinking becomes increasingly fragmentary and thus more and more distinct from communicative speech. Many of the items of information that would have to be transmitted to a listener are well known and not at issue when a thinker speaks to himself subvocally. So they, and the grammatical forms that embody them, can be left out. A man who is running through a familiar story in thought does not represent to himself every detail but simply reviews the highlights (Hebb, 1949, Ch. 9).

It is true that, whereas a response that originally came toward the end of a behavior chain, overt or symbolic, may occur anticipatorily, there are plenty of situations in which later responses are postponed until earlier portions of the chain have been completed. Some writers, like Osgood (1953), have maintained that whether or not a late response will come forward depends on whether it is "detachable" from the stimulus situation in which it first occurred. This criterion is, however, hard to apply. When is a response not detachable? Which elements of eating behavior are physically incapable of occurring in the absence of food? The point would seem rather to be that a response will not be performed anticipatorily if its premature performance delays or precludes reinforcement. If a rat takes a short cut or if he indulges in anticipatory salivation or chewing movements while running down a maze alley, his encounter with food will not be postponed and may very well be speeded up. If, on the other hand, he stands still and bends down (which is what he is used to doing in the goal box) when he is only halfway along the maze, or if he turns right before a choice-point is reached, his progress toward the goal will be hindered, and we can expect inhibition of delay to supervene and put an end to such maladaptive anticipatory responses. The occurrence of short-circuiting in directed thinking must surely be governed by similar factors.

MEDIATED RESPONSE GENERALIZATION. Figure 4-2 represents the mechanism of mediated response generalization. In this case, S_1 is associated with a mediating response, R_m, and the stimulus resulting

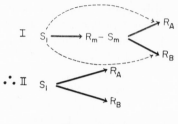

Figure 4-2

from R_m, S_m, possesses associations with both R_A and R_B. S_1 is therefore followed by R_A and R_B on different occasions.

It would appear that there is a form of semantic response generalization analogous to the semantic stimulus generalization that Ivanov-Smolenski (see Chapter 4) studied in the domain of stimulus generalization. Lovaas (1961, 1964) has found that the reinforcement of verbal aggressive responses or food-naming responses will increase, respectively, the subsequent incidence of overt aggressive behavior or the subsequent consumption of food.

By far the most important case of such mediated response generalization, both for behavior in general and for directed thinking in particular, is Hull's (1934) divergent hierarchy.

A divergent hierarchy (Figure 4-3,I) exists when we have a number of responses—the diagram represents three of them, R_N, R_P, and R_Q—that have all frequently, but at different times, been followed by a particular rewarding state of affairs. We use S_G to denote the goal situation (the stimulus situation that makes the reward possible). R_G stands for the goal response (the pattern of responses that habitually ensues upon the attainment of S_G).

R_G, being followed immediately by reinforcement, will, according to the reinforcement-gradient principle, be strengthened more than earlier responses in the chain. It will therefore have an extremely strong tendency to occur anticipatorily, and we may assume that some components of R_G will, in fact, be capable of occurring anticipatorily without detriment to the prospects of reaching the goal. These components form what Hull (1931) called the fractional anticipatory goal response (r_G). For Hull, r_G consisted of fractional and internal responses of muscles and glands, that is, part of the consummatory behavior pattern that actually gave rise to the enjoyment of the reward. We are, however, not committing ourselves to this conception; r_G may very well be purely cerebral in character, consisting of part of the neural processes that occur when the organism is faced with the goal situation, S_G.

The next step in the argument (represented by Figure 4-3,II) points out that r_G, like any other response, will give rise to distinctive feedback stimulation, which we represent by s_G (Hull's "goal stimulus"), since it acts as an internal representation or anticipation of the goal situation, S_G. An association can thus be expected to grow up, by a typical learning process, between s_G and each of the responses R_N, R_P, and R_Q.

This common bond with s_G, and through it with S_1, creates an equivalence between the three responses, R_N, R_P, and R_Q, no matter how dissimilar their physical forms may be. They are equivalent in so far as they are all ways of reaching S_G. And the r_G-s_G process acts as the lynch-pin, corresponding to the labeling response and labeling stimulus in secondary stimulus generalization.

Consequently, any stimulus, S_0, that acquires an association with one of the three equivalent responses, say R_N (Figure 4-3,III), will also acquire an association with each of the other responses in the equivalence class, in this case R_P and R_Q. This is because S_0 will come to evoke r_G as well as R_N, and s_G, resulting from r_G, will instigate R_P and R_Q (Figure 4-3,IV).

Such is the mechanism of the divergent response hierarchy. The fractional anticipatory goal response, r_G, qualifies as a symbolic response representing the goal situation in advance of its attainment. Human symbolic responses are, of course, capable of much more varied and detailed representation of anticipated end results than the kinds of r_G of which, say, a rat is capable.

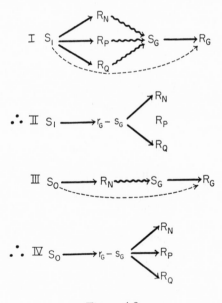

Figure 4-3

A habit-family hierarchy (Hull, 1934) is a form of divergent response hierarchy in which an equivalence exists between sequences of responses (behavior chains), rather than between single responses. The habit-family hierarchy is a special case of mediated response generalization, and we shall make abundant use of this concept in our subsequent discussion of directed thinking.

Habit-Family Hierarchies

A habit-family hierarchy (see Figure 4-4) consists of a set of behavior chains, such that (1) every chain is associated with, and thus can start out from, the same initial situation, S_0, and (2) every chain ends with the same goal situation, S_G.

The cement that binds the structure together is, once again, furnished by the fractional anticipatory goal response, r_G, since r_G will be evoked from the start by the combination of S_0 and an appropriate motivational condition and s_G will have an association with all the constituent chains of the hierarchy. It must be noted, once more, that the equivalences that underlie a habit-family hierarchy will, like stimulus equivalences, hold only with respect to particular internal (including motivational) conditions. So, although an organism may be said to possess a certain hierarchy all the time, it will utilize that hierarchy only when appropriate motivational and other internal conditions obtain.

The following characteristics of habit-family hierarchies must be noted in view of their bearing on our later discussion. A convenient example to bear in mind is that of a rat in a maze with several alternative routes leading from the starting box to the goal box, although any human situation in which there are several alternative courses of action, all of which would lead to the same desirable consequences, could just as well serve as an illustration.

1. While all the chains of a hierarchy can, at different times, be set off by the same S_0, they will, in general, not all be equally probable. They may, in fact, be listed in decreasing order of probability of occurrence, which is why the word "hierarchy" is used.

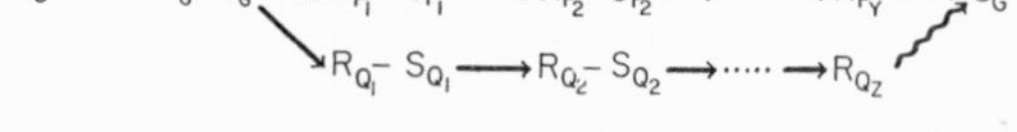

$$S_0 \longrightarrow r_G\text{-}s_G \underset{\displaystyle R_{Q_1}^-\text{-}S_{Q_1} \longrightarrow R_{Q_2}^-\text{-}S_{Q_2} \longrightarrow \cdots \longrightarrow R_{Q_Z}}{\overset{\displaystyle R_{N_1}^-\text{-}S_{N_1} \longrightarrow R_{N_2}^-\text{-}S_{N_2} \longrightarrow \cdots \longrightarrow R_{N_X}}{\longrightarrow R_{P_1}\text{-}S_{P_1} \longrightarrow R_{P_2}\text{-}S_{P_2} \longrightarrow \cdots \longrightarrow R_{P_Y}}} \longrightarrow S_G$$

Figure 4-4

Moreover, although they all lead to the same goal situation, they need not all be equally strongly reinforced. Some response sequences may extract larger quantities of reward from the same goal situation. Some will probably entail a greater cost than others, for example, in time to reach the goal situation or in effort. These factors, among others, will determine the relative strengths or probabilities of the various component chains.

A subject will most often embark on the dominant, or most probable, chain in the hierarchy. Random fluctuation [Hull's (1943) "behavioral oscillation"] may make him resort occasionally to other chains in accordance with their probability distribution. But various subsidiary stimuli and motivational conditions will also make their contributions. For example, a resident of Boston who has frequent occasion to visit New York may possess an elaborate hierarchy of ways of traveling between the two cities, involving different means of transportation and different routes. Going by air may be his prevalent practice. But he may go by bus instead when money is shorter than time, when his flight is canceled because of bad weather, when he has an additional errand necessitating a stop in New Haven, or simply when he is tired of the journey by air and would like a change [cf. the spontaneous alternation of rats in the T-maze (Berlyne, 1960a, Chap. 5; Dember and Fowler, 1958)].

2. When one chain of a habit-family hierarchy is reinforced (followed by reward), the hierarchy as a whole is reinforced. This is because r_G is reinforced and thus gives rise to a more intense s_G. There is consequently an increase in the likelihood that some chain or other belonging to the hierarchy will occur the next time that S_0 is combined with the appropriate motivational condition, but it will not necessarily be the same chain as originally led to the reward.

Thus, an animal in a familiar maze, having found food after following one of the lengthier routes to the goal box, may rush to the goal box by the most direct route the next time that he is placed in the starting box while hungry.

3. If a chain has habitually led the subject to a certain goal situation in the past but, from now on, the accustomed reward fails to materialize, two processes can be expected to result, namely, the weakening or extinction of the chain in question and the weakening or extinction of r_G.

The former will cause that chain to be relegated to a lower position in the hierarchy; it will become less probable, and its fellow members of the hierarchy will become relatively more probable. If the non-reinforced chain was formerly the dominant member, it may be deposed from the top of the hierarchy by the next strongest chain.

The weakening of r_G will, on the other hand, conduce to the weakening or extinction of the hierarchy as a whole, so that the subject will be less inclined, and finally not inclined at all, to utilize any of its component chains.

Which of these two processes will have the upper hand—whether one chain will give way to another or whether the whole hierarchy will be abandoned—must depend on many factors.

For one thing, the two processes may appear in turn. There are many situations in which the frustration of one chain will cause the subject to try out a few chains of a hierarchy and, then, after these have turned out to be of no avail, to desist from the whole hierarchy without going through all of its remaining members.

The decisive factor must sometimes be the point at which the usual sequence of events is interrupted. If a particular chain fails to bring about the goal situation, S_G, then some other chain of the same hierarchy may do so, for example, when a barrier is placed across one route by which a desired location can be reached. Suppose, on the other hand, that S_G is reached and R_G is performed but this time does not lead to reward. Then, we can expect R_G to succumb to extinction, with consequent weakening of r_G and eventual abandonment of the whole hierarchy. The goal situation, S_G, will then cease to be attractive, so that all behavior chains carrying the subject from S_0 to S_G will lose their appeal.

The habit-family hierarchies that concern us, that is, those playing a part in thinking, will generally consist of chains of implicit symbolic responses, that is, trains of thought.

Algebraic Equations and Habit-Family Hierarchies

We are now in a position to understand the psychological senses in which the two sides of an algebraic equation, such as $(x + y)^2 = x^2 + 2xy + y^2$, are equivalent. As Piaget (1947) has pointed out, the symbols in mathematical notation stand for actions, whether they be overt actions or the implicit actions that support thinking. Thus, $x^2 + 2xy + y^2$ can be held to represent a sequence of responses (a behavior chain): calculate the square of x, store the result of this calculation, multiply x by y, double this product, store the result of this doubling, calculate the square of y, add this square and the results of the two previous calculations. Similarly, $(x + y)^2$ represents a different behavior chain: add x to y, calculate the square of this sum.

The equivalence between these two behavior chains resides in their common membership of a number of habit-family hierarchies. The two chains are, in many situations, alternative ways of reaching the same goal situation. For example, if one begins with a square of side $(x + y)$ and is motivated to find the area of the square, the behavior chains denoted by $(x + y)^2$ and by $x^2 + 2xy + y^2$ will, either of them, lead to the quantity that is sought. In some conditions, $(x + y)^2$ will be the dominant member of the hierarchy, while in others $x^2 + 2xy + y^2$ will be dominant. But whichever is dominant, it can be replaced by the other if its implementation is, for any reason, hindered.

These hierarchies give rise, in their turn, to other hierarchies some of whose chains will include the writing down of $(x + y)^2$ followed by the writing down of $x^2 + 2xy + y^2$, or vice versa. The subject will thus be in possession of techniques like "removing parentheses" when handling equations such as $(x + y)^2 = x^2 + 2xy$ or "finding squares" when trying to solve equations such as $x^2 + 2xy + y^2 = 0$.

The concept of a habit-family hierarchy can also help us to understand quantitative invariants. But before we can show how, we must see how habit-family hierarchies can give rise to behavioral stimulus equivalences, and this in its turn must be left until we have gone a little further into some special properties of the hierarchies that participate in directed thinking.

Chapter 5

Situational thoughts and

transformational thoughts

EVER SINCE the beginnings of experimental work on thinking, psychologists have struggled to characterize the distinction (see Chapter 1) between autistic thinking, exemplified by reverie or by the "flight of ideas" reflected in the speech of some psychotics, and directed thinking, exemplified by the activity of a chess player, the efforts of a mathematician to prove a theorem, or the attempts of an inventor to contrive a device that will serve a practical need.

A prototype of the units out of which autistic thinking is built appears in the free-association experiment, originated by Galton (1879–1880), refined by Wundt's school, and most thoroughly developed by Jung (1906–1910). In this experiment, the subject is required to respond to a stimulus word by uttering the first word that occurs to him, no matter what it may be.

Wundt's associates introduced a variant of the free-association experiment, investigating what came to be called "controlled" or "constrained" associations. The first reported example appears to be Trautscholdt's (1883) study of what he called "subsumption judgments." The subject heard a number of nouns and had in each case to specify a class to which the named object belonged, for example, "newt" drew the response "animal," "z" the response "letter of the alphabet." Cattell (1888) used a wider assortment of tasks. For example, the subject might be given the name of a town and told to supply the name of the country in which it was located, or he might be given the name of an author and told to name the language in which he wrote.

These are cases of "completely constrained association," since only one response word is acceptable. Other tasks exemplify "partially constrained association," in which any of a number of words can serve as an acceptable response. Some of these were produced by reversing completely-constrained-association tasks, for example, giving the subject a country and requiring him to name a town within it, or giving the subject a language and requiring him to name an author writing in that language. Others consisted of giving the subject the name of a class and asking him to give the name of an object belonging to the class (for example, "river"—"Rhine") or giving him a verb and asking him to specify a possible object of the verb (for example, "write"—"letter").

A comparison between the constrained-association experiment and the free-association experiment brings out one characteristic that distinguishes directed thinking from autistic thinking quite sharply, and that is its greater selectivity. In autistic thinking or free association, each word or idea that occurs may be followed by any of thousands of words or ideas, all of which are associated with it. But in directed thinking or constrained association, all except a small number of ideas are excluded, since the response must stand in the specified relation to the stimulus, and there is often one response that occurs invariably.

Nevertheless, this difference in selectivity is not enough to account for the divergence between the two kinds of thinking. For one thing, it is only a difference in degree, and the two kinds of thinking seem to be divided in a more clear-cut and fundamental way than that. Second, the essential properties of directed thinking evidently depend on the way in which constrained associations are concatenated. It is true that virtually the only thoughts that generally occur in the course of directed thinking are ones that are "relevant" to the problem on hand, that is, ones that have a better-than-average chance of carrying the subject nearer to the goal. The only times when irrelevant thoughts or thoughts that have no likelihood whatever of being helpful intrude is when a subject is distracted or when frustration leads him to abandon serious efforts to solve the problem. But directed thinking is also marked by its directedness, that is, by the order in which the thoughts succeed one another. The thought process appears, on the whole, to be leading the subject step by step nearer and nearer to his goal, although he may be sidetracked into many false starts and blind alleys on the way. Once he has solved the problem, he will be in possession of the "solution chain," that is, a train of thought that proceeds without deviations from the initial situation to the desired goal situation.

Steps toward a Conceptualization of the Train of Directed Thought

We shall begin by tracing some of the stages through which psychological theory has passed in feeling its way toward an adequate representation of the trains of thought that participate in directed thinking. We shall then be in a position to consider some further modifications that might carry this search a little further forward.

1. The Associative Chain

The view of the course of thinking that was prevalent among the 19th-century associationists is most clearly expressed in the famous excerpt from James Mill's (1829) *Analysis of the Phenomena of the Human Mind.*

I see a horse: that is a sensation. Immediately I think of his master: that is an idea. The idea of his master makes me think of his office; he is a minister of state; that is another idea. The idea of a minister of state makes me think of public affairs; and I am led into a train of political ideas; when I am summoned to dinner.

In other words, the train of thought begins with the sensation produced by an external stimulus, and the sensation evokes an idea that is associated with it which, in its turn, evokes another idea associated with it, and so on (see Figure 5-1). The association between a sensation and an idea or between two ideas was generally held to result from habitual contiguity or from resemblance between the objects or events to which they corresponded, although Mill himself was rather more extreme than most associationists and regarded association by similarity as a special case of association by contiguity. The example just cited belongs to autistic thinking, except that the "train of political ideas" might have incorporated some directed thinking. However, as Mill's (1829) chapter on "ratiocination" and Bain's (1855) chapter on "constructive association" show, the associationists conceived all kinds of thinking after the same pattern.

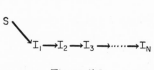

Figure 5-1

2. Early Behaviorist Theory

The behaviorist revolution introduced a refurbished version of the associationist account with certain improvements:

(a) It was realized that a thought process not only typically begins with a stimulus belonging to the external world, as the associationists recognized, but also typically ends with a motor response acting on the external world. It is true that sophisticated thinking is often de-

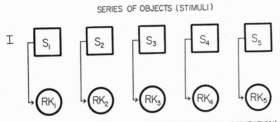

SERIES OF OBJECTS (STIMULI)

SERIES OF KINAESTHETIC RESPONSES (MANUAL ORGANIZATION)

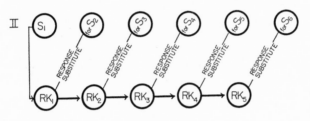

Figure 5-2

void of practical consequences, but thinking must have evolved in the first instance as an aid to adaptive interaction with physical reality.

(b) It was realized that the way in which a subject is conducted to a solution by a sequence of thoughts resembles the way in which a subject reaches a goal through a sequence of instrumental actions, the standard example being a rat reaching the goal box of a maze through execution of the correct sequence of runs along alleys and turns at choice points.

(c) It was realized that each thought is a response to the preceding external stimulus or thought and a stimulus to the succeeding thought or motor response, so that a thought can be represented as a combination of a response and a response-produced stimulus, r_i-s_i. Once this was seen, the age-old principles of association by contiguity and association by similarity could be equated with the principles of conditioning and stimulus generalization that appeared to govern the simplest forms of motor behavior.

Watson's (1924) account of the course of thought is depicted in Figure 5-2.* He cited as an illustration the process by which a pianist comes to play a piece from memory. At first, there is a series of external stimuli, that is, the notes on the sheet music, and these, being encountered in turn, evoke their corresponding responses. When this process has occurred a number of times, all the external stimuli with the exception of the first one (or some substitute for it) become superfluous. The music can be taken away, and each response is evoked, through conditioning, by the proprioceptive stimulation resulting from the immediately previous response. In thinking, the responses in question were held to consist of verbal, visceral, and other motor responses in an implicit form.

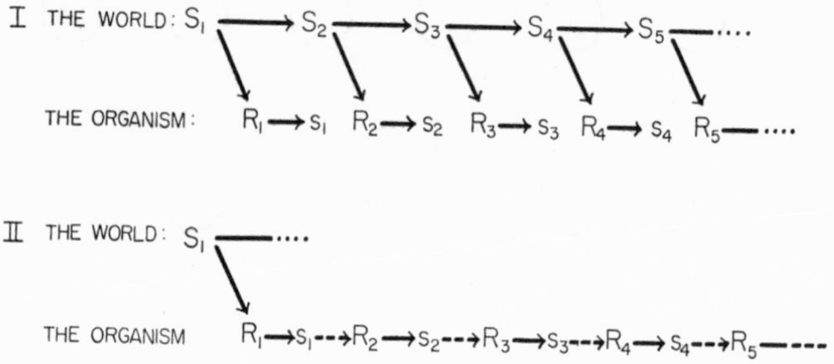

Figure 5-3

Hull's (1930) account, represented in Figure 5-3, is essentially the same, with the learning process described in a little more detail. We begin with a sequence of events in the external world, each of which evokes a response. After a number of repetitions of the sequence, the response sequence can be run off in the absence of, or in anticipation of, the stimuli from the external events, so that the subject is in possession of "a kind of replica of this world segment."

3. Secondary Laws of Association

These formulations, although they are more satisfactory from a contemporary point of view than their associationist forerunners, still suffer from some of the same deficiencies and leave some of the same questions unanswered. Perhaps the most obvious objection that can be aimed at both the older and the newer variants is that every thought or stimulus must have become associated with a multitude of other thoughts or responses. Any object or event must have been experienced in contiguity with scores of other objects or events and must resemble an even wider range of objects or events.

Watson's example of playing a piano piece from memory turns out to be rather unfortunately chosen from this point of view. Within the repertoire of an experienced pianist, a particular note must have been followed by virtually all the twelve notes of the octave at one time or another, although it will have been followed by some more frequently than by others. So, if each note were selected solely through association with the note before, a pianist would be quite unable to pick his way through a piece.

Neither the principles of association nor the more modern principles of learning evoked by Watson and Hull can, therefore, suffice to explain why a particular thought occurs at a particular juncture rather than any of the numerous other thoughts that are associated with the last thought.

A partial solution of this problem was offered in Brown's (1820) discussion of what he called the "secondary laws of association." Brown recognized that the outcome of competition among all the alternative thoughts that could be elicited through the operation of association by contiguity and similarity must depend on the relative strengths of associations. This means that laws determining how strong a particular association will be must be formulated. Brown did his best to satisfy this need by listing a number of "secondary" laws, according to which the strength of an association depended on, for example, the duration and vividness of the sensations involved, the frequency and recency with which they have been experienced in contiguity.

These laws have their equivalents among the laws that have been extracted from data on simple motor learning. And, as Hull (1943) put it, "When the reaction potentials to two or more incompatible reactions occur in an organism at the same time, only the reaction whose momentary effective reaction potential is greatest will be evoked." The "momentary effective reaction potential," or momentary strength of a response, fluctuates with a number of factors, including random "behavioral oscillation," but, on the whole, responses that correspond to stronger habits will be uppermost more often.

4. Motivational Conditions

Yet the incorporation of laws governing strength of association or habit strength is still not enough. Even when the existence of multiple associations, differing in strength, has been acknowledged, at least three deficiencies remain.

(a) Which thought is most likely to succeed a particular thought clearly varies with the nature of the task or problem at which the thought process is aimed. The course of thought is not therefore determined solely by the response-produced stimuli that succeed one another but by other internal conditions implanted in the organism by whatever factors imposed the task or set up the problem.

(b) This point links up with a further point that arises as soon as we attempt to pursue the relations between thinking and other forms of sequential behavior. It is by now clear that contiguity alone does not guarantee learning; numerous everyday experiences and experiments on remembering attest that we can perceive two events together or in close succession many times without the thought of one of them evoking the thought of the other. More generally, the performance of a response in the presence, or shortly after the presence, of a particular stimulus does not always lead to a strengthened association between the stimulus and the response. Learning requires, in addition, reinforcing agents. Neither the associationist nor the early behaviorist account of thinking tells us how the associations that carry thinking onward are reinforced.

The upshot of both these points is that motivational aspects of thinking were neglected in these accounts but must be brought in.

(c) The associative chains that we have considered thus far are examples of what, in probability theory, are called "Markov chains." These are sequences of "trials" or occasions, such that any of several alternative events (for example, thoughts or responses) can occur on each trial and the probability distribution of these events is determined solely by which event occurred on the immediately preceding trial.

Now, it is clear that the selection of a response does not always depend only on the nature of the last response that the organism made or, in general, on conditions obtaining just before a response is due to be executed. The choice of response may very well depend on something that happened several minutes ago or several items ago in the sequence.

Some of the most convincing proofs of this come from speech behavior. When we write or speak, the words in a sentence are arranged in a particular order, the letters in a word are written or typed in a particular order, and the phonemes that make up a word are pronounced in a particular order. But is each word, letter, or phoneme determined entirely by the one that comes just before it? If the selection of an item were postponed until a moment before that item appeared, there would be no way of distinguishing a man who was going to use a particular item (word, letter, or phoneme) from one who is not, until the immediately preceding item had appeared.

One reason for denying that this is the case is, as Lashley (1951) pointed out, the existence of anticipatory errors. A beginner at typing is apt to produce "hte" rather than "the." The fact that she was going to type "h" has therefore affected her before she has typed "t," the immediately preceding letter. Similarly, the famous Rev. W. A. Spooner is reported to have said "our queer old dean" when he meant to say "our dear old queen." He would surely have been much less likely to say "queer" if he had been intending to say "our dear old king."

Other evidence has come to light in the course of recent attempts to analyze grammatical structure (Chomsky, 1957; G. A. Miller, 1962). There is, for example, the possibility of indefinite "self-embedding" in speech. It is often permissible to insert verbal sequences of any desired length between two words of a sentence, A and B, and yet have B depend on A. We can say, for example, "The man who . . . came here." An adjectival clause replacing the . . . can contain any number of words without being ungrammatical, even though excessively long clauses may be considered inelegant and confusing. But no matter how long the sentence is, the word "came" occurs because the word "man" was the last word to occur before the insertion. Its probability does not depend in any way on what the last word of the inserted clause happens to be. Similarly we can say, "either . . . or . . ." Here, again, the insertions can be of any length, but the word "or" is made mandatory by the earlier occurrence of "either."

This point can be extended by recalling that, in many languages, the selection of a word may depend not on a word that occurred earlier but on a word that is to come later. The word that is yet to come may thus have been selected long before its place in the sentence has been reached. Thus, a Frenchman may say "Il a perdu sa . . ." Here the choice of the possessive adjective "sa" is due to the fact that a feminine noun is to follow.

THE WÜRZBURG SCHOOL AND "DETERMINING TENDENCIES." The only effective reply to the three criticisms discussed above is to concede that the selection of a response, in general, and of the kind of symbolic response on which thinking depends, in particular, is not determined solely by the external stimulus situation of the moment or by the feedback stimulus from the immediately prior response. It must be acknowledged that selection is determined jointly by these stimuli and internal stimuli corresponding to motivational conditions (s_M). A motivational condition can persist for a matter of minutes or hours. It can thus continue to operate throughout a long sequence of responses, having been set up by an event that took place some

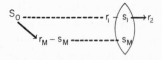

Figure 5-4

time ago. So, through its mediation, the influence of a temporally remote stimulus or response can be given some influence in determining the response that the subject is about to make. We thus have the kind of scheme depicted in Figure 5-4.

The first to credit motivational conditions (although they did not speak of them in this way) with part of the responsibility for directing thought were the members of the Würzburg school. The intensive introspective studies that they devoted both to prolonged thinking processes and to the more elemental processes of judgment and controlled association spotlighted the fact that, when the task or problem varies, the response—the thought that comes up—will also vary, even though the immediately precipitating stimulus pattern remains the same.

Suppose, for example, that the subject is told that names of countries will be read out and that he is to respond in each case with the name of the corresponding capital. If the subject is a person of normal education and intellectual endowment and, a few minutes later, hears the word "France," it can be predicted with assurance that he will reply "Paris." If he is told the next day that he will hear names of countries and must respond, in each case, with the name of the continent in which the country is situated, then exactly the same stimulus word will evoke the response "Europe." Ach (1905) provided a particularly graphic illustration of the same point in his experiment with arithmetical sums such as $\frac{8}{2}$; these numbers, printed on a card, can produce the responses "10," "6," or "16," according to whether a subject has been given a posthypnotic suggestion to add, subtract, or multiply. The problem of how this happens applies, of course, just as much to unhypnotized subjects who have been set to perform additions, subtractions, or multiplications in compliance with instructions from a teacher or an employer or with self-instructions.

The psychologists of the Würzburg school thus came to the conclusion that a response that figures in a thought process, whether it be implicit or overt, must depend jointly on the immediately preceding stimulus, whether it be external or produced by the preceding thought, and on an internal condition set up by instructions from an external agent or by whatever circumstances imposed the task or problem on the subject.

They referred to this internal condition by such names as *"Aufgabe"* (the German word for "task") and "determining tendency" and "idea of the goal," although they recognized subtle differences between the entities denoted by these terms. These are all instances of what psychologists used to call "sets." Contemporary psychologists would recognize them as motivational conditions productive of internal stimuli that supplement the external stimulus situation.

MOTIVATIONAL STIMULI IN NEOBEHAVIORIST THEORY. When Hull wrote the article from which Figure 5-3 is drawn, he had not gone very far in developing his behavior theory and, in particular, he did not yet attach the importance to motivational factors that characterized the theoretical system (Hull, 1943, 1952) for which he is best known.

Later, when he discussed situations such as maze-running, in which a sequence of responses is necessary if the goal is to be reached, he attributed the selection of each component response to the joint action of four kinds of stimuli. Two of these comprise the relatively fleeting stimuli that succeed one another as a behavior chain runs its course. They are (a) the external stimuli corresponding to the situations through which the subject passes, and (b) the proprioceptive stimuli that are produced by each response as it is executed. These correspond, of course, to the two kinds of stimuli that are held responsible for the responses in Figure 5-3, and the term "cue stimulus" may be used to refer to them both.

The other two kinds of stimuli are classifiable as "motivational," and they persist unchanged until the goal has been attained. They are (c) the drive-stimulus (S_D), corresponding to a state of physiological disequilibrium such as hunger or thirst or pain and associated with a broad class of responses that have potentialities for relieving the disequilibrium, and (d) the goal-stimulus, s_G, produced by the fractional anticipatory goal response, r_G, which we have already met when discussing the habit-family hierarchy. The drive-stimulus corresponds to a general kind of satisfaction that is being sought, for example, hunger reduction or termination of pain. The goal-stimulus is more specific in that it corresponds to a particular kind of satisfying situation, for example, a particular nutritive substance in a particular physical setting.

Cue stimuli and motivational stimuli are different and complementary in function. Motivational stimuli are ones that have, of course, special motivating properties: they tend to keep the subject at a high pitch of mobilization and incite him to continue the sequence of responses until the goal has been reached. These aspects of their role will be taken up in later chapters. Here we are concerned with the selection of responses, and, from this point of view, the special task of motivational stimuli is bound up with their having occurred in a large variety of situations, so that they will have become associated with a wide assortment of responses. They can thus serve to bring to the fore a fairly wide class of responses that are relevant to the kind of task in which the subject is engaged and more likely than most to conduce to the attainment of the goal.

The function of the cue stimuli is, on the other hand, to make a finer selection; they determine which member of the relatively numerous class made available by the motivational stimuli will actually be evoked. It is easy to see that factors classifiable as cue stimuli and motivational stimuli, with their distinguishable functions, must be at work in directed thinking as in other forms of serial behavior.

If response selection depends on motivational conditions as well as on cue stimuli, behavior does not form a Markov chain, since relatively long-lasting motivational conditions permit temporally remote stimuli and responses to exert an influence on the response of the moment. Since recognition of the role of motivational conditions goes back at least as far as the work of the Würzburg school in the first decade of the 20th century and since it has been firmly implanted in neobehaviorist theory since at least the early 1940's, recent criticisms of associative chains, supported by psycholinguistic arguments, have amounted in large measure to flogging a dead horse. They have, however, had the merit of drawing attention to issues that are by no means fully resolved.

THE CONSTELLATION THEORY. One essential problem to which some theorists (for example, those of the Würzburg school) gave little explicit consideration is how motivational and cue stimuli interact to produce a response. One solution to this problem is embodied in the "constellation theory" that was expounded by Müller (1913), in extension of some ideas that had been expressed by Bain (1868). According to this theory, the response that occurs in a constrained-association experiment, or more generally at some point in directed thinking, is one that possesses both an association with the motivational condition (or set) and an association with the cue stimulus (a stimulus word, an external stimulus, or an internal stimulus produced by preceding thought).

Thus, to hark back to an example given earlier, the word "France" is associated with, and thus tends to evoke, many words, including "French," "Paris," "Europe," "wine," etc. The motivational condition corresponding to the task of naming capital cities is associated with response words such as "London," "Rome," "Paris," "Madrid," etc. The word "Paris" is the only word that is associated with both the cue stimulus and the motivational condition and that consequently receives a double quota of strength. This is why it is the response that prevails over the others. If, on the other hand, the task is changed to that of naming continents, the motivational condition will instigate responses like "Europe," "Asia," "Africa," etc., and this time the word "Europe" will be the one that appears in both lists and therefore comes to the fore.

It is interesting that a behaviorist variant of the constellation theory was adopted by Hull (1935, 1952). In his discussions of animal reasoning in particular, he pointed out that a number of competing responses must be associated with the external stimulus situation that confronts the animal. The correct response, which is capable of leading the animal to its goal, will, he claimed, be associated not only with the external stimulus situation but also with the internal drive-stimulus and goal-stimulus corresponding to the animal's motivational condition. The correct response is evoked in preference to its competitors simply because it is the only one to be evoked both by the external stimulus situation and by the motivational stimuli.

5. Patterning

The constellation theory can hardly capture the distinction between directed and autistic thinking since, once again, it is equally applicable to both. As observations of writers as varied as Freud (1900) and Koffka (1912) show, free associations are likewise controlled not only by stimulus words or preceding thoughts but also by motivational conditions, enduring motivational dispositions, or specific tasks that subjects spontaneously set themselves. The only difference thus indicated by the constellation theory would be a quantitative one, such that the motivational conditions that induce directed thinking exercise a much more rigorous selection. This still fails to take account of the deep contrast that appears to divide the two kinds of thinking. Furthermore, a telling criticism of the constellation theory, which unfortunately failed to come to the attention of later behaviorist writers, was advanced quite early by Selz (1913).

The basis of Selz's objection was that the response that occurs—the correct response—need not be the only one that has associations with both the stimulus word or its equivalent and the motivational condition. An instructive counterexample is an experiment in which the subject is instructed to give opposites and the stimulus word is "dark." "Dark" can be presumed to instigate various responses, including "night," "day," "blind," etc. The task of supplying opposites must mobilize words that denote opposites, including "long" (the opposite of "short"), "light" (the opposite of "dark"), and "night" (the opposite of "day"). It will thus be seen that both "light" and "night" appear in both lists. If the constellation theory is correct, both of these responses will receive strength from the stimulus word and the set corresponding to the task, and both will therefore be equally likely to be uttered. Yet, the word "light" is, in fact, much more probable.

Although aimed at Müller's version of the constellation theory, Selz's telling objection is just as applicable to the behaviorist version advanced by Hull, and the grounds on which Deutsch (1956, 1960) has attacked Hull's theory of reasoning (to be discussed in Chapter 12) have actually a great deal in common with the argument offered by Selz. Deutsch likewise deduces that incorrect as well as correct responses will be associated with both the external cue and the internal motivational stimulus.

As a substitute for the constellation theory, Selz proposed his "complex-completion" theory. The subject is assumed to be in possession of items of knowledge called "complexes," of the form represented in Figure 5-5. The complex involves at least two elements and a relation between them, for example, the knowledge that "light" is the opposite of "dark." When the subject is given a constrained-association task, or when he gives himself an equivalent task in the course of directed thinking, he begins with an "anticipatory schema" as shown in Figure 5-6. There is an element and a relation specified by the task, and this pattern evokes the remaining element that is to fill in the blank.

The crux of Selz's objection is that the response does not necessarily have strong associations with the stimulus word and with the set. Its association with either of them may be very weak but its association with the combination of the two must be strong. Thus, the word "light" occurs not in response to "dark" and in response to "opposite" but in response to both of them appearing together or, perhaps, to

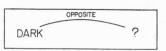

Figure 5-5   Figure 5-6

the whole phrase "opposite of 'dark.'" What this means in S-R terminology is that patterning is playing an important part.

Patterning, a well-established phenomenon in the literature on learning (Hull, 1943, Ch. XIX; Razran, 1939b), is said to take place when a subject has built up a discrimination between a combination of stimuli, $S_1 + S_2$, on the one hand, and either of the components, S_1 or S_2, appearing separately. Consequently, the response may be evoked by $S_1 + S_2$ but be inhibited in the presence of S_1 or S_2 separately. The contrary may also take place, and there can even be temporal patterning, such that a response is performed when a number of stimuli appear in a particular sequence but not when the same stimuli appear in a different sequence (cf. the discussion of natural relations in Chapter 3).

Selz's arguments carry us an appreciable step further toward understanding directed thinking, but they still leave us without a way of characterizing the differences between directed and autistic thinking. For one thing, the principle of patterning must also have some applicability to the latter. Thoughts that result from free association must often be determined by a combination or pattern of previous thoughts, although the patterning is incomparably less restrictive than that governing directed thinking.

In searching for the direction in which the next step should be made, we shall find it helpful to revert to our discussion at the end of the preceding chapter. There, the suggestion was made that Piaget's quantitative-invariant experiments offer an instructive paradigm for some essential aspects of directed thinking. One of their chief merits is to remind us that, in consequence of the intervention of thinking, we react to stimulus situations not simply in accordance with their present perceptible properties but rather in accordance with their present properties combined with representations of transformations that they have undergone.

Transformational Responses

When a subject is engaged in thinking, whether it be directed or autistic thinking, he is going through a series of symbolic responses representing stimulus situations other than the one in which he actually finds himself. The two kinds of thinking differ, however, in the way in which the subject passes from one symbolized situation to another. In autistic thinking, he leaps freely from one to another. How fully autistic thinking performs its functions depends solely on the content of the symbolizations and not on how the subject gets from one to the next or on how each is related to its predecessor. So a salient characteristic of autistic thinking, most dramatically illustrated in nocturnal dreams but found in every kind of free association, is the depiction of events in an order in which they could not possibly occur. There is no problem about the transition between each thought and the next. A prisoner can picture himself in paradise without having to decide where paradise is located or what means of escape or transportation could take him there. The symbolic pattern that represents it is simply evoked by the combination of external and internal stimuli present at the time.

The subject who indulges in directed thinking must satisfy additional requirements and restrictions. The end product of his thinking, if it is to be successful, will be a "solution chain." This is a train of thought consisting of a representation of an initial situation, a representation of a terminal situation, and a series of representations of intermediate situations, each of which must be joined to the last by a *legitimate step*. How he passes from one thought to the next is of critical importance and determines whether or not the aims of the thought process will be achieved. The conclusion to which we are driven is therefore this: directed thinking differs from autistic thinking in having to represent not only situations occurring in sequence but also the processes that lead from each situation to the next.

What constitutes a "legitimate step" will vary with the type of problem. In logical or mathematical reasoning, a legitimate step means an operation that obeys the rules of inference of the system and does not contradict the axioms. When one is dealing with practical problems, a legitimate step means a representation of an action that could change one stimulus situation into another. In scientific thinking, a legitimate step is a process that, in accordance with the laws of physics and chemistry, would cause one state of affairs to be succeeded by another. In chess, a legitimate step is a permissible move.

When a solution chain leading from the initial situation to the terminal situation by a sequence of legitimate steps has been formed, the thought process is over. Until then, some of the chain is missing.

Sometimes the starting point and the first few steps are given, but the end point has to be supplied. The thinker may have to select from a small list of easily specifiable alternative end points, as when a structural engineer has to determine whether or not a building with certain specifications will collapse or a meteorologist has to forecast tomorrow's weather. Which end point is to be identified as the valid one can only be ascertained after completion of the chain of calculations or anticipated changes in the weather map. At other times, the possible end points are far too numerous to specify in advance, as when a statesman or historian attempts to predict the remote repercussions of a foreign-policy move. If an appropriate series of predictable events can be pieced together, the nebulous remote consequences will take on a concrete form. These are all examples of what, following Bartlett (1958), we may call "extrapolative" thinking.

There are plenty of other cases in which the final item in the solution chain is known and fully describable from the outset. What is lacking is a sequence of legitimate steps to close the gap between it and the starting point. These cases of "interpolative" thinking are even more instructive with regard to the differences between directed and autistic thinking. A mathematician can easily repeat to himself or write down a proposition that is to be proved. But he has to find a string of valid inferences that will terminate with it. The chess player can picture to himself a position that will checkmate his opponent, but he has to work out a sequence of legal moves beginning with the present position that will have this result. The would-be designer of a flying machine can imagine devices of various shapes coursing through the air. But he has to conceive a sequence of processes that could actually cause this state of affairs and devise a series of actions that would cause these processes to take place. In all these instances, if directed thinking were essentially similar to autistic thinking, the thinker would have no difficulty in thinking about the end result right from the start, and if satisfaction depended solely on the nature of the situations that receive representation in thought, maximum reward would come from contemplating a gratifying situation without going through any laborious preliminaries. But the sequence of legitimate steps is what turns a considered fact into a believed fact or a desired end into an attainable end and thus fulfills the aims of directed thinking.

The next question to arise is: what form does the representation of a legitimate step, a process that changes one represented stimulus situation to another, take? A plausible answer is that it takes the form of an implicit derivative of an overt response that has regularly led to the replacement of one kind of stimulus situation with another kind. We thus arrive at a view of directed thinking as a process in which symbolic responses representing stimulus situations occur in sequence but a thought representing an admissible process of transition intervenes between each of these represented situations and its immediate successor.

Interestingly enough, two variants of this view have been worked out by two writers working outside the mainstream of German-language and English-language psychology, namely the 19th-century Russian physiologist, Sechenov, and the 20th-century Swiss psychologist, Piaget.

When we ask ourselves what kinds of overt responses regularly change one kind of external stimulus situation into another, two of them spring to mind immediately. First, there are receptor-adjusting responses, which cause one view of the external world to give way to another. They do not produce any changes in the physical environment, but they alter the distribution of stimuli among the organism's receptors and the selection of available information taken in through sensory channels. The role of implicit receptor-adjusting responses as a means of transition between situations contemplated in thought has been stressed by Sechenov and his Russian successors. On the other hand, one stimulus situation can be supplanted by another through the action of executive responses, which alter the stimulus field by effecting changes in the physical environment. The role of implicit executive responses in directed thinking has been stressed by Piaget.

These two views evidently complement one another, and we may hope to conceptualize directed thinking more satisfactorily if we draw on both of them. Let us first take a closer look at each of them in turn.

Sechenov's Theory of Thinking

Sechenov's position is best understood from his own translated work (1878). He refers to what we have called receptor-adjusting responses as "adaptive locomotor reactions of the body which help to increase the sensations." He says:

Here belong the movements of the head, eyes, or the body in the direction of strong light, a loud sound or strong smells, and in general all those movements which place the sensory mechanism in the best conditions for perception . . . the locomotor reactions not only increase the flow of vivid sensations but . . . the character of this flow changes with every movement of the head or body, or, more generally, with every change in the position of the sensory mechanisms. It is easy to see, for example, that our eyes will remain fixed on a definite group of objects only until there appears from another direction a new sensory impulse which is strong enough to evoke an adaptive reaction in this direction. In the course of this reaction the head changes its position, the eyes are transferred from the group of objects upon which they were fixed, towards some new group;

thus the former vivid impression is replaced by a new one, viz., by the impression which has led to the adaptive reaction.

Thus is produced "the disintegration of a sensory group into separate links separated by intervals during which locomotor reactions take place."
A little further on, he sums up:

Muscular sensations take place at the turning-points of the sensory chain, i.e., in the intervals between two different sensations; they not only serve as connective links, but also determine, in the course of the formation of objective impressions, the mutual relations of their substrate in time and space.

Sechenov is so far concerned with perception of actual external stimuli. Turning to thought, he states:

The thought is nothing else than the reproduction of a sensory group consisting of at least three separate reactions of perception. The two extreme ones correspond to the objects of thought, and the intermediate one is the link that connects them.

He explains what he means by "the link that connects them":

If the successive relations of perceptions are similar or dissimilar, the connective link between the objects of thought will be their similarity or dissimilarity; if the motor reactions of the observer take part in the substitution of one object for another (and they always do) the objects are connected by relations in space or time.

So we find Sechenov asserting that the basic unit of thinking (and what he says can be seen to refer particularly to directed thinking) is a triad consisting of a process representing a stimulus object or stimulus situation, followed by a process corresponding to a receptor-adjusting response, followed by a representation of a stimulus object or stimulus situation that would have replaced the first if the subject had actually been confronted with it and had performed that receptor-adjusting response. The receptor-adjusting response, he maintains, acts as a connecting link between the two and determines the spatial relation between them. What Sechenov writes elsewhere makes it clear that he thinks of all three components as the central portions of truncated reflexes, that is, as implicit responses. The vital role that Sechenov ascribed to exploratory responses in the organization of perception and thinking paralleled the vital functions that Pavlov saw for them in adaptation and learning.

Under the convergent influence of these two revered figures, contemporary Russian psychologists have developed further the conception of exploratory, particularly receptor-adjusting, activities in the higher and more rational forms of behavior. Zaporozhets (1954, 1958, 1960), one of the leading representatives of this trend, and his associates have paid special attention to the use of receptor-adjusting responses in the planning and control of voluntary behavior. They show how these responses can be evoked by conditioned stimuli in the absence of the objects that originally attracted them, how they become scaled down to an implicit form as they become habitual, and how they can thus take over a representational or symbolic function. Zaporozhets's arguments imply that, when we speak of a thinker "searching" or "hunting" for an idea or a solution, this is more than a mere metaphor, since the processes that he uses to gain access to the thoughts that he requires are, in large measure, implicit versions of the receptor-adjusting and other exploratory responses that he would use if he were actually searching or hunting for a concrete object in the external environment. In Zaporozhets's (1960, pp. 334–335) own words (translated):

Despite all the differences between orienting responses in sensation and in thought, they are united by a similarity of function and a genetic relationship. It can be assumed that the physiological mechanism of inner, covert orienting responses is prepared in the process of external, overt orientation. During an inner, ideational search, a focus of optimal excitation, like the beam of a searchlight, "rummages" through the cerebral cortex, seeking and reviving those traces of past experience that have a more or less close relation to the problem being solved by the subject at the present moment. This search has a selective character and is, in accordance with the circumstances, invariably directed into a definite channel, a particular itinerary, by the cues of inner speech. But how is this channel formed, how is this itinerary put together, through which internal, verbally controlled attention moves?

It is evidently put together in the first instance by the process of external, sensory attention, by the process of external overt orienting activity, aimed at the investigation of real, immediately perceived objects and situations. In coming up against their objective properties, the orienting response changes its form by a conditioning process and adopts an itinerary determined by them. And this itinerary, which is "traced out" in the cerebral cortex by movements of the sensory equipment and corresponds to the properties and interrelations of objects that have been inspected, is likewise followed by the inner search when a subject is concerned not with real objects but with objects that he is representing to himself and thinking about.

Piaget's Conception of the "Operation"

For Piaget, the unit of logical thinking is the "operation." And operations are "actions which are internalizable, reversible, and coordinated into systems characterized by laws which apply to the system as a whole" (Piaget, 1957).

What is meant by the characterization of operations as "reversible" and the nature of the laws that apply to systems of operations are matters that we shall postpone until Chapter 8.

When Piaget says that the elements of logical thinking are "internalized actions," he means that they are what other psychologists would call fractional, incipient, or implicit responses, that is, that they consist of incomplete versions—curtailed or scaled down—of processes that would otherwise culminate in overt responses.

The concept of "coordination" between "schemata" has long had a key position in Piaget's thinking. The term "schema" covers what we should refer to as "habits" or "response tendencies." He explained quite early (Piaget, 1936) that coordination occurs when a particular stimulus pattern evokes two or more response patterns, but in a later article (Piaget, 1959) he expatiates a little further on what the process entails. It can, he says, take either of two forms. The first is a means-end relation: since one of the evoked responses can be performed only after others have been completed, the child acquires the practice of carrying them out one after the other in a certain order, so that the earlier ones serve as means to the performance of the later ones. The second form of coordination consists of "class inclusions (emboîtements)": the various responses become substitutable for one another, so that "if one fails, the subject resorts to others considered as equivalent."

We can see here precisely the two kinds of relation between responses that define habit-family hierarchies, namely (1) the piecing together of responses into a behavior chain to reach a goal that cannot be reached by any of the responses singly, and (2) the equivalence of a number of responses or response chains as alternative means of reaching the same goal. If we therefore say that Piaget's operations are implicit responses organized in habit-family hierarchies, we have apparently captured the fundamentals of his conception. But hierarchies of operations have some important additional properties, to which we shall refer as our discussion advances.

Operations make possible what the Germans call a *"Gedanken-experiment"* (thought experiment). Piaget (1949b) uses the example of three beads of different colors, say, black, white, and red, strung on a wire. A child can rotate the wire through 180° (or watch somebody else rotating it) and see that the beads are now in the order of red, white, and black. He can then perform (or witness) a second rotation through 180° and see that the beads revert to their original order. Once he has mastered "operational" thinking, actual rotations can be replaced by imagined rotations; he can simply think of the wire being rotated and anticipate the order in which the beads would then appear. He can then perform a second rotation, or an indefinite number of them, in thought or imagination and predict what order would then result.

An operation is thus a transformation. It symbolizes a process that changes one stimulus situation into another, and, by representing to himself a transformation applied to a real or imagined stimulus situation, a subject can arrive at a representation of the stimulus situation that the transformation would bring about.

Transformational Chains

We are now in a position to propose a substantial modification of the conception of a train of thought that is found in the writings of Watson, Hull, and many of their successors. This modified conception takes account of the points made by Selz, Sechenov, and Piaget, among others, and it should prove more adequate to the treatment of directed thinking and more conducive to the formulation of productive hypotheses about it.

The traditional behaviorist account depicts a train of thought as a sequence of implicit response corresponding to successive events or stimulus situations. Each response produces its feedback stimulus to bring on the next response, so that we can represent the process as

$$S_0 \rightarrow r_1 - s_1 \rightarrow r_2 - s_2 \rightarrow \cdots \rightarrow r_{n-1} - s_{n-1} \rightarrow r_n - s_n \cdots$$

We shall call each of these responses representing an external stimulus situation a *situational response*, and we shall call the feedback stimulus that it produces a *situational stimulus*. For convenience, we shall use the notation u_k to stand for the combination of r_k and its feedback stimulus, s_k, and refer to this combination as a *situational thought.* The process as formulated by Watson and Hull can thus be represented as

$$S_0 \to u_1 \to u_2 \cdots \to u_{n-1} \to u_n \cdots$$

Our proposal is that, between each pair of successive situational responses, u_k and u_{k+1}, another symbolic response should be introduced to represent a transformation turning u_k into u_{k+1}. We shall call this intervening symbolic response a *transformational response.* It also will have its feedback stimulus, the *transformational stimulus,* and we shall use the notation "ϕ" to stand for a *transformational thought* comprising the two together.

So, to sum up, the chains that constitute the habit-family hierarchies on which directed thinking depends will be composed of alternating situational thoughts and transformational thoughts. They will take the form:

$$S_0 \to \phi_1 \to u_1 \to \phi_2 \to u_2 \to \phi_3 \to \cdots \to \phi_{n-1} \to u_n \to \phi_n \to \cdots$$

The transformational thoughts will constitute the "legitimate steps" that must link each situational thought with the next if the aims of directed thinking are to be fulfilled. The necessity of inserting an appropriate transformational thought or series of transformational thoughts between any two situational thoughts will thus be the factor that differentiates directed thinking from autistic thinking. In autistic thinking, the subject can contemplate one situation after another without thinking of a process that would cause the latter to follow the former, and the functions of autistic thinking can therefore be performed by situational responses alone.

Our conception of a *transformational chain,* as we shall call a train of thought built up of alternating situational and transformational thoughts, pays heed to Selz's arguments, reminding us of the role of patterning. Each situational response is determined jointly by the immediately preceding transformational and situational stimuli. If a preceding situational thought had been followed by another transformational thought, or if the same transformational thought had started out from a different situational thought, the subsequent situational thought would have taken a different form.

Transformational Thoughts as Mathematical Transformations

Our transformational responses are transformations in the sense in which mathematicians use the term. That is to say, we have a set of elements (in our case, situational thoughts), $U = \{u_i\}$, and a set of transformations, $\Phi = \{\phi_j\}$. For each transformation ϕ_j belonging to Φ, there is a subset of U called the *domain of* ϕ_j (that is, the subset of elements to which the transformation can be applied) and another subset of U called the *range* of ϕ_j (that is, the subset of elements that can result from the application of the transformation ϕ_j). To each pair consisting of a transformation, ϕ_j, and an element in its domain, u_i, there corresponds an element of the range which can be represented by $\phi_j(u_i)$. The latter is called the *transform* or the *image of* u_i *under* ϕ_j and is the element that replaces u_i when u_i has been subjected to transformation ϕ_j. The element from which the transformation starts out, u_i, is known as the *operand*.

It should be noted (1) that the domain and the range of a particular transformation may encompass the whole of U, (2) that the domain and the range may be identical, and (3) that $\phi_j(u_i)$ may be the same as u_i, in which case u_i remains unchanged by the transformation. When several transformations are applied in succession, they are customarily represented from right to left in the order in which they are effected. Thus, if ϕ_1 is applied to u_i and then ϕ_2 is applied to $\phi_1(u_i)$, the element that results is denoted by $\phi_2\phi_1(u_i)$.†

Ways of Specifying a Transformational Chain

As we have seen, we can specify a train of directed thought participating in a habit-family hierarchy by indicating all the situational responses and transformational responses through which the chain passes, for example,

$$S_0 \to \phi_1 \to u_1 \to \phi_2 \to u_2 \to \phi_3 \to \cdots \to \phi_{n-1} \to u_n \to \phi_n \to \cdots$$

But we do not have to do this, since every situational response is uniquely determined by the initial stimulus situation, S_0, and the sequence of transformational responses intervening between S_0 and it. So we need only indicate S_0 and the transformational responses, for example,

$$S_0 \to \phi_1 \to \phi_2 \to \phi_3{}^* \to \cdots \to \phi_{n-1} \to \phi_n$$

With this information, we can always identify the situational response that comes at any point as the image resulting from a string of

---

† A lucid account of the mathematical notion of a transformation is to be found in Birkhoff and MacLane (1953, pp. 119 ff.) and another, specially intended for behavioral scientists, is to be found in Ashby (1956, Ch. 2).

transformations. For example, the situational response that comes at the point marked * in the above illustration will be $\phi_3\phi_2\phi_1(S_0)$.

Each situational thought, although directly determined by the situational and transformational thoughts that come just before it, is therefore indirectly determined by the whole of the previous course of the train of thought. Unlike the behavior chains that make up the habit-family hierarchies of motor behavior (for example, maze-running in the rat), a train of directed thought is not guided by a succession of external cue stimuli. It might, of course, be affected or deflected by external stimuli that are incidentally encountered, or even deliberately sought out, while it is in progress. But on the whole, it must depend on the information contained in the subject's symbolic structures and cannot rely on periodic replenishments of information from the outside world.

Possession of Transformational Habit-Family Hierarchies

When we say that a subject is in possession of a certain habit-family hierarchy, this does not imply that the subject has learned each chain of the hierarchy as a unit or even that he has ever performed any of the constituent chains.

All that we are asserting is that the stimulus-response associations out of which the chains are built exist for that subject. The associations forming a particular chain may have been acquired at different times through a number of distinct learning experiences. Some of them may be innate (although this will rarely, if ever, be the case with symbolic hierarchies), and many of them are likely to stem from stimulus or response generalization.

With respect to transformational hierarchies (as we shall call those that are composed of transformational chains), the particular conditions are (1) that each situational stimulus (that is, the feedback stimulus from each situational response) must belong to the domain of the following transformational response, (2) that each situational stimulus must be associated with the following transformational response, and (3) that each situational stimulus must be the image of the preceding situation stimulus under the preceding transformation.

These criteria imply that, in symbolic behavior as in overt behavior dependent on habit-family hierarchies, the associations that a subject possesses may link up to produce a chain that he has never used before. In directed thinking, this may take the form of inference or of the random reshuffling to which a subject may resort when his established hierarchies leave him at a loss.

Transformation-Applying and Transformation-Selecting Habits

Directed thinking will depend, if our analysis is correct, on two kinds of habit, apart from the habits that simply link situational stimuli with the transformational responses that may come just after them.

One of these will be the kind of habit that enables the subject, when confronted with a situational thought and a transformational thought, to represent to himself the image of that situation under that transformation, that is, the situation that results from the application of the transformation to the situation in question. We may use a formula like $<u_1, \phi_1> \to u_2$ to indicate such a habit and we shall refer to it as a *transformation-applying habit*. The situational response corresponding to u_2 will be a product of patterning. Its discriminative stimulus condition will be the combination of u_1 *and* ϕ_1 in that order.

The other kind of habit enables the subject, when confronted with representations of two situations in a particular order, to represent to himself a transformation that would turn the first of these situations into the second. We may use a formula like $<u_1, u_2> \to \phi_1$ to indicate such a habit, and we shall refer to it as a *transformation-selecting habit*. This habit also will be an instance of patterning.

It should be noted that transformation-applying habits are *completely constrained associations,* while transformation-selecting habits are generally *partially constained associations.* Both mathematically and psychologically, the application of a particular transformation to a particular operand must always give rise to the same transform, but several transformations may lead from a particular operand to a particular transform. If, whether in actuality or in thought, we start at point A and walk 1 mile to the north, there is only one point, B, that we can reach. If we begin with the number 3 and add 6, the outcome can only be the number 9. On the other hand, there are several transformations (itineraries, means of transportation) that could take us from point A to point B and several arithmetic operations that could take us from 3 to 9 (for example, squaring, multiplying by 3).

The possession of transformation-applying and transformation-selecting habits does not, of course, imply that these habits will always be utilized. As with other associations, whether the responses in question will be evoked or not depends on whether appropriate motivational conditions are realized, on what other, incompatible responses are associated with the same stimulus situations, etc. We shall, however, be able to say that the response corresponding to a transformation-applying or transformation-selecting habit is "instigated" whenever the corresponding stimulus combination comes up.

Views of Other Writers

At this point, it is worthwhile to note how the conceptualization that we have been outlining makes contact with ideas expressed by a number of other writers, using various terminologies, and may thus bridge the gaps that have separated their work from the main body of S-R behavior theory.

First, let us note that, while we are developing the notions of the situational response and the transformational response with reference to directed thinking, an analogous distinction can often be drawn among processes governing other forms of behavior, including goal-directed and rationally planned motor behavior. These other forms of behavior can likewise depend on equivalents of our symbolic transformation-applying and transformation-selecting habits, controlling overt responses.

TOLMAN. For example, Tolman's (1932, 1959) theory of learned behavior holds that inferential processes, humbler prototypes of human directed thinking, underlie the doings of animals like the rat. When a certain response, R_1, performed in the presence of stimulus S_1, has been regularly followed by the appearance of stimulus S_2 (S_1 might be the sight of a certain maze alley, R_2 the action of running down that alley, and S_2 the visual and olfactory stimulation emanating from food), this concatenation of events, denoted by the formula (S_1R_1-S_2), gives rise, through learning, to a "means-end-readiness" in the subject, denoted by (s_1r_1-s_2). The means-end-readiness consists of an expectation that, whenever S_1 is present, the performance of R_1 will give rise to S_2. The entities s_1 and s_2 are evidently internal representatives of the external stimuli S_1 and S_2 and thus amount to what we have called situational responses. Likewise, r_1 is an internal representative of the overt response R_1, which can cause S_1 to be succeeded by S_2. It is thus an instance of a transformational response. And the means-end-readiness—(s_1r_1-s_2)—is plainly enough a transformation-applying habit.

Tolman does not have specific notation for anything corresponding to our transformation-selecting habit. But he uses the notation $\dot{S}_1$ and $\dot{S}_2$ to stand for the "perception" or "representation" of S_1 and S_2 respectively and states that the joint occurrence of $\dot{S}_1$ (brought on by the presence of S_1) and $\dot{S}_2$ (brought on by a drive state that S_2 would relieve) will cause R_1 to be performed. This is precisely the sort of process that we attribute to transformation-selecting habits.

HEAD. The neurologist Head (1926) was interested in how a human being can accurately select the movement necessary to bring him into a particular posture regardless of the posture that he was in the moment before. For example, as soon as a man notices the presence of an acquaintance who ought to be greeted, he holds out his hand to be shaken. The movements that result in an outstretched hand will be quite different according to whether he was just scratching his nose, feeling for something in his pocket, or letting his arm hang loosely by his side. Yet he produces whichever movement is required without difficulty or hesitation.

Head explained such commonplace phenomena with the help of what he called the "schema." This was a kind of model, representing the relative positions of the various parts of the body, which continually registered changes in posture as they took place, so that it was normally always up to date.

It can clearly be interpreted as a process whereby each bodily movement is apprehended as a transformation of posture; a representation of the subject's present posture together with a representation of a desired posture together determine the selection of a movement that will turn the one into the other. Head describes patients with cerebral lesions who can form a clear image of how an arm is placed but cannot tell where the arm is after it has been moved by somebody else while their eyes were closed. This appears to be evidence for the separateness of two functions corresponding to our situational responses and transformational responses.

BARTLETT. Bartlett's (1932) theory of remembering of meaningful material draws on Head's concept of a schema and invests it with wider significance. Each new perceptual experience is, Bartlett tells us, charged with a relation to what has gone before. A subject's reaction is determined by an organized mass of previous reactions, "with the last preceding reaction playing a dominant part." He stresses the "constructive" character of remembering. We find ourselves in possession of an emotional attitude and a few outstanding details of what we are trying to recall, and on this foundation we build up a detailed reproduction of past material. The constructive character of the process allows the organism to "turn round on its own schemata," "to rove more or less at will" over memories released from their chronological order. This is important in advanced forms of remembering, so that we can, for instance, assemble memories pertaining to a particular topic without having to trudge through irrelevant intervening material.

Bartlett's was one of the first bodies of work to convince psychologists of the profound distinctions between meaningful and rote remembering. Rote remembering appears to resemble autistic thinking in that situational responses—processes representing previously experienced stimulus patterns—are what we principally retain. It is true that rote memory can reproduce the order in which the experiences occurred if the task requires it, but, if a subject is left free to recall events in any order, he is likely to group together items that belong to a common theme rather than adhere to the original order. In much the same way, the free association of the psychotherapeutic session or of idle daydreaming is usually organized in clusters of thoughts concerned with particular types of subject matter, often bound together by an emotional attitude or interest. On the other hand, the recollection of something with a meaning that we understand depends primarily on retention of transformational responses. If we have a starting point and a series of transformations, we do not need to store detail. The detail can always be manufactured as required. But this economy and flexibility is achieved at the cost of some unreliability. Memory, as Bartlett's data illustrate, often distorts reality, since we are apt to replace the transformations that actually took place by more reasonable or more probable ones.

SPEARMAN. Turning to a writer specially concerned with thinking, we may recall Spearman's (1923) three basic processes of cognitive functioning: apprehension of experiences, eduction of relations, and eduction of correlates. His accounts of the second and third of these have had a great influence on the content of intelligence-test items. As he put it, "the presenting of any character together with any relation tends to evoke immediately the knowing of the correlative character," and this he called the eduction of correlates. The "correlative character" was the element that bore the specified relation to the first "character" or element. Since our transformational responses correspond to relations between stimulus patterns and the "correlative character" is equivalent to the image of a situational response under a transformation, we can recognize the ability to educe correlates as equivalent to the possession of transformation-applying habits. Similarly, eduction of relations corresponds to transformation-selecting habits; it is the process of specifying a relation when presented with two "characters" between which the relation obtains.

NEWELL, SHAW, AND SIMON. During the 1950's, several groups of researchers, realizing that the potentialities of high-speed electronic computers go far beyond arithmetical operations on numbers, began to develop techniques for programming them to emulate the more impressive activities of the human intellect. Newell, Shaw, and Simon (1958) have been among the most prominent and successful of these. They have made notable progress in programming computers to prove theorems in symbolic logic and to play chess, among other feats. About 1957 to 1958, they went beyond the construction of programs aimed at these specialized tasks and began to construct a "General Problem Solver," a language designed to permit simulation of the greatest possible variety of human thought processes.

The General Problem Solver works with "objects" and "operators." The objects that the computer handles are, of course, patterns of magnetization in ceramic cores, metal drums, plastic tapes, or whatever other forms of "hardware" constitute its "memory." These patterns of magnetization correspond to, and can be represented by, strings of 1's and 0's, which, in their turn, correspond to, and can stand for, expressions in symbolic logic, chess positions, or any other stimulus patterns with specifiable characteristics or components. The operators consist of procedures that produce one object or set of objects out of another. The close parallel between these objects and operators and our situational thoughts and transformational thoughts respectively is plain.

When presented with a problem, the General Problem Solver works on it by setting itself goals of three types, described by Newell and Simon (1961) as follows.

Goal type No. 1. Find a way to transform object a into object b (that is, a sequence of operators to accomplish the transformation).

Goal type No. 2. Apply operator Q to object a (or to an object attained from a by a transformation).

Goal type No. 3. Reduce the difference, D, between object a and object b by modifying a.

These goals are actually subgoals or intermediate steps that will bring nearer the ultimate goal of a solution to the problem. It can be seen that goal types 1 and 3 are rather similar, although, as far as the computer is concerned, they operate somewhat differently. In both cases, the computer possesses two objects, a and b, and it searches through a list of operators that are at its disposal, examining, in each case, the result of applying the operator to object a. If the result is identical with b (goal type No. 1) or possesses some specified characteristic that is found in b but not in a, that operator is retained, and the computer proceeds to the next goal. Otherwise, it passes to the next operator on its list, or, if it has come to the end of the list, it abandons that goal for another. On the other hand, in carrying out the procedures associated with goals of type No. 2, the computer takes cognizance of the object that results when operator Q is applied to object a.

The General Problem Solver, or computer programmed for simulation of creative intellectual work, thus depends on a capacity for procedures of two kinds. First, the computer must be able to perform operations on data brought out of storage and recognize properties of what results from these operations. This is, of course, what all computers do, whatever the purpose to which they are applied, and its correspondence to our transformation-applying habits is clear. The General Problem Solver must, however, also possess equivalents of our transformation-selecting habits. It must be able to identify an operation (a permissible reorganization of a logical formula, a legal chess move, etc.) that will take it from a given datum (for example, a set of axioms or a present chess position) to a desired datum (for example, a proposition to be proved or a stronger chess position).

Testable Implications

It is evident that a great deal more spadework will have to be done before rigorous and fruitful hypotheses about transformational thoughts can be laid down and predictions deduced from them can be tested. We have noted some of the properties that implicit transformational responses must possess. Other properties, with a close bearing on their mode of functioning, remain to be specified. Nevertheless, the notion of a transformational thought as we have sketched it and as it appears in the writings we have reviewed is already far from empirically vacuous. Transformational thoughts are conceived as derivatives of overt responses that regularly result in particular kinds of environmental change. Their possession enables the subject to represent to himself, and communicate to others, the stimulus situation that would result from a series of transformations, even when the transformations are not actually effected. Experimental study of the conditions in which subjects can specify possible transformations and anticipate their consequences is urgently needed and would surely form a signal contribution to the elucidation of directed thinking.

Chapter 6

Components of transformational chains:
imagery and language

WE MUST NOW CONSIDER what kinds of symbolic elements can serve as transformational and situational thoughts and thus as components of transformational trains of thought.

Classification of Symbolic Responses

Let us first consider some of the principal attempts that have been made to classify symbols. Three distinct bases of classification appear to have been used.

Classification by Significate

Morris (1946) divided signs and symbols into four classes differing in "modes of signifying."

1. A *designator* "signifies characteristics or stimulus-properties of stimulus-objects."

2. An *appraisor* "signifies something as having a preferential status for behavior."

3. A *prescriptor* "signifies the requiredness of certain response-sequences."

4. A *formator* modifies the way in which an organism responds to other signs or symbols that it accompanies. It includes grammatical and logical connectives such as "or" and "if," as well as qualifying terms like "all" and "perhaps."

This classification depends, therefore, on the nature of the significate, that is, on what it is that the sign conveys information about. Prescriptors or combinations of prescriptors and formators convey information about the kind of overt behavior that is appropriate. Designators and appraisors, accompanied or unaccompanied by formators, convey information about the two principal determinants of appropriateness of behavior, namely external stimulus properties and motivational conditions.

124

Other categories have been proposed along similar lines. Morris (1958) later added a fifth category of *expressive* signs, but this seems to be rather closely related to the appraisive category: an expressive sign conveys information about an organism's motivational condition, whereas an appraisor informs about the relation between an object and the organism's motivational condition, that is, the extent to which the presence of the object can aid or hinder gratification. Since, however, the way in which objects are appraised varies concomitantly with motivational condition, an appraisor must of necessity convey information about the latter. Ogden and Richards (1923) distinguish *referential* terms, which appear to correspond to Morris's designators, from *emotive* terms which appear to perform the functions of Morris's appraisors and prescriptors (Morris, 1946, pp. 69–72). Skinner (1957) recognizes a class of verbal responses that he calls *autoclitics*, which is very close to Morris's formators. Skinner's *tacts* are verbal responses (for example, descriptive terms, declarative sentences) whose performance is generally reinforced only in the presence of objects or events possessing certain characteristics. They thus convey information about stimulus properties. *Mands* are verbal responses reinforced by particular kinds of behavior on the part of the listener or reader. They therefore convey to the listener or reader information about their originator's motivational condition. Hamilton (1955) has expanded Morris's fourfold classification until it encompasses six major categories. Nevertheless, if one bears in mind the informational requirements of adaptation and recalls how information about external stimulus events, about motivational conditions, and about the nature of the optimal response must be used to guide the choice of the actual response, the categories marked out in Morris's original scheme would seem to have a fundamental validity.*

Classification by Origin

Morris (1946) calls "any sign which is similar in some respects to what it denotes" (p. 191) an *iconic* sign. This classification evidently cuts across the one just discussed, since designative signs, for example, can be either iconic or noniconic. Pictures and models are the clearest instances of external iconic signs. Images (p. 201) are considered to be internal iconic symbols.

The criterion that an iconic sign "resembles" or "has the properties of" (p. 349) its significate is hardly satisfactory. The resemblance

---

* In his most recent statement on the question, Morris recognizes a threefold division of signs into designators, appraisors, and prescriptors as basic. See his *Signification and significance*, Cambridge, Mass.: M.I.T. Press, 1964.

between a drawing or an image and what it depicts can at best be partial, and everything resembles everything else in at least some respects.

The iconic-noniconic dichotomy is surely better analyzed in terms of how a sign acquires its status as a sign. A sign, it will be recalled from Chapter 1, is a stimulus that evokes, if only in an implicit form, some of the behavior associated with its significate. This can presumably come about either through primary stimulus generalization or through conditioning, or, to use a more old-fashioned language, either through association by similarity or through association by contiguity. Iconic signs are stimulus patterns that have become signs through stimulus generalization. They will therefore include artifacts that have been deliberately made to resemble other objects, for example, drawings, sculptures, and photographs, as well as natural objects that owe their resemblance to a significate by chance (for example, the various mountains that are asserted by imaginative tourist guides to resemble human profiles). Among implicit symbolic processes, the ones that we can expect to be most capable of evoking responses by primary stimulus generalization will be those whose neural correlates bear the closest resemblance to the neural events occasioned by sensory processes, that is, images. Some images, it is true, will owe their meaning to conditioning, because they are images of objects that have frequently been perceived in contiguity with the significate.

The vast majority of signs produced by conditioning in human beings will, however, be ones that are traceable to social conditioning. The most important subclass of these will, of course, be verbal signs, from which implicit symbolic responses in the form of subvocal speech derive.

Classification by Informational Correspondence

Bruner (1964) has introduced a distinction between three "systems" or "modes of representation" that he calls *ikonic, symbolic,* and *enactive,* and this distinction suggests a third important basis of classification, relatively independent of the other two. Since we are reserving the terms "ikonic" (or "iconic") and "symbolic" for other usages, we shall replace them with the terms *schematic* and *onomastic* (Greek *onoma* = name), respectively.

Schematic, onomastic, and enactive symbols are best distinguished with reference to the notion of *informational correspondence.* This is a term that we shall use to denote the opposite of what Garner and McGill (McGill, 1954; Garner and McGill, 1956; and Garner, 1962) have called "positive interaction uncertainty." Whenever there is some degree of correspondence between combinations of output signals and combinations of input signals, the output pattern as a whole can be said to convey information about the input pattern as a whole. If a combination of output signals contains information that is not to be found in any of its components acting alone, there is positive interaction uncertainty. There is informational correspondence and an absence of positive interaction uncertainty to the extent that particular elements or properties of the output pattern convey information about particular elements or properties of the input pattern.

In order to make these concepts clearer, let us make use of an oversimplified example. In both of the cases depicted in Table 1, there are two input variables, x_1 and x_2, each of which can take on three values, and two output variables, y_1 and y_2, each of which likewise takes on three values. Let us assume, for the sake of simplicity, that the three alternative possibilities are equally likely in all instances.

In Case 1 as in Case 2, there are nine possible input combinations, so that the initial uncertainty about the input is equal to 3.17 (= $\log_2$ 9) bits.

In both cases, furthermore, a person who knew the values taken on by both output variables would be in a position to infer with complete assurance the values of both input variables. In other words, his input uncertainty would be reduced from 3.17 bits to 0, and T ($x_1,x_2:y_1,y_2$), which denotes the amount of information transmitted, would be equal to 3.17 bits.

Table 1

Case 1				Case 2			
Input		Output		Input		Output	
x_1	x_2	y_1	y_2	x_1	x_2	y_1	y_2
a	d	r	u	a	d	r	u
b	d	s	u	b	d	t	w
c	d	t	u	c	d	s	v
a	e	r	v	a	e	t	v
b	e	s	v	b	e	s	u
c	e	t	v	c	e	r	w
a	f	r	w	a	f	s	w
b	f	s	w	b	f	r	v
c	f	t	w	c	f	t	u

Suppose, however, that an observer knew either only the value of y_1 or only the value of y_2. Then, in Case 1, he would know the value of one or the other input variable for sure. In Case 2, however, he would be little better off than if he knew nothing at all about the output: knowledge of either output alone would leave him knowing that x_1 is equally likely to be a, b, or c, and that x_2 is equally likely to be d, e, or f, which is what he knew in the first place.

So, whereas, in Case 1, $T(x_1:y_1) = T(x_1:y_2) = 1.585$, in Case 2, $T(x_1:y_1) = T(x_1:y_2) = 0$. What Garner and McGill call the interaction uncertainty is $T(x_1:y_1,y_2) - [T(x_1:y_1) + T(x_1:y_2)]$, which equals 0 bits in Case 1 and 3.17 bits in Case 2. These statements hold true with x_2 substituted for x_1. Case 1 exemplifies, then, complete informational correspondence, but there is no informational correspondence at all in Case 2.

"Informational correspondence" is, it may be noted, a weaker concept than "isomorphism." An isomorphism, or identity of structure, between two patterns implies (1) a correspondence of elements, and (2) a correspondence of relations between elements. Informational correspondence does not imply a correspondence of relations and, since we are recognizing different degrees of informational correspondence, it may involve a correlation rather than a correspondence between particular elements of the two patterns. So, whereas isomorphism entails informational correspondence, the converse does not hold.

It is apparent that, of the three types of symbol suggested by Bruner's classification, schematic symbols are ones that possess a high degree of informational correspondence with stimulus patterns, enactive symbols possess a high degree of informational correspondence with response patterns, and onomastic symbols possess a high degree of informational correspondence with neither.*

---

* So-called "cognitive" theories hold that the behavior of human beings and higher animals is determined primarily by "cognitive structures," "cognitive maps," and the like, and cognitivist learning theories hold that learning consists primarily in the acquisition of them. These terms appear to denote implicit representational processes possessing a high degree of informational correspondence with sectors of the external world. The Gestalt psychologists, who were the forerunners of contemporary cognitive theorists, asserted explicitly that brain processes are isomorphic with perceived patterns. Later representatives of this tradition (for example, Miller, Galanter, and Pribram, 1960) posit "models" or "images" of external reality in a somewhat broader sense that seems to imply informational correspondence without necessarily attaining isomorphism. According to the point of view from which this book is written, there is evidence for schematic symbolic processes in higher animals, but these are not the only kinds of representational processes and far from outweighing all other determinants of behavior.

A good real-life example of a schematic symbol is a drawing of a house. If I have in front of me such a drawing, not only does the drawing as a whole help me to identify the house as a whole but the upper portion of the drawing gives me information about the roof, the left-hand edge of the drawing gives me information about the left-hand wall of the house, etc. Similarly, if I look at a map, I find that the number of black dots informs me about the number of towns in the corresponding terrain, the distances between the dots inform me about the distances between the towns, the nature of the lines connecting the dots informs me about the types of roads connecting the towns, and the color of the upper half of the map informs me about the distance above sea level of the northern sector of the terrain. Much the same can be said of images corresponding to drawings or maps.*

Gestures, such as licking the lips to represent food or rubbing fingers together to represent money, are enactive symbols, as are their implicit versions. They have informational correspondence with the response patterns that usually occur in the presence of the significate.

The symbols that are ideally suited for the onomastic role are clearly language symbols, including the specialized notations of logic and mathematics. They are capable of representing any distinguishable entity with unlimited accuracy, but they often do so, as we say, in a highly "abstract" way. There need be no correspondence at all between elements (phonemes, characters, words) of a linguistic formula and separable parts or characteristics of what they represent. If I am confronted with the number "17," the pair of numerals tells me the number of objects in a particular collection, but the "1" does not tell me how many elements there are in, say, the left-hand part of the collection and the "7" how many there are in the right-hand part. The word "elephant" designates an animal with a certain size, skin texture, color, form of proboscis, form of tusk, etc. But the "ele" does not identify some of these properties and the "phant" the remaining properties.

On the other hand, linguistic symbols are by no means confined to onomastic representation. They can be schematic, as illustrated by the following example of a teletype weather report such as airline pilots receive (Lehr, Burnett, and Zim, 1957, p. 115): DDC 90①E120

---

* A map is a good illustration of the difference between an *iconic* sign and a *schematic* sign. It is schematic without being iconic. It does not owe its usefulness to stimulus generalization resulting from its resemblance to the terrain it represents. On the contrary, prolonged training in map reading may be required before the information contained in it can be exploited.

⊕ 15R-166/67/64↓/18/009.   This contains symbols representing, in turn, the reporting station, the type of cloud cover, the cloud ceiling, visibility, weather, barometric pressure, temperature, dew point, wind direction, wind speed, and altimeter setting.   Enactive use of verbal symbols is exemplified by a culinary recipe.

After reviewing these over-all classifications, we must now spend some time on the two varieties of symbolic response that have been most widely discussed in connection with thinking, namely *images* and *words*.

Images

Some recent writers (for example, Miller, Galanter, and Pribram, 1960) have taken to using the word "image" to refer to any system of internal processes that represents what the subject knows or believes about a sector of external reality, whether perceived, remembered, or inferred.   We, on the other hand, must consider images in the more traditional and restricted sense of sensory images, that is, internal processes whose content and structure resemble those of sensory patterns and represent features of the external world that are apprehended through sense organs.

The 17th- and 18th-century empiricists and the 19th-century associationists depicted thought processes as sequences of "ideas" and, for writers like Hume and James Mill, "ideas" were what we now call "images."   Aristotle (*De Anima*) had stated that "when the mind is actively aware of anything it is necessarily aware of it along with an image," but, in an earlier passage in the same work, he had taken care to point out that thinking "is held to be in part imagination, in part judgment."

The introspective experiments of the Würzburg school and of Binet (1903) purported to demonstrate that, while images occupy prominent positions in any thought process, thinking does not consist of successions of images alone.   This work is still often cited as the classical body of evidence on the question, although the controversy it stirred up between the Würzburg psychologists and such authorities as Wundt and Titchener appeared to many later observers as an equally classical justification for discrediting introspective inquiry altogether.

Be that as it may, when we are inquiring into thinking as a contribution to the study of behavior, we need some behavioral criteria for the existence and description of images.   And when we seek them, it turns out to be extremely difficult to find any that will distinguish images sharply from other symbolic processes.

Plato, in the dialogue *Theaetetus*, compared perception to the process whereby a seal is pressed into a wax tablet, so that an image is comparable with the impression that is left behind when the seal is withdrawn. In line with this analogy, which was especially popular in the 18th century, writers from Hume on have regarded the image as something that differs from a sensation only in occurring when the corresponding external stimulus events are absent and in being fainter. This gave rise to a great deal of debate over such questions as whether an image of the sun is really fainter than the perception of a candle flame. But it received some encouragement from an experiment carried out by Perky (1910).

She seated subjects in front of a screen and instructed them to imagine pictures of a specified object projected on the screen. Sometimes, unknown to the subjects, the screen bore a faint actual picture of the object. The general finding was that subjects were unaware of the existence of the picture and showed every sign of believing that they had been experiencing nothing but products of their imaginations. Nevertheless, it was evident that they had been affected by the projected picture. For example, subjects told to imagine a banana described one in the same position as the one shown in the picture, and subjects facing a picture of a blue book claimed to be imagining a book that happened to be blue.

Despite this, we can readily distinguish images from perceptions, apart from the hallucinations that may occur in such abnormal states as psychosis and intoxication or in the perhaps even more unusual circumstances represented by Perky's experiments. A subject in possession of an image will, in many situations, behave like one who is perceiving the corresponding object. He will, for example, be able to give the same verbal description, point out an object that it matches, draw it, or communicate some of its properties by gestures. But when there is not an ecological equivalence between the existence of an image and the existence of an object in the immediate environment or in a determinate location, the behavior will not be the same. There are, furthermore, other differences that have been pointed out by J. G. Taylor (personal communication): ordinary visual images do not change their apparent size in concomitance with the distance of the surface at which the subject is looking, or blend in color with it, or otherwise interact with sensations that the subject is simultaneously deriving from the external visual field. These characteristics are, on the other hand, exhibited by afterimages, which are apparently due to excitation in the retina and in the visual cortex (Woodworth, 1938).

Loss of Information and Loss of Informational Correspondence

If we compare, from an information-theoretic point of view, the external stimulus situations that a subject encounters with the responses to which these situations give rise, two facts stand out:

1. Only a small part of the information contained in a stimulus situation is preserved in the subject's overt behavior. There is therefore considerable loss of information.

2. Despite the significant amount of information transmission between stimulus situation and overt response, there is little in the way of a one-to-one reflection of properties of the stimulus situation by properties of the response pattern. There is, that is to say, an even greater loss of informational correspondence.

So, between the impact of the external stimulus situation and the execution of the overt response, there must be a chain of neural events and intervening variables that progressively bring about these two characteristics of stimulus-response relations. As the chain proceeds, successive links will preserve less and less of the information contained in the stimulus field and come closer and closer to the sample of this information that will be reflected in the overt response pattern. Furthermore, links coming later and later will possess more and more informational correspondence with the response pattern and less and less informational correspondence with the stimulus pattern.

Many theoretical systems in psychology have found room for "percepts" as intermediate links that are at some distance from both ends of this chain. Percepts generally show an appreciable loss of information as compared with the corresponding stimulus patterns, since they have been subjected to the attrition that is effected by attention and abstraction. There is, on the other hand, as Brunswik's (1944) work indicated, a greater degree of correspondence (shown by higher correlation coefficients) between properties of the response and properties of the percept (for example, "distal" or apparent size) than between properties of the response and properties of the sensory pattern (for example, the "proximal" size or size of the retinal image). The existence of intermediate links in the chain receives further support from the data of neurophysiology.

Neurophysiological Findings

The principal portion of the cerebral cortex subserving vision is the striate area in the occipital lobe (Brodmann's area 4). The excitation that occurs in this area preserves a close approximation to a topological or point-by-point representation of retinal excitation. This means that it receives a large part of the information that the retina receives from the visible environment and that it maintains considerable informational correspondence with the visual field. Even at this stage, however, some selection and rearrangement of information is taking place, since microelectrode studies have revealed neurons that respond to the existence and angle of tilt of a light-dark boundary regardless of its location (Hubel and Wiesel, 1962).

Just beside the striate area, there are the so-called prestriate areas consisting of the peristriate area (Broadmann's area 18) and the parastriate area (Brodmann's area 19), which appear to have functions connected with interpretation of visual patterns. There is some evidence that animals with lesions in this region lose the effects of previous visual discrimination learning (Ades, 1946). Injuries to area 18 are said by Neilson (1946) to produce agnosia (inability to recognize seen objects) and injuries to area 19 to impair ability to visualize remembered objects.

There are fibers conducting excitation from the striate to the prestriate areas, but, once these are reached, point-by-point correspondence with the retina is lost. Fibers go from one point in area 17 to widely scattered points in area 18, and points from different parts of area 17 converge on the same point in area 18. This is precisely the kind of arrangement that we should expect if structures in area 18 had the task of sifting information coming in through the eyes, so that one center in area 18 responded to features that might be found in stimulus patterns impinging on different sectors of the retina or to relations between properties of stimuli reaching different sectors of the retina. The same sort of dispersion and convergence appears in the arrangement of fibers conveying excitation from area 18 to area 19 and from there to other parts of the cortex.

Penfield (1954) reports, with regard to electrical stimulation of the surface of the cortex:

Stimulation of sensory areas causes the patient to experience only the elements of sensation. In the somatic area it is tingling, numbness, sense of movement of some part of the body; in the visual area, lights, shadows, colored forms usually moving; in the auditory area, a buzzing, humming, knocking or ringing sound.

These are, it will be noted, not meaningful sensory patterns that represent well-defined stimulus situations.

On the other hand, as Pitts and McCulloch (1947) tell us:

During stimulation of a single spot in the parastriate cortex, human patients report receiving complete and well-defined objects but without a definite size or position, much as in ordinary mental imagery.

Here, therefore, there is considerable abstraction of properties from visual stimulus patterns, with corresponding loss of information (for example, regarding size and position) that sensory processes normally transmit.

Areas 18 and 19 receive fibers from other parts of the cortex, as well as from the brain stem. Through such fibers, conditioned responses can, no doubt, be evoked in the prestriate areas in the absence of the corresponding external stimuli. These conditioned cerebral responses will, of course, be able to serve as covert symbolic responses of a kind that we should class as imagery.

Although the investigations that we have been discussing have all concentrated on vision, there is every reason to believe that information originating in other modalities goes through analogous processing.

Criteria for Images

When we speak of sensory images, we mean central symbolic processes that are relatively near to the stimulus end of the chain with respect to richness of information content and to lack of feature-by-feature correspondence with motor behavior. Images in this sense can be said to exist in the highest mammals. There is, for example, an observation by Köhler (1921) that has often been cited. The ape Sultan was being tested in an experimental room in which a banana hung from the ceiling out of reach. After he had made a number of vain efforts to reach the fruit, he was led into a corridor outside the room, in which a ladder was visible, and brought back. He then engaged in some more unavailing attempts to gain possession of the banana, trying to climb on the backs of other apes that were present, until suddenly, he dashed out into the corridor and "reappeared dragging the ladder behind him."

Experiments that Beritov (1959, 1961) has been conducting for a number of years with cats and dogs illustrate phenomena that have a great deal in common with this one. A procedure that Beritov has frequently used begins by leading a blindfolded animal from one of several starting points in a room, or carrying him in a wheeled cage, by a circuitous route to a food tray. The animal is allowed to taste a little of the food and then is taken back to the starting point, where he is released. He then typically makes his way immediately and in a straight line to the place where he had eaten.

In some variants of the experiment, the animal is taken to two food trays before he is taken back to the starting point and, in such cases, he will generally go first to the location of a preferred foodstuff, to the place where a greater quantity of food is to be found, or to the nearer place, and later move on to the second food tray. The experimental conditions exclude guidance by smell, but the abilities in question disappear if the animal's vestibular organs are removed. They also disappear, significantly enough, after bilateral ablation of the prestriate areas of the cortex (Beritov, 1963).

These observations of Köhler and Beritov can therefore be regarded as evidence for implicit symbolic responses—Beritov actually uses the term "conditioned images"—which represent objects that have been perceived in the recent past but are now outside the stimulus field. These symbolic responses produce behavior resembling behavior that the sight of the objects would have produced. There is a high degree of correspondence or correlation between properties of the symbolic response and perceptible properties of the objects that they represent (including, in the case of Beritov's conditioned images, the quality and quantity of food). Their correlation with properties of the response must, however, be much lower, since the response will vary widely with other factors, such as the animal's location when the symbolic response occurs.

Human images, and probably animal images too, can evidently represent various stages along the route. Some will, for example, be nearer to the stimulus pattern and some nearer to the percept. As Perky (1910) put it, referring to the results of her introspective experiments on the imagery evoked by spoken words:

It soon appeared that a good proportion of the images thus aroused were of two sharply different kinds. There were, on the one hand, images of recognized and particular things, figuring in a particular spatial context, on a particular occasion, and with definite personal reference; and there were, on the other hand, images with no determination of context, occasion, or personal reference—images of things recognized, to be sure, but not recognized as this or that particular and individual object. The former were evidently "images of memory"; the latter, both by positive and by negative character, were "images of imagination."

One can certainly have an image of a man standing in the far distance with a minute apparent size, or one can have an image of the same man in no definite location with his normal "real" size. One can have an image of a specific coin or one can imagine, as Koffka's (1912) study showed, an abstract coin of no specific denomination. One can imagine a staircase without being able to tell how many stairs it contains, and one can imagine the front page of a newspaper without identifying a single word printed on it.

Everything considered, there appears to be no fully reliable way of telling whether a human being is using sensory images as distinct from other kinds of implicit symbolic responses, for example, subvocal words. Suppose that we are dealing with a man who is suspected of being a spy and of having assumed somebody else's identity. If he is really an impostor, he will have learned as much as he could about the present activities and past experience of the person he is professing to be, and he will have had to do this with the help of spoken or written material, possibly supplemented with photographs, drawings, etc. In this case, he can be expected to have stored this information in a primarily verbal form. If, on the other hand, he is not misrepresenting his identity, he will have stored information about his own present activities and past experience mainly in the form of memory imagery. The best that we could do to find out which he is would be to interrogate him and to apply precisely the two criteria that we have been discussing. We should attempt to elicit as much detailed information as possible, and the more he could supply, the more likely it would be that he is genuine and making use of memory images. We should also pay attention to his manner of expressing himself. If he gave answers to repeated or rephrased questions in an unvarying parrotlike manner, we should be more inclined to suspect that he has been coached verbally. This would imply that he acquired the information that he is now supplying in a form that possessed a great deal of informational correspondence with the responses that he was to give under interrogation and, consequently, relatively little informational correspondence with the stimulus events that he would be professing to have experienced. These tests could, however, never be foolproof.

So we can see that there is no way of drawing a hard-and-fast dividing line between images and other symbolic responses. Nor is there much point in trying to do so. All possible gradations in informational closeness to the significate evidently exist among symbolic responses. We can do no more than classify symbolic responses as more or less "imaginal."

Transformational Responses, Situational Responses, and Images

Implicit symbolic responses that maintain a relatively high degree of informational correspondence with stimulus properties and would thus generally be accepted as images can serve as both situational and transformational responses. There are, however, important differences between the images that perform these two functions, as some of Piaget's (Piaget and Inhelder, 1962) researches reveal. For one thing, the ability to imagine a transformation accurately appears later than the ability to imagine the situations that preceded and followed the transformation.

This is illustrated by an experiment using a cardboard tube, with one blue end and one red end, and a device that launches the tube into the air, where it rotates through 180°. Children of different ages are asked to draw the tube in its initial and final positions, and they are then shown a white tube and asked how the tube would have looked before and after the somersaulting movement if the two ends had been colored differently. The results of both tests are very similar: about one half of the 5-year-old subjects give correct answers in both cases, and the percentage increases with age until it reaches 100% at the age of eight. When, however, subjects are instructed to indicate, by drawing or by demonstration with tube in hand, the positions that the tube went through in the course of its rotation, the percentage of successes is 42 for the drawing test and 45 for the demonstration test with 7-year-olds, and the corresponding percentages are still only 60 and 70 at the age of eight.

In another experiment, the child sees two toy cars traveling at different speeds and then entering a long tunnel. He is asked to reproduce the movements that he has seen and then to anticipate how the cars will continue to move, and how their relative positions will change, while they are in the tunnel. The results show that the capacity for reproductive imagery is well in advance of the capacity for anticipatory imagery. Half of the subjects can correctly reproduce what they have already seen by the age of 7 to 8 but the percentage of successes in the anticipatory task does not reach 50 until 10 to 11 years.

These results thus favor the conclusion that images representing transformations do not occur simply as a result of witnessing the transformations in question. They are absent until the child can "understand" what the transformations involve, that is, until he has symbolic transformational responses that can represent them internally. Second, the discrepancy between the ages at which images can represent remembered and anticipated events conforms to what we should expect: components of a perceptual response can, through conditioning, be evoked by other stimuli in the absence of the stimulus events that the response depicts, provided that these events have already been perceived. But events that have not been perceived can only be represented in imagery if the subject has the transformational responses and transformation-applying habits that will enable him to represent them to himself.

IMAGERY AND IMITATION. Piaget (1945) makes much of the fact that, until the middle of the second year, the child shows no sign of possessing imagery and is unable to cope with situations in which imagery would be helpful, for example, knowing where to look for an object that has disappeared behind a screen. The middle of the second year is not only the time when language is just beginning to become a major element in the direction of behavior. It is also the time when what Piaget calls "deferred imitation," that is, imitation that occurs in the absence of the model and a long time after the model has been observed, is first in evidence. Piaget gives the example of the infant who watched in silent amazement the temper tantrum of a visiting child and then, the next day, convincingly re-enacted the tantrum. This is the time when we see the first signs of the make-believe games that will dominate the child's play during the next few years. Finally, it is the time when a child is first likely to use overt imitation in grappling with a frustrating task. A child who is having difficulty in opening a matchbox shows the instructive response of opening and closing his own mouth several times, after which he suddenly pokes his finger into the aperture and achieves success.

Piaget concludes that imagery is "internalized imitation." But to infer that images derive from imitative responses because both of them first appear at about the same time may be dangerous. One could conceive of the same evidence being cited in support of the opposite contention that the acquisition of imagery gives rise to deferred imitation. Imitation is certainly one form of activity by which a subject can gain access to stimuli that would otherwise not have occurred, including proprioceptive stimuli, interoceptive stimuli characteristic of affective states, auditory stimuli in the case of vocal imitation, and sometimes even visual stimuli. Implicit imitation can thus be a productive source of symbolic transformational responses, including ones that we should be inclined to class as images.

Since the early work of Jacobson (1932), it has been known that when a human being imagines himself executing a certain bodily movement, action currents occur in the muscles that the movement would use, even though the muscles are not contracting enough to produce a visible change in posture. It would be interesting to know whether similar action currents occur when one imagines, or thinks of, movements executed by other individuals. An experiment by Hull (1933) shows that tendencies to imitation occur when bodily movements of other individuals are observed. He found that standing subjects who watched others swaying backward and forward would unwittingly sway slightly themselves. It thus seems plausible that implicit imitative responses would be used to represent human actions that change one stimulus situation into another, and represent them as such without reference to a particular agent.

But imitation is not confined to living models, as many writers have reminded us. Lipps (1903–1906) explained the aesthetic qualities of architecture by postulating "empathetic" responses corresponding to attributes such as size and weight. Freud (1905) spoke of "ideational mimicry": we often, he pointed out, impress somebody with the huge size of a mountain by raising the hands above the head, by distending the eyes, or by raising the pitch of the voice.

Imitative responses can thus furnish transformational symbols through which a subject can represent to himself not merely actions of his own that can modify external stimuli but also physical processes in the environment that bring about changes independently of anything that he might do. At first, there is likely to be excessive generalization from representations of his own actions to representations of physical processes. From the animistic and anthropomorphic manners in which both primitive societies and children in our own society picture phenomena that depend on inanimate agencies, we can see how human actions provide the original models for conceptions of physical causality. Gradually, a widening experience of physical facts shows the inadequacy and essential maladaptiveness of representational processes of this sort, except possibly for a relief of anxiety when there is no other recourse. Discrimination learning cuts down the range of generalized responses until the recognition of structure, which is all that is ultimately needed, remains alone.

INTERMINGLING OF SITUATIONAL AND TRANSFORMATIONAL RESPONSES IN IMAGERY. Very often when we speak of an image, we are actually referring to a complex succession of events in which situational and transformational responses are intermingled. The participation of transformational responses, particularly in the form of implicit conditioned receptor-adjusting responses, is suggested by several lines of evidence. There have been introspective reports (Hebb, 1949; Rey, 1948; and J. G. Taylor, personal communication) that imagery, both visual and motor, is typically accompanied by awareness of eye movements, that it becomes more vivid when eye movements are deliberately intensified, and that it is hindered when they are inhibited. Action currents from oculomotor muscles are detectable during visual imagination and recollection (Jacobson, 1930).

Receptor-adjusting responses corresponding to absent stimuli are likely to appear in overt form in circumstances where we should expect imagery, especially if subjects are faced with a task that is new or intricate. Endovitskaia (cited in Zaporozhets, 1960) found this to be so when she gave instructions for a task involving an arrangement of cards bearing geometrical figures that had previously been visible but were now out of sight. Zinchenko's (1958) cinefilm records showed eye movements when subjects were instructed to imagine tracing a path through a familiar maze.

More direct evidence of alternating situational and transformational responses in imagery comes from experiments by Rey (1948) and Schifferli (1953). Rey asked his subjects to draw the pattern in Figure 6-1, and then asked them to close their eyes and imagine themselves drawing it. About 30% of them were seen to move an index finger, a hand, the head or the trunk, despite instructions to remain immobile while imagining the action. In a second experiment, the action of drawing was to be imagined while pressing rhythmically with the index finger. It then turned out that the two tasks could not be carried out simultaneously: either the pressing was disrupted or the imagining took place during the intervals between presses, which is further evidence for the dependence of motor imagery on responses, overt or covert, of the corresponding skeletal musculature.

Rey's major finding was that adults, but not children, take longer to imagine the drawing than to carry it out in actuality. He attributes this difference to the fact that

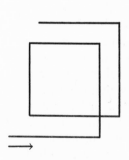

Figure 6-1

such a sequence of actions has to be guided by some sort of sensory feedback. When a subject is drawing a figure on a sheet of paper, he is concurrently receiving information regarding the progress and the correctness of his efforts through the visual channel. When, on the other hand, he is carrying out the task in imagination, he tells from the proprioceptive stimuli that follow each internalized movement which point he has reached and what is to be done next. This must necessitate a pause after each movement, which explains the slowing down, and we can see how this means an alternation between imagined actions (transformational responses) and apprehensions of outcomes (situational responses).

Schifferli told subjects to follow the outline of a specified geometrical shape with their eyes. He took cinefilms of their eyes while they were doing so. Eye movements, it was found, took the form of about five saccadic displacements per second with pauses separating them. This pattern has, of course, long been known to characterize reading and other visual activities. Morel, Burgermeister, and Dick (1955) mention that there must be little registration of visual information but a maximum of proprioception during a saccadic movement, while vision will predominate during a pause. What is interesting is that Schifferli's subjects showed the same pattern of eye movements with intervening pauses while they are imagining the shapes. In this case, the transformational responses, taking the form of saccadic movements, were overt, whereas the situational responses, occupying the pauses and representing the visual field that would follow each eye movement, were implicit.

Exploratory and other transformational responses must inevitably participate in imagery for at least two reasons. The first is that we often have to have a dynamic image of something that is undergoing continual changes and thus presenting a succession of stimulus situations. The other is that, just as perception involves some loss of information and selective attention to certain aspects or portions of the stimulus field, an image is subject to still more informational impoverishment due to selective attention and abstraction. Consequently, imagery will often not be detailed enough for the needs of a particular piece of thinking unless it represents different aspects or portions of a stimulus object or event in turn. There will thus be a succession of situational responses, in each of which a different selection of stimulus material is in focus and, if this succession is to make possible a unified representation of an object or event, each of the situational responses must be linked to the last by an appropriate transformational response, corresponding to the spatial and other relations between the elements that they bring into prominence. Receptor-adjusting responses are clearly more suited than any others to this function.

So if, for example, a man is asked to enumerate the states over which he would pass in flying from San Francisco to New York City, he will have to make use of imagery unless he has the names of the states readily available as a verbal sequence. But this latter contingency is unlikely to arise unless he has been asked the same question several times in the past or has otherwise had occasion to learn the names of these states by rote. No matter how complete his knowledge of the geography of the United States, he could hardly imagine a map in the form of a colored patchwork in which all the states appear equally clearly. He must first have an image in which the area around central California is in clear focus and the rest of the country is depicted rather vaguely. He will then see central California fade and the area immediately to the east of it come into view, allowing him to identify the next state as Nevada, and so on, until he finds himself picturing the approaches to New York City. These stages will be linked to one another by processes that are clearly equivalent to the eye movements, possibly accompanied by finger movements, that he would have used if he had been examining an actual map of the United States and reading off the names of the states from it.

That imagery often takes this form is demonstrated by a number of observations. Let us take, first, an example given by Rey (1958). With eyes closed, one imagines onself fixating a particular spot in a well-known room. One then moves the eyes to the left, and, Rey claims, this will inevitably cause the portion of the room to the left of the initial fixation point to become visible in imagination.

Another instructive phenomenon was reported by Müller (1917). Subjects were shown a square arrangement of numbers, like the one in Figure 6-2, and learned to remember the sequence of numbers read from left to right on each line. The figure was then withdrawn, and they were asked to name the numbers in a variety of orders, that is, not only from left to right but from top to bottom or diagonally. Even those who professed to be reading the numbers off from a clear visual image recited the numbers much more slowly when the order was different from the one in which they originally learned them. This would not have been the case if they had actually been reading the numbers from an image that was uniformly vivid in all its parts at once. They must have had to go through

2	6	4	3	0
5	9	7	I	8
0	8	3	9	5
4	I	6	2	7
9	4	0	5	3

Figure 6-2

stages in which different numbers were available to them, and they must have required transformational responses to lead from one of these stages to another. It is not surprising that these transformational responses were quicker and smoother when they reproduced the sequence of eye movements that had occurred when the figure was actually before them than when a different sequence had to be constructed.

Perky (1910) found that most visual images of memory were accompanied by reports of sensations of eye movement and by detectable eye movements, most auditory ones by faint laryngeal movements, and most olfactory ones by visible movements of the nostrils. These phenomena were generally absent during images of imagination. Shifts of gaze, laryngeal vocalization, and sniffing are, of course, responses that commonly change visual, auditory, and olfactory stimulation, respectively. With reference to images of memory, Perky remarks that "the observer was conscious of seeking them in a definite direction." "This point," she writes, "has been noticed by many investigators," and she lists five of them, beginning with Fechner.

Perhaps the fullest documentation for our assertions comes from experiments by Zaporozhets (1960) and his associates. Zaporozhets describes how, when children are faced with tasks such as moving a toy car through a maze or performing a sequence of key-pressing responses in correspondence with a sequence of signal lights, they have to learn to perform appropriate receptor-adjusting responses in an appropriate order. Their performance improves markedly when they are old enough to develop such systems of receptor-adjusting responses spontaneously or earlier if they are given special training to organize them. Once that has happened, the same pattern of receptor-adjusting responses can occur in the absence of the external stimuli that originally evoked it, and the child will then have an "image" of the situation that he can use to plan his activities in advance. He will also be in a better position to benefit from verbal instruction or demonstration. He will "understand" better what these instructions or demonstrations are about. This kind of image will contain elements representing the principal external stimuli that he will meet and to which he must pay attention in the course of performing the task, as well as the spatial and temporal relations that connect them.

It is worth noting that it is often impossible to distinguish exploratory from imitative responses. An imitative response is one that shares certain characteristics with the stimulus pattern that originally elicited it and that it may represent in its absence. A sequence of eye movements and manual exploratory responses used in the examination of a particular object must necessarily approximate the shape of the object. When these responses are evoked through conditioning in the absence of the object, they will represent the shape of the object; they will supply internal stimuli resembling the external stimuli that would have been received if the object had been present. This enables them to affect subsequent behavior in much the same way as stimuli from the object itself would have done. And thus from another point of view, the pattern of exploratory responses constitutes a behavioral reproduction of the object's structure. To some extent, all directed thinking must possess these two attributes: it imitates the structure of the events that it mirrors, and it consists of transformational responses that serve epistemic ends, that is, that are instrumental in the search for internal symbolic stimuli in much the same way as exploratory responses are instrumental in the search for informative external stimuli. And just as overt epistemic responses coincide in large measure with exploratory responses in human life, the implicit epistemic responses that bear the brunt of thinking must often be derivatives of the same exploratory responses.

Language and Directed Thinking

The relations between language and thinking have given rise to some of the most contentious and perennial problems of psychology. It is immediately obvious that these relations must be close. Linguistic responses—words, phrases, and sentences—commonly occur in the course of thinking. They usually occur implicitly, but they may also occur audibly when special instructions, stress, or solitude induce the subject to think out loud. Even when thinking has been silent, a subject is commonly able to utter a sequence of words representing the course his thinking took, although such reconstructions are notoriously incomplete and difficult.

The view that thinking consists of silent speech can be traced back at least to Plato, who, in the dialogue *The Sophist*, asked, "Is not thought the same as speech with this exception: thought is the unuttered conversation of the soul with herself?" In recent times, the inseparability of thought and language was first championed by one of the founders of modern linguistics, Max Müller (1887).

The American linguist Whorf (1940, 1941a, 1941b) has given some singularly impressive illustrations, both from his own experience as a fire-insurance inspector and from comparative linguistics, of the vastly dissimilar ways in which different groups of human beings can describe the same natural phenomenon. He has shown how these differences in verbal usage can make for profound differences in the content of thought as well as in overt behavior. He went so far as to suggest (1941a) that those who have been brought up to speak unrelated languages will have different "logics."

There is, however, room for dispute over how far Whorf's arguments can be pursued. For one thing, when Whorf speaks of differences in "logic," he appears to be referring to differences in the nature of the propositions constituting the content of logical thinking. He points out, validly enough, that members of different linguistic communities will differ in the concepts under which they classify objects. An untutored factory worker may see a pile of "scrap lead" and infer that this material, being a mass of metal, can be safely dumped beside a coal-fired melting pot. An individual with more training in fire hazards or in electronics will instead recognize lead sheets from old radio condensers with paraffin paper between them and realize that they must be kept away from fire. An American or European boy addresses both his father's brother and his mother's brother, as well as his parents' brothers-in-law, as "uncle" and does not show any noticeable distinction between them in his behavior and attitudes. Among the Trobriand Islanders (Malinowski, 1927), the maternal uncle is the person most directly responsible for disciplining a boy. He has a different title (*kada*) from a paternal uncle, and the power to evoke unique behavior and attitudes goes together with the title. Different languages mean not only different concepts and systems of classification but also vastly different grammatical structures to express relations and combinations of concepts, so that, for example, sentences of American Indian languages studied by Whorf do not have elements distinguishable as "subject" and "predicate."

It is clear that the content and grammatical form of propositions will affect the conclusions to which logical thinking leads. But Whorf's arguments do not demonstrate that there are differences, paralleling linguistic differences, between the rules by which propositions are pieced together to yield conclusions, and yet these rules form the essence of logic. As Whitehead and Russell (1910–1912) showed, the importance ascribed to the subject-predicate distinction by traditional Aristotelian formal logic is mistaken. Furthermore, several anthropologists (for example, Hoijer, 1953) maintain that virtually any thought or any distinction can be expressed in any language, although often at the cost of some inconvenience, just as an average American or European boy is quite capable of explaining exactly how a certain "uncle" is related to him.

In the U.S.S.R., emphasis on the role of language in thinking processes has received two powerful impetuses, one from Pavlov's belief in the crucial significance of the second signal system throughout the realm of human behavior and the second from the ideas of Vygotski, which form one of the major fountainheads of present-day Russian psychology. Vygotski (1956) depicted the human child as a creature whose behavior, soon after he begins to understand language, comes under the influence of verbal utterances from adults in the environment and who later comes to control his own behavior by producing analogous verbal patterns himself. This stress on the formative role of language was in accord with the Marxist view that the human intellect is essentially a product of interaction with material phenomena and that the forms taken by this interaction depend intimately on forms of social organization, particularly on the ways in which the members of a society are organized for economic activity. Language is singled out as the principal means of coordinating the work of different individuals and thus bringing the influence of society to bear on the psychological processes of each member.

Russian psychologists have accordingly devoted a great deal of effort to demonstrating effects of verbal behavior on perception, attention, concept formation, remembering and, above all, the direction and planning of voluntary behavior.

Nevertheless, to concede that thinking uses language and that thinking is strongly influenced by linguistic forms leaves open the question of whether there is any more to thinking than verbal responses and whether the ability to think is a direct product of the ability to speak and to understand what one hears spoken. Views that equate thinking with subvocal talking have been expressed by writers ranging from Plato to Watson. Twentieth-century English-speaking psychologists have derived some encouragement for this view from the logical-empiricist tenet that logic consists of using language in accordance with explicitly formulated rules. This encouragement is, however, perhaps derived from a misunderstanding, since the tenet was not intended as a contribution to the psychology of thinking but as an analysis of the meaning of statements belonging to logic and the criteria by which their truth or falsity is to be ascertained.

There are, in particular, three questions about relations between thinking and language that have played a part in the history of the psychology of thinking, and we must examine them in turn.

Does Thinking Consist of Responses in Peripheral Speech Organs?

By the beginning of the 1930's, a number of investigators (particularly Jacobson, 1932) had found evidence for minute movements or muscular action currents in the tongue, the lips, or the larynx when subjects were engaged in silent thinking. This work was, of course, done with the relatively crude apparatus that was available in those days, but the finding has been amply confirmed with the help of the more refined electromyographic (EMG) equipment that is at our disposal today. These observations naturally suggested that the processes of which thinking is constituted may be identifiable with fractional responses of the peripheral organs of articulation.

Evidence opposing this peripheralist hypothesis was reported by Thorson (1925) from a series of experiments in which slight movements of the tongue were registered. She found that the pattern of movements recorded during inner or silent speech did not regularly resemble the pattern obtained when the same words were pronounced aloud. There was not even a consistency between patterns recorded when the same words occurred silently on successive occasions. She found, moreover, that inner speech could still occur when the subject's peripheral speech organs were occupied in pronouncing the syllable "la" repeatedly and while he was tapping with his finger. Nevertheless, Thorson's findings did not put paid the hypothesis once and for all. Max (1934) criticized her recording technique and Jacobson (1929, p. 188) said that his subjects found inner speech to cease as soon as they relaxed the muscles of the mouth and throat.

A. N. Sokolov (1956) has pursued this line of research further, using modern EMG apparatus. He has investigated the effects of various kinds of interference on a number of tasks comprising (1) tachistoscopic recognition, (2) paired-associate learning, (3) mental arithmetic, and (4) translation from a foreign language. The last two of these, at least, must have entailed thinking in the strict sense. The interfering treatments were (1) suppression of articulatory movements by pressing the lips together and holding the tongue between the teeth, (2) simultaneous recitation of verse, (3) repeated pronunciation of the syllable "lia," and (4) listening to sentences uttered by the experimenter.

None of the interfering treatments completely precluded performance of the tasks. The actual degree of impairment increased with the complexity of the task; for example, it was greater with paired-associate learning of abstract words than with paired-associate learning of concrete words, greater when five numbers had to be added than when three or two numbers had to be added, and greater when difficult literary English was being translated than when simple stories designed for first-year students of English were being translated. Similarly, the degree of impairment increased with the complexity of the interference: it was greater when verse had to be uttered than when a single syllable had to be reiterated, greater when subjects were warned that they would have to reproduce what the experimenter said than when they were given no such warning. Prevention of articulation tended to produce the least impairment of all and sometimes even made for an improvement over performance in control conditions. Listening produced as much impairment as interfering treatments that involved the subject's articulatory organs. Impairment generally decreased with practice.

So the over-all indication is that, when the interfering treatments had a detrimental effect on thinking, it was not because they engaged, and made unavailable, organs of speech that thinking must utilize but rather because they occupied some of the limited information-processing capacity of the nervous system. This is compatible with the finding that the impairment increased with the informational demands of either the interfering treatment or the task. It decreased with increasing experience, which would be expected to bring about both a decrease in the information content of the stimulus material as it became familiar and an increase in the subject's capacity to process information of the kind in question.

A technique that permits a singularly thoroughgoing test of the peripheralist hypothesis consists in injecting an adult human subject with d-tubocurarine, a drug that induces such complete muscular paralysis that artificial respiration is required. Subjective reports obtained by Smith et al. (1947) stress the complete and uninterrupted normality of conscious processes. The cited article does not refer specifically to processes that we can accept as thinking or to inner speech, but the subject was able later on to recall events that he had perceived as well as to recall and answer questions that were put to him during the few minutes when he was totally immobile. All of this suggests strongly that thought processes proceeded as usual. Dr. D. Campbell of Queen's University has been conducting experiments of this nature more recently and even submitted to the paralyzing treatment himself. His memories, as reported in conversation, indicate that thinking in our sense of the term, for example, drawing inferences, occurred during the action of the drug.

The weight of evidence is therefore against the peripheralist view of thought, although there may still be room for some debate. K. Smith (1964) has, for example, expressed doubt that curare and related drugs completely exclude all skeletal muscular activity, although Black and Lang (1964) have found that curarization will eliminate detectable EMG potentials in the dog. Even if the peripheralist view is false, however, there still remains the second question.

Does Thinking Consist of Verbal Responses?

One hypothesis asserts that the processes that constitute thinking, whether they be central or peripheral, are verbal responses. They consist, that is to say, of curtailed forms of the neuromuscular chains of events that lead to audible speech, and they correspond to words or combinations of words.

Put this way, there are patent difficulties in the way of devising a test of the hypothesis. The obvious recourse is to introspective evidence, with all its hazards, and everyday experience supports the view that we do not think in words only. There is the familiar experience of having a thought and being at a loss for words to express it,* and the protocols collected by the Würzburg school when they used their method of systematic introspection in the early years of the present century were replete with references to much more elusive and shadowy thought elements than could be identified with verbal material. Even Watson (1924), despite his inclination to view thought as "largely subvocal talking," admitted that thinking can take place without words and with implicit manual or visceral responses predominating.

This hypothesis is, however, a special form of affirmative answer to the third question, which calls for a more prolonged and serious discussion. Arguments bearing on the third question will therefore be relevant to the second question also.

Is Thinking a Derivative of Verbal Behavior?

An affirmative answer to this question constitutes the hypothesis that thought processes, whether their components qualify as verbal responses or not, are by-products of the learning that enables us to respond appropriately to verbal stimuli and to string words together in appropriate sequences. This means that learning to use language is a necessary and sufficient preliminary to directed, and especially logical, thinking.

* In a correspondence with Galton published in the June 2, 1887, issue of *Nature*, Max Müller countered this argument with the contention that "Thoughts for which we cannot find appropriate words are thoughts expressed as yet by inappropriate, very often by very general, words."

Watson (1924) appears to have adopted this position when he referred to the nonverbal responses that can take part in thinking as "conditioned word substitutes." And several later American psychologists, without explicitly committing themselves to such a view, have evidently been strongly influenced by it in their attempts to find the key to the course of directed thinking in patterns of verbal association.

Nevertheless, Vygotski (1956), who initiated the current Russian insistence on studying intellectual processes in close conjunction with verbal behavior, asserted emphatically that, both phylogenetically and ontogenetically, "thought and speech have different roots." There is, he contended, a "prelinguistic phase in the development of thought and a preintellectual phase in the development of speech," but speech and thought become closely interconnected once they have both reached a certain stage of development.

In support of his belief in the independent origins of thought and speech, Vygotski cites Köhler's (1921) demonstration of insightful problem solution in the ape, which is evidently achieved without the use of the rudimentary vocabulary of communicative noises that apes have at their disposal. Yet the human capacity for thinking must have evolved out of the former function and the capacity for speech out of the latter. With reference to ontogenetic development, he cites analogous data from studies of infants. As Bühler (1928) showed, primitive reasoning resembling that shown by Köhler's apes appears in the human infant at the beginning of the second year. At about the same time, the infant is reacting to adult speech, babbling and even uttering his first words. But his first successes in reasoning, which gradually develop into more elaborate forms of thinking, and his first linguistic accomplishments have evidently nothing to do with each other.

Piaget (for example, Piaget and Inhelder, 1959) has been an even more adamant opponent of any attempt to reduce thinking to a by-product of linguistic functions. He bases his opposition on a variety of arguments but relies on three in particular.

1. He refers to the work of Oléron (1957) and Vincent (1956, 1957, 1959) showing the performance of deaf-mute children on various tests of intellectual functioning to be either not at all or at most a year or two behind those of normal children of the same age. These data are however extremely difficult to evaluate with reference to the relations between language and thinking. The deaf-mute subjects had been receiving training in lip reading and speaking, although

their linguistic capacities can hardly have been up to the normal level.   In any case, deaf-mute children generally possess gestural substitutes for vocal language, which are capable of performing at least some of its functions.   Finally, most of the tests used in these studies did not involve thinking as we have defined it but rather forms of discrimination, classification, and concept formation.

Although Piaget does not mention it, we might expect to find related evidence in studies of aphasics.   Hughlings Jackson (1874), refer-ring to the typical aphasic, wrote that he "can think, I suppose, because he has in automatic forms all the words he ever had; he will be lame in his thinking, because, not being able to revive words (to speak to himself), he will not be able to register new and complex experiences of things."   As Head (1926) puts it (p. 538), "The aphasic tends to fall back on images, so long as they do not express a formal relation, and on more primitive methods of temporal association."   "But," he writes in another passage (p. 521), "visual images are fragmentary and uncertain; each one of them may be vivid and full of detail but the connecting links with those which accompany or follow it are too weak to lead unaided to a definite intellectual conclusion."   One source of difficulty is, of course, the indefinite and variable criteria for thinking that are to be found in the writings of these early investiga-tors, as they are in everyday speech.   Head reports of one patient that "from the first he was able to play chess well and taught his sister the game.   He was extremely clever at draughts, 'fox and geese' and all games that did not demand expression or comprehension of names."   This was a patient who "may be said to have lost the power of recognizing verbal significance and of applying names to objects."   Yet the intellectual processes that are required for playing chess are widely accepted as prime examples of thinking, and they certainly fit our conception of thinking as a process in which absent or future stim-ulus situations are represented and behavior is adjusted to their char-acteristics.   Conclusions about the defects suffered by aphasics must, however, be drawn with caution, as Brain (1956) has warned.   He cites examples of patients with nominal aphasia who, although un-able to give objects or situations their correct names, could find al-ternative verbal formulas to convey either the same information or at least part of it.

Piaget's other two arguments seem rather more to the point.

2. He points out that, when logical thinking about classes and relations first appears at about the age of 7, the normal child has al-ready been in possession of all the linguistic resources that are needed to express the content of this thinking for some time.   He knows the

words that he will later use to refer to classes or to properties defining classes long before he can reason correctly about class membership and class inclusion. Words like "some" and "all" are understood and used to form grammatical and true sentences at a time when they will still figure in erroneous inferences.

Clearly there comes a change in the way in which he uses these items of language at the beginning of the stage of concrete operations. The changes that take place at this time certainly include ones that can be described as changes in ways of using language or as improvements in the understanding of language. Nevertheless, these changes must be the result of other factors than the kinds of learning by which new elements of vocabulary and new grammatical forms are acquired.

3. Piaget draws on his developmental studies to show that structures analogous to those that are used in logical thinking appear in sensorimotor behavior before symbolic functions have taken over the direction of behavior. This point resembles the point made by Vygotski, except that Piaget goes further. For him, forerunners of the logical relations that link thoughts are found well before the stage at which the infant can emulate the reasoning feats of apes. He claims, in fact, that an unbroken line of development can be traced from the earlier "coordinations" between motor responses that appear in the first month of life, as soon as the child is capable of more than simple reflexes and conditioned responses, and the techniques for combining symbolic operations on which logical thinking depends.

If there is any validity in the view of directed thinking (including logical thinking) that we are in the process of developing, then we must concur with this assertion of Piaget's, since, according to this view, thinking uses habit-family hierarchies that have much in common with those found in simple motor behavior. The symbolic transformational hierarchies that make such thinking possible have special properties, but these properties do not mark them off sharply from the simplest hierarchies, to which they must be linked by a whole continuum of intermediate cases.

Words and Transformational Thinking

As far as directed thinking is concerned, the signal limitation of verbal patterns is that they are ill equipped to represent transformations, although they may act as efficient enough situational responses. Words and combinations of words are especially suited to act as labeling responses by reason of their limitless multiplicity and their semantic and logical connections with one another. In this capacity, they are able to exert a powerful influence on the content and the itinerary of thought.

Transformational thoughts, as we have recognized, depend on internalized or covert forms of responses that, in their original overt forms, effected changes in the stimulus field. But words do not change the external environment, except in so far as they produce audible sounds and in so far as they bring about changes in other human beings with whom the speaker is communicating. This being so, words may be the elements of transformational chains of thought that are aimed, for example, at composing a persuasive speech or reconstructing social interaction. Their transformational role cannot, it would seem, extend far beyond such subject matter.

Nevertheless, thinking that consists simply of chains of verbal responses can and does occur. Such thinking must visually be of a nontransformational kind, which means either free association or reproduction of sequences learned by rote. Children can be taught to multiply and perform other mathematical operations by recitation of portions of the multiplication table or similar utilization of mechanical procedures acquired by drill. If, however, drill has not been supplemented by other procedures designed to promote "understanding" and transformational thinking, their education will suffer from some serious disadvantages, to be discussed in later chapters. Purely verbal trains of thought may also appear at a higher level of sophistication when mastery of the subject matter is profound. An expert who has worked out a procedure for solving a particular kind of problem by arduous transformational thinking in the past may subsequently resort to verbal strings evoking all the units of the procedure in the correct order.

Representation of Classes and Relations

Our final task in this chapter is to ask what kinds of symbolic responses support classificatory and relational thinking. Anything that we can find out about these kinds of thinking will, as we have seen, have a great deal of bearing on thinking that deals with numbers and other mathematical entities.

Classes

To recognize an object that is in front of one as a member of a particular class means, as we saw in Chapter 3, to perform, perhaps implicitly, a response that is associated with every member of the class. At the same time, it means recognizing the object as one individual member of the class, distinct from others, and this means performing another response peculiar to this object. So two kinds of labeling response are involved: one (the connotational response) corresponding to (and evoked by) the stimulus properties common to members of the class, and the other (the identifying response) corresponding to (and evoked by) stimulus properties peculiar to an individual member.

Besides these two kinds of labeling response, there may be a third kind (the denotational response) that functions when we recognize a collection of objects that is in front of us as a class. In this case, we perform a particular labeling response when the objects making up the collection are within the stimulus field and withhold it when only some of its members are present. Appropriate discrimination learning must make this denotational response depend solely on the combination of objects and not on their spatial or temporal arrangement, since the conditions in question will be ones in which the probability of reward depends only on the presence or existence of the class.

Now, thinking about class membership and class inclusion can take place when the objects and classes of objects that are concerned are absent from the immediate environment. They are not there to evoke their identifying, connotational, and denotational labeling responses, and so they must be represented by symbolic processes. But what kinds of symbolic processes actually take their place?

One possibility is that the labeling responses alone occur to represent the stimulus patterns with which they are associated. Another is that the objects or classes are represented in thought by names or sensory images and that these in their turn evoke the labeling responses. Whichever way it is, thinking of an object as a member of a particular class must mean performing in succession the identifying response corresponding to the object and either a connotational or denotational response corresponding to the class.

This kind of view is in line with the early accounts of thinking given by Watson and by Hull that we have already reviewed. Skinner (1957) and Mowrer (1954) have more recently offered similar answers to the related question of what happens inside a subject when he hears or reads a sentence stating that a particular object is a member of a particular class. Presumably, what happens then is much the same as what happens when a subject remembers or realizes, in the course of directed thinking, that an object belongs to a class.

For Skinner, the sentence "All swans are white" is apparently equivalent to "It is always possible to say 'white' when one sees a swan" and has the effect of modifying the hearer's verbal behavior on future occasions when he meets a swan. There may, however, be a modification of more than merely verbal behavior, as Skinner recognizes with reference to the sentence "There is gold in the Klondike" (presumably equivalent to "The Klondike is a place where gold is to be found"). He says that this sentence induces in the subject "either a verbal response or a resulting nonverbal tendency (to go to the Klondike where gold is reported)," which, in either case, makes his behavior resemble that of the speaker.

Whereas Skinner describes the declarative sentence as a means of initiating an association between verbal responses (or overt motor responses) and stimulus objects of the kind mentioned in the sentence, Mowrer sees a sentence as a means of transferring "meaning" from one set of stimuli to another. He takes meaning, in a manner compatible with Osgood's analysis, to consist of implicit components of overt response patterns. So the effect of hearing a sentence like "Tom is a thief," to take the example that Mowrer uses, is to produce one-trial conditioning, in consequence of which the mediator corresponding to the concept of a thief becomes associated both with the name "Tom" and with the sight of the person who is identified by this name. Through the action of this mediator, the sight of Tom will, in future, evoke the overt behavior that the hearer reserves for thieves. He may, for instance, feel uneasy in Tom's company, lock up his belongings when Tom is in the vicinity, or blackball Tom's application for membership of his club.

Now this analysis must indisputably have its share of truth. When somebody is told that Tom is a thief, this certainly changes the way that he behaves toward Tom, feels about Tom, speaks about Tom, or thinks about Tom. The new behavior that is evoked by the perception of Tom, or by symbols standing for Tom, consists largely of responses that previous learning has associated with thieves and thoughts of thieves; so we can infer that secondary stimulus generalization is at work and that implicit mediators of some kind must be serving as labeling responses.

A series of experiments by Staats and associates (for example, Staats and Staats, 1957; Staats, Staats, and Heard, 1961) have been claimed as support for this kind of view. Student subjects looked at printed nonsense syllables while hearing words spoken. Each nonsense syllable appeared several times, interspersed with other syllables, and every time it appeared, it was paired with a different word. But when all the words paired with a particular syllable had some element of meaning in common, such as "goodness" or "angularity," it was later found, with the help of Osgood's semantic-differential test (Osgood, Suci, and Tannenbaum, 1957), that some of this element of meaning adhered to the syllable.

Analyses such as Skinner and Mowrer have offered have, however, come in for some criticism (for example, Mandler, 1961). More than contiguity of the words "Tom" and "thief" is obviously needed to effect the changes in behavior attendant on believing that Tom is a thief. There are many situations in which these words would occur in close contiguity without implanting this belief. One might, for example, have occasion to say, "I have a friend called Tom. A thief once stole his wallet." Staats's experiments produced significant but relatively weak effects. If subjects had been told that "XEH is angular" or that "XEH means zigzag," they would presumably have shown more striking changes in their reactions to "XEH."

In other words, there must be some psychological process corresponding to, and resulting from, the word "is," the copula. It is true that in some languages, such as Russian and Hebrew, the present tense of the verb "to be" is generally omitted, so that "Tom is a thief" would be expressed as "Tom thief." But even in these languages, the context makes clear when the verb "to be" is to be understood, and not all utterances in which the words "Tom" and "thief" occur in close succession are taken to assert that Tom is a thief.

When we turn from listening or reading to thinking, there is the analogous problem of what happens when we judge that Tom is a thief or think of Tom as a member of the class of thieves. To say that we think to ourselves the words "Tom is a thief" cannot be the answer or at least not the whole answer. There are many circumstances in which we may be induced to think of such a sentence without espousing the judgment or belief corresponding to the sentence and performing the pertinent overt behavior.

An alternative answer that offers itself is that, when we judge that Tom is a thief, we have a succession of symbolic responses, including the thought of Tom and the thought of the class of thieves or of theft. But although this may be the case, it can hardly be the whole story. When we think of somebody called Tom, an association may set us thinking immediately afterward of tomcats, but to think of Tom and then of tomcats is not at all the same as to think of Tom as a tomcat or to subscribe to the view that Tom is a tomcat.

We are therefore faced with precisely the kind of problem that makes it necessary to invoke transformational responses. If directed thinking is to have the orderly controlled character that is necessary for it to reach its objectives, there must be some kind of symbolic process that conveys us from a contemplation of an object, say Tom, to a contemplation of that object as a member of a particular class, say the class of thieves. In this way, a succession of thoughts, representing an object as a member of a particular class, will be distinct from other situations in which two thoughts follow one another.

But from what kind of response could the kind of transformational thought that we are seeking be derived? The thought of an object is, according to our previous arguments, derived from the reactions that accompany the experience of perceiving the object, and similarly the thought of a class must derive from the reactions that accompany the experience of a collection of objects with a class-defining property in common. So the responses that fulfill our requirements must be responses that change a stimulus situation in which we perceive and attend to a particular object into a situation in which we perceive the object in the midst of a collection of similar objects.

We are led, then, to the hypothesis that Piaget has emphatically advocated, namely that thinking about class membership or judging, in thought, that an object is a member of a class is an internalized derivative of such actions as physically gathering together objects with a certain property in common. When we think, say, of all thieves collectively, this is an implicit equivalent of the kind of overt response that we should use, say, to pick all the yellow objects out of a heap and assemble them in one location. And when, in thought, we "put" Tom into the category of thieves, this is an implicit equivalent of a response such as taking hold of a yellow object and laying it down in the midst of an assemblage of yellow objects.

This view of Piaget's is the result of many years of experimentation on classificatory behavior in children. And while we must be chary of inferring from the successive appearance of two phenomena that they must be causally connected, the course of development that he has traced is certainly compatible with this view.

The most relevant experimental situation (Piaget and Inhelder, 1959) is one in which the child is presented with a pile of elements (pieces of wood or plastic differing in color, size, and geometrical shape, or toy models of familiar objects) and the task is simply to place together the ones that are "alike." Between the ages of about $2\frac{1}{2}$ and 5 years, the subject produces what Piaget calls "figural collections." He assembles unlike objects that form pleasing patterns or unlike objects that he feels ought to go together because they are frequently seen together; for example, he may put some chairs together with a table, because that is the arrangement he sees every day at home.

At this stage, therefore, the child is capable of reacting to a collection of objects as a unit, and, as other observations show, he is capable of associating a common reaction with objects that have a perceptible property in common. But so far, he is not coordinating or combining these two abilities, as he must if he is to carry out the task correctly. To do this, he must reserve a discriminative response for a collection of objects, all of which he can recognize and respond to as similar, and place an object in the collection only if it has the properties that characterize those already in the collection.

Between the ages of about 5½ and 7 comes the second stage, in which the child can gather together objects that are alike in some easily identifiable respect, such as shape or color or size or a combination of these. It may seem, therefore, that he has now acquired a full understanding of class membership, but other tests show that his understanding is still not complete. Some of these tests (already mentioned in Chapter 4) involve verbal behavior in response to questions. He may still make invalid statements using the words "all" and "some," and he may not realize that, if class B includes all the objects in class A as well as some objects that are not in A, then B must contain more elements than A.

These limitations disappear at about the age of 7, when the stage of concrete operations is beginning, and, at about the same time, the child begins to cope with other tasks that are even more revealing.

In one type of experiment, the child is handed some additional objects after he has finished grouping together the ones that he already has, and these new objects call for a change in the classifications that he has already made. For example, the instructions may require objects to be placed in two boxes only, and, after the child has dealt with a heap of green circles and green crosses, he is handed some yellow stars, so that a division according to color has to replace the division according to shape. This necessitates being able to undo what has already been done and to anticipate an alternative manner of grouping that will accommodate both the old objects and the new ones.

In another type of experiment, the child is given miscellaneous objects and told that he must place like objects in one envelope. He is then asked how many envelopes he will need, what should be written on the envelopes, and which objects will be placed in each. So once again, he must foresee how he will divide up the objects before actually handling them. The anticipatory capacities that are needed by these two types of experiments are first in evidence, significantly enough, at the age when the child is first able to answer questions about class membership and class inclusion correctly and, in general, to think logically about classification.

All these experiments demonstrate, then, that the ability to gather similar objects together takes some time to appear but that it precedes the ability to think correctly about objects as members of classes and about classes as parts of broader classes. Furthermore, they show that the ability to think of similar objects as members of a class—even when the objects are visible, let alone when they are merely represented in thought—comes into existence relatively late. At first, the child does not react to a class of objects as a whole or recognize a class to which the particular object belongs, unless the class forms a perceptual whole. Then comes a time when he can form them into a perceptual whole by moving them close together and separating them from other objects. Later still, he can recognize and think about a class when the objects that make up the class are spatially separated and mingled with other objects and even when some or all of the objects in the class are out of sight. The presumption is that, when this final stage has been reached, implicit derivatives of assembling responses lead to symbolic situational responses through which a class can be contemplated as a whole and in isolation from things that do not belong to it. A thought about class inclusion is presumably derived in much the same way from actions such as pushing two collections of similar objects (for example, blue squares and red squares) together to form a larger collection that embraces them both.

Relations

Thinking about relations raises comparable problems. In Chapter 3, we concluded that to recognize a relation means to possess an equivalence class of ordered pairs of stimulus objects, such that every ordered pair belonging to the class is associated with a common response. The stimulus objects in question can be ordered spatially or temporally or both, and the pairs that are instances of a relation may have a natural similarity, so that primary stimulus generalization can account for their instigating similar behavior, or else the similar behavior can result from labeling responses that give rise to mediated relations.

An adult subject or a child older than about 7 can think about, and make inferences about, relations between pairs of objects that are not spatially or temporally ordered. Two objects between which a relation (for example, "greater than") is recognized to hold may not be contiguous at all, so that they cannot be readily perceived as a pair. Alternatively, the relation may be recognized between objects that are absent altogether from the stimulus field.

From arguments that are essentially the same as those adduced in connection with thinking about classes, we can see that transformational responses must represent the process of relating one object to another in a certain way or "putting" two objects in a certain relation to each other. And if we pursue the analogy with classificatory thinking further, we should expect such transformational responses to derive from overt actions that result in the appearance of ordered pairs of stimulus objects exemplifying particular relations.

Since a pair of stimulus objects that exemplifies a relation can be ordered spatially or temporally or both, we must look for the origins of relational transformational thoughts either in responses that present us with two objects side by side or in responses that present us with two objects in close succession.

The first of these alternatives forms the basis for Piaget's (Piaget and Szeminska, 1941; Piaget and Inhelder, 1959) hypothesis regarding the origins of relational thinking. In his view, the operations that relate objects in thought originate in actions such as placing sticks side by side in order of increasing length. As we have already seen, he has found that the child is not capable of carrying out this arrangement systematically and efficiently before the start of the stage of concrete operations, although he might succeed at it by dint of trial and error a year or two earlier. At about the same time as he is beginning to master this task, he first shows himself capable of anticipating the pattern that will result from his efforts and drawing sticks of different colors as they will appear when he has finished. So, as in the case of classification, ability to carry out the required action on the motor level precedes the ability to anticipate the end product of the action, which presumably means the ability to use implicit equivalents of the same actions to arrive at symbolic representations of their consequences.

However, this hypothesis of Piaget's and the experimental work associated with it neglect another likely source of transformational responses corresponding to relations. This is one that has received extensive consideration in Russian writings. The ordering responses that Piaget considers produce patterns of spatially ordered simultaneous stimuli. But relations could also be represented by responses that result in temporally ordered stimulus pairs, that is, that lead us from a stimulus situation in which one object is in view to a situation in which another object, related to the first in a particular way, has replaced it. The obvious candidates for this function are exploratory responses changing the orientation of sense organs.

It will be remembered from Chapter 5 that Sechenov (1878) referred to motor reactions leading from one sensation to another. He contended that the "elements of the muscular sense" that are produced by, and therefore correspond to, these reactions, "placed in the intervals between the members of the group or chain, determine the relations between the members of the group or chain in space and time."

We have also seen how the experiments of Zaporozhets's (1960) group draw attention to the role of eye movements and manual exploratory responses in, first of all, helping the child to recognize the spatial and the temporal relations between the stimuli that he encounters in the course of carrying out a task. At a later stage, the subject can plan his activities in advance with the help of these same exploratory responses, which occur in the absence of the stimuli but provide information about where they stand in relation to one another and about the temporal intervals that separate them. They are well suited for this function, since the form of an exploratory response must vary closely with direction, distance, and time interval between the stimulus that is in focus when it starts and the stimulus that is to be brought into focus when it is concluded.

According to Taylor's (1962) analysis, responses that bring the subject into contact with objects at various locations in his environment are responsible even for the perceptual location of objects in space. He describes the gradually widening assortment of such responses that become available from infancy onward and shows how they ensure the formation of an ever widening unified perceptual space in which objects perceived through different receptors are localized and spatially related to one another. First, we have ocular pursuit movements, which are fairly accurate within a few weeks of birth. Movements of the head soon occur in conjunction with them and increase their range. Soon afterward, reaching movements acquire an accuracy that enables them to bring the hand into contact, by the quickest possible route, with any object that is in sight and sufficiently close to the body. Their scope is soon augmented by bending movements of the trunk, and finally locomotion affords access to environmental objects that are well out of reach of the hands and permits the child to attribute a spatial location to objects that appear in the distance.

All of these responses are delicately adjusted to distance and direction and, when they occur in anticipation of meeting an object that is not yet in view, to time intervals. Implicit versions of them could therefore serve as transformational responses representing spatial relations among objects that are contemplated in thought.

Such responses, like the responses on which Piaget's studies of ordering have concentrated, give rise to pairs of stimuli, occurring simultaneously or in succession, that possess particular spatial relations. But, as we have seen, all relations can be defined in terms of ordered pairs, and a class of ordered pairs that corresponds to a nonspatial relation is one in which the nonspatial relation is correlated with the spatial or temporal ordering relation. In this way, transformational responses that, in the first instance, represent spatial relations can be used to represent other relations also, as common language shows so abundantly. Thus, we say that "A is higher than B in status," that "C is behind D in attainment," and that "E is more deeply immersed in vice than F," or that "G is nearer to bankruptcy than H."

Mathematical Thinking

The transformational responses that participate in mathematical thinking must overlap both with those that underlie classificatory thinking and with those that underlie relational thinking. We must have implicit equivalents of responses that gather objects together to form collections to which numbers are attached, and we also need transformational responses to express the ordering relations that exist between numbers and between objects that are counted or measured. When we count, we usually have to perform pointing movements or eye movements or head-nodding movements that transfer our attention from one object to the next. Whenever possible, we usually find it helpful to gather together in one spot the objects that we are to count. It is plausible that such responses occur in an implicit form when we count objects in thought or when we think about objects or sets to which numbers are attached.

Arithmetical and algebraic operations, such as addition, subtraction, substitution, and transposition, are all easily recognizable, if only from the fact that these terms are used to refer to them, as symbolic equivalents of physical actions that move objects about in relation to one another.

Chapter 7

Stimulus-response equivalences and tree structures

Logical Inference

Let us consider syllogisms such as "All men are mortal, Socrates is a man, therefore Socrates is mortal" or, to adapt a more up-to-date example given by Wertheimer, "Smith lives in Palo Alto, Palo Alto is in the area handled by the San Francisco Internal Revenue Office, therefore Smith's income tax problems should be discussed with the San Francisco Internal Revenue Office." These, like all forms of reasoning, are examples of learning. They give rise to knowledge, which will be retained and which may therefore influence the thinker's behavior in relevant circumstances for an indefinite period.

Yet the ability to reason in these ways is itself a product of learning. As Piaget and other students of child behavior have fully demonstrated, the ability to reason logically takes some time to appear, and we have to assume that learning and maturation are jointly responsible for its emergence. So we have here learning processes of great generality. They equip the subject with techniques of reasoning that make other, much more specific learning processes possible and lead to the acquisition of particular items of knowledge or symbolic response patterns. The whole value of logical reasoning lies in the fact that a familiar structure, such as the syllogism, can be used on material to which a subject has never before applied them to generate conclusions that he has never before entertained. They might very well give rise to conclusions that no member of the human race has ever formulated before, as happens every day in logical and mathematical research.

These facts have led Apostel (1959) to compare the learning that produces logical reasoning to the formation of "learning sets" (Harlow, 1949), which have been described as instances of "learning to learn." It is true that logical reasoning, like all reasoning, consists of learning that influences later learning, but the analogy with learning sets is not otherwise very close. An animal is said to form a learning set when he is exposed to a succession of discrimination problems and solves them with increasing rapidity as his experience of them accumulates. So the learning set is a special kind of learning to learn, which is rather different from reasoning.

There are other sectors of behavior in which we find evidence for intellectual acquisitions that are infinitely transferable, and so it may be enlightening to have a look at some of them.

Counting and Mathematical Induction

The French mathematician Poincaré (1902) was greatly impressed with "the faculty of conceiving that a unit may be added to a collection of units." He went on to say:

> We have had the opportunity of exercising this faculty and are conscious of it; but from this fact we feel that our power is unlimited, and that we can count indefinitely, although we have never had to count more than a finite number of objects.

He refers to "the power of the mind which knows it can conceive of the indefinite repetition of the same act, when the act is once possible," and he maintains that "the mind has a direct intuition of this power."

It is true that the normal child comes to realize, after a few years of tuition in arithmetic, that there is no such thing as the largest of all numbers. He knows that, no matter how large a number may be, a still larger number can always be found. He knows how to form (by naming it or writing it down) the number that comes after any number with which he is presented, even though it may be one that he has never seen before. Yet being able to count indefinitely and being able to supply the number that should come after any given number does not mean repeating the same action indefinitely. It means producing a different pattern of behavior (spoken or written) each time, depending on the stimulus pattern derived from the immediately previous number.

Poincaré refers to reasoning by mathematical induction or recursion as "mathematical reasoning *par excellence*." This is a kind of reasoning that enables us to conclude that a formula (for example, $a + 1 = 1 + a$) holds when a is any conceivable number, by recognizing (1) that it holds when $a = 1$, and (2) that, if it holds when $a = n$, it must hold with $a = n + 1$. Mathematical induction,

Poincaré says, "contains, condensed, so to speak, in a single formula, an infinite number of syllogisms" which "follow one another, if one may use the expression, in a cascade."

The hypothetical syllogisms in question are the following. The theorem is true of the number 1. If it is true of 1, it is true of 2; therefore it is true of 2. If it is true of 2, it is true of 3; therefore it is true of 3; and so on. It is clear that the process also gives rise to an infinity of stimulus-response associations. Having recognized that the formula $a + 1 = 1 + a$ is true for all numbers, we shall, in suitable motivational conditions, write down "$= 1 + 31$" on seeing "$31 + 1$," "$= 1 + 102$" on seeing "$102 + 1$," etc. Poincaré appears to attribute the ability to use reasoning of this sort to a "direct intuition" of the mind.

Inhelder and Piaget (1963) have found evidence for reasoning by recursion in children approaching the age of six. For example, if an experimenter drops a single bead into glass A and then keeps on dropping single beads into glasses A and B simultaneously, these children will recognize that glass A must always contain one more bead than glass B. At a slightly earlier stage, however, children abandon this belief as the collections of beads in the two glasses come to look more and more alike. According to data gathered by Gréco (1963) and by Matalon (1963), a child is not capable of more advanced forms of such recursive reasoning, depending on the notion of an order of succession, until the age of nine or ten. We must, therefore, conclude that the infinitely fruitful resources of mathematical induction and analogous kinds of inference are products of learning processes combined with maturation.

Grammar

Writers with an interest in psycholinguistics (for example, Chomsky, 1957; Brown and Fraser, 1963) have recently been making much of the fact that the normal human adult, and even the child who has mastered language, is capable of constructing sentences that he has never heard anybody utter but that are perfectly consistent with the rules of grammar. He can similarly recognize whether a sentence uttered by another person is grammatically correct, even though it differs from any sentence he has encountered in the past. Knowledge of grammar is obviously a fruit of learning, but this learning is transferable to an infinite variety of unprecedented situations, each of which calls for its own unprecedented sequence of verbal responses.

So in all these cases, as in many instances of directed thinking, we have learning processes that involve the performance of certain responses in certain stimulus situations, and these learning experiences result in the establishment of an infinite number of new associations between quite different responses and quite different stimulus situations.

Rules

Considerations of this sort have led a number of writers in recent years to recommend that S-R formulations be abandoned. To take the place of these, they have imported into psychology a new type of unit of analysis and zealously promoted it under several different names. Those influenced by game theory have spoken of "strategies" (for example, Bruner, Goodnow, and Austin, 1956). Those interested in linguistic problems, especially ones related to grammar, have assigned onerous responsibilities to the concepts of "structure" (for example, G. A. Miller, 1962) and "rule" (for example, Brown and Fraser, 1963). Successes achieved in computer simulation of psychological processes have encouraged wide diffusion of the word "program" (for example, Newell, Shaw, and Simon, 1958). Perhaps the most ambitious effluent of this current has been the proposal (Miller, Galanter, and Pribram, 1960) to reconstruct virtually the whole of psychology using "plans" as the building blocks. The Gestalt psychologists of an earlier generation (for example, Wertheimer, 1945) favored the term "principle." In the U.S.S.R., Shevarev (1958) has won lively interest for his suggestion that thinking depends on "generalized associations," described as "rule-conforming associations," each of which can be actualized through a variety of stimulus-response pairings. Piaget's (1936) "schema" belongs to this category also.

We shall use the word "rule'" as a means of referring to concepts of this kind collectively. "Strategies," "structures," "programs," and "plans" can be regarded without excessive misrepresentation as systems of rules. The devotees of "rules" have done a great service in pointing out some problems that face S-R conceptualizations, especially in the analysis of thinking, and many of these are undoubtedly problems to which S-R psychologists have given insufficient heed in the past. But to find deficiencies in an existing body of theory is one thing, and to find an alternative brand of theory that can do both what established theories cannot do and what they have been able to do is another thing.

The principal differences between a rule and a S-R association would seem to be this. If we know that a particular organism possesses an association between stimulus situations of class A and responses of class X, this will enable us to predict its behavior (in the sense of giving a better-than-chance guess) only if we know that a stimulus situation of class A will occur. Concepts like "rule," however, equip us with a prediction about behavior for any stimulus situation that is likely to confront the organism.

A person with an adequate strategy will have a response available for any of the possible configurations of events that may face him in the course of a game or battle. If we know his strategy, we cannot say what he will do without knowing what contingencies he will meet, but we can say what action each conceivable contingency will draw from him.

In English grammar there is a rule stating that if we wish to negate any declarative sentence with a third-person singular subject and a verb in the present tense other than "is" or "have," we insert "does" immediately before the verb and replace the indicative form of the verb by its infinitive. If we know that a person has mastered grammatical English, we can tell in advance how he will phrase the negative of any such sentence that could possibly arise.

A program that is fed into a computer must make clear exactly what is to happen at any stage. The nature of the operation to be performed, however, must depend on what is in the memory cells at the time. If we could not specify an operation without knowing beforehand what would be stored in every cell when the operation became due, we could not take advantage of the high-speed capacities of computers. But programs can be devised to leave no ambiguity about what is to be done at any point and yet make each operation contingent on the outcome of what precedes it.

So a strategy or rule or program conveys information that could otherwise be conveyed in a less succinct form by listing all the possible stimulus situations and stating the response to which each would give rise. In other words, it means giving a list, which would probably be extremely, perhaps even infinitely, long, of S-R associations.

There is, of course, more to it than that. One of the main points made by partisans of rules is that S-R associations are not acquired singly. When one of the higher animals undergoes a learning experience in a particular situation, he does not gain merely an enhanced tendency to make a certain kind of response in that kind of situation. He may well profit from this learning in other, vastly different situations, and the effect of the learning experience may be to make him perform vastly different responses in those situations.

So it is urged that, instead of describing learning as a matter of strengthening S-R associations, we should say that an animal, when he learns, comes into possession of a rule and that thereafter he applies this rule in a variety of situations. Applying the same rule in the one situation is likely, however, to mean outwardly different behavior from applying it in another.

Nevertheless, this usage presents difficulties. If applying the same rule in different stimulus situations means performing different responses, how does the subject select the response that is the appropriate representative of a particular rule in a given situation? How can an external observer predict which response the subject will perform from a knowledge of the rules that he has acquired?

Two kinds of solution have been proposed for this problem. One solution is to say that all the responses that are instances of a particular rule have some consequence in common and that the subject performs whichever response is going to be an effective means of achieving this consequence in the situation in question. This clearly fits the facts in many cases, but it does not, of course, give a satisfactory answer to the question of how the effective response is to be distinguished and selected.

The other kind of answer, characteristic of the Gestalt school and writers influenced by it, has been that the response, although topographically different from another response performed in another situation, will give rise to the same structure or system of relations. It might be a matter of performing a pattern of actions with a particular structure, or it may be that the structure formed by the stimulus situation and the behavior together, that is, the system of relations embracing stimulus elements and response elements, is isomorphic with what has occurred in other stimulus situations. In either case, this criterion is very difficult to apply rigorously. The actual structures that are realized are not usually clearly defined, and there will often be several alternative responses that give rise to some kind of isomorphism with structures encountered during previous learning experiences.

Stimulus-Response Generalization

We shall, therefore, have recourse to another way of handling these phenomena and the unavoidable problems that they present. In his book *Principles of Behavior,* Hull (1943) distinguished three kinds of generalization:

1. The reaction involved in the original conditioning becomes connected with a considerable zone of stimuli other than, but adjacent to, the stimulus

conventionally involved in the original conditioning; this is called *stimulus generalization.*

2. The stimulus involved in the original conditioning becomes connected with a considerable zone of reactions other than, but related to, the reaction conventionally involved in the original reinforcement; this may be called *response generalization.*

3. Stimuli not involved in the original reinforcement but lying in the zone related to it become connected with reactions not involved in the original reinforcement but lying in a zone related to it; this may be called *stimulus-response generalization.**

Stimulus generalization, in which a response, R_A, having become associated with stimulus situation S_1, is found also to have acquired an association with stimulus situation S_2, which is similar to S_1, was discussed in Chapter 3, and an enormous body of experimental work has been devoted to it. Response generalization, in which, when S_1 becomes associated with R_A, S_1 is found to have acquired an association also with R_B, a response similar to R_A, was discussed in Chapter 4, and, as was mentioned then, some experimental work, but not much, has been devoted to it. Stimulus-response generalization, in which the formation of an association between S_1 and R_A results in the formation of an association between S_2 and R_B, has, on the other hand, scarcely been investigated at all.

Nevertheless, we shall suggest that the phenomena that we have been considering and that other writers have preferred to discuss in terms of rules, etc., are best regarded as cases of stimulus-response generalization. The structures that form the basis of directed thinking, notably transformational chains, are, we suggest further, distinguished by their extreme susceptibility to stimulus-response generalization, which gives them their wide usefulness in a variety of environmental circumstances.

Despite the paucity of experimental studies specifically concerned with stimulus-response generalization, several examples of behavior that fits this category can be cited.

First, we may consider an experiment by Wickens (1938). His subjects were seated with the hand lying palm downward and the fingers touching an electrode, and he trained them to make a conditioned finger-extension response by sounding a buzzer shortly before the delivery of an electric shock. Once this response had been established, the subjects laid their hands palm upward, so that the dorsal surfaces of the fingers were now in contact with the electrode, and, without

* Reprinted with permission from C. L. Hull: *Principles of Behavior.* Copyright 1943 by Appleton-Century-Crofts.

further training, they responded to the buzzer with finger flexion. As a consequence of the initial training, which established an association between the extension response and stimulus situations including the sound of a buzzer and tactual stimulation to the volar surface, an association was established between the flexion response and stimulus situations that included the sound of the buzzer and tactual stimulation of the dorsal surface.

Then, let us look at a series of experiments carried out by Naroditskaia (1934) in the laboratory directed by Ivanov-Smolenski. The subjects were children varying between five and twelve years of age, and Ivanov-Smolenski's motor-conditioning technique was used. The response consisted of pressing a rubber bulb with the fingers. The initial conditioned stimulus consisted of illumination of a red square, the unconditioned stimulus being the word "Press!" uttered by the experimenter. If the response was performed on receipt of the conditioned stimulus, reinforcement was delivered in the form of a brief appearance of a picture.

Naroditskaia studied generalization by changing from the original conditioned stimulus to a green rectangle and then, while retaining the same conditioned stimulus, changing the kind of bulb that had to be pressed. In one variant, the red square that had originally served as the conditioned stimulus was replaced by an orange sector and the nature of the required response was simultaneously changed by replacing the original pear-shaped bulb, whose sides had to be squeezed between the thumb and the fingers, with a conical bulb, whose base had to be pressed with the thumb. It was found that subjects who had undergone the initial training procedure generally performed this new response to this new conditioned stimulus, the percentage of successes being greater with older children. These data were claimed as evidence for (to quote the title of the chapter in which the experiments were reported) "the formation of new conditioned connections in childhood without prior elaboration."

Coming a little nearer to the topic of directed thinking, we find stimulus-response generalization illustrated by some of the observations that Köhler (1921) made in the course of his work with chimpanzees. One female ape, Tschego, had learned to take a stick and use it to push a bunch of bananas within reach. Some hours later, she achieved the same effect by flapping the fruit toward her with a blanket. Köhler did not carry out control experiments to demonstrate that she did this because of her previous success with the stick. But the presumption is that it represented transfer from that piece of learning.

We find perhaps even more convincing evidence of stimulus-response generalization, often overlooked because of its very familiarity, in grammar. The child or the foreigner makes errors like "I brang," and "I goed." He has never heard anybody utter these forms, but he uses them because he has heard and learned to use forms like "I sang" and "I walked." Such errors are quaint enough to attract our notice. Nevertheless, correct grammatical speech depends on similar use of earlier learning experiences in which other stimulus situations became associated with other response patterns.

It is easy to see that all R-reasoning must involve stimulus-response generalization. As we noted in Chapter 3, S-reasoning is identifiable as a form of secondary stimulus generalization, since it establishes an association between the new stimulus situation and a response that was already associated with other stimulus situations. But R-reasoning associates a new stimulus situation with a new response pattern. It cannot be attributed to response generalization, since, like all reasoning, it results from the prior establishment of at least two distinct stimulus-response associations. The new response pattern must differ from at least one of the responses that participated in these preceding associations. Likewise, the stimulus situation in which the new response pattern occurs must differ from the stimulus term in at least one of the preceding associations. So it follows that stimulus-response generalization must be at work.

S-R Generalization versus Application of Rules

Whether we say that an animal learns response R_A in stimulus situation S_1 and, as a result of stimulus-response generalization, performs response R_B in stimulus situation S_2 or whether we say that he learns a certain rule in S_1 and applies the same rule in S_2, which gives rise to a different response, we are expressing the same facts.

The former description, using the language of stimulus-response generalization, raises undeniable problems. There is, first, the problem of what determines which new response will be performed in the new stimulus situation. Coupled with this is the question of why S_2, being similar to S_1, does not evoke R_A (as the principle of primary stimulus generalization would lead us to expect) rather than a different response, R_B.

Nevertheless, two arguments can be offered for preferring analysis in terms of stimulus-response generalization to analysis in terms of rules.

1. When we say that an organism learns a rule, which expresses itself in the performance of different responses in different stimulus situations, we are obscuring the fact that the rule is acquired as a result of specific learning experiences in specific stimulus situations and that these learning experiences cause other specific responses to be performed in other, equally specific stimulus situations.

Rules can, of course, be acquired in either of two ways. One way is by exposure to a sample of the situations to which the rule is applicable and training in a sample of the responses that exemplify the rule. Some process of induction then causes the rule to be abstracted from its exemplars, so that the response that represents the rule in any new situation can be selected. This is how animals have to learn rules. It is also how a human child has to learn the grammatical rules of his native language or an adult learns the grammatical rules of a foreign language when taught by the "direct method."

The other way is by having the rule as such imparted in a verbal form. An adult is told how to form the past tense of a verb when he studies a foreign language by traditional methods. Schoolchildren are told to find the area of a parallelogram by constructing a rectangle that is equal to it in area.

In both these cases, the subject gains possession of the rule by performing specific responses in specific stimulus situations. In the former case, the stimulus situations that occur during training resemble in some way those in which the rule will be applied later, and the responses performed during training resemble in some way the responses that the rule will cause him to perform in the new situations. The second way means exposure to stimulus patterns, that is, verbal formulas, that are probably quite unlike those that would call for the use of the rule, and the responses, namely those (mostly covert) that constitute understanding of language, will be quite different from those that exemplify the rule. But the essential fact, namely, that the performance of certain responses in certain situations leads to performance of other responses in other situations, holds in both cases and is masked by reference to learning rules.

2. If what the subject learns is a rule or principle or structure, applicable to a vast range of stimulus situations, then he should surely perform the response that represents that rule with equal mastery in all these situations. On the other hand, if what happens is the acquisition of certain stimulus-response associations by direct learning and the emergence of other stimulus-response associations by stimulus-response generalization, then we should expect a generalization decrement, such as is found with stimulus generalization and with response

generalization. The strength of the response that occurs through generalization should be less than that of the original response that occurred during training, since conditions have changed. The difference in strength should increase with the degree of dissimilarity separating the original stimulus situation and response from the new stimulus situation and response.

Now, the experimental work that should be devoted to this question has not been done on the scale that is required, but there are already many indications that generalization decrements exist in the kinds of situation that some writers would analyze in terms of rules. For example, Lashley (1951) points out:

> Patterns of coordinating movement may often be transferred directly to other motor systems than the ones practised. In such transfer, as to the left hand for writing, an analysis of the movements shows that there is not a reduplication of the muscular patterns on the two sides, but a reproduction of movements in relation to the space coordinates of the body. Try upside-down mirror writing with the left hand and with eyes closed for evidence of this. The associative linkage is not of specific movements but of directions of movements.

That one can do this upside-down mirror writing with the left hand is a fact and an important one. But it is an equally noteworthy fact that this writing will be markedly less regular and less rapid than normal writing. If directions of movement relative to space coordinates were what we acquired when we first learned to write, then it would surely not be unreasonable to expect perfect transfer when the hand is changed and the axes defining these spatial coordinates are rotated through 180°.

An experiment that was explicitly designed to demonstrate "the 'genericizing' of learning into a principle applicable to new instances" was carried out by Bruner, Mandler, O'Dowd, and Wallach (1958). Rats were trained to make a single-alternation sequence of turns (for example, left-right-left-right) in a four-unit straight-alley maze. After reaching a criterion of mastery, they were then tested with the maze changed so that the opposite sequence of movements (for example, right-left-right-left) was required. This reversed-alternation sequence certainly possessed the same structure as the original sequence, both in the rigorous mathematical sense and in any everyday sense. There is clearly a perfect isomorphism between the two. Yet, among the various combinations of conditions—degrees of food deprivation and amounts of training—that were tried, only those that entailed moderate (12-hour) deprivation during either or both phases of the experiment produced positive transfer, manifested by a saving in the time taken to master the sequence over the time taken to master the first. Subjects with 36-hour deprivation and subjects with lesser amounts of training showed no transfer. Furthermore, even those groups that showed positive transfer, while they learned the second response sequence more quickly than they had learned the first, showed far from perfect positive transfer. These data would seem to fit the concept of stimulus-response generalization much better than the concept of learning rules.

So, while talk of stimulus-response generalization raises problems, talk of learning rules, etc., may be said to conceal problems. The laws that govern stimulus-response generalization and would enable us to predict which new response will occur in any new situation as a result of this kind of generalization must await empirical study. But even at this stage, we can venture to suggest some familiar mechanisms that could account for the phenomenon of stimulus-response generalization, using as examples the illustrative cases that we have already examined.

Mechanisms that May Contribute to Stimulus-Response Generalization

To recapitulate, then, we have to account for situations in which the establishment of an association between S_1 and R_A leads to performance of R_B in a similar situation, S_2. S_1 and S_2 resemble each other, as do R_A and R_B, but these resemblances are coupled with important differences. We have to consider two related problems. The first is why S_2 did not evoke R_A by stimulus generalization instead of R_B. The second is how the response R_B, which occurs in place of R_1, is selected.

Conditioned Inhibition

If the change from S_1 to S_2 involves simply a shift along a generalization continuum—if, say, a stimulus object, O, belonging to S_1 is replaced by an object, O′, that differs from O in some respects but is otherwise like it—we should, as a rule, expect primary stimulus generalization to give rise to the performance of R_A in S_2.

The obvious exception would be the case where the subject has learned a discrimination between the presence of O and the presence of O′, so that the effects of primary stimulus generalization are undone. We must exclude the case where the subject has learned in the past to perform R_A in the presence of O and R_B in the presence of O', since we are now considering stimulus-response generalization, that is, cases where R_B occurs immediately on encountering S_2 and where its occurrence can be ascribed to the previous establishment of the S_1-R_A association.

There is, however, another variant of discrimination learning that may well be to the point. This is conditioned inhibition. The subject may have found in the past that the performance of R_A in the presence of O' is not reinforced, so that he will have learned to inhibit R_A when O' is present. This will explain why he does not perform R_A in S_2, but we still have to explain how the existence of the S_1-R_A association leads him to select R_B rather than some other response when next he finds himself in S_2.

We have already noted (in Chapter 4) how the presence of an external impediment to the execution of the response most strongly associated with a particular stimulus situation can occasion recourse to another response, which means response generalization. External impediments to responses that might otherwise have taken place through primary stimulus generalization are to be found in many of the illustrative situations discussed above. A subject who has learned to extend a finger on hearing a buzzer is physically unable to extend the same finger when his hand is lying on a hard surface palm upward. Köhler's apes thrust their arms between the bars of the cage, but the banana was too distant to grasp in this way.

If, however, the impeding condition is accompanied by some characteristic form of stimulation, the regular failure of reinforcement in its presence will cause this feature to become a conditioned inhibitor. Consequently, once there has been opportunity for learning, the unavailing response will not be attempted when this feature is in evidence. Köhler's apes gave up trying to reach the banana through the bars after a while, just as a human infant stretches out his hand at first toward objects that are beyond his reach but quickly comes to confine this response to objects that are within his grasp. It is doubtful whether Wickens's adult subjects actually tried to extend the finger when the hand was lying palm upward. The strong pressure sensations coming from the dorsal surface of the finger will surely have precluded any such attempt. Naroditskaia's subjects will presumably have been deterred from pressing the hard sides of the new bulb on recognizing the imperviousness of these sides to deformation under pressure.

The distinction between response generalization and stimulus-response generalization often turns on a distinction between a change from the original stimulus situation S_1 to a new stimulus situation S_2 and a change from S_1 to S_1 coupled with an external impediment. When the external impediment is not accompanied by characteristic stimulation, for example, when it takes the form of an invisible glass barrier, the latter description is patently appropriate. But these instances are, no doubt, rare, so that the distinction between response generalization and stimulus-response generalization will sometimes be rather arbitrary.

Response Chaining

One source of confusion in discussion of the phenomena with which we are concerned is the ambiguity with which the "response to" a stimulus situation is identified. Sometimes, what is described as the response, R_B, to S_2 is actually a sequence of responses. The same applies to behavior that is cited as an application of a rule. The alternating sequence of right and left movements in the experiment by Bruner et al. is a case in point. So is the construction of a grammatical sentence.

There are reasons for believing that combinations or sequences of elemental responses often become "integrated" (Mandler, 1954), so that the response pattern is evoked as a whole by the stimulus situation. But in other cases, each response in the sequence gives rise to stimuli that are needed as cues to the next response. Such would seem to be the case with the experiment by Bruner et al., as with many other examples of experiments in which animals have learned to alternate responses. The existence of some positive transfer shows that the alternating sequence receives some strength from prior learning of the opposite sequence and is not just a product of a separate learning process. The rats may, nevertheless, have learned to change the direction of movement at the first choice point as a response to finding the door, through which they had formerly passed, locked. From then on, the proprioceptive and other cues resulting from passage through a right-hand door will, because of the original training, evoke movement toward the left-hand door at the next choice point, and vice versa. The new sequence can thus be built up in a way that permits one to regard it as a by-product of the original training of the opposite sequence and yet to describe it as a new response pattern presenting a variant of the "alternation rule."

In even more cases, what is called the "response to" S_2 is actually the final item or final outcome of a behavior chain evoked by S_2. S_2

is likely to appear in different external conditions from S_1.   So, even though S_2 may evoke the same initial response as S_1, the cues that result from this initial response may be different when S_2 has been experienced, because the external environment is different.   These cues determine the form taken by subsquent responses in the sequence, and so the end-product may well be other than the one that might have eventuated if S_1 had been present instead of S_2.   It is especially easy to overlook the role of receptor-adjusting and perhaps other exploratory responses in providing cues that vary when the situation varies and that can thus set behavior off on a radically different course when the initial configuration of stimuli is altered.

Thus, Naroditskaia's subjects presumably had their gaze attracted to the new bulb because of its similarity in appearance and position with the familiar bulb.   Primary stimulus generalization must likewise have produced the response of stretching out the arm toward it and taking hold of it.   At that point, the tactual and visual cues emanating from the bulb will have differed from those that the original bulb provided.   These cues will have evoked the response of pressing the bottom, since prior learning will have enabled the subject to recognize this as the part that would yield to pressure.

Köhler's ape, Tschego, may have been prompted to look at and then pick up the blanket in much the same way, although it is likely that anticipation of the end result played a part here.   But once she felt the blanket in her hands, her learning history will have made her more likely to shake the blanket than to attempt to poke it between the bars as if it were a stick.

We can perhaps see these points even more clearly if we consider the child's ability to write down the number coming after any number that may be shown to him, even if it be one that he has never met before.   This must in practice depend on quite a complex succession of events, utilizing a number of distinct habits.   He must begin by looking at the number whose successor he is to find, which probably means that his eyes will come to rest focused somewhere toward the middle of it.   He must then move his eyes digit by digit to the right.   Whenever he finds his eyes focused on a digit, he shifts his gaze a further step to the right.   If he finds himself looking at blank paper, he shifts his gaze to the left, so that he will now be fixating the last digit.   If this digit is a 0, he replaces it by 1.   If it is a 1, he replaces it by 2, etc.   If it is a 9 he replaces it by a 0, shifts his gaze to the next digit on its left, and resumes the procedure.   Having made all the changes that he is prompted to make, he leaves the remaining digits of the original number unchanged and then writes down or names the new number that he has formulated in this way.

An investigation by Eritsian (1962) suggests that syllogistic reasoning may work in a similar manner. He showed, first, that subjects could arrive at correct conclusions invariably if they made use of some nine "generalized associations" (in Shevarev's sense, discussed earlier). One example is putting "not" in the conclusion when "not" appears in either of the premises. Another is prefacing the conclusion with "some" when either premise starts with "some." Protocols obtained by questioning subjects faced with pairs of premises verified that these "generalized associations" are in fact used. The implication is that syllogistic reasoning depends on learning, first, to look for words like "not" and "no" signifying negation, for quantifiers like "some" and "all," for the middle term which is common to the two premises, etc., and then, having found such features, to incorporate the appropriate elements in the conclusion.

This is, of course, very much how computers operate. They have rules either built into them and inherent in their wiring or fed into them as elements of a "source program" or "interpreter." Different inputs will cause the computer to yield different outputs, even though, in all cases, it is applying the same rules. What actually happens is that it is using procedures for finding numbers (stored in the form of strings of 1's and 0's), comparing numbers, and changing numbers, in accordance with the outcomes of previous operations. So every time that it carries out a particular operation or applies a particular rule, it comes up with a different output, because the output depends on what it encounters while going through its computation procedures and what it encounters varies with the input data.

Programmers find it convenient to represent the activities of computers by block diagrams, and writers (for example, Miller, Galanter, and Pribram, 1960) who are partial to analogies between computer operations and human behavior have indicated the possibility of representing many human activities with similar block diagrams (for example, Figure 7-1). Those who use these diagrams are right to insist that the sequence of responses that occurs is not

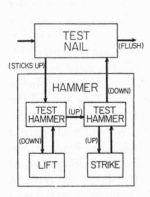

Figure 7-1   Reproduced with permission from Miller, Galanter, and Pribram (1960).

one that has simply been associated with the initial situation by the kind of learning that associates specific response classes with specific classes of stimulus situations. It may, on the other hand, arise as a result of learned associations that involve not only the initial situation but the stimulus situations that are encountered subsequently. Thus, each block in the diagram may be held to represent a response with its corresponding response-produced stimulation (or the stimulus situation resulting from the response, regarded as a transformation) and each arrow a stimulus-response association.

To sum up, the cases that we have been considering are ones in which learning has caused S_1 to be followed closely by R_A, and so we are entitled to speak of an association between S_1 and R_A. The establishment of this association is shown to increase the probability that R_B will occur shortly after S_2 has been experienced. We can therefore legitimately speak of an association between S_2 and R_B. But, on closer analysis, we find that these two processes are more accurately represented by $S_1 \to R_X\text{-}S_3 \to R_A$ and $S_2 \to R_X\text{-}S_4 \to R_B$, where R_X is a response that possesses a learned association with S_1 and is evoked, through stimulus generalization, by S_2 also. S_3 is a stimulus pattern that depends jointly on the nature of R_X and the nature of the external stimulus situation. It is replaced by S_4 after S_2 has been encountered, since the external environment will be different. R_X can be appropriately regarded as a transformational response, in which case, S_3 and S_4 are transforms that result when the transformation is applied to different operands. $S_3 \to R_A$ and $S_4 \to R_B$ are then already existing associations, deposited by prior learning. Long sequences of responses and stimuli rather than a single response and stimulus may, of course, intervene between S_1 and R_A or between S_2 and R_B, making for infinitely wider flexibility.

Symbolic Mediating Processes

The crucial steering role of intermediary stimuli and responses is sometimes overlooked through failure to take account of features of behavior that are fully observable. This failure has probably been encouraged by the fact that alternative ways of achieving a particular end result, for example, reaching the end of a maze alley or depressing a lever (to mention some of the simplest instances), appear to be equivalent as far as the functional analysis of behavior is concerned. The subject resorts to them interchangeably, and the theoretician appears to lose nothing if he ignores the differences between them. This has fostered the view that responses need be defined only in terms of their end results. But in other situations, the end result is the culmination of a succession of responses and stimulus situations, each of which leaves its imprint on what happens subsequently.

In some cases, including those that concern directed thinking, the end product (for example, a statement of the solution to a problem) may be the first observable event that occurs after the subject has been exposed to the initial stimulus situation (for example, a statement of the problem). The intermediary processes are not directly observable at all, unless by some such means as asking the subject to think out loud. They consist of symbolic processes, which normally occur in a covert form. These symbolic intermediary processes can bring about stimulus-response generalization, and thus act as vehicles for productive thinking, by the same sort of mechanism as we have just been discussing in connection with overt intermediary processes. There are, however, two special cases to which we must draw attention.

1. One essential intermediary response (corresponding to R_X above) must, in reasoning, be a representation of the end product or goal situation. This is, in fact, what Hull meant by the "fractional anticipatory goal response (r_G)," whose feedback stimulus, s_G (Hull's "goal stimulus"), serves as a representation of the goal situation.

So what happens when the subject finds himself in stimulus-situation S_2 is that S_2 evokes a symbolic response representing the goal situation. This will occur through stimulus generalization from S_1. We then have the conditions for utilization of a transformation-selecting habit, namely the presence of an initial stimulus situation (or a representation of an initial stimulus situation) and a representation of a consequent stimulus situation. The response that is then selected, R_B, may be one that previous learning has associated with the combination of S_2 and s_G, or it may be the result of stimulus generalization from some other experiences not involving S_1. In either event, S_2 would not have given rise to R_B had it not been for the learning experience involving S_1, because, without it, S_2 would not have been accompanied by s_G. But the strength of R_B, when evoked jointly by S_2 and s_G, may well exceed the strength of R_A, instigated by S_2 through stimulus generalization.

Thus, as far as Tschego was concerned, the major gain from the previous experience with the stick was that it caused her, when she saw the blanket, to represent to herself a situation in which the blanket extended over the gap between her hands and the banana and in which movements of her hands in contact with the near end of the blanket caused the banana to move nearer to her. The sight and feel of the blanket combined with this representation of a desired and anticipated situation brought out the flapping response much more strongly than the poking response.

In Wickens's experiment, we may presume that expectations and representations of consequences did not play much part, because the finger movement must have occurred quickly and automatically. But one can well imagine this kind of mechanism working in somewhat different circumstances. A subject may have learned to frighten away a mosquito that approaches his hand lying palm downward, by extending the middle finger suddenly. If a mosquito approaches the same finger on a future occasion when his hand is lying palm upward, a flexion of the same finger is likely to ensue. This is because the main thing that is carried over from the learning experience to the new situation is a representation of the finger sticking up and the mosquito flying away. The combination of the hand position and this anticipatory representation evokes the appropriate movement.

2. The second case that we must consider is the application of rules in contexts such as grammar, logical thinking, or mathematical thinking (whether carried out by mathematicians or by computers). Those rules all involve "operations," such as adding elements, subtracting elements, transposing elements, and substituting elements for one another. These are obviously spatial terms and, in the light of our previous discussion, it may reasonably be supposed that the intellectual processes corresponding to them are internalized variants of the overt movements that shift objects about in space. This being so, we have clear examples of implicit transformational responses. We can understand how existing habits and stimulus generalization can cause appropriate spatial transformations to be selected and how, once they have been selected, transformation-applying habits can bring about representations of appropriate end products. Consequently, grammatically correct sentences (or sentences exhibiting the kinds of error that depend on failure to recognize exceptions to grammatical rules) are constructed, and valid logico-mathematical formulas are written down.

Mechanical versus Intelligent Learning

In his book *Productive Thinking* (1945), Wertheimer dwelt on the contrast between two methods that can be used to teach schoolchildren how to find the area of a parallelogram. If a child is taught to deal with a parallelogram such as that in Figure 7-2 by dropping

Figure 7-2   Figure 7-3

perpendiculars, he will be at a loss when faced with a parallelogram like that in Figure 7-3. If, on the other hand, he has been told to construct a rectangle with the same area as the parallelogram and then to find the area of this rectangle by multiplying the lengths of its sides, he will "grasp the principle" and be able to cope with a parallelogram in any orientation.

According to Wertheimer, these two teaching methods were illustrative of two types of learning. One is what he called "structurally sensible" learning of "type alpha," which "focuses on developing structural insight, structural mastery and meaningful learning in the real sense of the word." The other, belonging to "type gamma," is "structurally blind"; it "corresponds to learning by drill, by external associations, by external conditioning, by memorizing, by blind trial and error." These two types of learning foster two types of thinking, consisting of "A-responses" and "B-responses," of which the former are characterized by a fuller understanding of a problem and, once a problem has been solved, by greater possibilities of fruitful generalization to other problems.

It is evident that one salient difference between the two kinds of learning, which we may call *mechanical* and *intelligent* (Latin *intelligens* = understanding) learning respectively, is that the latter opens up far more extensive possibilities of stimulus-response generalization. The profound contrasts between mechanical and intelligent learning have been made yet more evident by a series of experiments carried out at Piaget's behest in 1957–1958 (Gréco and Piaget, 1959; Apostel et al., 1959; Morf et al., 1959; and Goustard et al., 1959). The general aim of these experiments was to find out whether special training procedures could make the kinds of thinking characteristic of the stage of concrete operations appear earlier than they would otherwise. The principal technique consisted in asking a child a question about objects or phenomena in front of him and then allowing him to witness a demonstration that revealed the correctness or incorrectness of his answer.

This technique was applied to some of the situations that were described in previous chapters when the differences between the stage of intuitive thinking and the stage of concrete operations were discussed. In general, it was found that the training produced some tendency, but a relatively slight one, for subjects to change from the erroneous answers characteristic of the intuitive stage to the correct answers that normally come with the stage of concrete operations. Presumably, the children could have been persuaded even more effectively to give the right answers if somebody had stood over them with a whip and coached them in what they were to say. But there are striking differences between children who are led to give the correct answers precociously by such training procedures and children who have reached the age when the correct answers are given spontaneously. After training, the younger children may give the answers that older children give without training, but they, unlike the older children, have not acquired an "understanding" of what is involved. This is shown in three ways:

1. The trained younger children give the correct answers in the situations that figured in their training but are unable to recognize new situations to which their answers should be generalized.

For example, Gréco (1959) studied the situation in which a rod bearing a black, a white, and a red bead is inserted into a cardboard tube and the tube is turned one or more times through 180°. The subject has to predict the order in which the beads will emerge, and he is given opportunities to see that the original order is reversed after one turn but restored after two turns. Children who have not reached the stage of concrete operations are generally unable to predict the consequences of three, four, or five turns. They may think that the white bead must sometimes have a turn at coming out first. The older child, who understands what is happening and why, realizes that any odd number of turns produces the one order and any even number the other order.

In a later experiment, Gréco (1960) tested the ability to learn that odd and even numbers alternate. The principle was given a concrete form by building two parallel columns of counters and adding one to each column in turn, so that the columns were equal in length when the total number was even but one column projected above the other when the number was odd. A typical result, obtained with a six-year-old boy (who claimed that he could count up to 114!), was acceptance of the principle for numbers up to 17 but not for larger numbers.

2. The trained younger child, having been persuaded by empirical observations to accept a certain belief, can just as easily be led to give

up the belief if he encounters an experience that seems incompatible with it.

Smedslund (1959) attempted to teach children in the stage of intuitive thinking that, when one of two identical balls of plasticine is elongated, its weight does not change. His method was to demonstrate the equality of weight between the changed and unchanged masses of plasticine on a balance, and he obtained a limited measure of success with a limited proportion of his subjects. In one experiment (Smedslund, 1961a), he surreptitiously broke a piece off the elongated mass before the weighing. All the children who had been persuaded to accept conservation of weight as a result of the training procedure showed little surprise and reverted to their belief in nonconservation. On the other hand, six out of thirteen children who had come spontaneously to believe in conservation of weight resisted the temptation to give up this belief, maintaining that some plasticine must have fallen off without being seen.

The same marked refusal to consider giving up logical or mathematical beliefs is illustrated by everyday behavior in adults. To adapt an example given by Britton (1953), suppose that we count 25 cows in one meadow and 26 cows in another meadow and then, after the latter have been driven into the first meadow, count 50 cows. We might conclude that we must have miscounted earlier or that a cow must have disappeared without our noticing it. But no number of experiences of this sort will cause a normal person to wonder whether he has been right all these years to believe that $26 + 25 = 51$!

3. Finally, there is a contrast between the ways in which the younger trained children and the older children justify their beliefs when they are asked why what they have said is true (Smedslund, 1959). Younger children give explanations in terms of empirical findings. They treat a logical or mathematical principle as something that is to be accepted because phenomena that they have witnessed show that it happens to be true. The older child, like the adult, will, in contrast, give deductive explanations without appeal to the evidence of external events. He will show how the principle follows from general considerations and why it must necessarily be true.

These sharp differences between mechanical and intelligent learning raise many interesting and fundamental questions. They show the inadequacy of treatments of thinking that ignore them. There is the obvious question of why the child changes with relative abruptness from one kind of thinking to the other, when dealing with logical and mathematical matters, at about the age of seven. The difficulty of accelerating the change by training procedures and the spectacular modifications that evidently appear, often within a period of six months or a year without special training, argue for a major role of maturational processes. But to say this does not tell us much, and there is always the possibility that other training methods than those used in the experiments just mentioned may be much more effective in hastening the changeover. First, however, must come the task of characterizing more rigorously the differences that divide the less mature from the more mature ways of dealing with these situations. It must be partly a motivational question, and this aspect will be taken up in later chapters.

We can readily recognize that mechanical learning gives rise to the kind of thinking that uses sequences of verbal, and perhaps other, symbolic responses each of which is linked to the last by direct association. Intelligent learning, or learning with "understanding," seems, on the other hand, to engender the kind of thinking that makes use of transformational chains. And one of the hallmarks of transformational thinking is evidently its ability to promote far-reaching and effective stimulus-response generalization.

Tree Structures

As an improvement on analyzing behavior in terms of sequences of stimuli and associated responses, more and more writers are turning to analyses that emphasize the so-called "hierarchical" organization of behavior. Since the "hierarchical" aspects of behavior that are in question here are quite distinct from the aspects that Hull meant to indicate when he coined the term "habit-family hierarchy," we had better avoid confusion from the outset and employ the term "tree structure" to refer to what these writers have in mind.

A *tree* in this specialized sense is a special kind of *graph* in the sense in which this word is used in the branch of topology known as "graph theory," that is, to signify a set of points ("nodes" or "vertices"), any pair of which may or may not be joined by a line (a "branch" or an "edge").[*] A tree, of which an example is depicted in Figure 7-4, is a graph whose nodes are distributed among a number of levels. The number of nodes at each level is less than, or equal to, the number of nodes at each lower level. Every node belonging to each level except the highest is joined by a branch to one and only one node

[*] For simple introductions to graph theory, see Harary and Norman (1953) and Ore (1963).

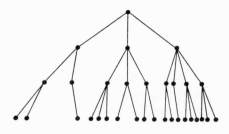

Figure 7-4

of the level next above, and each node at each level except the lowest is joined to one or more nodes of the level next below.*

Miller, Galanter, and Pribram (1960), who have been the most explicit advocates of the tree structure as the most promising key to understanding the organization of human behavior, maintain that most human activities are governed by "plans" composed of decisions proceeding from higher to lower levels. The higher levels select among broader categories of activity and bear on more extensive segments of behavior. Each successive lower level breaks the segments down into smaller units and narrows down further the kind of activity that shall occur.

The wide validity of this view is unmistakable. For example, a housewife, in planning how she will spend her day, may decide that the morning is to be spent on "housework," followed by "doing lunch," with the afternoon spent on "shopping." Doing housework may comprise "doing the bedrooms," then "doing the laundry," and finally "doing the living room." Doing the bedrooms means "making the beds," "clearing up," "dusting," etc. And this process of making progressively more specific decisions can obviously be continued until the precise degree of contraction of any muscle at any moment during the day has been determined.

Sometimes, activities are clearly planned, in the sense of "thought out," in this manner, although planning ahead will stop far short of anticipating particular muscular contractions. The presumption is, however, that even when a person goes through a daily routine automatically, some equivalent kind of planning is carried out by his

* A technical definition of a *tree* is "a connected subgraph of a connected graph which contains all the vertices of the graph but is free of circuits." (From the *International Dictionary of Applied Mathematics*. Princeton, N.J.: Van Nostrand, 1960.)

nervous system, which maps out the broad outlines of a sequence of actions in advance and then fills in the details in time for the motor system to carry out its task smoothly.

Now, tree structures have cropped up in an astonishing variety of specialized areas of study in behavioral science. Figures 7-5 and 7-6 are diagrams used by Tinbergen (1951) to depict the organization of instinctive behavior in the three-spined stickleback. First, the animal comes under the sway of one of several instincts that correspond to biological requirements. This instinct, the reproductive instinct, brings to the fore a number of activities, such as fighting, mating, etc. Each of these activities, in its turn, is composed of a variety of response patterns, and so on, until the contributions of individual muscle fibers are prescribed.

Tinbergen's view receives support from the ethologically inspired neurophysiological investigations of von Holst and von Saint Paul (1960, 1962) on the domestic hen. These investigators found, for example, one area in the hen's brain stem whose strong stimulation provoked escape behavior and whose weaker stimulation provoked threatening and attacking behavior. It seems, therefore, that this area coordinates activities constituting behavior in the face of an enemy. Stimulation of another area produced only escape behavior, consisting of cackling, running round, and flying away in succession.

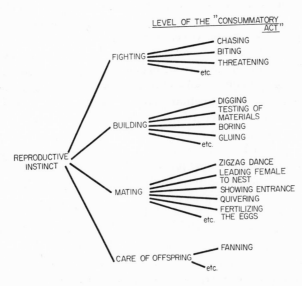

Figure 7-5   Reproduced with permission from Tinbergen (1951).

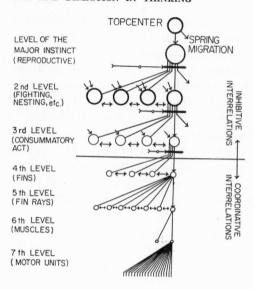

Figure 7-6　Reproduced with permission from Tinbergen (1951).

Finally, there were two areas whose stimulation gave rise to cackling alone.

In the mammalian nervous system also, points controlling specific muscular contractions and points controlling more comprehensive combinations of responses have been located (Chang, Ruch, and Ward, 1947; Morgan and Stellar, 1950; and Ruch, 1951). So there is some support for the view that motor behavior depends on the selection, first, of a broad class of behavior and, then, of more specific classes or components, until particular motor units are mobilized. This would mean the activation in turn of neural centers arranged in a hierarchy of levels of coordination, as Weiss (1941) held. If such gradual narrowing down is characteristic of motor functioning, it is likely to be even more typical of thinking. So yet another link is established between thought processes and overt behavior, adding to the plausibility that motor responses and implicit symbolic "responses" are governed by common principles.

To move on to a very different field of study, Chomsky (1957) has argued that the way in which grammatical speech is constructed conforms to a diagram such as Figure 7-7. The speaker begins with the intention of formulating a sentence. He then uses rules such as those listed in Figure 7-8 to carry out a series of substitutions (the notation

"$X \to Y$" is equivalent to "rewrite X as Y"), which gradually delineate the major portions of the sentence together with their mutual relations, subsequently filling in their contents.

Mehler (cited by G. A. Miller, 1962) has presented subjects with sentences of various grammatical forms and asked them to state the "kernel sentence" (that is, the affirmative, active, indicative sentence) that underlies each of them. The task takes longer to perform with sentences that, according to the theory, are removed from the kernel sentence by a greater number of transformations. This provides some corroboration for the view that processes corresponding to transformations (which can be identified as transformational responses from our point of view) occur in succession when a sentence is heard or read.

The tree structures that are most evidently germane to thinking, and the ones by which Miller, Galanter, and Pribram (1960) confess themselves to have been most deeply impressed, are those that have come out of work with computers. When a human programmer wants a computer to carry out a task for him, he usually finds it helpful to begin with a block diagram, in which he takes care to include the main steps that must be completed, indicating their temporal order. He also identifies the points at which decisions between alternative ways of continuing the process must be made, depending on the out-

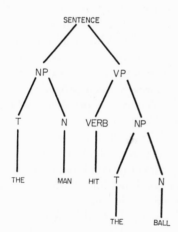

(i) SENTENCE ⟶ NP+VP

(ii) NP ⟶ T+N

(iii) VP ⟶ VERB+NP

(iv) T ⟶ THE

(v) N ⟶ MAN, BALL, etc.

(vi) VERB ⟶ HIT, TOOK, etc.

Figure 7-7 Reproduced with permission from Chomsky (1957).

Figure 7-8 Reproduced with permission from Chomsky (1957).

p implies ((p implies q) implies q)

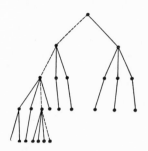

Figure 7-9   Reproduced with permission from Newell, Shaw, and Simon (1957).

come of the previous step. Each of the major steps then gives rise to perhaps several dozen source-program instructions. When these are fed into the computer, each of them will generally give rise to some hundreds or thousands of individual operations. So there are commonly at least three distinguishable levels in the programming of the computer, and many more can often be discerned.

When a computer is used to simulate creative human thinking, for example, by means of the Information-Processing Language (IPL) of Newell, Shaw, and Simon (1957), the computer itself has to carry out a search for an acceptable solution to the problem with which it is presented, and that means that it must organize its own activities according to a tree structure. Such programs, which go through all the branches belonging to one level of a tree in turn but take up every subbranch attached to a particular branch before passing on to the next branch, are known as "recursive" programs (Green, 1963).

Figure 7-9 represents the manner in which the Logic Theory Machine, a computer programmed to prove theorems in logic, achieved one of its successes. The machine starts off with a theorem that needs to be proved, the five axioms laid down by Whitehead and Russell in *Principia Mathematica* (1910–1912), and three rules of inference. It has at its disposal three methods of generating new expressions from axioms or from theorems that have already been proved.

The computer works by first selecting a problem, whether it be the original problem or a subproblem that promises to contribute to the solution of the original problem. It then selects one of its three methods, and finally it tries out this method on a theorem (that is, an axiom or an already proved lemma) or combination of theorems. It runs through all the theorems or combinations of theorems that are available to it in turn. If it succeeds with none of these, it turns to another method. If none of the methods leads anywhere, it runs through the routine again with a new subproblem. And so it continues until it has generated the expression to be proved from the axioms by a series of steps that are in accord with the rules of inference or until it has exhausted its stock of subproblems, methods, and theorems.

Compound Habit-Family Hierarchies

Champions of tree structures claim, then, that the use of tree diagrams to represent behavior episodes is markedly superior to the use of diagrams presenting chains of stimuli and responses. Which of these representations is actually superior depends, of course, on the purposes to which they are applied. The unmatched appropriateness of chain diagrams can hardly be gainsaid if one is concerned simply to depict events in their order of occurrence, since stimuli and responses must occur in time, and time is unidirectional and unidimensional. Nevertheless, some properties of behavior, connected particularly with the principles by which responses are selected, can be clarified with the help of tree diagrams. A question that thus arises is whether the neoassociationist kind of analysis that this book has espoused is able to take due account to these aspects of behavior.

The first step toward answering this question is to consider the concept of the *compound habit-family hierarchy* that has been introduced by Maltzman (1955) with special reference to thinking. A compound habit-family hierarchy is a habit-family hierarchy whose components, instead of being behavior chains, are themselves habit-family hierarchies (Figure 7-10). It is thus, as Maltzman puts it, "a hierarchy of habit-family hierarchies or a class of classes of stimulus-response relationships." As far as thinking is concerned, a constituent hierarchy of a compound habit-family hierarchy represents a general "approach" or method of attack on a problem, and the extreme fruitfulness of Maltzman's notion will be explored more fully in later chapters.

The notion is, however, by no means confined to thinking. And the compound habit-family hierarchy need not be restricted to two levels. The hierarchies that are joined together in a compound habit-family hierarchy may themselves be built up of subhierarchies, and so on, until a specific behavior chain is reached.

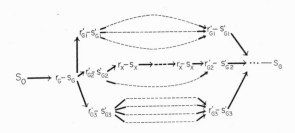

Figure 7-10

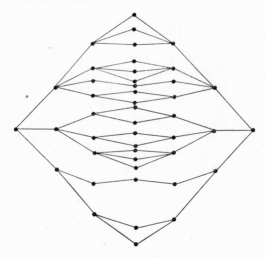

Figure 7-11

If we then take a tree diagram, arrange it so that its root is on the left (instead of at the top or bottom as in most representations), and fill in its mirror image on the right, we can see immediately that the structure corresponding to a compound habit-family hierarchy is formed (Figure 7-11).

When stimulus-response associations are organized in this fashion, the selection of a course of action (overt or implicit) depends on the selection of a compound hierarchy of the highest level, then of a sub-hierarchy belonging to this compound hierarchy, then of a sub-sub-hierarchy belonging to this subhierarchy, and so on, until a particular behavior chain is embarked on.

Each hierarchy of whatever level thus corresponds to a condition of the organism, that is, a class of states in which that particular hierarchy is dominant. When we say that a certain hierarchy is dominant, we mean that the probability that the organism will execute some chain belonging to that hierarchy is higher than it would have been otherwise. The over-all probability that some component or other of the hierarchy will become dominant is distributed among the components in accordance with their positions in the hierarchy. As hierarchies of lower and lower levels are successively selected, narrower and narrower ranges of behavior have their probabilities raised, and finally one response, initiating a specific behavior chain, becomes prepotent.

Corresponding to every hierarchy of whatever level, there must be a mediator, a response whose response-produced stimulus puts the subject into the state in which that hierarchy becomes dominant. We may call it a *switching mediator* (composed of a *switching response* and a response-produced *switching stimulus*). In the case of a simple habit-family hierarchy, the switching response is the fractional anticipatory goal response, r_G, a representation of the goal situation to which all chains in the hierarchy lead. Being conceived as a fractional form of the characteristic response pattern evoked by the goal situation, it represents a common final response of every chain.

In the case of a subhierarchy belonging to a compound hierarchy, the switching response must represent the stimulus situation with which all components of the subhierarchy terminate (r'_{G1}, r'_{G2}, or r'_{G3} in Figure 7-10). This may be regarded as a subgoal whose attainment contributes to the attainment of the final goal situation which is common to the whole compound hierarchy. The process of selecting hierarchies of lower and lower levels depends on the occurrence of a succession of switching mediators, making more and more restricted classes of behavior dominant. The final culmination is the advent of a state in which the subject is committed to a specific behavior chain.

Such a state is launched by the occurrence of a response that is peculiar to that chain. Sometimes, this response will take the form of an anticipatory representation of the last stimulus situation traversed by the chain that is not shared by other chains in the same subhierarchy (r_X in Figure 7-10). At other times (for example, when transformational chains are used in directed thinking and the later situational responses to which the chain will conduct the subject cannot be specified until the chain has run its course) the response whose execution commits the subject to the chain will be its initial response.

A switching response will presumably correspond to the activation of a neural center whose excitation brings a certain kind of behavior to the fore. The switching stimulus will correspond to the influence of this center on other structures with which it is connected. If it is a center of the lowest level, this will mean innervating particular muscles or glands. Otherwise, it will mean the activation of centers of the next highest level, controlling more restricted classes of behavior.

Two Kinds of Compound Habit-Family Hierarchy

Among the varied forms of behavior for which tree structures have been invoked, there is actually an important dichotomy whose bearing on the ways in which the corresponding compound habit-family hierarchies work must not be overlooked. The differences between the two kinds of compound hierarchy that emerge must hinge on differences in the functioning of switching mediators.

Searching Hierarchies

In some instances, the subject selects hierarchies of lower and lower levels (or nodes of lower and lower levels, if we use the terminology of tree graphs) until a single behavior chain with properties appropriate to his present motivational condition is found. If, after proceeding through one pathway of the tree graph to the lowest level (or, in other words, proceeding through a series of more and more specific switching responses until a specific behavior chain has come to the fore), the appropriate conditions are not met and the motivational condition is not relieved, the subject will, at some level, give up the node or hierarchy that he has been trying out in favor of another one belonging to the same level. But as soon as an appropriate behavior chain has been found, there is no point in taking up any of the branches of the tree that have not yet been tried out; all the rest of the compound habit-family hierarchy can be dropped.

This is what happens when directed thinking occurs, whether on the part of human beings or on the part of computers programmed by Newell, Shaw, and Simon. The process of trying out and giving up alternative operations continues until a behavior chain recognizable as a solution—one that constitutes an acceptable proof of the theorem or one that brings about the desired practical end—is formulated, or until all the resources of the thinker have been exhausted without success.

Hierarchies of this sort may be called *searching hierarchies*. When a particular behavior chain or a particular subhierarchy of a certain level has emerged and been found wanting, its switching response is evidently inhibited. This causes the next component of the hierarchy to which the chain or the subhierarchy belongs to become prepotent, and the process continues in this manner. Switching responses of successively higher levels are inhibited, so that the alternative possibilities can be systematically sampled.

As Newell, Shaw, and Simon (1957) point out, it is important for a human or an electronic thinker to sample the possibilities in order of decreasing probability of being fruitful. A "heuristic," that is, a procedure attuned in this manner to probabilities, is inherent in the program that the computer receives but is likely to be a product of learning in man.

When, on the other hand, a behavior chain that fulfills the pre-requisites of a solution is reached, then the highest-level switching response ceases and the whole compound habit-family hierarchy is switched off, no doubt because the highest-level switching mediator is closely identified with the motivational condition that impelled the whole thinking process.

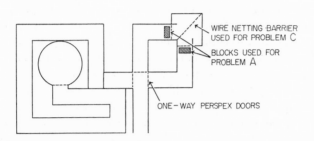

Figure 7-12   Reprinted from *Structural Basis of Behavior* by J. A. Deutsch by permission of The University of Chicago Press. Copyright 1960 by The University of Chicago.

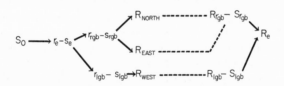

Figure 7-13

As an illustration of how searching hierarchies work, let us consider an experiment by Deutsch and Clarkson (1959). They studied rats in a maze whose shape is shown in Figure 7-12. An animal can take a long path to the left-hand goal box or either of two short paths to the right-hand goal box. The behavior chains corresponding to following the two short paths share, as their final link, the response of entering the right-hand goal box, R_{rgb} (see Figure 7-13). An antici-patory representation of R_{rgb}, r_{rgb}, will therefore serve as the switching mediator for this subhierarchy. This subhierarchy, together with the behavior chain corresponding to following the longer path, will then form a higher-order hierarchy, converging on the common terminus of eating, R_e, so that r_e, an anticipatory representation of eating (which is likely to occur during hunger), will act as a switching mediator for the higher-order hierarchy.

Deutsch and Clarkson set their subjects three problems. In Problem A (see Figure 7-12), the animals found a barrier blocking the entrance to the right-hand goal box after going down one of the shorter paths. On the next trial, most of them went down the other shorter path. In Problem B, the animals found the right-hand goal box empty on entering it, with the result that most of them went to the left-hand goal box on the next trial. In Problem C, the animals found a wire-mesh barrier separating them from food, which they could see, in the right-hand goal box. On the next trial, most of them went to the left-hand goal box. We can interpret these findings as follows. In Problem A, one behavior chain belonging to the subhierarchy failed to terminate with its usual final response, R_{rgb}. This means that while r_{rgb}, the switching response for the subhierarchy, was not inhibited, the behavior chain that had just been tried was weakened, making the other chain belonging to the subhierarchy dominant. In Problems B and C, on the other hand, R_{rgb} was able to complete itself, but R_e was prevented from occurring. Our assumption is that, when a subgoal response like R_{rgb} occurs without being followed by reinforcement (that is, the attainment of the ultimate goal), its corresponding switching mediator is inhibited. Consequently, the subhierarchy as a whole is weakened, so that the remaining member of the over-all hierarchy, namely the response sequence of going down the longer path to the left-hand goal box (beginning with $r_{lgb}-s_{lgb}$), is brought to the fore.

The hierarchies involved in this illustration consist of overt behavior chains, but we may suppose that the implicit symbolic chains that participate in thinking are organized and work in an analogous manner.

Coordinating Hierarchies

In other instances, the subject must go through the whole tree or compound hierarchy, no matter what the outcome or nature of the behavior chains through which he goes. The housewife must complete the entire series of responses that make up the day's housekeeping. The speaker must utter all the words that make up the sentence. So, when these coordinating hierarchies are used, the completion of a particular behavior chain or of a particular subhierarchy of a certain level must simply inhibit its own switching response, causing a shift to another element belonging to the same level. The underlying motivational state is not relieved, and so the highest-level switching response is not inhibited, until all elements at all levels have been traversed.

The tree structures discerned by Tinbergen in the instinctive behavior of lower animals seem to be partly of the coordinating and partly of the searching kind. An animal that is under the dominance of the reproductive "instinct" or drive must normally go through all the activities—fighting, courtship and mating, care of young—that are subsumed under that instinct. And the same goes for the classes of behavior belonging to the lower levels of Figure 7-5. The order in which the elements of one level are taken up need not always be fixed. When, exactly, fighting or courtship will occur will depend on the perception of a potential rival or a potential mate. On the other hand, instinctive behavior seems in part to be a matter of searching through alternative possibilities until a means of relief is found. This is shown by the phenomenon of displacement, whose role is depicted in Figure 7-6. If the dominant element of one level is blocked by frustration (absence of the appropriate releasing stimulus) or by conflict, an animal may show behavior corresponding to another element at the same level. If the direct expression of an instinct is prevented, behavior characteristic of a quite different instinct may appear.

Conclusions

It appears, therefore, that, far from being diametrically at variance with contemporary neoassociationist analysis of behavior, tree-structure analyses are fully in tune with them. Some of their characteristic properties may, in fact, be expected of structures of stimulus-response associations when certain conditions, which we have no reason to regard as exceptional or implausible, are fulfilled.

There is good reason to believe that composite blocks of behavior, represented by nodes belonging to levels other than the lowest level of a tree or by subhierarchies of a compound habit-family hierarchy, act in important respects like unitary responses. It is, in fact, hard to tell what unitary responses are, since the responses that psychologists discuss are invariably grosser than single muscle-fiber contractions and therefore analyzable into smaller components. As Osgood (1963) has pointed out, several composite blocks of behavior can apparently have different strengths of association with a particular stimulus condition and thus be elicited by that condition with different probabilities. And as N. E. Miller (1963) has pointed out, the completion of a composite block of behavior apparently means the attainment of a corresponding subgoal and is thus subject to reinforcement.

But what, it may be asked, is the point of referring to tree structures in S-R terminology? If we show that the arguments that advocates of tree structures have been urging can be translated into the kind of language to which certain other psychologists are partial, what have we done except to repeat the points that they have made and admit their justice?

In answer to this, it can be urged that, when we attempt a reconciliation between tree-structure concepts and S-R concepts, we are attempting something that is necessary for a number of reasons. We are certainly not aiming to disparage the insights of those who have been struck by the prevalence of tree structures in behavior. But we are attempting to go beyond pointing out that concepts that have been found useful for the analysis of the simplest forms of behavior must prove inadequate to the most complex forms of behavior without considerable modification and extension, as if anybody ever believed otherwise. We are attempting an analysis that will make manifest both the similarities and the differences between the structures that underlie the most complex and the simplest forms of behavior. A great deal of empirical spadework will have to be done before we can deduce the detailed working of compound habit-family hierarchies from their peculiar attributes and the basic principles of behavior. To recognize at the outset that compound habit-family hierarchies are involved may, however, help us to see some of the dependent variables that are worth examining and some of the factors whose influence on them is likely to repay investigation.

Chapter 8

Group structures and equilibrium

THE HABIT-FAMILY HIERARCHIES originally envisaged by Hull were quite simple in structure. They consisted of parallel strands, joined together at their beginnings (since they all started out from a common initial stimulus situation) and at their ends (since they all had led to a common goal situation). Hull was thinking particularly of the rat's behavior in a maze offering a number of alternative paths from goal box to end box (1934) and of the behavior of a human child locomoting over a plane surface, with many alternative ways of traveling between any two points (1938). In these cases, alternative itineraries, comprising different chains belonging to one hierarchy, might well have segments in common, but their general form was that represented in Figure 8-1.

The symbolic habit-family hierarchies that participate in thinking can, however, be much more varied and much more complex in structure. Otherwise thinking would be less useful and versatile than it is. Even some of the hierarchies that underlie the most advanced systems of motor behavior must possess structures that are not adequately represented in a diagram such as Figure 8-1.

We saw in the last chapter how Maltzman's (1955) notion of a compound habit-family hierarchy constitutes an important advance. It allows for some of the needed additional complications, and we noted, in particular, its fruitfulness for the treatment of directed thinking. But the recognition of compound hierarchies corresponding to tree structures with any number of levels is hardly enough. Symbolic structures can reach such high levels of complexity and take on so many specialized forms, whose peculiarities must be taken into account, that

Figure 8-1

we must have recourse to mathematical languages to represent them. And as long as we are dealing with habit-family hierarchies whose chains consist of alternating situational and transformational thoughts, there are two mathematical languages that promise to be particularly useful.

Graphs

One of these languages is provided by graph theory, which was discussed in the last chapter in connection with tree structures. Graph theory has already been tried out in several psychological contexts, for example, by Harary and Norman (1953), Cartwright and Harary (1956), and Apostel (1957).

A graph, it will be recalled, consists of a set of points ("nodes" or "vertices") and connecting lines ("branches" or "edges"). For our purposes, a node can stand for a situational thought and a branch for a transformational thought leading from one situational thought to another. Our graphs would have to be what are called "oriented" or "directed" graphs, that is, each branch would have to bear an arrow indicating its direction, since a transformation may lead from u_1 to u_2 but not vice versa. A branch will, in other words, represent an ordered pair of situations. Sometimes, there will be a transformation taking us from u_1 to u_2, but no transformation linking the situations in the opposite direction, but at other times there will be two lines, going from u_1 to u_2 and from u_2 to u_1 respectively, to stand for two transformations, having opposite effects.

Furthermore, we shall have to have some means (for example, coloring the lines differently) of showing which branches represent instances of the same transformation. A branch going from u_1 to u_2 and a branch going from u_3 to u_4 might, psychologically, represent the application of the same transformational response beginning with different starting points and thus having different consequences.

Finally, our graph will have to be a "doubly rooted" graph. This means that two of its nodes will have to be marked in such a way as to distinguish them, for example, one may be enclosed in a small circle and the other in a small square. This is, of course, because one node will have to represent the initial situation and the other the terminal situation or goal situation, both of which have their special properties.

Groups of Transformations

Another mathematical language that comes naturally to hand and can be used in conjunction with graph theory is that of the algebra of transformations. This deals with systems in which there is a set of transformations and a set of entities to which the transformations can be applied. Among the various types of structure that it recognizes, the one known as the "group of transformations" is the one whose study has proved most fertile.

A group of transformations (Birkhoff and MacLane, 1953, pp. 119 ff.) is characterized by the validity of four rules. Familiar systems that obey these four rules are movements in space and the arithmetical operations of addition and subtraction. But in order to show that the concept of a group of transformations has a much wider range of application, we may illustrate the rules not only with reference to addition and subtraction and movements in space but also with reference to an example given by Birkhoff and MacLane, namely rotations of a square.

Figure 8-2

If we think of the square depicted in Figure 8-2, we can recognize three rotations that will leave the square with a similar appearance but with the corners, A,B,C,D, in different locations. We can rotate the square through 90°, leaving the corners located

$$\begin{array}{cc} D & A, \\ C & B \end{array}$$

through 180°, leaving the corners located

$$\begin{array}{cc} C & D, \\ B & A \end{array}$$

and through 270°, leaving the corners located

$$\begin{array}{cc} B & C. \\ A & D \end{array}$$

These rotations may be called R_{90}, R_{180}, and R_{270}, respectively. For completeness, we must recognize a fourth rotation, which consists of rotating the square through 360° (R_{360}) so that its corners remain in the arrangement

$$\begin{array}{cc} A & B, \\ D & C \end{array}$$

with which it started.

The four rules defining a group of transformations are, then, as follows.

1. *Closure.* If we apply any two transformations belonging to the group in a particular order, say ϕ_1 followed by ϕ_2, there must always be a third transformation, ϕ_3, which is equivalent to this combination, so that we can write $\phi_3 = (\phi_2\phi_1)$.

It will be remembered from Chapter 5 that transformations are usually denoted from right to left in the order in which they are applied. When we say that ϕ_3 is equivalent to $(\phi_2\phi_1)$, we mean that if ϕ_3 is applied to a certain entity, the outcome will be the same as would have resulted, had ϕ_1 and then ϕ_2 been applied to the same entity. It should be noted that if ϕ_3 is the single transformation corresponding to ϕ_1 followed by ϕ_2, ϕ_3 will not necessarily be the single transformation corresponding to ϕ_2 followed by ϕ_1. Furthermore, ϕ_1, ϕ_2, and ϕ_3 need not necessarily be three different transformations.

The applicability of the rule of closure to movements in space, arithmetical operations of addition or subtraction, and rotations of the square can readily be appreciated. For any two successive movements we can make, there is always one movement in a straight line that would have had the same effect. For example, if we walk 1 mile due north and 2.4 miles due east, the single rectilinear movement that would have brought us to the same final location is a movement of 2.6 miles to the east-northeast. Similarly, there is always one addition or subtraction that would have the same outcome as any two of such operations performed successfully. For example, corresponding to adding 6 followed by subtracting 2, there is the single operation of adding 4. As for the rotations of the square, there is invariably one rotation equivalent to any two successive rotations. For example, R_{90} is equivalent to R_{270} followed by R_{180}.

2. *Identity.* In a group of transformations, there is always a transformation called the "identity" or "null" transformation, ϕ_0, with a property that sets it apart from all others: when the identity transformation is combined with any transformation of the group, ϕ_i, whether it is applied before ϕ_i or after it, the outcome is the same as if ϕ_i had been applied alone. The identity transformation is one that, when applied to any entity, leaves that entity unchanged. In other words, it is the transformation that makes no difference: $(\phi_i\phi_0) = (\phi_0\phi_i)$ $= \phi_i$.

To turn to our examples, the "movement" of standing still is an identity movement, since standing still followed by any movement in a straight line turns out the same as performing the rectilinear movement alone, and the same holds if we stand still after a rectilinear movement. In the same way, adding (or subtracting) zero before or after the addition or subtraction of another number does not affect the result. And finally, the rotation through 360°, R_{360}, can be performed before or after any of the other rotations without altering the terminal arrangement of the corners of the square.

3. *Inverse.* Having defined an identity transformation, we can now make sense out of the third rule, stating that every transformation belonging to the group must have a corresponding inverse transformation. An inverse transformation for ϕ_i is a transformation which, when applied in conjunction with ϕ_i, makes the outcome the same as if the identity transformation had been applied instead of this combination.

Strictly speaking, we should distinguish between a "right inverse" and "left inverse." A right inverse, ϕ_r, is one which leads back to the starting point when applied before ϕ_i, so that $(\phi_i\phi_r) = \phi_0$. A left inverse, ϕ_l, is a transformation which leads back to the starting point when applied after ϕ_i, so that $(\phi_l\phi_i) = \phi_0$. But in many cases, including the ones we have taken as examples, the right inverse and the left inverse are always the same, so that we can talk simply of an inverse.

Thus, the (right or left) inverse of walking 4 miles to the southwest is walking 4 miles to the northeast, since doing one after the other in either order would have the same effect as standing still. The inverse of adding 4 is subtracting 4, and vice versa. As for the rotations of the square, R_{90} and R_{270} are inverses of each other, but R_{180} has itself as its own inverse, as does R_{360}.

4. *Associativity.* The last rule states that, for any three (not necessarily distinct) transformations, ϕ_1, ϕ_2, and ϕ_3, the following holds: $\phi_3(\phi_2\phi_1) = (\phi_3\phi_2)\phi_1$. In this case, $(\phi_2\phi_1)$ refers to the single transformation that is equivalent to the combination of ϕ_1 followed by ϕ_2.

Illustrations of this rule are the following. In moving about on a plane surface, we reach the same place (Q in Figure 8-3) whether we travel 1 mile to the north (S to P, equivalent to traveling 1 mile to the east, S to R, and then 1.4 miles to the northwest, R to P) and then 1.4 miles to the northeast (P to Q), or whether we travel 1 mile to the east (S to R) and then 2 miles to the north (R to Q, equivalent to traveling 1.4 miles to the northwest R to P and

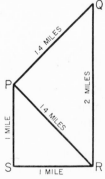

Figure 8-3

then 1.4 miles to the northeast, P to Q). In arithmetic, we obtain the same answer whether we add 11 ($= 8 + 3$) to 2 or whether we add 8 to 5 ($= 3 + 2$). And in rotating the square, R_{270} (which is equivalent to $R_{90} + R_{180}$) followed by R_{180} produces the same result as R_{90} followed by R_{360} (the last rotation being equivalent to $R_{180} + R_{180}$).

Groups and Behavior

Equivalent Chains of Transformations

What we have just reviewed are the defining characteristics of groups. There are, however, other important characteristics that can be deduced from these. For example, if there is a single transformation equivalent to any pair of transformations combined, it follows that there will be a single transformation corresponding to any combination of more than two transformations. This can be seen from the following considerations. If we have three transformations, ϕ_1, ϕ_2, ϕ_3, applied in succession, there will be a transformation, denoted by ($\phi_2\phi_1$), that is equivalent to the successive application of ϕ_1 and ϕ_2. There must then be a single transformation, ϕ_4, that is equivalent to ($\phi_1\phi_2$) followed by ϕ_3. The transformation ϕ_4 will therefore be equivalent to the successive application of ϕ_1, ϕ_2, and ϕ_3.

Similarly, if there are equivalences between, on the one hand, combinations of transformations and, on the other hand, single transformations, there must necessarily also be equivalences between combinations of different numbers of transformations. To revert to the example just considered, there must be a transformation equivalent to ($\phi_3\phi_2$), and ϕ_4 will be equivalent to the successive application of ϕ_1 and ($\phi_3\phi_2$) as well as to the successive application of ($\phi_2\phi_1$) and ϕ_3. These last two combinations must consequently be equivalent to each other.

So we can see that groups of transformations possess the salient characteristic of transformational habit-family hierarchies, that is, the possibility of forming chains of transformations of varying lengths and regarding them as equivalent to one another. When transformational responses consist of responses acting on the external environment, the equivalence will reside in the fact that the alternative chains terminate in the same practical outcome. When we are considering symbolic transformational hierarchies, this criterion cannot hold, since symbolic responses do not effect external changes by themselves. The basis of the equivalence between the alternative chains will, instead, be the recognition of a behavioral equivalence between the situational stimuli with which the chains terminate.

These are also, as we saw in Chapter 5, among the defining attributes of the "operation" for Piaget. Moreover, they come near to the properties characterizing what Tolman (1932) called a "means-end-field."

Reversibility

The group has, however, an additional feature that is not by any means essential to the habit-family hierarchy, namely the existence of inverses. Inverses engender the "reversibility" that Piaget has constantly stressed as the very touchstone of rationality and intelligence, achieved in greater and greater measure as the child grows up. And it must be remembered that, in order to give a meaning to the relation between the transformation and its inverse, we have first to define an identity transformation as the ϕ_0 which, combined with any other transformation, ϕ_i, produces ϕ_i, that is, $(\phi_0\phi_i) = \phi_i$. Then, for each ϕ_i, we define the inverse as ϕ_j such that $(\phi_i\phi_j) = \phi_0$. Strictly speaking, we are here defining a right inverse only, but we might as well confine ourselves to cases where right and left inverses are identical, to avoid unnecessary complication.

CANCELLATION AND COMPENSATION. In the physical world there are many situations that could be represented mathematically by a formula such as $(\phi_i\phi_j) = \phi_0$. The ϕ_i, the ϕ_j, the ϕ_0, and the equals sign in this formula, as well as the denoted combination of ϕ_i and ϕ_j, can all correspond to a variety of physical phenomena and relations between physical phenomena. But in general there are two broad classes of situations that the formula can appropriately cover. These are the cases that can be called *cancellation* and *compensation* respectively.

In the cancellation case, we have a process that changes some variable in the situation into something different, followed by a second process that changes the same variable back to its initial value and thus restores the initial situation. An example would be walking 100 yards to the north followed by walking 100 yards to the south. Another example would be turning a knob so as to halve the volume of sound coming from a radio set and then turning the knob in the opposite direction until the original volume is restored.

Compensation occurs when the effect of a change in one variable, say x, is undone by an appropriate change in another variable, say y. So, if we start out with a combination of values of these two variables, (x_1, y_1), we end up with a combination of different values,

(x_2, y_2), which is, in the respect that is important to us, equivalent to (x_1, y_1). This may come about, for example, if something depends on the sum of x and y or on the product of x and y. In the former case, if x_2 is changed to ($x_2 + a$), this change will be compensated if y_2 is changed to ($y_2 - a$), leaving the sum invariant. In the latter case, a change from x_2 to ax_2 can, of course, be compensated if y_2 is changed to y_2/a. The changes that constitute compensation may occur successively or simultaneously. An example might be somebody walking backward the length of a slowly moving train. As long as he is moving at the same speed as the train, although in the opposite direction, his position with respect to a point on the station platform will remain constant. Similarly a person might arrange for somebody to turn up the volume of a radio set while he is walking away from it, and as long as the two processes are correctly timed, the audibility of what is being broadcast will remain unchanged.

REVERSIBILITY AND BIOLOGICAL ADAPTATION. In psychology, as in physiology and biology generally, many situations conforming to the ($x_i x_j$) = x_0 formula and belonging to both the cancellation and the compensation categories occur. These situations are closely connected with the maintenance and restoration of psychophysiological equilibrium, in the sense of the conditions that must be kept constant within narrow limits if an organism is to remain alive. Piaget attaches great importance to the analogies between biological and psychological equilibrium and the states of equilibrium (defined as states in which a system can persist indefinitely) that figure in the physical sciences.

When we speak of equilibrium in the biological sciences, we are usually thinking not so much of a state in which an organism can persist indefinitely as of a state in which it can remain alive. This means that certain critical variables (for example, those relating to the temperature and the chemistry of the blood) must remain constant within quite narrow limits, although other characteristics of the organism, for example, those defining its posture, may vary widely and freely (Cannon, 1932; Ashby, 1952).

Biological equilibrium or, as it is often called, "homeostasis" has certainly much to do with reversibility. Events impinging on the organism from the external environment and events within the organism are constantly threatening survival and well-being by tending to drive critical variables away from their desirable values. The organism can survive and maintain its equilibrium only if it responds to these sources of disturbance by behavior (that is, changes in its state), which counteracts them. Its reactions can thus be regarded as inverse transformations with reference to the transformations that would result from the disturbances if they were allowed to exert their influence unhindered.

We have cases of both cancellation and compensation. For example, the depletion of foodstuffs within the body is followed by processes leading to the ingestion of food. If something happens to knock an animal over on to its side or to turn it upside down, righting reflexes intervene to restore the normal upright posture. But in cases of compensation where the remedial measures are contemporaneous with the disturbances, so that the critical variables are prevented from departing from their desirable values, adaptation is more satisfactory. Thus, if an event chances to pull an organism over toward one side and its impact is relatively moderate and gradual, the compensatory contraction of muscles on the opposite side is likely to supervene early enough to forestall any noticeable leaning over. And, as soon as events inside or outside the body threaten to lower body temperature below the normal level, a variety of processes from vasoconstriction in the superficial blood vessels to the action of lighting a fire will generally suffice to keep temperature unchanged throughout.

In all these cases of relatively primitive and direct reaction to biological threat, the relation of reversibility holds between two events belonging to different universes: one is an environmental event, which occurs independently of any action of the organism, whereas the second event, which acts as the inverse of the first and counteracts it, belongs to the behavior of the organism.

REVERSIBILITY AND THINKING. Psychologically, and especially as far as the psychology of thinking is concerned, the most interesting cases of reversibility are, however, those where the relation obtains between two responses of the organism. For example, an organism with symbolic capacities can think back over previous experiences of environmental threat or disturbance and over the measures it took to remedy these. Alternatively, it can plan ahead, representing to itself possible future disturbances or threats and the measures that can be taken to deal with them. In these cases, both the disturbing event and the disturbance-removing event must be represented by symbolic responses of the organism, and therefore one response stands in the relation of inverse to the other.

The possibilities of preparing in advance for emergencies that such capacities offer are valuable enough. But, as Piaget points out, reversibility in the sense of an inverse relation between two responses, particularly two symbolic responses, is essential to thinking in other respects also.

For example, it has often been pointed out that part of the advantages of thinking lies in the ability to substitute implicit trial and error for overt trial and error (Dewey, 1910; Claparède, 1933). In thought, one can represent to oneself a sequence of possible ways of solving a problem until one lights upon a course of action that will lead to success. At the level of overt trial and error, exemplified by the cat in Thorndike's puzzle box or the rat in the Skinner box, each possible solution must be tried out physically, whereas, in thought, it need be sampled only in a symbolic form in order to be rejected or retained. This means at least a saving in time and effort compared with what would be required to perform each response overtly, and, in many instances, it avoids danger that might result from a mistaken course of action.

Consequently, once a particular response pattern has been contemplated and then rejected as inappropriate, the organism can resume its search for a solution without being affected by this false start. But just as "the spoken word can never be recalled," an item of thought, having once been entertained, can hardly be completely wiped out in an organism that is equipped with capacity to remember; as in perceptual or motor functions, the traces of processes that have just occurred must remain to contaminate and modify succeeding processes for at least a few minutes. But if a thought element is followed by a thought element that cancels it, the combined influence of traces of both of these elements can be equivalent to zero, that is, the organism, having entertained both of them in turn, is comparable to an organism that had not entertained either, as far as the possibilities now open to it are concerned.

A pattern like this can be helpful in other contexts than those involving implicit trial and error. Let us take an experiment (Piaget and Szeminska, 1941) that was mentioned in Chapter 3. A child is shown about 20 wooden beads, most of which are brown and the remainder of which are white. He is then asked whether there are more wooden beads or brown beads. Up to about the age of seven, "the child almost always replies that there are more brown beads 'because there are only two or three white ones'" (Piaget, 1947). Having counted the larger part of the beads as "brown beads," he is evidently incapable of regarding them also as "wooden beads," so that, as far as he is concerned, the only wooden beads to compare with the brown beads are the white beads. An older child can, of course, answer this question correctly.

According to Piaget, what the younger child lacks is a form of reversibility. He does not realize that a particular bead can be counted as both a brown and a wooden bead and that, in order to answer the question, he must count it, first, as a member of the class of brown beads and, second, as a member of the class of wooden beads. This requires, Piaget says, some process by which, after the brown beads have been gathered together to be considered as a class, the class of brown beads is then dissolved and the class of wooden beads constituted and considered, with the beads that made up the class of brown beads included in it. There must therefore be some process that corresponds to the dissolution or inversion of the gathering together in thought of the brown beads. Such a process will act as an inverse of the process that presents to thought the class of brown beads. This would seem to illustrate the need to link each step to the next by a transformational response, so that the orderly character of directive thinking can be maintained.

Finally, Piaget (1949a) states that, in logic, the reversibility relation is the foundation of all consistency in the form of the law of contradiction. This law states that a proposition, p, and its denial, not-p, cannot both be true. In other words, logical thinking requires a recognition of an inverse relation between two incompatible propositions, each of which entails the nonvalidity of the other.

In this case, contradiction or impossibility has to be regarded as a null element. But it does not conform to the definition of a null element given in the second rule defining groups. To assert a proposition, p, together with some other proposition that is contradictory or impossible is hardly equivalent to asserting p alone.

We have to conclude from this and other instances, that, despite the valuable service that Piaget has performed in spotlighting the importance of inverse processes, his eagerness to demonstrate the ubiquity and centrality of reversibility throughout intellectual functioning has led him to interpret reversibility with a great deal of flexibility and, at times, a little procrusteanly. We shall come back to these points a little later in this chapter.

Groups and Psychological Development

Groups and Motor Behavior

The first writer to stress the importance of group structures in behavior was apparently the French mathematician Poincaré (1914). Being interested in the psychological foundations of mathematics,

Poincaré came to consider how knowledge of spatial relations might originate in the child. He pointed out that a spatial change, that is, a movement undergone by an environmental object, differs from every other kind of environmental change in one important respect, namely that it can always be canceled out, and the object restored to its initial apparent location, by a bodily movement of the subject. The bodily movement must, of course, be equal in extent and opposite in direction to the movement of the external object. Furthermore, Poincaré showed that the movements open to objects in the environment and the bodily movements open to the subject each form a group.

Piaget (1937), building on these ideas of Poincaré, found evidence for the gradual formation of a group structure in the child's understanding of space. His observations of his own children showed that, as far as overt movements are concerned, group structures became completed during the first half of the second year. At this stage, the child shows that he can recognize equivalences between different successions of movements, whether his own or those of other objects. Having watched an object undergo a succession of displacements from one location to another, he knows which single movement of his eyes or of his body will bring him back into contact with it.

During the second half of the second year, imagined or represented movements can participate in groups together with perceived movements. This is the stage where the child can, for example, select detours to bring him beyond barriers. This means that he recognizes the succession of movements comprising the detour as equivalent to the direct movement that would be made if the barrier were not present. He can also anticipate where he will find an object that went out of sight while it was in motion or that was placed under a cover which in its turn was placed under another cover and so on. He can select a series of bodily movements that will gain access as quickly as possible to the hidden object.

Even the maze learning of the rat shows features adapted to the group structure of movements in space. The rat's behavior shows, for instance, a recognition that the end points of two itineraries may be identical, making the two itineraries equivalent as alternative ways of reaching the same place. This may be seen from the fact that he follows the two itineraries about equally often on different occasions (Dashiell, 1930). When a rat learns to avoid going down a blind alley, as in Figure 8-4, he can be said to have learned that the

Figure 8-4

point at which he arrived after going down the blind

alley and back up it again is the same as the point at which he found himself before going down the blind alley, so that the shortest path to the goal box lies straight ahead (Hull, 1932).

When a rat has learned how to proceed from the starting box to the goal box of a maze, this learning reduces the time needed to learn to take the same route in the opposite direction when the starting box and the goal box are interchanged (Bunch and Lund, 1932; Dorcus, 1932). In an experiment by Lukaszewska (1961), rats were taught by a preliminary training procedure not to eat food as soon as they found it outside the home cage but to take it back to the cage and eat it there. The cage was then placed on the starting platform of one or other of four one-choice-point mazes of differing designs. On the first trial, about 90% of the rats, after reaching the goal box, found their way back to the starting platform without making a wrong turn at the choice points.

So we can see the rudiments of reversibility even at this level. We can understand how the group structures that are immanent in human locomotor behavior may have grown out of capacities that are in evidence in the simple learning of the rat, coupled with the superior capacities for forming expectations and representations that are at the disposal of the human subject.

Groups and Symbolic Behavior

Group structures come into their own, however, when the child is old enough to make fertile use of his symbolic functions. As Wiener (1948) has written:

> For the existence of any science, it is necessary that there exist phenomena which do not stand isolated. In a world ruled by a succession of miracles performed by an irrational God subject to sudden whims, we should be forced to await each new catastrophe in a state of perplexed passiveness. . . . The essence of an effective rule for a game or useful law of physics is that it be stateable in advance, and that it apply to more than one case. Ideally, it should represent a property of the system discussed which remains the same under the flux of particular circumstances. In the simplest case, it is a property which is invariant to a set of transformations to which the system is subject. We are thus led to the notions of transformation, transformation-group, and invariant.

A high proportion of the systems of physical events that can be represented in thought possess group structures. Several combinations of factors, simultaneous or successive, can have the same outcome. And a given factor can have its effect undone by an inverse factor whether acting at the same time in a compensatory manner or afterwards so as to bring about cancellation.

Inhelder and Piaget (1955) have made a painstaking study of the development of the ability to conceptualize physical problems of this nature. They show that the child's capacity to cope with them is limited at first but gradually approaches a stage (the stage of formal operations, reached by the age of 14 or 15) at which the subject can conceive the possible ways in which the operative variables may interact, can design conclusive experiments to ascertain how they actually interact, and can draw valid conclusions from the findings yielded by these experiments.

Piaget is inclined to attach particular importance to systems of phenomena that have the same structure as a group of four transformations known to algebraists as the "four group" (Birkhoff and MacLane, 1953, p. 138). In the systems in question, each change that could be introduced into the situation has two opposites, an inverse (which produces cancellation) and a reciprocal (which produces compensation). Thus, if we have two equal weights in the pans of a balance and if we increase the weight in the left-hand pan, we shall bring about an asymmetry in the positions of the two pans. But the original symmetry can be restored, either by the inverse change of removing the excess weight that was added to the left-hand pan or by the reciprocal change of moving the right-hand pan farther away from the fulcrum. To take another example, if we have a ring casting a shadow on a screen, an increase in the diameter of the ring will cause an increase in the diameter of the shadow. Once again, we can cancel this change by reducing the ring to its original size or compensate for it by moving the ring farther away from the screen.

Parsons (1960) has pointed out that, strictly speaking, these systems of phenomena do not always conform to the four group. They do not always have only two opposites. In the case of the balance, for example, there are at least two other ways of reinstating the initial state of affairs besides those mentioned: one can increase the weight in the right-hand pan by as much as the left-hand weight was increased, or one can move the left-hand pan nearer to the fulcrum. Be that as it may, and even if the four group is not so predominant as Piaget makes out, it cannot be denied that group structures are found in many sectors of the physical world, so that symbolic responses that mirror these sectors satisfactorily will need themselves to be organized in group structures.

As far as logic is concerned, groups can certainly be formed out of selected logical elements and operations. Piaget (Piaget, 1949a; Inhelder and Piaget, 1955) shows how the sixteen binary relations between two propositions recognized by modern logic form a group isomorphic with the four group. For example, the compound proposition "*p* implies *q*" can be said to have two opposites in the form of an inverse, "*p* does not imply *q*," and a reciprocal, "*q* implies *p*." The inverse of the reciprocal forms the correlative, "*q* does not imply *p*." But he supplies no evidence that the utilization of these relations between propositions is in any way essential to logical thinking. The protocols of the experiments just discussed abound with illustrations of thinking that reflects group structures. But these group structures, including equivalences among chains of processes and inverse relations, reflect the physical phenomena upon which the thinking is brought to bear. There is nothing to show that they are indispensable to the application of the propositional calculus.

Groupings

One drawback of the group as a device for describing thought structures is, as Piaget recognizes, the fact that the members of the group, for example, transformations, must be completely distinct from one another, whereas many of the entities that figure in thought overlap with one another or include one another.

This is true of classes, relations, and propositions. The class of vertebrates is included in the class of animals, whereas bipeds overlap with mammals. The relation "larger than" includes the relation "twice as large as," and there is an overlap between "cousin of" and "female relative of." If we take the series of propositions, "*p* or *q*," "*p*," "*p* and *q*," we can see that the cases where the second is true are included among the cases where the first is true and that the cases where the third is true are included among the cases where the second is true. Each successive member of the series supplies part of the information that is supplied by its successors and defines a subset of the situations defined by its predecessors.

To handle the thought structures whose elements are related in such ways, Piaget has introduced the concept of the "grouping (*groupement*)" or imperfect group (see Chapter 3). He has not defined the grouping rigorously enough to satisfy mathematicians or logicians, although Grize (1960) has attempted to provide a formalization for groupings of classes and relations. But one can say that a grouping is a structure in which the defining characteristics of a group are partly but not completely realized. The relations of overlapping and inclusion give rise to certain equivalences that would be anomalous in a group. For example, we have cases where $(A + B) = A$ even though B is not zero; for instance, the class consisting of all mammals and all kangaroos is the same as the class consisting of all mammals. Then we have $(A + A) = A$; for instance, the class consisting of all kangaroos and all kangaroos is equivalent to the class of all kangaroos. Furthermore, only some pairs of elements of a grouping can be combined to produce another element that also belongs to the grouping. For example, the class of all vertebrates and the class of all invertebrates can be combined to produce the class of animals, but the class of invertebrates combined with the class of kangaroos does not give rise to a recognized class. Similarly, the relations "father of" and "mother of" can be combined to form the relation "parent of," but there is no relation corresponding to the combination (logical sum) of "son of" and "mother-in-law of."

It should be noted that this last limitation is a purely psychological one. From the point of view of a mathematician interested in set theory, the conjunction of the set of kangaroos and the set of invertebrates defines a set that is as good as any other. But the class of all kangaroos plus all invertebrates does not form a psychological class for most people, because the members of this conjunction do not possess an ecological equivalence that nonmembers of the conjunction do not possess: there are no conditions in which a particular response would be appropriate in the presence of a kangaroo or of an invertebrate but inappropriate in the presence of other stimulus objects. An ecological equivalence could, of course, be artificially produced, for example, by offering a child a reward every time he points either to a kangaroo or to an invertebrate. The child could be trained to treat the conjunction as a class and, for example, to give it a name. But until this is done, the conjunction does not form a class in the psychological sense, and so the law of closure applicable to groups is not fulfilled.

Habit-Family Hierarchies and Groups

We have already remarked that any system of behavior that possesses a group structure possesses the essential properties of a habit-family hierarchy. But the converse is not true; not all habit-family hierarchies have group structure. We must therefore show how conditions corresponding to the defining characteristics of a group of transformations can obtain in some habit-family hierarchies. In doing this, we shall show how these properties give rise to new behavioral equivalences among represented stimulus situations. There is, of necessity, an equivalence among the terminal situations or end points of the constituent chains of a transformational hierarchy. This is implied by the very definition of a habit-family hierarchy. But in addition to these equivalences, behavioral equivalences can arise, as the result of group properties, between intermediate points of different chains of a hierarchy or between two points reached by one and the same chain at different stages. These additional equivalences can constitute some of the most valuable fruits of thinking that utilizes symbolic habit-family hierarchies possessing a group structure.

The formation of new bases of behavioral equivalence results from what we have called (Chapter 3) the principle of secondary generalization. It will be remembered that the phenomenon of secondary stimulus generalization occurs whenever two stimuli, S_1 and S_2, happen to be associated with a common response, R_A. Then, when any new response, R_B, becomes associated with S_1, it will generalize to S_2. This is because both S_1 and S_2 will now be accompanied by the feedback stimulation resulting from the performance of R_A, and any new response that is associated with one of these external stimuli will become associated also with the feedback stimulation from R_A and thus tend to occur also whenever the other external stimulus is encountered.

A special case of the conditions for secondary stimulus generalization will obtain whenever two stimuli are associated with a common chain of responses. This will be the case, for example, whenever we have a transformational habit-family hierarchy containing two chains whose early members differ but which are identical from a certain point to the termination, that is, whenever we have two chains of the form $S_0 \to \phi_a \to \cdots \to \phi_j \overset{*}{\to} \phi_n \to \phi_{n+1} \to \cdots \to \phi_G$ and $S_0 \to \phi_b \to \cdots \phi_k \overset{*}{\to} \phi_n \to \phi_{n+1} \to \cdots \to \phi_G$. There will then be a basis of behavioral equivalence between the stimulus situations corresponding to the points marked with asterisks.

We shall now set forth the properties that can occur in transformational habit-family hierarchies to correspond to the properties of a group, using the following notations. The sign $\longleftrightarrow$ will indicate that, for the hierarchy in question, if a chain having the form indicated to the left of the sign belongs to the hierarchy, then the corresponding chain indicated to the right of the sign will also belong to the hierarchy, and vice versa. And, in each formula, asterisks will indicate the stimulus situations between which a basis for behavioral equivalence will exist in consequence of the principle of secondary stimulus generalization.

1. *Closure.* We shall say that $\phi_c = (\phi_b\phi_a)$ if and only if

$$S_0 \rightarrow \phi_1 \rightarrow \cdots \rightarrow \phi_k \rightarrow \phi_a \rightarrow \phi_b \xrightarrow{*} \phi_m \rightarrow \cdots \rightarrow \phi_G \leftrightarrow$$

$$S_0 \rightarrow \phi_1 \rightarrow \cdots \rightarrow \phi_k \rightarrow \phi_c \xrightarrow{*} \phi_m \rightarrow \cdots \rightarrow \phi_G.$$

2. *Associativity.* We shall say that $\phi_c(\phi_b\phi_a) = (\phi_c\phi_b)\phi_a$, if and only if

$$S_0 \rightarrow \phi_1 \rightarrow \cdots \rightarrow \phi_k \rightarrow (\phi_b\phi_a) \rightarrow \phi_c \xrightarrow{*} \phi_m \rightarrow \cdots \rightarrow \phi_G \leftrightarrow$$

$$S_0 \rightarrow \phi_1 \rightarrow \cdots \rightarrow \phi_k \rightarrow \phi_a \rightarrow (\phi_c\phi_b) \xrightarrow{*} \phi_m \rightarrow \cdots \rightarrow \phi_G.$$

The notation $(\phi_b\phi_a)$ stands, of course, for a single transformational response that is equal to $(\phi_b\phi_a)$ according to the definition just given under *Closure.*

3. *Identity.* We shall say that ϕ_0 is an identity or null transformation of the family, if and only if

$$S_0 \rightarrow \phi_1 \rightarrow \cdots \rightarrow \phi_k \xrightarrow{*} \phi_0 \xrightarrow{*} \phi_m \rightarrow \cdots \phi_G \leftrightarrow$$

$$S_0 \rightarrow \phi_1 \rightarrow \cdots \rightarrow \phi_k \xrightarrow{*} \phi_m \rightarrow \cdots \rightarrow \phi_G.$$

4. *Inverse.* We shall say that $\phi_{a'}$ is a left inverse of ϕ_a and that ϕ_a is a right inverse of $\phi_{a'}$, if and only if

$$S_0 \rightarrow \phi_1 \rightarrow \cdots \rightarrow \phi_k \xrightarrow{*} \phi_a \rightarrow \phi_{a'} \xrightarrow{*} \phi_m \rightarrow \cdots \rightarrow \phi_G \leftrightarrow$$

$$S_0 \rightarrow \phi_1 \rightarrow \cdots \rightarrow \phi_k \xrightarrow{*} \phi_m \rightarrow \cdots \rightarrow \phi_G.$$

If the family possesses an identity, ϕ_0, it follows that

$$S_0 \rightarrow \phi_1 \rightarrow \cdots \rightarrow \phi_k \xrightarrow{*} \phi_a \rightarrow \phi_{a'} \xrightarrow{*} \phi_m \rightarrow \cdots \rightarrow \phi_G \leftrightarrow$$

$$S_0 \rightarrow \phi_1 \rightarrow \cdots \rightarrow \phi_k \xrightarrow{*} \phi_0 \xrightarrow{*} \phi_m \rightarrow \cdots \rightarrow \phi_G,$$

and we shall be able to say that $(\phi_{a'}\phi_a) = \phi_0$.

In most cases, left inverses will also be right inverses, so that

$$S_0 \rightarrow \phi_1 \rightarrow \cdots \rightarrow \phi_k \xrightarrow{*} \phi_a \rightarrow \phi_{a'} \xrightarrow{*} \phi_m \rightarrow \cdots \rightarrow \phi_G \leftrightarrow$$

$$S_0 \rightarrow \phi_1 \rightarrow \cdots \rightarrow \phi_k \xrightarrow{*} \phi_{a'} \rightarrow \phi_a \xrightarrow{*} \phi_m \rightarrow \cdots \rightarrow \phi_G,$$

and it will follow that

$$(\phi_{a'}\phi_a) = (\phi_a\phi_{a'}).$$

It should be noted that $\phi_{a'}$ will sometimes be a response that changes back a variable changed by ϕ_a to its initial value, in which case we shall have cancellation. In other cases, $\phi_{a'}$ will not affect the variable changed by ϕ_a but will, instead, introduce an alteration in the value of another variable that compensates the effect of ϕ_a. Sometimes, the mutually compensating changes in two variables may be effected by a single response rather than by two consecutive responses. If we use the notation $\phi_{x'y'}$ to denote a response that simultaneously changes the value of variable X from x to x' and the value of variable Y from y to y', the combination $x'y'$ being behaviorally equivalent to the combination xy, we shall have the following property:

$$S_0 \rightarrow \phi_1 \rightarrow \cdots \rightarrow \phi_k \xrightarrow{*} \phi_{x'y'} \xrightarrow{*} \phi_m \rightarrow \cdots \rightarrow \phi_G \longleftrightarrow$$

$$S_0 \rightarrow \phi_1 \rightarrow \cdots \rightarrow \phi_k \xrightarrow{*} \phi_m \rightarrow \cdots \rightarrow \phi_G.$$

This kind of situation will play an important part in our later discussion of quantitative invariants.

These properties of habit-family hierarchies correspond to characteristics of groups, but the rules defining groups impose some stringent requirements that must be fulfilled if we are to recognize a hierarchy as one with a group structure:

(1) There must be, for *every* ordered pair of transformational responses, ϕ_a and ϕ_b, a single transformational response, ϕ_c, that is equivalent to the ordered pair in the sense discussed under *Closure*.

(2) The associativity property, $\phi_c(\phi_b\phi_a) = (\phi_c\phi_b)\phi_a$, must hold for *any* three transformational responses, ϕ_a, ϕ_b, and ϕ_c.

(3) *Every* transformational response must have an inverse.

(4) There must be an identity transformational response.

We can see, therefore, how one habit-family hierarchy might conform fully to the rules defining a group, while, in another habit-family hierarchy, the group properties that we have described might apply to certain combinations of transformational responses but not hold universally so as to satisfy the requirements for a group. In cases of the latter sort, it is understandable that habit-family hierarchies might represent various degrees of approximation to group structures, for example, imperfect group structures represented by Piaget's groupings.

Quantitative Invariants and Group Properties

We must now return to the situations exemplified by Piaget's experiments on quantitative invariants, which appear to be instructive paradigms for the process of establishing equivalences by thinking. As we observed in Chapter 4, the ability to recognize quantitative invariants and to behave in accordance with them means to be able to distinguish transformations that leave these quantitative properties (for example, size, amount, or number) invariant from transformations that modify them. When this discrimination has been mastered, the stimulus situation that results from a transformation of the former sort will possess a basis of behavioral equivalence with the stimulus situation that preceded this transformation or with the stimulus situation that would have resulted from any other transformation of the same class. There must thus be responses that would be equally adaptive in all the stimulus situations, provided that there is an appropriate motivational condition, that is, one in which the value of the consequences of the response depends solely on the quantitative property in question.

A subject recognizing a quantitative invariant will possess a number of habit-family hierarchies of the following kind: all constituent chains will end with a common sequence of acts (for example, selecting a particular vessel as containing just enough liquid to quench one's thirst and then consuming its contents), but the earlier parts of different claims, preceding this final sequence, will consist of all possible successive combinations of transformations preserving the quantitative property, for example, all possible successive pourings of a mass of liquid from container to container.

The subject's hierarchies will also show the following characteristic, using the same notation as before:

$$S_0 \rightarrow \phi_1 \rightarrow \cdots \rightarrow \phi_k \xrightarrow{*} \phi_x \xrightarrow{*} \phi_m \rightarrow \cdots \rightarrow \phi_G \longleftrightarrow$$

$$S_0 \rightarrow \phi_1 \rightarrow \cdots \rightarrow \phi_k \xrightarrow{*} \phi_m \rightarrow \cdots \rightarrow \phi_G,$$

where ϕ_x represents any transformation that preserves the quantitative property, provided that the satisfaction of the motivation subserved by the hierarchy depends on this quantitative property. It follows that this property holds when ϕ_x is replaced by any sequence whatever of transformations preserving the quantitative property.

Such a transformation may modify some variable that bears no relation to the property of interest, for example, moving a vessel containing a certain amount of liquid about in space. Alternatively, it may introduce a modification in some variable that would entail a change in the quantitative property unless accompanied by a compensating modification of another variable. In such cases, an invariant-preserving transformation will be one that produces changes in two or more variables that offset one another. For example, an increase in the height of a column of liquid would necessarily imply an increase in quantity unless accompanied by a decrease in width. But pouring the liquid into a narrow vessel constitutes a transformation of the type noted by $\phi_{x'y'}$ on page 217, since it increases height while decreasing width and so leaves the amount of liquid unchanged.

Origins of Quantitative-Invariant-Conserving Habit-Family Hierarchies

We have shown how the existence of group structure in a habit-family hierarchy can generate bases for behavioral equivalence. We must suppose that the converse can also occur and that combinations of transformational responses will become equivalent when behavioral equivalences between represented stimulus situations are brought about by other means.

For example, let u_i be any represented stimulus situation and let there be a natural similarity between the stimulus situations denoted by $\phi_c(u_i)$ and $\phi_b\phi_a(u_i)$. The subject will then possess transformation-selecting habits associating ϕ_c with the stimulus combination $<u_i,$ $\phi_c(u_i)>$ and associating the sequence $<\phi_a, \phi_b>$ with the combination $<u_i, \phi_b\phi_a(u_i)>$. But by primary stimulus generalization, the combination $<u_i, \phi_c(u_i)>$ will also possess an association with the response sequence $<\phi_a, \phi_b>$ and, similarly, the combination $<u_i, \phi_b\phi_a(u_i)>$ will become associated with the transformational response ϕ_c.

Consequently, any hierarchy that has ϕ_c in a certain location in one of its chains will also possess the corresponding chain with ϕ_c replaced by $\phi_a \to \phi_b$, and the converse will also hold.

Much the same may result from secondary stimulus generalization. If a certain labeling response becomes attached to both $\phi_c(u_i)$ and $\phi_b\phi_a(u_i)$, then the combination of u_i and the feedback stimulus corresponding to the labeling response can be expected to instigate alternatively the response sequence, $<\phi_a, \phi_b>$ and the single response ϕ_c, with the same consequence for the constitution of habit-family hierarchies. Instead of the attachment of a common labeling response to the stimulus situations, there may be a mediating response producing a secondary equivalence relation between them, that is, some such verbal response as "same," "equal," etc.

In analogous ways, habit-family hierarchies might acquire the properties corresponding to other characteristics of groups than closure.

It seems that processes of this sort play a large part in the establishment of the habit-family hierarchies that underlie quantitative invariants from the age of about seven on. Some of these notions appear before others. According to Piaget's data, quantity precedes weight, and weight precedes volume (Piaget and Inhelder, 1941). The notions are, however, generally absent in younger children but firmly established and virtually universal once the relevant point of development has been reached. In between, there may be a surprisingly brief period of transition, lasting perhaps a few months or a year, when the child is vacillating and suggestible. But once he has passed the turning point, he will confidently assert, for example, that a mass of liquid does not change in quantity when it is poured into a thinner glass, and it will be hard to believe that the same child, when tested a year before, was maintaining just as firmly that the quantity increased.

Reversibility and Quantitative Invariants

Both kinds of reversibility, cancellation and compensation, play a manifest part among the transformations that leave quantitative properties invariant. We can take the pouring of a liquid from one vessel into another as an example.

When children who answer correctly are asked how they know that the narrower vessel contains the same amount of liquid as the wider vessel, they will reply in a variety of ways. Many will be unable to give any reason for their judgment. Of those who are articulate enough to reply, some will point out that no liquid was added or removed when the pouring took place, so that the amount must be the same. Most will, however, refer to one or other of the forms of reversibility that exist in the situation. Some will say that the amount must be the same because one could easily pour the liquid back into the wider vessel, whereupon things would be as they were at the beginning. Others will observe that, although the height of the liquid has gone up, the width has gone down.

Piaget, on the basis of these facts, has singled out reversibility as the decisive factor. He has stated repeatedly that children younger than about seven years fail to appreciate that the amount of liquid must remain unchanged, because they lack reversibility. This error is abandoned, he maintains, when the child acquires "reversible operations."

Yet, neither recognition of the possibility of cancellation nor recognition of the compensatory relation between the changes in height and in width can be the cause of the shift to judgments of equality.

Let us take cancellation first. If a child is shown two identical rubber bands side by side, sees one being elongated, and is then asked how the length of the elongated band compares with the length of the other, it would clearly be absurd for him to answer that the bands must now be equally long because one could always release the elongated band, causing it to resume its original appearance! Surely, few, if any, children would answer in this way. Similarly, to revert to the experiment with the liquids, suppose that, instead of asking whether the liquid has increased or decreased in quantity, we ask whether it has increased or decreased in height after being poured from the wider into the narrower vessel. No child who has entered the stage of concrete operations will conclude that the height of the column must be the same as it was before the pouring on the grounds that the original configuration could be restored by pouring the liquid back again! The child who understands quantitative invariants appreciates that a transformation leaves some properties unaltered but alters others, and it is clearly a matter of knowing which properties are affected and which are not. Recognition of the possibility of cancellation does not in itself equip the child with the ability to make this distinction.

Unpublished observations of my own, which Piaget concedes agree with his experience, suggest that most 5- or 6-year-old children who believe that the amount of liquid increases after pouring into the narrower vessel can correctly predict that, if the liquid were poured back into the wider vessel, the column would have the same height as before. Even those who do not make this prediction can be taught to make it with the help of a few demonstrations. Nevertheless, many of them persist in asserting that there is more liquid after pouring into the wider vessel and that the liquid becomes less again when returned to the wider vessel. So, anticipation of the possibility of cancellation does not lead immediately to recognition of conservation of quantity.

As for compensation, we have already noted (in Chapter 4) that the sight of increased height together with decreased width cannot be what leads an older child or an adult to conclude that quantity is unchanged. It would indeed be fallacious to draw such a conclusion on this basis, since a simultaneous increase in height and decrease in width does not imply unchanged volume. A decrease in width has to be accompanied by just the right degree of increase in height if it is to be compensated, and normal life experience does not enable us to recognize at a glance whether an increase in height is large enough or too large or too small to compensate a decrease in width. The conclusion that quantity has not changed is clearly based not on the comparison between the change in height and the change in width but on a recognition of the kind of transformation that has brought a new stimulus pattern into being.

There are grounds for believing rather that, when a child realizes that changes in height and in width can compensate each other, this simply removes an obstacle to judgment of unchanged quantity. A younger child is apt to assume that an increase in height necessarily means an increase in amount. When he has learned that height can go up while width goes down, and that both of these factors must be taken into account, he is free to separate his assessments of quantity from his assessments of height.

There is some confirmation of this interpretation in some experiments by Franck reported by Bruner (1964). She used cylindrical vessels with opaque coverings, so that, while the lesser width of the second vessel was clearly visible, the height of the column was not. Under these conditions, judgments of unchanged quantity could be drawn from younger children who would not otherwise have given them.

An experiment by Taponier (Piaget and Inhelder, 1962b) shows, on the other hand, that anticipation of compensating changes in different dimensions can occur without recognition of invariance of quantity. She showed the narrower vessel to her subjects, ranging in age from four to eight years, and asked them to indicate how high they thought the liquid would come if it were poured into this vessel from the wider vessel. The pouring was then actually carried out, and the usual question was put about the amount of liquid that was now to be seen in the narrow vessel. Of all her subjects, 23% predicted that the level would rise but failed to conclude that the quantity was unchanged, while only 5% believed in invariance of quantity without predicting a rise in level.

When children realize that one process can undo the effects of another without recognizing a quantitative invariant, Piaget prefers to speak of "revertibility (*renversabilité*)" or "empirical return (*retour empirique*)" rather than of "reversibility (*réversibilité*)." The distinction between *réversibilité* and *renversabilité* was introduced by Duhem (1893), a French physicist of the turn of the century, who reserved the former term for cases where a process passes from state A through a number of intermediate states to state B and then goes from B to A, passing through the same intermediate states in the opposite order. There was *renversabilité* when the return from B to A went through different intermediate states. Piaget (1957, p. 44) offers the following definitions (translated).

We shall call "reversibility" the capacity to carry out one and the same action in both directions, with an awareness that it is a matter of one and the same action. . . .

We shall say that an action is "revertible" or that there is empirical return to the starting point when the subject comes back to the latter without an awareness of the identity of the action carried out in both directions.

But it is difficult to see how these distinctions can be made to fit the difference between the child who recognizes a quantitative invariant and the child who does not. There is no evidence that the older child recognizes an identity between pouring the liquid from the wider to the narrower vessel and pouring it back again in a way that the younger child does not. Nor does an identification of the intermediate states through which the liquid goes in the course of the two pourings seem to play any part.

It seems rather that the cases to which Piaget confines the term "reversibility" are ones in which the inverse relation between two responses, overt or symbolic, coexists with the other conditions that define groups. As was pointed out earlier, the transformations that preserve quantitative properties invariably form groups, and the habit-family hierarchies that incorporate responses representing such transformations will possess the properties that correspond to properties of groups.

We shall therefore dissent from Piaget's insistence on reversibility as the prime source of recognition of quantitative invariants. We shall, moreover, dispute the central role that he sees for it in logical thinking in general. Instead, we shall suggest that the factor in these symbolic structures is the existence of transformational habit-family hierarchies possessing the properties that characterize groups of transformations. Reversibility is, of course, one, but only one, of these properties. Finally, we shall suggest that a major feature of the habit-family hierarchies used by the highest forms of thinking, including those that lead us to recognize quantitative invariants, is that they have the structure of *transitive* groups.

Transitive-Group Habit-Family Hierarchies

A transitive group (Bourbaki, 1940) is a group with the peculiarity that, for any two of its elements u_1 and u_2, there is always some transformation, ϕ, such that u_2 equals $\phi(u_1)$. In other words, it is always possible to get from any element to any other element through one transformation. It follows from the principle of closure that whenever it is at all possible to get from one element to any other element by a sequence of transformations belonging to the group, we can get from the one element to the other in one transformation. The only groups that are not transitive groups are those whose elements are divided into two or more subsets, such that it is impossible, in any number of transformations, to get from a member of one subset of elements to a member of another subset.

A transitive group corresponds to what is called a *trivial* or *complete graph,* which is a graph with every node joined to every other node. Since transformational habit-family hierarchies have to be represented by directed graphs, we shall actually have to have two lines connecting every pair of nodes, going in the two directions. Furthermore, to take care of identity transformations, we shall have to have a line linking each node with itself—what König, the founder of graph theory, called a *"Schlinge* (loop)."

Advantages of Transitive-Group Habit-Family Hierarchies

If we are right in supposing that habit-family hierarchies with structures corresponding to transitive groups and complete graphs occupy a unique position in the most advanced forms of thinking, we must ask ourselves how this comes about. This means asking what special advantages hierarchies of this kind could offer.

One way of answering this question might be simply to point out that the world contains many systems of phenomena with transitive-group structure, that those systems of symbolic responses that possess a similar structure will therefore be most adaptive in reacting to them, and that the isomorphism between such symbolic structures and the sectors of reality on which they bear is responsible for the reinforcement that has caused the former to become established through learning.

But other factors, more instrinsic to the nature of transitive-group hierarchies, are likely to be of importance also. For one thing, the fact that one can go from any represented situation to any other in one move means a substantial saving in time. Bartlett (1932) describes how a witness, called before an African native court, was asked to relate what happened at the time that the offense was committed. He could reply only by going in detail and in order over everything that happened between the time he awoke on the morning of the day in question and the moment of interest. Bartlett contrasts this behavior with the capacity that most members of our society would have in similar circumstances to go straight back to a landmark not too far distant from the relevant point in the past and to recall what happened then without having to work their way through so much irrelevant intervening material. When symbolic content is organized in a transitive group, for example, in mathematical or in geographical thinking, we do not even have to go to the length of selecting a reference point that is near the situation of interest and groping our way toward it from there. A transformation-selecting habit will take us straight to the target situation with no fumbling at all.

The consequent advantages are comparable to those that we derive from our ability to select a motor response that will take us directly from our present posture to any intended posture (cf. Head's theory of the "schema" discussed in Chapter 5). For example, Hess (1954) mentions how "man and the higher vertebrates are capable of looking from every momentary position of the eyes into any other direction using the shortest possible way. With perfect aim and accuracy they can combine the tensions of their muscles in accord with the continually changing directions of their pull."

Still other advantages must underlie Piaget's long-standing contention that reversibility is a necessary and sufficient condition for "equilibrium" in psychology as in physics. If attention is to be focused, as we suggest, on transitive-group structure as a whole, rather than on the reversibility that is one feature of this structure, we must inquire in what senses transitive-group hierarchies can contribute to equilibrium, with special reference to thinking. Here, we cannot go very far without coming up against motivational problems, with which any notion of psychological equilibrium is inextricably linked. We shall, however, have to postpone a full airing of these motivational problems to later chapters.

Transitive-Group Hierarchies and Equilibrium

The concepts of "equilibrium" and "stability," which originally belonged to physics, have been given abstract analyses that make them fully applicable to biology and psychology, for example, by Ashby (1952, 1956) and by Mandelbrot (1956).

A body is said to be in "stable equilibrium" when it has the following property: if an external agent subjects it to a disturbance that changes its state, the body undergoes a second modification which cancels the effect of the disturbance. In other words, the body is capable of spontaneously making its way back to the state in which it would have been, had the disturbance not occurred.

STATIC AND DYNAMIC EQUILIBRIUM. There are cases of static equilibrium, in which the state to which the body returns is the same as the state it was in before the disturbance. But there are also cases of dynamic equilibrium, in which a body was in the process of evolving in some direction when the disturbance reached it, so that the state which it attains after reacting to the disturbance—the state in which it would have been if the disturbance had not occurred—is different from its previous state.

Transitive-group habit-family hierarchies ensure that organisms possessing them will respond with maximum efficiency when beset by analogous disturbances. As we have seen, the utilization of a behavior chain belonging to such a hierarchy means passing through a sequence of stimulus situations, actual or symbolically represented, resulting from a sequence of transformational responses. But if the organism should chance to find itself in one of these situations through the action of an external agent, that is, without having reached it through its own actions, the remainder of the behavior chain, or a portion of the remainder, can be executed as if the organism had reached that situation spontaneously, since each stimulus situation has an association with the succeeding pattern of responses. Because of this, both static and dynamic equilibrium can be realized, provided that the conditions for the transitive group are fulfilled. There will then be a transformation available to take the organism from any situation to which a disturbance brought it either to the situation it occupied previously or to the one it would have occupied if left undisturbed. The rest of its behavior can be run off from that point as if nothing untoward had taken place.

Let us suppose that a traveling salesman possesses a transitive-group habit-family hierarchy comprising all possible itineraries in the vicinity of Lake Geneva in Switzerland (see Figure 8-5), through having traveled over them repeatedly or through having studied a map. If, one day when he is staying at Montreux, he is abducted by gangsters, who blindfold him, convey him to Lausanne, and release

Figure 8-5

him there, his habit-family hierarchy will enable him to recognize where he is and return to Montreux by the quickest route.

This is a case of static equilibrium, but the same habit-family hierarchy will furnish dynamic equilibrium as well. If the salesman is kidnapped while passing through Lausanne on his way from Montreux to Geneva, and the gangsters this time carry him over the lake to Thonon and leave him there, he will be able to go directly to Geneva and resume his itinerary there without needing to return to Lausanne. In these cases, we have been speaking of actual, if unlikely, situations and actual responses. But the symbolic responses corresponding to the situation and to the actions would be made available by the corresponding symbolic habit-family hierarchy if the salesman needed to figure out what to do after the kidnapping had taken place or if he wanted to plan in advance for such predicaments. He would have the benefits not only of rapid recovery from the uncomfortable effects of the disturbance but also freedom from conflict, due to the availability of a clearly prepotent response for each contingency.

Piaget's Criteria for Equilibrium

We are now in a position to reinterpret some of the points that Piaget has repeatedly made with respect to the nature of equilibrium and the criteria for completeness of equilibrium (for example, 1947, 1957).

"Since operations are actions," he writes (1947, p. 40, in the English translation), "the equilibrium of operational thought is in no way a state of rest, but a system of balancing interchanges, alterations which are being continually compensated by others. It is the equilibrium of polyphony and not that of a system of inert masses. . . ." He writes further (p. 48) that it is "an equilibrium, both mobile and permanent, such that the structure of operational wholes is conserved while they assimilate new elements."

In perception and in the "intuitive" thinking of the 5- or 6-year-old child (which suffers from some of the same kinds of limitations as perception), the relations between the elements making up a pattern or, in other words, the structure of a pattern may vary with the point of view, the internal condition, and the direction of attention of the subject. But in more mature and more objective forms of thinking, the structure remains unchanged, no matter which portions of it are being contemplated or what the condition of the subject may be. A journey between two cities may seem longer or shorter according to all kinds of illusion-provoking external and internal factors. But geographical relations—distances and directions—worked out by computational procedures or stored in the form of knowledge are strikingly resistant to fluctuation.

But in what sense does a transitive-group habit-family hierarchy "preserve its structure" when the focus of attention shifts from one element to another or even when it incorporates new elements? The structure of a transformational habit-family hierarchy is defined by specifying, for every stimulus situation, what other stimulus situations are accessible in one move and which transformation leads to each of them. As long as we have a transitive group, every situation belonging to the group is accessible immediately from every other situation. So the situations accessible in one move are always the same, whatever the point that the subject's thinking has reached, and, consequently, the transformational responses available on the next move but one are always the same.

"VIRTUAL MOVEMENTS." Piaget (1941) describes psychological equilibrium as a state in which the algebraic sum of "virtual movements" is zero. He points out the analogy between this notion and the notion of equilibrium in mechanics, where any force that tends to impel a body in one direction is exactly counterbalanced by the forces that tend to impel it in other directions, so that the body remains stationary. But what corresponds to these virtual movements in psychology?

Our conception of a transitive-group habit-family hierarchy allows us to answer. It will be recalled that all the transformations starting out from a certain stimulus situation are responses having an association with that situation. In accordance with the terminology that we have adopted, only one of a set of mutually exclusive responses associated with a particular stimulus situation can be evoked or performed, but all of them are instigated.

"Virtual" responses are thus responses that are instigated without being performed. If a habit-family hierarchy has a transitive-group structure, this network of instigated responses will lead simultaneously in all directions, to all portions of the structure. They will thus safeguard the structure by compensating each other while opening up a multiplicity of opportunities for mobility. This would not be the case if the transformations setting out from a particular situation were directed to some portions of a structure but not others.

COMPENSATION AND REVERSIBILITY. In discussing the mechanisms that maintain equilibrium, Piaget (1941, 1947) distinguishes between "rhythms," "regulations," and "reversibility."

Rhythm, which characterizes many elementary physiological processes, gives rise to a periodic alternation of opposite changes. The rhythms of breathing and walking are clear examples.

Regulation entails the intervention of a corrective change as soon as a deviation from a normal state is recorded. This is characteristic of the self-correcting devices with negative feedback studied by cybernetics. Regulation possesses the drawback, common to many negative-feedback systems, that the corrective process is not always quantitatively adjusted to the need and that the beginning and end of its action are subject to some delay. There is consequently apt to be some oscillation or fluctuation about the optimal state, which dies down relatively quickly in the most favorable cases but persists in certain morbid psychological or sociological conditions (as in the electronic circuits to which the term "feedback" was originally applied).

Reversibility, on the other hand, is realized when the change is accompanied simultaneously and precisely by a compensating process which prevents some of the effects that would otherwise have occurred. There seem to be two types of relevant cases.

In the first type, the combination of two simultaneously occurring compensatory transformations causes a certain *property* of an object to remain unchanged. This is generally so when quantitative invariants are involved. For example, when liquid is transferred from a wider to a narrower vessel, the increase in height is accompanied by a decrease in width, and, if the subject is mature enough to take account of both changes at once, he will recognize that the simultaneous occurrence of these two changes makes it possible for the amount of liquid to remain invariant. We have already considered such phenomena from the point of view of habit-family hierarchies, and we have seen how the subject has to form equivalence classes of transformations that preserve quantitative properties. An expansion along some dimensions combined with a shrinkage along other dimensions appears to be a necessary feature of a transformation belonging to this category, although the converse is not true.

In cases of the other type, the combination of simultaneously occurring opposite transformations serves to maintain the *structure* of a system. The system contains one element which is undergoing a change and other elements which remain constant. As the change unfolds, the relations between the changing element and the constant elements are modified in such a way that the mutual relations between the constant elements are preserved intact.

Thus, if we think of somebody moving between New York and San Francisco, we recognize that the distance between the traveler and San Francisco decreases concomitantly as the distance between New

York and the traveler increases. The represented distance between New York and San Francisco can thus persist without modification.

As Piaget (1961) has pointed out with the support of his studies of visual illusions, this is not always the case with perception. If the inner of two concentric circles is expanded, the apparent distance between the circles is not diminished by the same amount, so that the circumference of the outer circle will appear to change.

In a transitive-group habit-family hierarchy, the simultaneous inverse operation that is so essential is a transformational response that is instigated without being evoked. If we begin with a stimulus situation, u_1, and if we pass by means of a transformational response, ϕ_x, to another situation, u_2, then the inverse of ϕ_x, that is, the response that leads from u_2 to u_1, will be one of the responses associated with u_2 and thus instigated whenever u_2 is encountered. And if thought follows a train that belongs to such a hierarchy, passing from u_2 to a sequence of other situations, there will always be an instigated response which would lead back to u_1, but this response will take different forms as the thinker passes from one represented situation to another.

This transformational response, which, even if not performed, is always available to lead back to the starting point, is likewise a key factor in the maintenance of the structure of the hierarchy. Because of it, the subject can always return to the starting point in one move, and the transformations that are capable of leading from this starting point to any other situation are not affected by the actual course of thinking.

The same applies to the relations between the situation that is being represented at the moment and any other stimulus situation belonging to the hierarchy. What corresponds to the relation between two situations is the transformational response that connects one with the other. As the relation between the represented situation, u_2, and the starting-point, u_1, changes, the relations between u_2 and all other situations undergo corresponding changes. Thanks to these changes, any situation belonging to the hierarchy is invariably accessible without delay, and the possibilities that are open thereafter are always the same.

Decentering

Perceptual and conceptual processes are, as Piaget has repeatedly stressed, highly susceptible to distortions due to "centering." The properties of objects, as perceived or symbolically represented, are apt to change with the position and condition of the subject in ways that impede adaptive behavior. Complete immunity from errors due to centering can never be achieved, but the gradual advance toward intellectual maturity, the ascent to higher and higher levels of "intelligence," consists in large part, as Piaget has shown, of a progressive adoption of devices for minimizing these errors.

The purest illustrations of centering come from study of perception (Piaget, 1961). They stem from the essential nonhomogeneity of the perceptual field. To concentrate on vision, the retina has an area of maximum discriminative power in the fovea and areas of minimal discriminative power in the periphery. In addition to these unevennesses, there are others due to selective attention. All these factors cause visual illusions to occur. Some of the more dramatic ones have been known for some time and intensively studied by psychologists. Others are not so striking but nevertheless pervade everyday perception. There is the "error of the standard" (Piaget and Lambercier, 1942–1943), which causes stimulus objects on which attention is fixed to be overestimated in size or intensity, and there are differences in clarity, of which everyone is aware.

Analogous forms of centering result from changes in the stimulus field due to locomotion. First, a child is apparently unable to distinguish movements of the objects that surround him from apparent movements of objects that remain stationary while he moves about. When a five-year-old child is shown a model of a mountain and asked to select a picture showing what the mountain would look like to somebody standing on the other side of it, he tends to select a picture of what he is now seeing (Piaget and Inhelder, 1948).

The errors characteristic of the stage of intuitive thinking, for example, the belief that a column of water increases in quantity when it is poured into a narrower vessel, represents centering on a symbolic plane. The child's judgment is based on one circumstance to which he is paying attention, namely the increase in height, while ignoring another equally relevant circumstance, namely the compensating decrease in width.

Social interaction is susceptible to a kind of centering about which Piaget had a great deal to say in his earlier writings (for example, 1923, 1925) under the term "egocentrism." He says (1962, p. 4):

Egocentrism . . . stems from a lack of differentiation between one's own point of view and the other possible ones . . . reactions such as jealousy, envy, vanity, which are doubtless universal, can certainly be considered various types of systematic error in the individual's emotional perspective. In the field of thinking, the whole history of science from geocentrism to the Copernican revolution, from the false absolutes of Aristotle's physics to the relativity of Galileo's principle of inertia and to Einstein's theory of relativity, shows that it has taken centuries to liberate us from the systematic errors, from the illusions caused by the immediate point of view as opposed to the "decentered" systematic thinking. And this liberation is far from complete.*

A young child cannot, for instance, engage in conversation effectively, because he cannot appreciate the effects of his speech on his interlocutor; he does not understand that facts familiar to himself may be unknown to the other person and require explanation or that what he says may be misunderstood (Piaget, 1923). If asked how many brothers his brother has, he is likely not to count himself, failing to realize that, from his brother's point of view, he himself is a brother (Piaget, 1925).

These various forms of centering have three disadvantages in particular. First, the information that is selected to occupy the limited channel capacity of the nervous system is taken predominantly from certain sectors of the stimulus field, perceptual or representational, whereas (as we pointed out in Chapter 2) the information that is needed to bring the actual response into line with the optimal response is usually dispersed, so that proper selection requires abstraction rather than merely selective attention. Second, precious channel capacity is taken up by information about the subject's momentary condition and location that is irrelevant, that is, that does not help in identifying the optimal response. It is true that adaptive action requires us to take account of certain facts about our condition and location, for example, about our motivational condition, our posture, and our distance and direction from biologically important objects. But much of the information that reflects (that is, varies with) our receptor-adjusting responses and our locomotion will lead us astray in our search for effective courses of action. Similarly, if our behavior transmits too much information from (that is, is unduly influenced by) our own vanity and selfish desires, we shall be deflected from the pursuit of socially optimal behavior. Third, the changes due to successive centerings produce inconsistencies of judgment and appearance, and these will disturb a nervous system that can preserve incoming in-

---

* Reprinted from *Comments on Vygotski's Thought and Language* by J. Piaget, by permission of The Massachusetts Institute of Technology Press. Copyright 1962 by The Massachusetts Institute of Technology.

formation long enough for outcomes of successive centerings to be compared.

The only way to overcome these deficiencies is to collate the information received from a number of different centerings. This is what Piaget calls "decentering." It makes a more "objective" view of the world possible. The child learns to withhold judgment until he has let his gaze roam over all portions of an object. He may walk around the object until he has seen what it looks like from a representative variety of angles. The effectiveness of these "perceptual activities" is augmented by the ability to retain traces of what was seen a few moments ago from a different point of view and to anticipate the view that will result from a change in fixation or locomotion before the change in fixation or locomotion is actually executed.

As we have noted, Poincaré held that the ability to distinguish one's own movements in space from movements of other objects depends on the recognition that we can always undo apparent movements in external objects that are due to our own locomotion by walking back to the starting place. After sufficient experience, we can simply anticipate this undoing without having to walk back in reality, and this anticipation helps us to view ourselves as one object among the many that people the world, all of which are capable of moving independently in their common space.

Egocentrism is shaken by clashes between one's own judgments and those expressed by other people. As Piaget (1925) puts it:

What then gives rise to the need for verification? Surely it must be the shock of our thought coming into contact with that of others, which produces doubt and the desire to prove.

Social and moral development is not complete until an individual sees himself as a member of a community of equals, with reciprocal rights and duties, realizing that others are affected by his actions in the same way as he is affected by theirs. He concedes that his interests are no more or less important than those of another individual, both being subordinate to the shared interests of the community. This cannot come about until he has acquired the ability to "put himself in somebody else's shoes," that is, to represent to himself how things look and feel from another individual's point of view. Signs of the ability to do this appear once the stage of concrete operations has been entered. After reaching the age of seven or eight, a child is able to regard rules of games or moral rules as conventions voluntarily accepted by members of a group in order to facilitate social interaction and prevent unfairness, rather than as absolute imperatives laid down by adult or supernatural authorities. "Egocentric speech," during which "he does not bother to know to whom he is speaking nor whether he is being listened to. . . . chiefly because he does not attempt to place himself at the point of view of his hearer" (Piaget, 1923) is abandoned or internalized (Vygotski, 1956). He indulges instead in genuine conversation or discussion, "which consists principally in knowing how to place one's self at the point of view of one's partner in order to convince him on his own ground" (Piaget, 1962).

He becomes susceptible to such feelings as gratitude (Piaget, 1953–1954); being uncomfortable at the thought that somebody has done him an unreciprocated favor, he is anxious to restore the balance by conferring some benefit on his benefactor; he no longer behaves like a spoiled child or despotic monarch who feels that his unique importance entitles him to the services with which he is showered.

Decentering is thus a product of transformational thinking. It means using transformational responses to arrive at a representation of what would be perceived from a point of view that the subject himself might occupy at another time or that another individual might be occupying now. The subject must also keep track of the relations between a location and condition that is being contemplated and the subject's present location and condition. This is done with the help of transformations that lead from the latter to the former and whose form therefore corresponds to the relation between the two.

But to have an objective view of the world or of some part of it means more than to be able to consider it from a number of points of view in turn. The limitations of centering can be fully overcome only if the selection of a response is determined by an "all-round view," that is, a conception that contains items of information accessible from a number of different points of view at once. We are thus led to much the same conclusions as we reached in our earlier discussion of equilibrium.

In developing his theory of perception, Taylor (1962) argues that any stimulus field must contain a vast number of stimulus conditions associated with different responses. Only a few of these responses, at most, can be performed, but, Taylor holds, the "engrams corresponding to all of them are activated." By an "engram" he means (p. 38) a "neural link . . . connecting the cortical termini of the afferent processes with the relevant motor centers." "The activation of an engram," he writes (p. 340), "puts the subject into a state of readiness for the appropriate response." It is "identical with an element of perception" and "with knowledge that the object has such-and-such a property." Perception of spatial relations, for example, involves holding in readiness the bodily movements that would be required to make contact with any object that is at present perceptible. Extending Taylor's conception, we are assuming that whenever our intellectual powers are brought to bear on a stimulus pattern, whether physically present or contemplated in thought, the transformational responses that could start out from that pattern are all simultaneously instigated. The information contents of the situational thoughts to which they would all lead are thus simultaneously made available to be taken into account in the selection of the motor response.

Once again, we can see how the special properties of transitive-group hierarchies, and particularly the fact that the same range of situational thoughts can be reached immediately from any situation belonging to the hierarchy, ensure stability and consistency.

Transitive-Group versus Tree Hierarchies

The habit-family hierarchies with transitive-group structure that have been discussed in this chapter will, of course, be distinct from the compound habit-family hierarchies with tree structure that were discussed in the last chapter. Tree hierarchies of the searching variety will represent the frontier regions of knowledge. They will, we may suppose, be the prime instruments of productive thinking, although they will also have some part to play in reproductive thinking. Transitive-group hierarchies, on the other hand, will represent the most highly developed settlements of knowledge—those organized around the most advanced logical or mathematical models. They will bear the brunt of reproductive thinking when productive thinking and other epistemic activities have reached their utmost limits of penetration. Tree hierarchies of the coordinating variety and other compound hierarchies, with structures depending on the factual contents of particular areas of knowledge, will occupy intermediate positions and contribute to both productive and reproductive thinking.

Chapter 9

The motivation of directed thinking:

conceptual conflict

ONE THING that sharply distinguishes the psychologists of today from
their predecessors of 50 or more years ago, apart from a few pioneers
like Freud and McDougall, is their interest in motivational questions.
Many of those who shun words like "motivation" and "motivational"
are nevertheless concerned with problems that fall within the domains
to which others would apply these words. There is, however, considerable divergence among ways of demarcating and analyzing the
phenomena that are to be classed as "motivational."

For many English-speaking psychologists, problems of motivation
center round the concept of "drive," but the word "drive" has
vastly different connotations for different individuals. At one extreme, Thorpe (1956) defines "drive" as "the complex of internal
and external states and stimuli leading to a given behavior." This
definition appears to cover everything that could incline an organism
toward one response rather than another. At the other extreme,
Brown (1961) favors reserving the word "drive" for a "broadly acting,
nondirective factor" with a "capacity to facilitate all behavior." He
feels that it should not be applied to factors that strengthen particular
patterns of behavior selectively. Most writers who use the word
give it a connotation somewhat broader than Brown's and narrower
than Thorpe's, although there is no unanimity. Some prefer other
words like "need" or "motive." Russian writers use Ukhtomski's noun
"dominant" or Pavlov's expression "difficult condition" to express similar notions. Still other writers have attempted to remodel the whole
approach to motivational problems by conceptualizing them in radically different ways, while some have sought to thread their way among
these same problems without becoming entangled in them. Be that
as it may, most modern psychologists would feel that no psychology

with an aspiration to completeness can afford to ignore the questions that underlie the term "motivation," whatever the terminology in which they are discussed.

The phenomena that are generally regarded as "motivational"—the ones in whose investigation concepts like "drive" are meant to help—fall into three classes:

1. ACTIVATION. In the early days of motivation theory, motivational factors were considered necessary to start an organism acting. One widely held view, put forward by Freud (1915) and echoed by Miller and Dollard (1941), depicted an organism that remained quiescent until animated by stimulation, whether external or internal in origin. Its behavior was aimed at terminating the stimulation and restoring quiescence as quickly as possible. In his book *Organization of Behavior* (1949), Hebb pointed out that higher animal organisms do not need motivating stimulation to make them active. Unless they are fatigued, asleep, or ill, they are rarely immobile for more than a moment. Harlow (1959) has criticized theoretical treatments of phenomena like discrimination learning that start out by asking what makes an animal respond. Higher animals such as the monkey will, he reminds us, invariably do something when a stimulus object makes its appearance. Discrimination learning is mainly a matter of eliminating incorrect responses so that the correct response can have a free run. As the EEG shows, there is continuous electrical activity in the central nervous system, except in such abnormal conditions as extremely low body temperature.

Nevertheless, even though animals are always active, they are not always active to the same degree. And, even if it is unnecessary to look for factors that initiate activity, we must still identify factors that make an organism more or less active, as Hebb acknowledged, under the influence of more recent psychophysiological research, in an article published a few years later (1955). So there is a place for a concept of "drive" as a variable with a general energizing function, such as Hull (1943) assigned to his "*D*." The way in which the closely related concept of "arousal" or "activation" has arisen out of recent psychophysiological and neurophysiological research (see Berlyne, 1960a, 1963; Duffy, 1962; and Malmo, 1957, 1959) provides further arguments for the usefulness of such a concept.

Drive, then, is conceived as a variable whose value can be raised by a variety of internal and external factors. Its fluctuations are reflected in varying ways according to circumstances. In situations where there is one predominant unlearned or learned response, an increase in drive means an increase in the strength of that response, as shown by such measures as probability, resistance to extinction, and amplitude. When there are a number of responses of about equal strength in competition, an increase in drive means an increase in the time taken for an effective response to come to the fore and an increase in stress and disruption of behavior. When there are no pre-potent responses, as with a newborn animal in most situations or an adult animal that finds himself in an unprecedented situation, an increase in drive means an increase in restlessness and random activity.

Sometimes, a condition that is recognized as drive-heightening may lead to reduced mobility rather than to a rise in overt bodily movements. This frequently happens when an animal is in pain or frightened (for example, Brown and Jacobs, 1949). Inordinately strong motivation of any kind can sometimes leave a subject paralyzed or dazed, possibly through the effects of conflict between responses or through what Pavlov called "supramaximal inhibition." For these reasons, among others, more attention is currently being paid to less overt indices of level of arousal or activation, such as skeletal muscular tension, EEG desynchronization, and the various effects of auto-nomic innervation. These are held to indicate the degree to which the organism is alerted or mobilized and the rate at which it is ex-pending energy, regardless of how far the energy is contributing to effective, coordinated bodily activity.

2. DIRECTION. Since behavior depends jointly on the nature of ex-ternal stimulation and on the condition of the organism and since, as Hebb (1949) has pointed out, behavior becomes more and more au-tonomous and less dependent on the external environment as we as-cend the evolutionary scale, there is a need to consider the internal variables that play a part in the selection of the response and how their values are determined.

There are, however, several kinds of internal directive factor at work in higher mammals, including implicit symbolic responses. It is therefore incumbent on us to seek criteria by which those that are to be described as "motivational" or as forms of "drive" (although some writers, for example Brown, object to this usage) can be dis-tinguished.

On the one hand, a motivational condition is thought of as a condition that inclines the organism toward a broad class of behavior, often as-sociated with a particular biological need. Structures and processes controlling such broad classes of behavior have been identified in the central nervous system, for example, in the hypothalamus and the limbic system. They may also exist in the brain-stem reticular formation (Anokhin, 1959). Another way of looking at the matter is to remember that any pattern of cues, whether external or internal, must be associated with a number of alternative responses, so that it leaves considerable residual uncertainty regarding what the organism will do. Directive motivational factors are factors that remove the uncertainty left by such a stimulus pattern and determine which of the several responses instigated by it shall actually be performed.

3. REINFORCEMENT. At least some learned responses, namely, those that are known as "operants" or "instrumental conditioned responses," are reinforced by events closely following them, which are therefore classified as "rewards." One desideratum for a psychological theory is thus an account of the conditions that determine whether a certain event will function as a reward and, if so, how effectively. It is a matter of ascertaining what rewards have in common to give them the power of reinforcing responses that they all share.

Questions that relate to the functioning of rewards are coupled with other motivational questions for a number of reasons. One is that whether a particular event will act as a reward, and how potent its reinforcing effect will be, often depend on internal conditions. In particular, rewards often consist of termination or alleviation of so-called "aversive" conditions. Whether all rewarding agents work by reducing drive or removing aversive conditions is, however, still an open question. It is also far from established whether all states in which drive is high, as judged by energizing and directive effects, are also aversive states. There seem to be some conditions, for example, pleasant emotions, sexual excitement, and perhaps mild hunger, that possess the energizing and directive hallmarks of heightened drive without always prompting efforts to escape from them or avoid them.

As well as being strengthened when closely followed by rewards, responses are often, but not invariably, weakened when closely followed by punishment. According to some usages, punishing agents are called "negative reinforcers." Some theorists have held that punishment exerts its inhibiting effects indirectly through reward: an incompatible response is reinforced by cessation of pain or fear. Anyhow, questions regarding the adverse influence of noxious events on response strength are generally also counted as motivational.

Motivational Problems Specific to Directed Thinking

The motivational problems that concern directed thinking are essentially those that confront behavior in general, although the peculiarities of symbolic behavior introduce some specialized forms of them. In general, anyone who inquires into the motivation of directed thinking must, among other things, seek factors that determine when a bout of directed thinking will start, what course the thinking will take, and when it will come to an end.

A thinking process can come to either of two kinds of end, namely successful and unsuccessful. Sometimes, it terminates because the subject has reached a symbolic pattern that he accepts as a solution. So the theory of motivational aspects of thinking must include some explanation of how a subject recognizes when he has found what he was seeking. At other times, a thinking process is cut short before it has reached its goal, because the subject is discouraged or because he judges that the chances of success are too small to warrant his continuing. The process undergoes, in other words, some kind of inhibition akin to extinction. At yet other times, a bout of thinking ceases because something, either external or internal, occurs to distract the subject or to impose the overriding claim of some other activity (for example, thinking about some other topic) that precludes the continuation of the thinking that is already going on. These last two cases are, however, closely related; the probability that a thinking process will give way to some competing activity must depend on the relative strength of factors (for example, hopes of a successful conclusion within a reasonable time) supporting persistence with it and factors favoring engagement in activities that are incompatible with it. The variables that we cover when we speak of the "motivation of thinking" must therefore include those that determine how resistant to extinction or distraction a thought process will be.

We can now take each of the three main groups of motivational problems in turn and see what special subproblems emerge when they are considered with reference to directed thinking.

1. ACTIVATION. Intensity of thinking possesses a proverbial negative relation with bodily activity. The thinker, as portrayed, for example, by Michelangelo or Rodin, sits frozen in one posture, oblivious to the world around. Immobility is, in fact, so unusual in higher animals that we are apt to attribute deep reflection to anybody who, while obviously not asleep, remains motionless for more than a few seconds. Fixity of posture makes even infants and domestic animals appear to be "immersed in thought."

So degree of overt motor activity can scarcely serve as an index of intensity of involvement or of drive level during thinking. On the other hand, directed thinking can certainly be carried on with more or less effort, concentration, and force. It seems likely, although this remains to be demonstrated, that the degree to which these are present will be related to the persistence with which the subject carries out the thinking process and to his ability to ward off distraction and discouragement. Presumably, the various covert indices of arousal will have varying values in the course of thinking and will supply useful and valid information about the extent to which the subject's energies are committed.

2. DIRECTION. The need to seek motivational factors to account for selection among alternative kinds of symbolic material arises at several different levels. We must identify the internal conditions that determine whether the subject will engage in thinking about a particular matter in a particular external stimulus situation. If he does so, thinking has been selected among many mutually exclusive activities that the situation might have evoked, and the topic has been selected among the many topics to which thinking might have been devoted.

At the opposite pole from this high-level selection of behavior, motivational conditions must play a part in the evocation of specific symbolic responses. In the simplest forms of behavior, the external stimulus pattern bears the chief onus of selecting the response. In other words, a higher proportion of the information inherent in the response is traceable to the external stimulus pattern than to any other source. In thinking and other behavior that depends to a major extent on internal symbolic stimuli, the equivalent role devolves on the symbolic stimulus, which is, of course, defined by its function as a substitute. In either case, the principal determinant, whether it be an external or an internal stimulus pattern, generally leaves appreciable residual uncertainty concerning which response will actually occur since, even when the range of possibilities is narrowed down to responses that are associated with it, there will almost always be many of them. So in thinking, as in nonsymbolic behavior, motivational conditions must provide the final quota of information needed for response selection and decide which of the instigated responses will prevail. The mechanisms responsible for this fine-grain direction of thinking have already been discussed in Chapter 5. So here, we may content ourselves with noting their place among the various motivational aspects of thinking.

Between these two extremes, there are many other levels at which choice-points succeed one another and thinking could go off in any of a number of directions. Factors that we recognize as "motivational" must arbitrate among the divergent routes.

Finally, the choice between continuing with the thought process on hand, thinking about something quite different, or abandoning thinking for some nonsymbolic activity exists at all stages and not only at the beginning of the thought process. Here again, motivational factors must have a primary say in determining which of these occurs at any time.

3. REINFORCEMENT. The achievement of a symbolic sequence or pattern that the subject regards as a successful conclusion of the thinking process is clearly analogous to the attainment of a reinforcing state of affairs or a goal situation in motor learning. When the subject feels that he has arrived at a solution, the particular piece of thinking in which he was engaged ceases and gives way to some other activity. The final product of the process, the solution, is retained and is likely to come promptly to the fore when the subject finds himself faced with a similar situation in future. The reinforcement-gradient principle and the anticipatory-response mechanism ensure that the end product will come up immediately next time and that the intermediate steps that led up to its initial appearance will be omitted.

The achievement of a solution must thus be followed by a rewarding condition. This condition is likely not only to reinforce the particular pattern of symbolic responses that immediately preceded it but also to reinforce the more general modes of symbolic behavior, such as lines of thought or strategies of thinking, that led to this satisfactory result. It will make the subject a little more likely to try them in preference to others in subsequent spells of thinking. We must therefore inquire into the nature of this reinforcing condition and ask how it might be related to the conditions that supply reinforcement for instrumental learning in general.

These then are the principal motivational problems of directed thinking. They have, for the most part, been lamentably neglected throughout the history of experimental work on thought processes, largely because traditional experimental techniques have bypassed them. Subjects have invariably been presented with problems to think about and instructed to start thinking. Almost always, they do their best to comply. In this way, the conditions that determine when human beings embark on thinking in everyday life and explain why they think about one matter rather than another have been obscured. Subjects have sometimes been left free to decide of their own accord when they have solved their problems. Occasionally, they have been permitted to give up the search for a solution at any time if they felt it to be hopeless. Most often, however, experimenters have arbitrarily set limits to the time available for the thought process and stopped subjects when it has run out. They and not the subjects generally decide whether the subject's solutions are correct. Their decision, as in many concept-formation experiments, may be highly arbitrary. In some situations (for example, when subjects are required to think aloud, to answer specific questions one after another, or to report on their progress at specified stages), the experimenter decides at each point whether they have completed their thinking or whether they have more to do. The choice among alternative lines of thought between the beginning and the conclusion of a thought process is about the only aspect of the process that natural motivational factors are left free to influence. This is virtually the only part of their functioning that has received much study, although not always under the heading of "motivation."

The specular advances due to computer simulation have only encouraged this neglect of motivational questions. Computers have to be given some means of deciding when they have completed the task assigned to them, since their high speed of operation precludes their reporting back at intervals to a human taskmaster. They are likewise left to their own devices, or to the devices inherent in their programs, when it comes to choosing a direction to take at points where there are alternatives. When a computer starts to attack a problem and which problem it attacks are matters over which it exercises no discretion at all. Its assignments are imposed on it by its human associates, and this is one glaring respect in which computer simulation of human thinking has thus far been deficient. It is, no doubt, merely a temporary deficiency. The time will certainly come when computers will formulate their own problems and identify the ones on which their time can most profitably be spent.

When we come to ask what motivational conditions can influence directed thinking and perform the various functions that fall to the lot of motivational factors, it is clear that most of the sources of motivation that are familiar from other areas of psychology may have a part to play. Thinking can certainly be initiated and guided by hunger, fear of pain, desire for wealth, and social ambition. But might there not be certain sources of motivation that possess particularly close ties with thinking and are at work in conjunction with these other factors, even when their influence is prominent? Perhaps the best way of starting the search for an answer to this question is to consider the kind of nonsymbolic behavior that comes closest to epistemic behavior, of which directed thinking is one form. The nonsymbolic behavior in question is exploratory behavior, at least some varieties of which, like epistemic behavior, have the acquisition of information as their principal function. The chief difference between the two (and they often overlap in human life) is that the information that becomes available as a result of exploration is embodied for the most part in external stimulus patterns and not in stored symbolic structures. Let us therefore recall briefly what recent research (reviewed in Berlyne, 1960a, 1963) has revealed about the motivation of exploratory behavior.

The Motivation of Exploratory Behavior

Although there has been steadily increasing interest in exploratory behavior in both Western and East European countries since about 1950, the term has been used with reference to a highly variegated assortment of phenomena. We shall, no doubt, have to await the results of many more years of research before we shall be in a position to identify the essential subdivisions within this somewhat adventitiously marked out class of behavior. There is, however, one important distinction that was overlooked in much of the past literature but is clearly one that should be recognized from the start. This is the distinction between specific and diversive exploration.

Specific exploration is behavior aimed at, and reinforced by, the prolongation or intensification of stimulation from particular sources. It is exemplified by the behavior of an animal that sees something novel in the distance and advances to give it a close examination, or by that of a man who turns his head and moves his eyes to fixate somebody who addresses him. The indications are that specific exploration is occasioned by an aversive condition of a kind that may be called "perceptual curiosity." This condition is brought on by incomplete perception of a sector of the stimulus field, which leaves the subject with some uncertainty regarding its characteristics. The exploratory responses afford access to additional information, which reduces the uncertainty and thus relieves the perceptual curiosity.

Diversive exploration, on the other hand, has the function of introducing stimulation from any source that is "interesting" or "entertaining." It is exemplified by the various activities through which human beings seek "amusement," "diversion," or "aesthetic experience," as well by the behavior of a rat that presses a bar to produce a momentary change in illumination or that of a monkey that opens a door to see what is going on outside the box in which he is confined. Whenever the external environment is inordinately dull or monotonous, diversive exploration is likely to occur, and other activities are likely to take on a form that couples a diversive function with their other functions. Diversive behavior seems to be especially strong when an animal has spent some time in dull surroundings, in which case we may speak of an aversive condition of "boredom." Diversive exploration, like specific exploration, can evidently be reinforced by the stimulation that results from it, and relief of boredom may be one factor contributing to its reward value.

Whenever a stimulation coming from a particular source is introduced, intensified, or prolonged, there is an increment in the subject's intake of information from that source. Both kinds of exploratory behavior are strongly affected by the informational properties of the stimulation to which they give rise, although other stimulus properties may play their part also, especially in the case of diversive exploration. But there is an important difference in that specific exploration is prompted by a condition arising from uncertainty about a specific environmental object. Consequently, specific exploration can be reinforced only by information that is capable of reducing that uncertainty, that is, information coming from the object to which the uncertainty relates. Stimulation coming from elsewhere will be of no avail, whatever its information content. So *specific* exploration is clearly akin to *directed* thinking, which is likewise initiated by concern with a specific topic and is not successfully concluded until a symbolic formula that can eliminate specific uncertainties has been reached. *Diversive* exploration is apparently more closely related to *autistic* thinking.

Collative Variables

The probability and direction of specific exploratory responses can apparently be influenced by many properties of external stimulation, as well as by many intraorganismic variables. They can, no doubt, be influenced by stimulus intensity, color, pitch, and association with biological gratification and punishment, although these are likely to bulk larger in the regulation of diversive exploration. The paramount determinants of specific exploration are, however, a group of stimulus properties to which we commonly refer by such words as "novelty," "change," "surprisingness," "incongruity," "complexity," "ambiguity," and "indistinctness." Some of these words cover a number of logically separable variables. In any case, there is a great deal of overlap and a great deal of empirical correlation among the properties that they denote. Nevertheless, there are two things about them that are worth noting.

The first is that these properties possess close links with the concepts of information theory, and they can, in fact, all be discussed in information-theoretic terminology. In the case of "ambiguity" and "indistinctness," there is uncertainty due to a gap in available information. In some forms of "novelty" and "complexity," there is uncertainty about how a pattern should be categorized, that is, what labeling responses should be attached to it and what overt response is appropriate to it. When one portion of a "complex" pattern or of a sequence of "novel" stimuli is perceived, there is uncertainty about what will be perceived next. In the case of "surprisingness" and "incongruity," there is discrepancy between information embodied in expectations and information embodied in what is perceived. For these reasons, the term "collative" is proposed as an epithet to denote all these stimulus properties collectively, since they all depend on collation or comparison of information from different stimulus elements, whether they be elements belonging to the present and the past or elements that are simultaneously present in different parts of one stimulus field.

It should be pointed out that the uncertainty we are discussing here is "subjective uncertainty," which is a function of subjective probabilities, analogous to the "objective" uncertainty (that is, the standard information-theoretic concept of uncertainty) that is a function of objective probabilities.

The second, and perhaps even more noteworthy, peculiarity of collative stimulus properties is that they can all be argued to entail conflict. By conflict, we mean the simultaneous instigation of incompatible responses. It can be said to occur whenever we have stimulus conditions that are associated with incompatible responses. This means that, although conflict is conceived as a condition of the organism, its nature must be deduced from a knowledge of what stimuli are acting on the organism and of the kinds of behavior that these stimuli evoke when they occur singly.

When a subject is beset by discrepant items of information, responses corresponding to each of them will presumably be instigated, but these responses must necessarily compete with one another. A subject is placed in a condition of uncertainty whenever he is exposed to a situation that might, in the light of previous experience, be followed by any of a number of mutually exclusive stimulus events, each having its probability. In such circumstances, mutually incompatible responses, corresponding to these possible impending stimulus events, must be held in readiness. When a subject has a high level of conflict owing to collative properties of his external environment, there will be a high degree of (objective) uncertainty about which of the instigated responses will actually be performed.

In passing, it should be noted that the motivational effects of collative stimulus properties are not confined to initiation and direction of exploratory behavior. They have a great deal to do also with the conditions controlling fear, creation of, and response to, humor, and creation of, and response to, works of art (Berlyne, 1960a). The far-reaching influences that they may exercise over child development, socal interaction and behavior abnormality, as well as over evaluative processes in general, are gradually coming to light (Berlyne, 1963).

It will be realized that conflict, thus conceived, is not something that the subject is either in or not in. He will always have some degree of conflict, at least while he is awake. He will invariably be surrounded by stimulus objects each of which is associated with at least one response, verbal, locomotor, or manual, and he will not be able to perform all these responses at once. But the degree of conflict will vary from moment to moment. Most of the time, it will be quite moderate, but there are times when it will be intense.

Our conception of conflict is closely related to uncertainty, the central concept of information theory, as we can see in a number of ways. For one thing, situations in which characteristics of behavior have turned out to be simple functions of information-theoretic variables (Attneave, 1959; Garner, 1962; and Luce, 1960), for example, situations involving choice reaction time, discrimination, concept formation, and remembering, are ones in which conflict must be playing a major role. Second, degree of conflict will, all things being equal, be positively related to uncertainty about how the subject will behave. But with uncertainty constant, conflict may still vary, since uncertainty reflects only probabilities, and therefore relative strengths, of alternative responses, whereas conflict must depend also on absolute strengths.

Alternative Views

At this point, it will be as well to compare the hypothesis that the special motivational effects of collative stimulus properties depend primarily on conflict with alternative views that other writers concerned with similar problems have offered.

1. DISPARITY.   Some writers attribute special motivational effects to some kind of disparity between the nature of incoming stimulation and the kind of stimulation for which the organism is prepared (for example, Anokhin, 1955; Hebb, 1949; McClelland et al., 1953; and Sokolov, 1963). What the organism is prepared to receive—the "anticipatory excitation," "expectation," "adaptation level," or "nervous

model"—may depend on its motivational condition, on what it has been experiencing in the immediate past, or on what has, in its previous history, followed what it is now experiencing. Processes indicative of a smoothly functioning nervous system are supposed to be set off when what the organism expects or wants and what it receives coincide. When they fail to tally, other processes, indicative of disturbance, take place.

This view is more restrictive in scope than the conflict hypothesis; being therefore less audacious, it might be thought to have a better chance of being correct. Nevertheless, we have two reasons for preferring the conflict hypothesis at the present stage of inquiry.

◥ (a) The notion of disparity may fit variables like novelty, surprisingness, incongruity, and frustration very well, but it does not seem so potentially useful for the treatment of complexity or ambiguity or indistinctness.

(b) Disparity is a relation that holds between two entities. The discrepancy figuring in the hypothesis that we are now considering exists between a kind of stimulation that is represented centrally and a kind that the sense organs are receiving. But we need also to have some way of including situations in which this inharmonious relation can exist between three or more processes, central or environmental. There can, we may presume, be conflict among any number of competing responses, just as uncertainty can arise from situations in which more than two alternative events are possible. As we shall see, conflict among a large number of competing processes is particularly likely in the course of directed thinking.

2. INCONSISTENCY. The second sort of hypothesis lays the onus on inconsistency between available items of information, whether contained in sensory inputs or stored in symbolic structures. Inconsistency is a different matter from disparity (that is, physical dissimilarity between anticipated and received stimulation), since signals of differing physical form can have either consistent (that is, overlapping or unrelated) or inconsistent (that is, mutually contradictory) information contents.

Discomforts due to disagreements between simultaneously held beliefs or evaluations have been prominent in recent social psychology (Abelson and Rosenberg, 1958; Festinger, 1957; Heider, 1946; and Osgood and Tannenbaum, 1955). Hunt (1963) has specified "incongruity" as the characteristic of sensory inputs that has most to do with the occurrence of exploratory and related behavior. According to McReynolds (1956), exploration or anxiety may be induced by "unassimilated percepts." "By *assimilation*," he explains, "I mean that process whereby percepts enter meaningfully and harmoniously into systematic conjunction with other percepts."

There is plenty of evidence that inconsistency between items of incoming information or between items of information summoned from storage can be disturbing and provoke remedial measures. We shall, however, adopt the admittedly speculative position that inconsistent inputs or thoughts are disturbing because they tend to cause incompatibility between outputs or motor responses, that is, conflict. This speculation is offered in an attempt to answer the following three questions, which inconsistency hypotheses leave unanswered.

(a) How has the subject learned to recognize which inputs or items of information are inconsistent with one another?

(b) From a biological point of view, why should such inconsistencies be so disturbing?

(c) Since mutually inconsistent items of information can have widely varying content, their neural correlates must confront one another in widely scattered points in the brain. Yet there must be one neural structure through which their common motivational effects are ultimately channeled. How can mobilization notices be delivered to this structure from such a diversity of locations?

In response to these questions, we should first recall that the brain is originally and ultimately, as Sperry (1952) reminds us, a device for selecting motor processes. It is suggested, accordingly, that the organism learns to recognize certain configurations of information as inconsistent, and to react to them as threats, because of their association with interresponse conflict, which, in its turn, jeopardizes the organism's ability to react effectively. For a tentative explanation of how disparate events meeting in different parts of the cerebral cortex could lead to a common motivational discharge, we shall have to wait until we have discussed the relations between collative variables and arousal.

3. STIMULUS CHANGE. Last, we must consider efforts to reduce all collative properties to stimulus change (Dember and Earl, 1957; Earl, 1961; and Musselman, 1963). According to this view, novelty is "temporal change" and complexity is "spatial change." The two are regarded as equivalent on the grounds that "spatial change implies some sort of scanning process . . . the scanning of a spatially heterogeneous stimulus is equivalent to movement by the stimulus, over time, past the 'stationary' individual" (Dember and Earl, 1957). Andrew

(1963, in press) singles out "stimulus contrast" as a condition that evokes attentive responses, defensive responses giving rise to facial expressions, vocalization in animals, and laughter in human beings. "Stimuli may have this characteristic," he writes, "because they contrast with background stimulation (for example, a sudden sound or a moving object)" (1963, p. 6). He applies the term "stimulus contrast" also to "certain patterns of stimulation, which depart from normal or sought after stimulation . . . (for example, cold surroundings or absence of the imprinting object in chicks)," as well as to stimuli that are readily perceived and stand out "because the animal is looking for them" (for example, stimuli preceding food delivery when chicks have been deprived of food for some time). Of these three conditions, only the first is, of course, relevant to the stimulus-change hypothesis. The second is an instance of what we have called "disparity," while the third is not primarily a collative condition at all.

Stimulus-change hypotheses seem inadequate for the following reasons:

(a) The assumption, made by Dember and Earl, that perception of a multipartite stimulus pattern requires scanning (that is, perception of elements in turn, so that differences between elements are experienced as changes) is certainly valid in some instances. Its universal validity is, however, far from established. The nervous system may well be able to compare properties of different sectors of the stimulus field simultaneously without having to register them one by one.

(b) Collative properties depend not only on the degree of difference between stimulus elements but also on the condition of the organism. Dember and Earl acknowledge this in postulating that an animal will, if offered a choice, expose himself to something a little more complex than what he has recently been experiencing. But other internal conditions must play some part also. Response to surprisingness or incongruity depends on the kinds of previous learning that build up expectations (other than the expectation that what has just been experienced will be repeated) that may be contradicted. Other kinds of learning yield the ability to recognize inconsistencies that are not correlated with differences in physicochemical nature. Still other kinds may reduce complexity by causing elements to be grouped into meaningful subunits.

(c) Stimulus change occurs when adjacent stimulus elements are different. Novelty and complexity can, however, arise out of relations between temporally or spatially separated elements. How novel something is is not simply a matter of how it compares with what immediately preceded it; it may be rather dependent on whether similar stimuli have been encountered at any time during the last hour or during the whole previous life history. How complex it is may depend on the number and heterogeneity of widely scattered elements. For example, a pattern composed of ABC is more complex than one composed of ABA. Yet the total amount of change from A to B and then from B to C need not exceed the total amount of change from A to B and then from B to A.

Dember and Earl recognize, it is true, that a difference between two stimulus patterns that do not occur in immediate succession but are separated by a temporal interval may be effective. They cite, for example, an experiment in which a rat is taken out of a maze and put back into it a few minutes later to find that an arm that had been black before is now white or vice versa. If "stimulus change" is conceived in this broad manner, then the stimulus-change hypothesis turns into a version of the discrepancy hypothesis.

To sum up, then, the disparity, inconsistency, and stimulus-change hypotheses seem each to cover some of the collative conditions that are motivationally important, while leaving others out of account. The conflict hypothesis concedes that the factors to which all these hypotheses have drawn attention must play significant parts. It proposes, however, an answer to the question of what all the collative factors have in common, and it offers speculations on how these factors acquire their motivational effects.*

Arousal

A substantial body of experimentation, most of which has gone on in the U.S.S.R., although some of it has been done by Western investigators, has demonstrated that at least some forms of exploratory behavior coincide with a complex of psychophysiological changes collectively known as the "orientation reaction." They include EEG desynchronization, vegetative changes associated with activity of the

---

* For the sake of completeness, it should be mentioned that, whereas most, if not all, instances of novelty affecting human adults can be argued to involve conflict, "absolutely novel" forms of stimulation (see Berlyne, 1960a, p. 19), such as human infants or lower animals might encounter, may be exceptions. They are likely to owe their disturbing effects to the fact that the subject has not yet had time to become accustomed to them, so that the prolonged or repeated exposure to them that results from exploratory behavior may have the function of relieving the disturbance through simple habituation.

sympathetic nervous system, increases in skeletal muscular tension, and processes in sense organs that make for improved sensitivity. These processes coincide remarkably with those that have been shown to accompany activation of the brain-stem reticular formation and with recognized indices of heightened "arousal" or "activation." The level of arousal is a variable representing how "alert," "mobilized," or "wide-awake" the organism is, and its value appears to depend principally on interaction between the reticular formation and the cerebral cortex.

It may be concluded, therefore, that exploratory behavior is commonly accompanied by increased arousal, as evidenced by the component processes of the orientation reaction. One of my experiments (Berlyne, 1961) has shown the magnitude of one of these processes, namely the GSR, to increase with degree of conflict. Conflict, it will be recalled, is what we have assumed to be the essential factor behind the motivational effects of collative variables. Experimental data have also shown specific collative variables (that is, novelty, surprisingness, complexity, and incongruity) to affect the incidence and magnitude of the GSR (Berlyne, 1961; Berlyne, Craw, Salapatek, and Lewis, 1963) and the incidence and duration of EEG alpha blocking (Berlyne, 1960a, Ch. 7; Berlyne and McDonnell, in press).

The comparatively new concept of arousal has obviously much in common with the long established concept of "drive." It certainly seems to be associated with general activating or energizing effects like those that have been held to characterize drive. As far as the roles of drive in direction of behavior and in reinforcement are concerned, there are indications that arousal may exist in a variety of forms, mobilizing activities that correspond to different motivational conditions, and that high arousal may act as an aversive state whose alleviation can be rewarding (Berlyne, 1963).

Drive increases when an organism is subjected to a physiological disturbance, such as those accompanying hunger, thirst, and sexual excitement, or to noxious external agents. It can also be raised by stimuli, external or internal, that have been regularly paired with such disturbances. These motivating conditions, which involve organs other than the sense organs and the nervous system, may be called "sources of extrinsic motivation." They can undoubtedly actuate exploratory or epistemic behavior, as when a person seeks information for the solution of a practical problem or for the social status that erudition will bring him. There are, however, other, "intrinsic" forms of motivation which collaborate with extrinsic motivation in regulating exploratory or epistemic activity but are also capable of actuating exploratory or epistemic activity on their own. Intrinsic motivation depends primarily on the collative properties of the external environment.

When drive or arousal is driven upward by an encounter with an exceptionally novel, surprising, complex, or puzzling stimulus pattern, exploratory behavior is likely to supervene, and the intensification of stimulation and accrual of information that result serve to bring the drive or arousal down again. This reduction in drive (perceptual curiosity) may provide reinforcement facilitating the retention of the information in question and strengthening the subject's inclination to engage in exploratory activity in comparable situations.

Elsewhere (Berlyne, 1960a, pp. 179–182), I have drawn on neurophysiological findings to speculate how this might come about. It appears that the reticular formation becomes less active, which means that arousal is reduced, largely in response to inhibitory impulses from fibers connecting it with the cerebral cortex. Once activated by incoming stimulation, the reticular formation must be expected to remain at a high level of excitation until either the stimulation is withdrawn or the cerebral cortex inhibits it. The latter event will, we may surmise, occur as soon as the stimulus pattern has been recognized as innocuous or insignificant or until a response has been selected to become prepotent over its competitors, which is another way of saying that conflict has been diminished.

We are led, in this way, to postulate that human beings and other higher animals will take action to lower arousal, once it has been raised by environmental events with collative properties productive of intense conflict. This can be done by acting to terminate the stimulation, for example, by escaping from it or withdrawing attention from it. It can also be done by acting to augment the stimulation for a while until either habituation makes it less disturbing or an additional influx of information decreases uncertainty, mitigating conflict.

The symbolic capacities with which human beings are so well endowed makes the expedient of seeking to relieve conflict by acquisition of information by far the most effective as a rule. One reason for this is the fact that symbolic representations of stimulus patterns are apt to linger after they have left the stimulus field and to prolong any disturbance to which the stimulus patterns gave rise. Conflict due to discrepant or inconsistent relations among symbolic processes can presumably be reduced only by modifying symbolic structures and injecting new information into them. This extension or reorganization of symbolic structures is what we mean in everyday speech by "acquisition of knowledge." A state of high drive induced by conflict traceable to disharmonious symbolic processes constitutes *epistemic curiosity* (Berlyne, 1954a). This is a condition that can be relieved by the acquisition of knowledge and that therefore leads to epistemic behavior, which includes directed thinking.

Another reason why it is usually preferable to seek information rather than to shun conflict-inducing stimulus patterns is that these patterns are likely to recur. Behavior that equips us with new information to be stored in the form of knowledge can rob the disturbing stimulus patterns of their power to generate conflict in case they should be encountered again.

So we can see how specific exploratory behavior grows into epistemic behavior, how the processes that bring about the one must overlap with the processes that bring about the other, and how the two commonly occur in conjunction. The human nervous system is so made that, when stimulation is sought for the relief of perceptual curiosity, the characteristics of the stimulation are represented in memory and the information contained in it leaves its lasting mark on the subject's knowledge structures. In any case, the time-honored picture of the thinker who shuts himself off from the world and muses in his study is hardly typical of reality. The real-life thinker is apt to be surrounded by stimulus events which may at any time interrupt or deflect his thought processes. Rapt cogitation is more than likely to alternate with overt kinds of epistemic activity, such as asking questions of people who may be present. The lawyer planning his presentation of a case periodically consults his law books. The scientist may postpone his conclusions until he has obtained more experimental data. The creative artist may dash off a sketch to see what it looks like or try out the sound of a phrase on the piano. The choice between pursuing the quest for a solution through thinking and interrupting thought to seek information from the external world is, in fact, dangled before the thinker throughout his inquiry.

The assumptions that have just been outlined must not be taken to imply that human beings will never seek to increase the collative properties of external stimulation that are so often responsible for rises in arousal. There are patently times when they do so. One reason for this may be that arousal rises not only when the external environment is inordinately rich in collative properties but also when its collative properties fall inordinately low, for example, when a stimulation is monotonous or scanty. The resulting state of distress, which is, of course, what we call "boredom," is relieved by receipt of stimulation from virtually any source, provided that it brings the collative properties of the environment up toward an optimal level. This optimal level is apparently the minimum arousal of which the organism is at the time capable (Berlyne, 1960a, 1963). In other circumstances, stimulation productive of a transient rise in arousal may be sought out for the sake of the reduction in arousal that follows. These mechanisms are, however, likely to have more to do with diversive than with specific exploration and more to do with autistic than with directed thinking.   GO TO P. 179

Conceptual Conflict

The kind of conflict that affects directed thinking and other forms of epistemic behavior most directly will be *conceptual conflict*. This is conflict between incompatible symbolic response patterns, that is, beliefs, attitudes, thoughts, ideas. Conceptual conflict will, we hypothesize, be the principal, but not necessarily the only, factor producing epistemic curiosity.

Of the various ways in which responses can become incompatible, innate antagonism can hardly play much part in covert symbolic behavior. We no longer believe that there is an innate ability to see that two ideas or propositions are inconsistent, but there may possibly be some minor element of innate incompatibility involved in the evaluative or affective aspects of thought, that is, between incipient approach and withdrawal responses or between neural processes corresponding to pleasantness and unpleasantness. Conceptual conflict could sometimes stem from occlusion or congestion, that is, overloading of information-handling capacity. This may be related to what Bruner, Goodnow, and Austin (1956) have called "cognitive strain."

Nevertheless, most conceptual conflict by far must depend on learned antagonisms. Two symbolic response patterns will be incompatible when each is associated with the inhibition of the other. The inhibitory bonds may result directly from symbolic learning (including directed thinking processes belonging to the past), as when a child is told that nice people do not swear or a mathematician has convinced himself that a matrix with a zero determinant cannot have an inverse. In other cases, an incompatibility between symbolic responses will be a by-product of an incompatibility between motor or other nonsymbolic (for example, affective) responses associated with the stimulus patterns that the symbolic responses represent.

Degree of conceptual conflict, like degree of conflict in general, is assumed to increase with the following:

(1) the number of competing responses,

(2) how nearly equal in strength the competing responses are,

(3) the total absolute strength of the competing responses.

The first two of these are reflected in uncertainty, when probabilities of responses are regarded as measures of response strength. These three determinants of degree of conflict apply to conflicts between responses that are altogether mutually exclusive. When we come to consider conceptual conflict, we have to allow for the possibility that two responses will be partially incompatible, which will, no doubt, occur also in some forms of motor conflict. This being so, we have to recognize a fourth determinant of degree of conceptual conflict:

(4) degree of incompatibility between competing responses.

Degree of incompatibility between two responses, R_1 and R_2, may be identified with the strength with which the stimulus produced by R_1 inhibits R_2 or with the extent to which the occurrence of R_1 lessens the probability of R_2 [that is, $p(R_2) - p(R_2|R_1)$].

This list of determinants of degree of conflict was first suggested (Berlyne, 1954b, 1957) by Brown and Farber's (1951) article on the problem of measuring conflict (although they called it "frustration") between two completely incompatible responses. It seemed desirable to extend the conception to cases where there is more than one conflicting response and to cases of partial incompatibility. There are, however, striking similarities between the presumed determinants of degree of conflict and the factors that students of "cognitive dissonance" (Festinger, 1957; Brehm and Cohen, 1962) have enumerated as determinants of this variable. Their list comprises the relative number of factors working in a positive and a negative direction (cf. relative strengths of competing responses), the importance to the subject of the issues involved (cf. absolute strengths of competing responses), and the degree to which the alternatives among which the subject has to choose possess common elements (cf. degree of incompatibility).

Major Types of Conceptual Conflict

There is no end to the heterogeneity that can exist in the field of conceptual conflict, but a number of special cases stand out by virtue of their prevalence and their special properties.

1. DOUBT. This is conflict between tendencies to believe and to disbelieve a proposition or between tendencies to ascribe and to deny reality to a phenomenon. There are many objective tests of belief that could be recognized, including content and manner of verbal utterance, autonomic processes (used, for example, in lie detection), etc. But, following writers from Bain (1880) to Morris (1946), as well as common everyday practice, we may regard action as the acid test. This means that a subject is held to believe a proposition or to believe in the reality of a phenomenon to the extent that he will perform the actions that would occur if his sense organs showed the proposition to be true or the phenomenon to exist. Doubt thus entails conflict between excitation and inhibition of these actions.

2. PERPLEXITY. This kind of conflict occurs when there are factors inclining the subject toward each of a set of mutually exclusive beliefs. It is, of course, the kind of situation to which we can most properly apply the notion of subjective uncertainty. There will also be objective uncertainty regarding how the subject will behave overtly, since mutually incompatible overt responses must correspond to the alternative beliefs.

3. CONTRADICTION. This is a particularly intense kind of conflict, perhaps forming the limiting case of doubt. The subject is under the influence of factors that not merely favor but imperatively force on him two incompatible beliefs. He is, to view the matter differently, committed to propositions implying that a particular proposition both is and is not true.

4. CONCEPTUAL INCONGRUITY. This occurs when a subject believes that two properties, A and B, never occur together, or are unlikely to occur together, and yet factors are present that lead him to believe that a certain object possesses both. There are, no doubt, cases where conceptual incongruity and contradiction come together, but there is an important difference between the two. Contradiction involves the belief that something both has a property A and does not have it. Conceptual incongruity is a matter of at least two properties, and the reluctance to believe that they can be coupled is usually the result of empirical experience, which can be belied by further experience. An example would be the condition of a person who hears about a fish (the mudskipper) that walks on dry land when he has been trained to believe that no fish can survive or move about after leaving the water.

5. CONFUSION. This condition is produced by information whose implications are not clear. A subject who perceives an external stimulus object in far from ideal circumstances might be left with a gap in his belief system, such that he does not know what value to ascribe to some variable descriptive of the object. Ambiguous verbal material might have a similar effect. Confusion will overlap with perplexity whenever the subject recognizes a number of alternative possibilities and the information he receives from without is insufficient to specify the correct one. At other times, however, he may be left wondering what the truth could possibly be, without being able to name any alternatives.

6. IRRELEVANCE. This kind of perceptual conflict is extremely hard to define or analyze. It can apparently be distressing and motivate searches for means of escape from it in the course of directed thinking, for example, when thoughts that appear unlikely to carry the subject nearer to a solution obtrude themselves.

One hypothesis previously put forward (Berlyne, 1954b, 1960a) is that irrelevance accounts for some of the discomfort of bafflement. Whenever a subject is faced with a question to which he can supply no possible answer whatever, or whenever he sets out to think of a solution to a problem and finds himself utterly at a loss with no leads to follow, we assume that he will not be entirely bereft of thoughts, or at least not for long. Some symbolic material will inevitably be conjured up by associative processes. These processes can be expected, however, to produce a large number of responses of about equal strength, most or all of which will be irrelevant. We can thus infer that there will be a high degree of conflict due to irrelevance. There will, of course, also be discomfort due to the persistence and the frustration of the motive that originally actuated the search for a solution.

Ways of Relieving Conceptual Conflict

Directed thinking, as we have seen, has both information-rejecting and information-gathering aspects. The information-rejecting function of thinking will obviously reduce conceptual conflict whenever the thinker is subjected to items of information with disparate implications for behavior. He may, for example, be contemplating an object with many attributes corresponding to mutually exclusive lines of action. In any case, he is unlikely to be able to react to all the attributes at once, so that conflict due to occlusion will occur, quite apart from innate and learned antagonisms. Such conflict among motor responses will involve conflict among symbolic responses, for example, alternative labeling responses or beliefs.

We must now consider how conceptual conflict can be relieved, and, in particular, how information provided by directed thinking can relieve it:

1. DISEQUALIZATION. Degree of conflict will be reduced if either the number of competing responses or their nearness to equality of strength is reduced. We may take these together, since reducing the number is really a limiting case of making strengths more unequal: when one member of a set of alternatives is eliminated, its probability falls to zero and the probabilities of the other members are correspondingly raised. New information may very well strengthen one response while weakening or eliminating others, thus producing disequalization. Perplexity may be removed when evidence pointing to the correct alternative is made available. Doubt will be terminated when new information causes the subject to believe either the proposition in question or its converse definitively.

2. SWAMPING. There is, however, another manner in which conflict between a number of responses of about equal strength can give way to a situation in which one response is overwhelmingly stronger than any of its competitors. This is by the introduction of a new response, which was not among those entertained previously but exceeds them all in strength. Such a process may be called swamping. It is the usual way of alleviating conflict due to irrelevance, resulting, for example, from confusion or bafflement. The mass of unhelpful thoughts that obtrude themselves yields to a new line of thought that is more promising and, from then on, possesses a prepotent association with the stimulus pattern that is at work.

Problems that give rise to directed thinking often involve several requirements that, at first sight, appear inconsistent with one other. All the thoughts suggested by one appear at variance with those suggested by the others and vice versa, until finally some means of satisfying them all is discovered. In Duncker's (1945) well-known experiment, the subject is instructed to think of a way of destroying a tumor, located well below the surface of the body, without destroying the surrounding tissues. Before hitting on the answer, the subject considers various ways of bringing the radiation to bear on the tumor, but they can all be seen to entail destruction of other tissues. He also considers ways of circumventing other tissues, but they can all be seen to preclude the concentration of sufficient radiation on the tumor. Finally, the expedient of directing beams from different angles to converge on the tumor is discovered, and it is seen to satisfy both requirements at once. If ever the subject encounters this or an analogous problem in future, thoughts about converging beams will, no doubt, supplant all other lines of thought.

3. CONCILIATION. *Degree of incompatibility* will be reduced if new information reveals that two beliefs need not be treated as incompatible (conciliation). A person who is told about mudskippers will henceforth no longer think of fishes as creatures that can, in no circumstances, leave the water and survive. Likewise, subjects who have solved Duncker's problem will no longer believe that it is impossible to focus a certain quantity of radiation on a spot in the interior of the body without delivering the same quality to intervening tissues.

4. SUPPRESSION. *Total absolute strength* of competing responses can hardly be reduced by accumulating information, unless it be information that reveals the whole issue to be less important than it seemed at first. Total absolute strength can, however, be reduced by suppressing thoughts about conflict-ridden subject matter or avoiding stimuli that tend to evoke such thoughts. This will normally be a desperate measure, adopted when the first efforts to solve a problem are not encouraging. Its effectiveness is, moreover, likely to be short-lived, since troublesome thoughts are apt to return sooner or later. Nevertheless, some personalities, for example, those high in "intolerance of ambiguity," may be prone to this kind of behavior.

Alternatives to Unbiased Information Gathering

When directed thinking is used effectively for the relief of conceptual conflict, it seeks information without bias. Its quest will generally be confined to material with a bearing on the problem, but, within the limits of relevance, it will garner information where it can. The content of the information that it yields and the nature of the overt response that will emerge as prepotent cannot be specified in advance, since epistemic curiosity is a condition in which the subject cannot identify the most adaptive response.

There will, however, be times when unbiased information gathering aggravates conflict. When, for example, one symbolic response pattern is stronger than its rivals but not strong enough to establish its paramountcy decisively, epistemic behavior runs the risk of supplying information that strengthens one of the weaker alternatives.

This will tend to equalize response strengths and thus to increase the degree of conflict, at least temporarily until the initially weak response achieves unchallengeable prepotency. A person may already have committed himself to a course of action or a system of beliefs, but external or internal factors may raise doubts about the correctness of his decision (Festinger's "cognitive dissonance"). Alternatively, the extrinsic motivational factors that predispose a person to prejudice or to wishful thinking may make him loth to surrender a cherished belief or evaluation, no matter how much information is arrayed against it. Persons in these plights may selectively expose themselves to sources of information from which support for their hard-pressed predilections can be expected (Festinger, 1957). Otherwise, conflict may be reduced, independently of epistemic behavior, through spontaneous reorganization of attitudes, beliefs, and interpretations (Festinger, 1957; Abelson, 1959).

Evidence for Motivating Effects of Conceptual Conflict

The foregoing discussion is based largely on extrapolation from general principles of behavior theory and from presumed similarities between exploratory and epistemic behavior. Several lines of evidence tend, however, to confirm that conceptual conflict can generate epistemic curiosity and motivate epistemic behavior and that relief of conceptual conflict can provide reinforcement for the learning processes through which knowledge is acquired. Our next step must be to review these.

Determinants of Conceptual Conflict and Reports of Epistemic Curiosity

One kind of experiment (Berlyne, 1954b, 1962) has taken the postulated determinants of conceptual conflict and tested their effects on epistemic curiosity, measured through verbal reports.

In the first such study (Berlyne, 1954b), high-school students were presented with multiple-choice questions about invertebrate animals. They were asked to indicate the 12 questions out of 48 to which they would most like to know the answers. Questions about familiar animals, it was found, induced more reported curiosity than questions about nonfamiliar animals. This variable had been introduced because it was assumed that the competing thoughts evoked by questions about familiar animals would be both more numerous and greater in absolute strength. More reported curiosity occurred, moreover, in response to questions that subjects said they found surprising and also to questions that, according to a group of judges, attributed particular characteristics to animals that seemed unlikely to possess them. These last two variables were assumed to reflect degree of incompatibility. In more recent experiments (Berlyne, 1962b), high-school students were exposed to a succession of quotations, each coupled with the names of two or three famous persons, one of whom, it was falsely stated, was its author. Each name was accompanied by a number, purporting to show how many of a group of 100 teachers had chosen it as the name of the correct author. The students were instructed to mark the 12 quotations out of 28 whose true authors they would most like to know and then to rank-order these 12.

One experiment showed more epistemic curiosity, as revealed by this procedure, to derive from quotations coupled with three authors than from quotations coupled with two. Another experiment showed more epistemic curiosity to occur when the fictitious teachers' guesses were evenly distributed among the names than when they were preponderantly allotted to one name.

It was assumed that the distribution of fictitious teachers would influence the relative strengths of the subjects' tendencies to select as correct the various names coupled with each quotation. Some subjects were, in fact, required to indicate their own guesses, and the data confirmed that the probabilities of subjects' guesses were influenced by the numbers printed next to the names. The experiment verified that epistemic curiosity increases with two of the postulated determinants of degree of conceptual conflict, namely nearness to equality of strength, and number of competing responses. These are the two determinants reflected in the concept of uncertainty, and, since the remaining determinant, absolute response strength, figured in the first study, all three have now been found to influence reported curiosity.

Findings related to these were obtained by Maas (cited by Peel, 1961), who showed subjects some exotic objects borrowed from museums. She went through them three times, giving more information with each successive appearance. Subjects were required to indicate on a five-point scale the extent to which they wanted to know more about each object, and there was a significant tendency for more curiosity to be expressed in this manner over the three presentations. Once again, we have some indication that epistemic curiosity is not at its maximum with complete ignorance but increases, up to a point, with increasing knowledge. As long as knowledge is incomplete, the more there is of it, the more scope there presumably is for conflicting symbolic response tendencies.

Morozova's Work on "Interest" in Children

Morozova and her associates have devoted a number of studies to "interest" in schoolchildren. In one study (Morozova, 1955), different groups of schoolchildren, ranging in age from 11 to 15, were shown variants of a written passage designed to acquaint them with means of finding latitude and longitude. She endeavored to find out how far they had mastered the details of the content and its general theme. She also measured interest, as judged by the following criteria: (1) concentrated, "absorbed" reading, (2) the occurrence of emotional verbal utterances, for example, "How interesting!", (3) the number of spontaneous questions about the material and expressions of desire to know more about its subject matter. The variant that was much more successful than any of the others in eliciting both understanding and interest was one in which there was a child hero who was faced with the practical problem of finding his location and had thus to experience and solve the various difficulties that this problem presented. On the basis of this and similar studies (for example, Triger, 1955), she concludes that interest depends on the following conditions:

(1) What is read must raise a question that the reader finds hard to answer.

(2) There is a hero who is faced with the question.

(3) The hero is engaged in an active search for an answer.

(4) There is a central element of "struggle" against difficulties and perplexities.

There must, therefore, be the makings of conceptual conflict, and the possibility of identifying with a hero enables the reader to experience the conflict vicariously. The hero's successful efforts to overcome the difficulties and resolve the conflict appear not only to satisfy the reader's desire to know the answers to the specific questions involved but also to stimulate an eagerness for further knowledge about the same topic.

Morozova also inquired which books were and were not in heavy demand in the school library. The books for which there was not a great call consisted largely of declarative statements, simply purveying information; they raised few questions, offered few chances to guess answers, and required no thought on the part of the child. The books for which there was a great demand, and which the children presumably found interesting, were ones that raised questions and stimulated efforts to think out answers to the questions before the information to be assimilated was supplied.

As Morozova's work has continued (personal communication), there has been still more emphasis on the key role of conflict or "struggle." She stresses the pedagogical and interest-inducing value of first giving children some information and then acquainting them with facts that apparently discord with the information. They may, for example, hear about Spartacus and what a stalwart leader of the Roman slave population he was. But then they are told that he hesitated to lead a revolt against the patricians. They may be told how plants require sunlight for the photochemical processes on which their growth and survival depend. It is then pointed out to them that there are plants, namely fungi, that can live in the dark. Once they have been confronted with these apparently inconsistent facts and have made some attempts to resolve the conflict, they are given the appropriate explanations and, it is reported, both interest and retention are thereby brought to a peak.

Discovery Methods in Education

In the course of the search for improved teaching methods that is now proceeding in many countries, educationists are finding that immense wells of intrinsic motivation lie within the normal child, which are capable of lending powerful support to the teacher's efforts when properly tapped but are all too often stopped up by traditional techniques of instruction.

An early experiment that helped to launch the movement in favor of "discovery methods" was performed by McConnell (1934). Two groups of about 500 second-grade pupils were taught elementary arithmetic by different methods. Those taught by method A were told the correct answers to a number of simple problems with maximum appeal to the authority of the teacher and of the text book. They were then given prolonged and repetitive drill on the same and similar problems. Method B used, instead, a work book presenting pictorial patterns with whose help the children were encouraged to discover the answers to the problems by themselves. Tests inserted at various points during the period of instruction (which involved a total time of 35 to 40 hours) and at the end revealed that method A produced greater accuracy and speed with the actual problems on which the pupils were trained but that method B produced more transfer to other problems and more "maturity in manipulating number facts."

Since then, there has been a great surge of interest in devising radically new curricula and techniques of instruction in a variety of school subjects. Most of the new techniques whose early trials have been encouraging rely heavily on stimulating independent discovery of facts and development of individual judgment, as distinct from passive absorption.

Ausubel (1961) has warned against the overhasty conclusion that discovery methods are superior to others in all circumstances and for all subject matters. He reminds us that carefully controlled investigations are needed before the merits imputed to these methods by their devotees can be regarded as demonstrated and that these remain to be done. Nevertheless, discovery methods can apparently cause children to assimilate material that would formerly have been thought utterly beyond them and to show enthusiasm for topics that, when taught by traditional methods, are usually found "as dry as dust." These new pedagogical methods appear to work largely by manipulating conceptual conflict. To illustrate this, let us consider some examples.

I once witnessed a demonstration by Professor D. A. Page, Director of the University of Illinois Arithmetic Project. He was acquainting third-grade children with the proposition that the difference between the square of an integer and the square of the preceding integer (that is, $(n + 1)^2 - n^2$) must be an odd number. He showed this to be the case with 2^2 and 3^2, then with 3^2 and 4^2, etc. Would it work with 4^2 and 5^2, 5^2 and 6^2, etc.? The tension with which the moment of revelation was awaited and the excitement on finding the principle vindicated once more grew visibly with each succeeding instance. Questions asked by Professor Page elicited all the standard signs of schoolroom zeal—climbing on desks, hissing, stretching of hands toward the ceiling. After enough specific instances had been examined and it was becoming clear that the proposition was true throughout the number system, the question of why it was true was raised, and the equivalent of a proof was presented with the help of colored blocks of wood. Thus, curiosity regarding the reason for the phenomenon, presumably coupled with curiosity arising from the last lingering doubts about its general validity, was resolved as a final culmination.

To turn from mathematics to science, we can consider the "inquiry training" that is the subject of a research project directed by Suchman

(1961). The procedure begins with a short film in which a surprising physical phenomenon is demonstrated: a brass ball that is just small enough to slip through a brass ring is heated and then sits on the ring without being able to pass through it; an empty varnish can, having been heated and then allowed to cool, collapses because condensation of moisture reduces the internal pressure. The child is then invited to ask the teacher questions that can be answered "yes" or "no." At first, the questions concern properties of the objects and events that they have seen on the film, but, as the questioning proceeds, the child is encouraged to think of possible explanations and of an experiment by which the validity of each explanation could be tested. He asks the teacher whether a particular outcome would occur if the experiment described were carried out.

Experience with the technique suggests that "the inquiry skills of fifth-grade children can be improved over a 15-week period" by this technique. Their ability to note properties of objects accurately, to formulate explanatory hypotheses, and to design experimental tests improves markedly. Controlled studies (Suchman, 1959, 1962) indicate that the number of fruitful questions asked is significantly increased. Once again, we can see how epistemic curiosity is stirred up by an experience that contradicts expectations or leaves the subject perplexed. Questions elicit answers that reduce the resulting conceptual conflict progressively, and differential reinforcement evidently guides the subject toward the most fruitful strategies of interrogation.

To take an example from social studies, Bruner (1960) tells of an experiment carried out by the Harvard Cognition Project:

A sixth-grade class, having been through a conventional unit of the social and economic geography of the south-eastern States, was introduced to the north-central region by being asked to locate the major cities of the area on a map containing physical features, natural resources, but no place names. The resulting class discussion very rapidly produced a variety of plausible theories concerning the requirements of a city . . . the level of interest as well as the level of conceptual sophistication was far above that of control classes.

There was, he reports, "pleasure and excitement in the pursuit of the question . . ." One can see that there must have been a great deal of conceptual conflict among symbolic responses corresponding to possible locations and possible operative factors from the start. Once a guess had been made, there must, in addition, have been doubt, with attendant curiosity concerning the rightness or wrongness of the guess.

Finally, to show that interest in discovery methods is not just a vogue confined to North America, let us cite two Russian experiments. In one by Zankov (1957), one class of 11-year-old children examined the cellular structure of a leaf through a microscope while the teacher described features that were to be seen. Another class simply heard the teacher ask questions about the leaf whose answers were to be found in its microscopic appearance. Children in the latter class were able to answer many more questions correctly after the lesson. Similar results are reported for lessons on the leaf's external structure (although the difference was less pronounced) and for lessons with other subject matter.

Milerian (1960) studied transfer of skill from operating a lathe to operating milling and drilling machines. A control group was trained on the lathe by the traditional method: they were told about the structure of the machine and shown how to use it. The experimental group was trained by a method by which "the pupils independently determine the general principles of work on machines and then make active practical use of this knowledge." Transfer was markedly more successful in the experimental group, of whom 15 out of 17 were able to operate the milling machine as compared with 2 out of 10 control subjects. By the end of the experiment, which lasted two months, the number of subjects expressing interest in industrial processes had increased from 2 to 7 in the experimental group but only from 3 to 4 in the control group. Milerian reports that "transfer usually begins with attempts to apply existing knowledge and skills directly in the conditions of the new task." When these attempts are unsuccessful (which must mean frustration, surprise, and perplexity), subjects engage in "intellectual activity" which is focused on the differences between the new task and the old one and finally gives rise to "a generalized representation of the practical actions" that are required.

All of these new methods of instruction seem clearly to motivate children by subjecting them to conceptual conflict in the form of surprise, doubt, incongruity, perplexity, and confusion, depending on the peculiarities of the subject matter. Effective learning, susceptible of wide and fruitful stimulus-response generalization, is promoted by exploiting the reinforcing potentialities of conflict reduction. This learning encompasses not only mastery of the specific facts and skills that constitute the subject matter but also epistemic habits that foster independent inquiry and verification and afford protection against passive credulity. Kersch (1958, 1962) has, in fact, gathered evidence that such advantage as discovery methods have over traditional methods in the teaching of arithmetical techniques derives from their power to motivate the student more effectively and, in particular, to induce him to practice what he has learned in his own time.

The distinction between the new or discovery methods of education and the older methods is clearly very close to the distinction between intelligent and mechanical learning that was discussed in Chapter 8. The newer methods are clearly aimed at fostering "understanding," and they often show every sign of doing this successfully. It will be remembered that two of the distinguishing characteristics of beliefs derived from intelligent learning are that they are difficult to shake by exposure to phenomena that apparently contradict them and that the subject justifies them deductively, that is, by showing that they follow of necessity from general principles rather than by appealing to empirical evidence. The stubbornness with which beliefs accompanied by "understanding" are upheld suggests that they have some source of reinforcement on which they continue to draw when external support is lacking, so that extinction is resisted. If the reasons that the subject gives in justifying his belief have anything to do with the factors that are actually responsible for his acceptance of it, we can see where these sources of intrinsic reinforcement must lie. Beliefs are evidently reinforced with great effectiveness when they are deduced from firmly established principles. According to logicians, a "necessary" proposition is one whose denial would mean contradiction of the axioms or rules of inference of the system. The psychological phenomenon corresponding to this is evidently the way in which deductive support of a belief eliminates conceptual conflict. The reduction of conflict when a belief is deductively arrived at and the recrudescence of conflict when a deductively justified belief is questioned may thus hold the key to the tenacity with such a belief is maintained. The distinctive properties of intelligent learning are thus likely to depend in large measure on the distinctive forms of motivation and reinforcement that they utilize.

Ever since Herbart (1835), educationists have recognized the importance of presenting new material in such a way that its relations with what the child already knows are clear and that it fits in harmoniously with his "apperceptive mass." Recent pedagogical experiments suggest that, before this is done, it is as well to motivate him by doing the opposite, that is, presenting the new material in such a way that it challenges the child's existing beliefs and expectations and makes him sensible of the gaps and inadequacies in his present knowledge structures. The contrast between the very atmosphere of a classroom in which this is done and that of the more traditional classroom, in which information is meekly imbibed, lends further credibility to the postulated drive-inducing power of conceptual conflict.

Learning Reinforced by Reduction of Epistemic Curiosity

There have been regrettably few experiments directly aimed at the hypothesis that reduction of epistemic curiosity, resulting from diminution of conceptual conflict, will reinforce learned responses.

In the experiment of mine (Berlyne, 1954c) that was mentioned earlier, an experimental group was exposed to a series of factual multiple-choice questions (assumed to induce curiosity), then to a series of facts including answers to the questions (assumed to relieve curiosity), and finally to an after-questionnaire in which the questions were repeated in an open-ended form. Subjects in this group recalled significantly more of the facts during the after-questionnaire than a control group that went through the same procedure except for the fore-questionnaire. It was also found that subjects were more likely to remember the answers to the questions that they had marked in the fore-questionnaire as the 12 whose answers they would most like to know. This finding had been predicted on the assumption that receiving the answer to a question that has induced a high degree of epistemic curiosity will produce a large amount of curiosity reduction and thus be strongly reinforced.

Mittman and Terrell (1963) designed an experiment to ascertain whether relief of epistemic curiosity would reinforce discrimination of shape and size. Every time a correct choice among three stimulus objects was made, a child was allowed to draw in one more connection on a dot drawing. Degree of epistemic curiosity was varied among groups by placing a copy of the completed drawing in sight after different numbers of connections had been made. It was found, in accordance with the prediction, that the number of errors in the discrimination task was greater, the earlier the completed drawing was exhibited. This was presumably because, once a child saw the completed drawing, there was no more uncertainty, and hence no more epistemic curiosity, to be reduced by adding another connection.

Pitting the Reward Value of Epistemic Curiosity Reduction against a Cost

One indirect way to gauge the reward value of the consequences of a response is to impose some condition that deters the subject from making that response and to observe how much of the behavior in question will appear in the face of a given amount of deterrent. Data relevant to epistemic curiosity have been obtained in a number of experiments using guessing games, in which chances of monetary rewards depended on the correctness of a guess and subjects could supply themselves with items of information that increased their chances of guessing correctly before making their final decisions.

Irwin and Smith (1957) showed subjects a series of numbers and required them to guess whether the mean of the population from which the numbers were taken was positive or negative. The guess could be made after seeing as many or as few numbers as they wished, and they had to pay $\frac{1}{2}\phi$ or 1ϕ for each number that they saw. Subjects who were offered a prize of $1 for guessing correctly chose to see more numbers than those who stood to win 50ϕ. This is precisely what we should expect if uncertainty, and thus epistemic curiosity, has to be reduced to a certain threshold value before a subject is prepared to make a guess. The greater the prize at stake, the greater the desire to win and the fear of losing, the greater therefore the absolute strength of the opposed tendencies to voice a guess and to refrain from voicing it, and the greater therefore the initial level of conceptual conflict. It was also found that subjects looked at more numbers when the population mean was ±0.5 than when it was ±1.5 and when the standard deviation was 7.5 than when it was 2.0. The closer the mean to zero and the smaller the standard deviation, the less effective the sight of a succession of numbers of a given length will be in reducing uncertainty. It will therefore be necessary to see more of them before uncertainty and the associated curiosity will have dropped to the threshold.

Becker (1958) allowed his subjects to press a switch which caused either a left-hand or a right-hand counter to advance. They were told that the movements of the two counters were events randomly selected from two of a set of populations, containing different proportions of left-hand and right-hand counter movements, which were described to them. After any number of switch presses, subjects could guess from which population the events were taken, and their chances of winning a monetary prize was, they were told, an increasing function of the ratio that the excess of correct over incorrect guesses bore to the number of times the switch was pressed. It was thus in the subject's interest to minimize the number of counter movements to which he exposed himself before guessing, and this number turned out to be greater when the populations between which he had to choose were similar in statistical properties than when they were far apart and when the number of alternative populations presented was greater. These findings likewise fit our conception of epistemic curiosity. The more alike the populations, the more nearly equal in strength the competing response-tendencies must have been, and the more numerous the populations, the greater the number of competing response tendencies must have been. So two of the determinants of conceptual conflict are represented here. The greater the initial level of conceptual conflict, the greater the number of items of information supplied by epistemic responses that will be needed before epistemic curiosity can be brought down to a level compatible with commitment to action.

Two more recent experiments (Lanzetta, 1962; Lanzetta and Kanareff, 1962) corroborate our hypotheses further. In one experiment, subjects were confronted with a series of problems, each associated with six alternative solutions. Before selecting a solution, a subject could ask for up to five items of information, making it progressively easier for him to identify the correct solution. For example, one problem concerned alternative treatments for a patient in a psychiatric hospital, and the items of information described more and more abnormal ways in which he had been observed to behave. Different sums of money were offered for correct solutions, and different costs per item of information sought were imposed, but in all cases the subjects' expected gain went up with the number of items of information received. Despite this, most subjects stopped short of asking for all five items, and the mean number requested was inversely related to the cost per item. This is compatible with the view that epistemic curiosity will impel subjects to ask for information but that the net strength of the epistemic behavior will diminish as its cost grows. Measures of subjective uncertainty were derived for each problem from the proportion of subjects opting for each solution and from verbal ratings of confidence. According to both measures, the number of items of information requested was found to bear a positive relation to the level of the initial subjective uncertainty. An analogous finding was yielded also by a second experiment, using a concept-attainment task; initial uncertainty was manipulated by varying the set of alternative concepts, and subjects could supply themselves with helpful items of information by asking to see instances of each concept.

Conceptual Conflict and Attitude Change

Having for many years studied how single attitudes originate and how they can be changed, social psychologists are now beginning to face the fact that an individual's attitudes are generally organized in systems and apt to interact. Sometimes, the way in which two or more attitudes interact will be such as to make their possessor uncomfortable and to promote attitude change as a means of relief. Since attitudes are associated with symbolic responses, the discomfort that results when coexisting attitudes do not get on well together may be classified as an aversive condition involving conceptual conflict. Changes consequent on such a condition may thus be regarded with some plausibility as learning processes reinforced by conflict reduction.

Two of the groups of investigators concerned with this line of inquiry have concentrated on special cases of conflict between evaluations. Osgood and Tannenbaum (1955) apply the term "incongruity" to situations in which a respected person speaks in favor of a despised object or vice versa. They predict that the evaluations of both the originator and the object of the communication will then be changed so as to bring them closer together, and some empirical support for this prediction has been obtained (Tannenbaum, 1953).

Abelson and Rosenberg (1958) have developed a theory of "cognitive imbalance," which extends a concept first introduced by Heider (1946). Two persons, objects, or states of affairs that a subject values positively or negatively may be related either associatively (for example, A favors B, A promotes B, etc.) or dissociatively (for example, A dislikes B, A prevents B, etc.). There will be imbalance whenever the subject recognizes that two favored objects are dissociatively related, that two disfavored objects are dissociatively related, or that a favored and a disfavored object are associatively related. Evaluations or beliefs can then be changed or reorganized in various ways to remedy this anomalous state of affairs. Some of the ways have been described by Abelson (1959), and a number of experiments have confirmed that changes are likely to occur as predicted (for example, Rosenberg, 1960).

Festinger's (1957) theory of "cognitive dissonance" is much broader in potential scope than the two theories just discussed and has won a wider hearing. Two "cognitions" or "items of information" are said to generate dissonance when "A psychologically implies not-B" (Lawrence and Festinger, 1962). The term "cognition" covers evaluation, beliefs, and elements of knowledge and thus denotes implicit symbolic processes. If "A psychologically implies not-B," the stimulation stemming from A will presumably be associated with inhibition of the response corresponding to B. So what is involved is evidently a learned antagonism between two symbolic response patterns.

Although "dissonance" has been given such a far-ranging definition, its exponents have actually confined their attention to one class of situations, namely those in which a subject has already committed himself, either spontaneously or under pressure, to some action or expression of opinion and has reasons for disliking or questioning what he has done. Support from a sizable body of work (Festinger and Bramel, 1962; Brehm and Cohen, 1962) is claimed for the view that he is then likely to mitigate this predicament by modifying some of his attitudes, although the evidence has come in for some criticism (for example, Chapanis and Chapanis, 1964). The subject, it is contended, usually becomes more favorably disposed toward whatever he has committed himself to. He may, in addition, resort to other devices, such as seeking social approval of his position or selectively seeking exposure to information that will encourage him in the belief that he has done right, while avoiding information that might strengthen his doubts.

Those who are partial to the concept of "dissonance" have generally been eager to distinguish dissonance, which occurs after a decision has been made, from conflict, which they conceive as a condition preceding decision. It would seem, however, that both of these conditions fit our conception of conflict. It is true that the conflict takes different forms before and after the decision since, in the former case, there is a conflict between alternative overt courses of action and, in the latter case, there is conflict between evaluations of the action that has been taken and of other actions that might have been taken instead. These two conflicts must necessarily be isomorphic and correlated in degree, since there will be a postdecisional evaluative response corresponding to every course of action that was instigated before the decision was made and the strength of each response tendency before decision must be correlated with the strength of the tendency to evaluate that response favorably afterward. It is, nevertheless, not surprising that predecisional and postdecisional conflicts will have different effects, since different devices will be effective in relieving them.

"Equilibration" and Child Development

We have already devoted some discussion to connotations of Piaget's conception of psychological "equilibrium" as something most fully realized by intellectual operations that conform to the principles governing group structures. The main driving force of the whole perceptual and intellectual development of the child is, in his view (Piaget, 1957, 1959), an autonomous tendency for interacting processes to gravitate from lesser to greater equilibrium. He calls this trend "equilibration" and has been inclined to distinguish it sharply from both learning and maturation, although he concedes that it must work in conjunction with these two factors.

The concept of "equilibration" is certainly in need of more elaboration. But Piaget's writings contain plenty of indications that it refers to a kind of learning motivated by conflict, particularly conceptual conflict, and reinforced by conflict reduction (Berlyne, 1960b). For example, he describes (Piaget, 1957) the advance toward greater equilibrium as productive of a gain in "ability to predict" and *"sécurité"* (translatable either as "assurance" or as "safety"). Furthermore, "equilibrium" is stated to depend on balance between the two complementary but potentially opposite processes of "assimilation" and "accommodation." Disequilibrium results from an insufficiency of either of these. "Assimilation" covers processes that enable incoming stimulation to evoke a response that fits in with what is already in the organism, for example, effects of previous learning. A failure of assimilation must therefore entail conflict due to novelty (when stimulus generalization does not give rise to a clear-cut prepotent response), to uncertainty (when no unequivocal expectation of what will follow is possible), or to occlusion (when the limits of information-handling capacity are overstepped because familiar sequences and patterns are absent). "Accommodation" covers processes whereby a subject is made to behave in a way that fits what is in the external environment. When it is deficient, we can expect conflict from surprise (when the subject responds in accordance with expectations that disagree with what is actually experienced) or frustration (when the subject responds in accordance with existing habits but rewards appropriate to his motivational condition fail to materialize).

Some evidence that changes ascribed by Piaget to equilibration are actually induced by conceptual conflict has come from a series of quantitative-invariant experiments by Smedslund. These have been concerned with the development of the recognition that deformations do not alter weight. Children are shown two identical balls of plasticine and then, after one ball has been elongated, they are asked whether this ball weighs more than the other or whether they weigh the same.

Demonstrating by means of a balance that the two masses of plasticine were of equal weight (1961a) produced no more changes from judgments of inequality (characteristic of the intuitive stage) to judgments of equality (characteristic of the stage of concrete operations) than occurred in a control group of children who received no special treatment. Those children who came to believe in conservation of weight were easily persuaded to relinquish this belief by a fake demonstration (1961b), in which the experimenter surreptitiously took a piece off one of the masses of plasticine before weighing them.

In a subsequent experiment (1961c), Smedslund adopted an expedient that could be expected to produce conflict. Having elongated one mass of plasticine, he broke a piece off it before asking for the comparison. A conflict, he assumed, would then be set up between the tendency to judge the elongated mass heavier, because of its greater length, and the tendency to judge it lighter, because part of it had been removed. Four out of 13 subjects were in this way led to see that a change in shape leaves weight unchanged when nothing is added or subtracted. Furthermore, they gave logical, as distinct from empirical, reasons for this belief in the post-test. Although the procedure was successful with only a minority of the children to whom it was administered, the occurrence of 4 successes out of 13 contrasts with the occurrence of only 5 conversions to conservation of weight justified by logical arguments among more than 100 children subjected to other treatments. Smedslund (1961d) later tried the same kind of procedure with discontinuous material. This consisted of two compact piles of small pieces of linoleum, one of which was spread out before asking whether the two assemblages contained the same amount of linoleum. Taking away a piece from one of the assemblages before asking for a judgment induced about one third of the subjects to recognize conservation of quantity.

Chapter 10
The initiation of directed thinking

WE MUST NOW ask what support can be mustered for the view that conceptual conflict is a major influence in the initiation of directed thinking. We shall first consider some reasons for believing that conflict is bound up with the very nature of thinking. Then, we shall review evidence that conflict tends to make those animals that are capable of them resort to symbolic and epistemic activities in general. Finally, we shall discuss the conditions in which human directed thinking in particular is likely to start. We shall throughout concentrate on intrinsic motivational factors. This is not to deny that extrinsic motivation has an important say in the initiation and course of thinking. Such familiar and intensively studied motivational conditions as fear and frustration appear to affect symbolic responses in much the same way as they affect other behavior (Maltzman, 1962; Osgood, 1957), but intrinsic factors have received little investigation.

Thinking and Inhibition of Motor Responses

We have already seen how writers with such diverse backgrounds as Sechenov, Watson, and Piaget have arrived at the conclusion that thoughts consist of internalized (that is, attenuated or curtailed) actions. Thinking makes use of neural processes that, if allowed to complete themselves, would issue in bodily movements. These processes are, however, modified and abbreviated, so that, if they reach the muscles at all, they produce only weak muscular innervations that are not sufficient to move the structures to which the muscles are attached. There are factors present, in other words, that, if operating alone, would give rise to overt activity, but other factors are opposing them and preventing the motor processes from reaching fruition. Simultaneous instigation and inhibition of a motor response, which means conflict, is thus inferable as an indissociable accompaniment of thinking.

The same inference is no less inescapable when we focus on the role of a thought as a stimulus. Any external stimulus acting on a human being must be associated with some motor response or other. Stimulus generalization or higher-order conditioning must ensure that the same motor response becomes associated with an internal symbolic stimulus representing the external stimulus. This is, in fact, essential to the definition of a "sign" that, following Morris and Osgood, we have adopted. Countless Russian experiments have shown how a response associated with an external conditioned stimulus general-izes (through what Ivanov-Smolenski calls "elective irradiation") to the sound or sight of a word describing it. A similar transfer must surely occur when a subject thinks a word to himself. N. E. Miller (1951) has verified that, if the sight of a letter "T," which the subject is instructed to name, is regularly accompanied by electric shock, the thought of "T" will evoke a stronger galvanic skin response than the thought of the number "4," which has never been coupled with pain. The same kind of transfer will, no doubt, occur with skeletal, as well as with vegetative, responses and with images and other symbolic stimuli as well as with subvocal words.

Yet it is clear that the overt responses associated with the vast ma-jority of links in a train of thought, apart perhaps for the concluding link, are not performed. The conditioned responses that make up the mediator, r_m, are usually restricted to a covert form. William James (1890) used the expression "ideo-motor action" to allude to the tendency for a movement follow "unhesitatingly and immediately" on an idea. Thurstone (1924) characterized thinking in these terms:

. . . the basic relation, when there is no conflict or deliberation, is that of an idea which issues forthwith into the action that corresponds with the idea. . . . It is only when there is a conflict between two unfinished or proposed actions, two conflicting ideas, that the effect of ideo-motor action is withheld.

Thinking is universally identified with suspension of activity. En-gagement in thought means interruption of whatever course of ac-tivity was previously in motion, presumably by a neural process of the kind that Pavlov called "negative induction." Epistemic behavior thus appears to be analogous to the exploratory behavior that Pavlov as-sociated with the "orientation reaction" and held to be responsible for the phenomenon of external inhibition.

Put differently, thinking involves suspension of belief. The thinker has to contemplate states of affairs and possible actions without be-lieving that the states of affairs are, or ever will be, real or that the actions are advisable. Inhelder and Piaget (1955) have concluded from their developmental studies that the capacity for hypothetico-deductive reasoning is not fully formed before adolescence. This kind of reasoning requires one to consider, and draw conclusions from, propositions without accepting them as true. By examining their consequences, their truth or desirability can be determined. Not only does hypothetico-deductive reasoning appear relatively late in the individual's development; the scepticism and willingness to postpone judgment that are indispensable to the systematic hypothetico-deductive procedures of science have appeared relatively late in the history of human society. As Bain (1880) wrote, "preparedness to act upon what we affirm is admitted on all hands to be the sole, the genuine, the unmistakable criterion of belief." The process of entertaining a thought in such a way that the logical and other associations that lead from it to other thoughts are allowed full play, while desisting from the overt actions to which the thought must point, entails a conflict between responses corresponding to what Bain called "primitive credulity" and "acquired scepticism," even though the conflict may not be an equal one and the latter may prevail.

This conflict, an example of those that we have subsumed under "doubt," will be strongest when the tendencies to believe and to disbelieve are of comparable strength. But we can infer some degree of conflict even when the subject contemplates a proposition of whose falsity he is thoroughly convinced. To quote Russell (1940, p. 266), "Negation expresses a state of mind in which certain impulses exist but are inhibited. . . ."

Conflict and Recourse to Symbolic and Epistemic Behavior

According to the definitions adopted by information theory, there can be no information without prior uncertainty. The amount of information in an event (not to be confused with the amount of information transmitted from one set of events to another) is defined as a function of the probability of that event, namely $\log_2 (1/p)$, and a probability cannot be assigned to an event unless it is an element of a "sample space" or "ensemble," that is, a set of alternative events, any one of which might have occurred and each of which has its relative frequency or probability. If a sample space can be specified, it will be possible to assign an uncertainty value to it.

The mathematical truth that information implies prior uncertainty corresponds to the biological and psychological truth that the role of information in animal life is contingent on conflict, the behavioral equivalent of uncertainty. Information will be valuable to an animal only when it prevents or relieves conflict, that is, when a maladaptive chaos of competing responses would occur in its absence. So we can expect animals to seek information when they suffer for lack of it, that is, when there is a condition of disturbance or high drive that information could allay, which must mean a condition of which conflict is a major ingredient.

This state of affairs can arise in a number of ways. There may be lacunae in available information, in the sense of questions that have no answer. We can then expect a mass of relatively weak competing responses to be thrust forward by virtue of their association with stimulus elements that are present or by virtue of stimulus generalization. If, however, none of these proves adequate, each will be subject to inhibition as well as to excitation. An organism may be beset by contradictory items of information that point to mutually incompatible responses or that prescribe and contraindicate one and the same response. Additional information is then required to determine which of the discrepant items is to have precedence or how the inconsistency between them may be resolved. Finally, an organism may suffer from congestion or information overload. It may be faced with a stimulus pattern possessing a large number of attributes and need guidance in determining which attributes should form a basis for selecting a response or, put differently, in determining to which class of patterns the present pattern is ecologically equivalent. As we have already noted, this means ignoring other attributes and thus discarding information.

Now, directed thinking is both epistemic behavior and symbolic behavior. Epistemic behavior, like exploratory behavior, consists of activities by which information is sought, and symbolic responses are devices for bringing information out of storage to supplement what is coming in through exteroceptors. Our line of discussion would, therefore, lead us to expect that symbolic behavior will most likely emerge when information coming from the external environment gives rise to conflict.

As many writers have remarked, thinking does not occur when things follow a smooth, accustomed course. Automatized sequences of habitual or instinctive responses can then supply what is required more efficiently and less arduously. But when something occurs to interfere with these responses, symbolic processes obtrude themselves without delay.

Vygotski (1956) refers to some experiments of his in which children were subjected to "a series of frustrations and difficulties." "For instance," he writes, "when a child was getting ready to draw, he would suddenly find there was no paper, or no pencil of the color he needed. In other words, by obstructing his free activity we made him face problems." "A younger child," he reports, "would try to grasp and to remedy the situation in talking to himself . . ." When an older child was faced with a similar situation, he often "examined the situation in silence and then found a solution. When asked what he was thinking about, he gave answers that were quite close to the thinking aloud of the preschooler." The speech that occurred was of the kind that Piaget (1923) has called "egocentric speech." Vygotski argues that this is the kind of verbal behavior that gradually turns into "inner speech" and is used by a child to control his own behavior through thinking.

It is instructive to compare what Vygotski had to say about the use of verbal symbols with the conclusions that Bartlett (1925) expressed after studying another kind of symbolic response, namely the image. "Unpleasing feelings," he writes, "are a 'sign' of a clash and holdup of tendencies. They thus accompany what we in general term 'states of indecision.'" A little later, he goes on:

Although a feeling arises as a first tentative step towards supplanting a mere blind struggle among adaptive tendencies, it achieves but a small step forward, and is a bad guide in practice. How is this difficulty dealt with? It is dealt with by an attempt further to define the conflict of which the affect is a sign. There appears to be one way only in which this can be done. That way is by calling upon cognitive tendencies for help, and by attempting a more conscious discrimination of the situations which have aroused the antagonistic tendencies. The most straightforward method of doing this is to effect as direct a reproduction as possible of these situations. Thus comes the image . . .

But images themselves have their limitations. The principal one that Bartlett sees is the possibility that, through reproducing in full detail a past situation that resembles the present situation in some respects but not in others, it may foist on the subject an action that was appropriate then but will be of no avail now. So we use thinking to "carry further the processes of discrimination which begin in perceiving and issue in imaging. We find our solution by careful analysis of the situation which provokes the conflict. The analysis proceeds by isolating and generalizing the elements which gave rise to the check, and the solution secured is on the whole a more adequate one because it gets farther away from the accidents of a particular environment."

Bartlett's conception of the image reminds us of Piaget's (1945) child who opened and closed her mouth when her efforts to open a matchbox were unsuccessful. We have already seen how such overt imitation is one of the roots of imagery.

In Chapter 6, Beritov's (1959) experiments on spatial learning in cats and dogs were mentioned. It will be recalled that, in some of these experiments, the animal was blindfolded and either carried in a cage or led to a place where he was allowed to eat a little food. He was then able to find his way back to this place from any starting point. Beritov found, however, that if an animal had been taken repeatedly for a large number of trials to the same place to be fed, "psychoneural" behavior, utilizing symbolic responses, would be replaced by automatized behavior. This can be seen from the way in which the animal initially behaved when a change was introduced into the experimental conditions. If the food was moved in his sight from its customary location to a new location, the sound of the bell (signaling the start of a new trial) made him rush to the old location. If the bell had always been placed next to the food but was moved elsewhere while he was blindfolded, he would run to the bell instead of to the food, as soon as it rang. However, when this response brought him to a spot where no food was to be found, he would sniff, look around and, evidently reverting to the use of his symbolic capacities, make his way to the new location. So, once again, conflict, taking the form in this instance of surprise coupled with frustration, seems to have been the cause of symbolic activity.

Problems and Problematicity

The word most commonly used to describe the kind of situation in which directed thinking is likely to be launched is "problem." A problem is often spoken of as something that exists in the outside world. It is presented to a subject on a piece of paper, or he discerns it in some part of nature. However, what will constitute a problem for one individual may not be a problem at all for another; despite identical external situations, a problem is more properly thought of as a condition of the organism.

What are, then, the criteria by which we recognize that a problem exists?

1. Some writers tend to apply the word "problem" to any situation in which an animal has *high drive and lacks a readily available drive-relieving response*. Mowrer (1947) once distinguished between

"conditioning" (that is, classical conditioning) and "problem solving" (that is, instrumental or operant conditioning). But this usage clashes with the widespread practice of reserving the term "problem-solving behavior" for a narrower class of learning processes, that is, those that make use of symbols and involve something approaching reasoning.

2. Other writers have resorted to *metaphors taken from physics*. Claparède (1933), for example, refers to "disequilibrium." Wertheimer (1945) writes of "stresses and strains" in thought structures. A state of disequilibrium is a state in which a system cannot remain indefinitely and so a state in which some change is bound to occur. Stresses and strains are, of course, conditions which, unless exactly compensated by other stresses and strains, create disequilibrium. Now, the kinds of situation in which human beings begin to think obviously resemble states of physical disequilibrium in that they are states in which something has to happen. If they were not, nothing, including thinking, would happen. So we still have to ascertain the differences between these situations and those in which the subject dispenses with thought.

3. Bartlett (1958) refers to the kind of situation in which "information is given, and then more information, and between there is a gap" as the starting point of one kind of thinking, namely "interpolation." Koffka (1935) had already used words like "gap" to characterize conditions that initiate action in general and impel it to continue until "closure" has been attained.

A *gap* implies that something is absent and that the subject would somehow be better off if it were present. But it still remains to tell how we can distinguish situations in which something important is missing from situations that are, in essentials, complete. Above all, we need to know how we can specify the conditions in which a subject will recognize a gap, be disturbed by it, and set about filling it in.

4. Maier (1945) singles out *variability of behavior* as the earmark of a problem. When behavior is highly variable, its form is difficult to predict, and so there is, from an external observer's point of view, considerable uncertainty about it. From the organism's point of view, there are a number of responses whose momentary strengths fluctuate but whose mean strengths are close together. This is, of course, exactly the state of affairs that is denoted by a "high level of conflict."

5. Then there are writers who have selected *frustration* as the essential element. Van de Geer (1957) develops a conception of a

"problem situation" based on Johnson's (1955) statement to the effect that "A problem arises if a subject is motivated towards a goal and his first attempt at reaching this goal is unsuccessful." Skinner (1953, p. 246) writes:

There appears to be no problem for the organism which is not in a state of deprivation or aversive stimulation, but something more is involved . . . In the true "problem situation" the organism has no behavior immediately available which will reduce the deprivation or provide escape from aversive stimulation.

He goes on to say, "This condition may be expressed more generally. We need not specify the deprivation or aversive condition if we can demonstrate that *a response exists in strength which cannot be emitted.*"

6. Finally, there are writers who refer explicitly to *conflict*. For Dewey (1910), what starts thinking off is a "felt difficulty." "The difficulty must then be located and defined, but these two processes often fuse into one conflict between conditions at hand and a desired and intended result, between an end and a means of reaching it." Duncker (1945) likewise recognizes conflict as a central feature of problem situations. "Analysis of the situation," he writes, "is . . . primarily analysis of a conflict."

In attempting to collate all these views, we can see a fair measure of agreement that a problem implies a condition of high drive which is not promptly relieved. And a condition of high drive means a "critical state" (Ashby, 1952), that is, a state that represents an ultimate threat to the integrity of an organism and that will therefore be followed inevitably by sharp changes. Comparisons with physical states of disequilibrium have therefore some validity. Some of the writers we have cited (and notably those in the last two categories) recognize further that something is happening to prevent a response that could relieve the drive state. Of these, a few have explicitly pointed to conflict as the obstructive factor.

One thing that is clear is that a problem can be more or less of a problem. Some problems are more "problematical" or, to use a commoner word, more "difficult" than others. The fewness of subjects in a population who can perform a task satisfactorily has occasionally been regarded as an objective measure of difficulty, for example, by Davis (1938) and by constructors of intelligence tests. A difficult problem is thus one that an individual subject has a relatively small probability of solving. Posner (1962) found that the more "difficult a task was judged to be the greater the probability of error, both of these variables being directly related to the amount of information reduction that was required" (see Chapter 2).

A response that would bring about drive reduction and thus be reinforced may be unlikely to occur for any of a number of reasons. It might be overshadowed by some prepotent response that the situation calls forth, as in experiments on "fixation." This response, not being conducive to a solution of the problem, will, however, be followed by nonreinforcement, frustration, or punishment, so that processes promoting its performance have to contend with processes militating against it. Another possibility is that the correct response exists in appreciable strength but some factor specific to it is inhibiting it. Finally, the subject's learning history may have left him with no predominant response associated with the situation that confronts him, so that a vast array of competing responses of about equal strength, most of them irrelevant, will be instigated.

A difficult problem situation will leave an external observer at a loss to foretell what responses (including verbal responses when a subject is asked to think aloud) will actually be forthcoming. So, to sum up, we have a reasonable case for identifying the degree of "difficulty" or "problematicity" possessed by a problem with degree of conflict. Degree of conflict will, in its turn, vary with the four determinants already listed. It will be possible to represent it by the formula $\Sigma E \times U$, where ΣE represents the total strength of competing responses and U represents uncertainty regarding the subject's behavior.[*]

Of these two factors, U may be regarded as a measure of the extent to which the situation fails to call forth one response with overriding strength. ΣE can, on the other hand, be regarded as an "importance" factor—a measure of the extent to which the subject is committed to the problem, which is a matter of the extent to which strong responses are involved. This, in its turn, will be affected by the level of drive. Even though U may be high, if ΣE is low, that is, if the subject is unable to find a prompt appropriate response to a situation but the situation is of little concern or interest to him so that the consequences of delay in finding a solution are not serious, we can say that the situation "does not constitute much of a problem" as far as he is concerned.

[*] I am indebted to R. D. Luce, who made some points in correspondence that indicated this formula.

Questions

Another word that is often used in connection with the initiation of thinking is "question." This word is, in its wider sense, used more or less synonymously with "problem" or "difficulty" or "topic." But in its narrower sense it means, of course, a verbal utterance in interrogative form. Such an utterance is generally what Skinner (1957) calls a "thematic probe," that is, a stimulus pattern with the function of eliciting verbal behavior from a listener or reader. In the case of a thematic probe, as contrasted with a "thematic prompt" (and questions occasionally serve as thematic prompts rather than probes), the questioner is unable to specify in advance what answer will be elicited. He is, in other words, in a state of uncertainty. But he will be able to narrow down to some degree the range of items from which the answer will be selected.

If his question is a "yes-or-no question," the alternative answers can be divided into two classes, equivalent to "yes" and "no" respectively, and strengths or subjective probabilities will normally be assignable to the expectations corresponding to these two alternatives. With "specific interrogations" (Bloch and Trager, 1942, p. 52), that is, questions beginning with interrogative adverbs or their equivalents, the alternative answers will be more numerous, but they will still be restricted to a particular set. Questions begining with the word "where" demand answers specifying locations, questions beginning with "why" demand answers specifying reasons, etc. The questioner will commonly be able to enumerate in advance a much more limited range of locations, reasons, etc., to which the answer is likely to belong, and he will, as often as not, be able to assign subjective probabilities to these alternatives.

In other words, the questioner will be faced with a set of alternative events to which an uncertainty value can be assigned. Samson (1954) has, in fact, developed a calculus for allotting uncertainty values and related measures to questions. A questioner is, we may surely assume, driven to put the question (an epistemic response) under the pressure of his subjective uncertainty or conceptual conflict.

The listener or reader may respond to the question with an immediate answer. This will be so when one answer is prepotently associated with the question, as a consequence either of rote learning (for example, studying a catechism) or of a previous successful thought process. Otherwise, the question will instigate a set of alternative, competing responses in him, and he will be placed in a condition of conceptual conflict paralleling that of the questioner. This conflict, probably augmented by such extrinsic factors as desire to oblige the questioner, embarrassment at the possibility of being found ignorant, etc., will incite him likewise to seek an answer.

We all know how cogently motivating a question can be. It is extremely difficult to ignore a question without at least attempting to make some sort of reply. And it has often happened in the history of science, mathematics, philosophy, or even art that the mere recognition of an unanswered question has driven a person to the intellectual labor from which an epoch-making innovation sprang.

Why-Questions and Explanations

The frequency of questions beginning with "why" is especially significant. As Piaget (1926) shrewdly remarks:

. . . its very abundance leads us to look upon the "why" as the maid-of-all-work among questions, as an undifferentiated question, which in reality has several heterogeneous meanings.

Some why-questions, in both children and adults, are simply expressions of astonishment, disappointment, or dismay ("Why should this happen to me?" "Why can't you look where you're going?"). They either require no answer at all or call for reassurance and remedy. But most why-questions, even in the young child, are means of seeking information that will relate the event or property of interest to other events or properties. Answers to questions of this sort are what we call "explanations."

All explanations can be regarded as devices that link the phenomena to be explained to other phenomena through transformational links. The tracing can proceed backward or forward. A physical event can be traced back to a preceding cause or factor, a human action to a motive, a mathematical, moral, or grammatical rule to a system of axioms or basic principles. In these cases, the explanation makes clear the transformations that have led from these antecedent conditions to the phenomenon of interest, whether they take the form of physicochemical, psychological, or logico-mathematical processes. Some explanations, for example, those that refer to intentions or functions, relate the phenomenon of interest to something that will or may happen in the future, specifying, or leaving to be understood, the transformational processes that will lead from the present stimulus pattern to those that will replace it.

So, when we explain an occurrence, we indicate its place in a transformational chain that has proceeded through recognizable transformations from previous states of affairs to the stimulus pattern that is under examination and that will in due course lead on from it to succeeding situations.

While writers like Piaget (1926) and Nagel (1961) have analyzed the content of why-questions and classified the explanations that are offered in answer to them, Isaacs (1930) has sought to identify the motivating conditions in which why-questions occur. The essential factor, he concludes, after collecting instances from children, is "a certain clash, gap or disparity between our present experience and any present event. Some factor is met which is contrary to expectation, or unexpected or creates confusion or difficulty as to what to expect next. Something has gone wrong with our knowledge or assumptions. We need to find out what it is and to put it right. We are pulled up, thrown out of our course, caught unprepared, or left without any clear guidance, and we have to deal with the obstruction." This is, of course, the kind of situation characterized by collative properties like novelty, surprisingness, and incongruity, and we can see Isaacs approaching the conclusion that the root of the disturbance is a conflict between discrepant motor response tendencies.

It is clear that, as the child grows up, the urge to find an explanation extends to all phenomena that are unaccounted for, and not merely those that are at variance with specific expectations. In explaining how the "epistemic question" arises, Isaacs goes on to describe how the "immediate experience turns into a sense of something wrong with knowledge, some unsuspected error, insufficiency, or confusion—or of something wrong with the perception of the supposed fact."

He continues, "There is accordingly generated a striving or endeavour to locate what is wrong and to put it right. Is there a definite error, or something missing, or something ambiguous or unclear? If any of these, it must according to the case be corrected, supplied or cleared up. If none of these, then what has happened?"

There could be no better testimony to the pervasive importance of transformational thinking in human behavior than the readiness with which a human being, from the age of three onward, can be driven to ask "why?" and the compelling force that the urge to have something explained can possess. Much, if not most, of the time, our responses do not depend solely on an external stimulus pattern that is facing us or even on one that we are contemplating in thought. They are determined by the present stimulus situation (external or internally symbolized) plus a representation of the process by which this situation has developed out of foregoing situations, whether these were accessible to our observation or not. In addition, we are constantly forming anticipatory representations of the changes that are likely, in their turn, to start out from the situation of the moment, basing our behavior to a large extent on them.

If we have only a momentary stimulus situation to go by—if we have access only to one phase of a development whose past and future course is concealed from us—then we are usually at a loss and in conflict. We are thus prone to ask why-questions or engage in other kinds of epistemic behavior in order to complete our knowledge of the past and future fates of the objects with which we have to interact.

A moment's reflection will reveal how universal this phenomenon is. If somebody hears an unusual sound coming from the engine of his car, he inquires why it is occurring: he tries to think out what might be causing it, he inspects the engine, or he consults a mechanic. It might signify nothing of consequence, it might be a warning of serious trouble, or it could conceivably mean that the car is working better than it has been working before. Only knowledge of its antecedents can reveal whether an unexpected physical phenomenon is good, bad, or indifferent as far as our interests are concerned and indicate how to remove or prevent it should it be harmful and how to prolong or restore it should it be beneficial.

If an acquaintance asks us to give him five dollars, it is a safe bet that our first response will be to ask why he wants it. There are a number of possibilities. He may be collecting money for a deserving charity, he may be shamelessly sponging, he may be having a joke, or he may have gone out of his mind. All of these call for distinct courses of action on our part, and the fact that he is asking for the five dollars does not enable us to select the appropriate one until it has been supplemented with an explanation.

In the history of mathematics, there have been a number of instances of theorems whose truth is generally believed in, although no proof of them, that is, no account of why they are true, has been discovered. For example, nobody has yet devised a map that requires more than four colors for no two adjacent regions to be colored alike. Yet no topologist has yet succeeded in proving that four colors must be sufficient for any map, or, in other words, in showing why four colors are sufficient.

Such states of affairs leave mathematicians unhappy and stimulate vigorous efforts to remedy them. Until a proof has been found, there is always some small possibility that the theorem is not true and that an exception to it will eventually be found. Furthermore, until the theorem has been related to other mathematical principles, it is not clear how it can be built on to arrive at further mathematical discoveries.

The Role of Factors other than Uncertainty

We have so far laid particular stress on subjective uncertainty as a form of conflict that generates epistemic curiosity and thus plays a leading part in determining when thought processes will be launched and how long they will continue. We must not, however, suppose that uncertainty is the only decisive factor.

Importance

For one thing, we must remember that, while degree of conflict increases with degree of uncertainty when everything else is held constant, it can nevertheless increase with uncertainty left unchanged. This is because uncertainty does not reflect all the determinants of degree of conflict; in particular it does not reflect absolute response strength. As we saw earlier, to represent degree of conflict, we need to use some such formula as $\Sigma E \times U$, where U is uncertainty and ΣE is the sum of the absolute strengths of the responses involved or the "importance" factor. ΣE will reflect such variables as how strongly rooted the habits associated with the competing responses are, how much drive is coming in from extrinsic sources, what rewards and punishments are at stake for the subject, etc.

Prokasy (1956) found that rats would tend to enter an arm of a T-maze containing cues that indicated whether or not food would be forthcoming, in preference to an arm in which similiar cues were uncorrelated with the availability of food. A later experiment by Wehling and Prokasy (1962) found this preference to be greater under 20 hours, than under 12 hours, of food deprivation. It was pointed out (Berlyne, 1962a) that this result is what one would expect if the preferential turning habit were reinforced by the reduction of conflict to a threshold value and if the initial degree of conflict varied directly with total absolute response strength, which, in its turn, could be assumed to be greater with the longer period of deprivation. So we have here some confirmation for the view that conflict increases with extrinsic motivation when uncertainty remains constant.

If such variables can have such a strong influence over this particular kind of exploratory behavior, it is reasonable to assume that they would influence epistemic behavior, including directed thinking, in much the same way. Some measure of support for this assumption is to be found in an experiment by Caron (1963). High-school students were first given some personality tests and then allowed to read a short passage presenting a theory of risk-taking behavior. They were told that this material would help them to understand the results of the tests that they had just taken. Subsequently, they were tested for recall of information contained in the passage and also for comprehension, gauged by asking them to apply the principles expounded in it to new problems. In one of the tests administered before the reading of the passage, subjects were required to indicate how badly they would feel if they heard friends describing them as "cowardly." This measure of "cowardliness-involvement" was assumed to contribute to the importance (ΣE) aspect of conceptual conflict. It was, in fact, verified that subjects possessing it to a high degree performed significantly better than others on the comprehension test and somewhat better, but not significantly so, on the rote test. This can plausibly be attributed to more intensive epistemic behavior in the form of reading the material and thinking about its content until it was clear. It is revealing that "cowardliness-involvement" had no effect on either rote recall or comprehension in another group of subjects, who were told to read the passage for the sake of a subsequent aptitude test whose results would be entered on their records.

Subjective Probability of Success

Even bearing in mind the dependence of epistemic curiosity on factors other than uncertainty, we must be careful not to assume that readiness to engage in a thought process and persistence in it depend solely on the strength of the motivation that would be satisfied if the problem were solved. This would imply that we are more likely to start thinking about a problem the more difficult the problem is, which is patently not so. We can all list questions that it would be highly gratifying to have answered but that we can never imagine ourselves thinking about for long because thinking has no prospect of leading us to reliable answers.

Thinking entails a cost in time, in effort, and often in risk of mortification and frustration if the thought process turns out to be fruitless. As Henry Ford once said, "Thinking is the hardest work there is, which is the probable reason why so few engage in it." So we can expect that engagement and persistence in thinking, as in so many other human activities, will depend on the resultant of a number of interacting forces, of which some will favor the thought process and some will inhibit it. In other words, some of the phenomena that have given rise to discussions of "level of aspiration" (Hoppe, 1930; Lewin et al., 1944) will appear here as in other departments of human behavior.

Of particular consequence will be the subjective probability of succeeding. Processes corresponding to this subjective probability will come up in at least two ways. First, the relative strength of dispositions to embark on, or continue, thinking and to refrain or desist from thinking must vary with the estimated likelihood of success. Apart from this, the degree of satisfaction to be derived from solving a problem can be expected to vary directly, and the degree of humiliation that would result from failing to solve it can be expected to vary inversely, with the difficulty of the problem, which means with the initial improbability of succeeding with it.

Atkinson (1957) has developed a theory of risk-taking behavior, which could be as fully applicable to thinking as to other enterprises with uncertain outcomes. He deduces that both motivation to seek achievement and fear of failure will reach a maximum when the subjective probability of success is equal to .5. The bearing of subjective probability of success on satisfaction with achievement and disappointment at failure must, one imagines, arise largely from the way in which social commendation and disapproval depend on relations between performance and task difficulty. But it seems not impossible that epistemic curiosity about whether or not one will succeed may be an operative factor. In view of the special place of probabilities of .5 in Atkinson's theory, it is interesting that uncertainty, and hence perceptual conflict, will be at a maximum, all other things equal, when the chances of success and failure are judged equal.

Feather (1961) has tested deductions from Atkinson's theory regarding the length of time that a subject will persist with an insoluble problem. His subjects were set to find a way of tracing the lines of a figure without taking the pencil from the paper or going over any line twice. He recorded how much time was spent on a figure that was actually not unicursal (although this could not easily be recognized) before giving up, and he found all his predictions verified. They concerned the interactions among subjects' prevailing motivation for achievement, their fear of failure, and the estimated chances of success that were imparted to them before they began.

How hopeful a subject is of success and how strongly inclined to undertake a problem must depend in a large measure on his previous experiences of success with similar problems, working through rein-forcement of pertinent habits and stimulus-response generalization. Investigations by Ponomarev (1960) illustrate how potent such a factor can be. When subjects were shown a pattern of 144 dots arranged in a square and asked to find a way of connecting the dots with 22 lines, they declined to try. Other subjects were shown how to solve similar problems with 9 dots, then 16, then 25, then 36, and finally 49. After these preliminaries, they were willing to apply themselves to the problem with 144 dots. Ponomarev reports that willing-ness to attempt a problem, and persistence with it once it has been taken up, depend on whether the problem appears soluble. For ex-ample, a subject would invariably attack the problem of connecting 4 dots arranged in a square with a cycle of 3 lines, although no subject out of more than 600 tested without special preliminary training suc-ceeded with this soluble problem. When told to connect a pattern of 41 haphazardly arranged dots with 40 lines, subjects did not hesitate, but they generally refused to undertake the task of joining the 41 dots with 7 lines, even though this was perfectly feasible.

Whereas Ponomarev's observations related to the effects of experi-enced success and failure on readiness to attack a problem, an experi-ment by Rhine (1957) dealt with the effects on the likelihood of solv-ing a problem, which must largely depend on degree of persistence. His subjects were given 15 training anagrams, followed without a break by 20 test anagrams. Different groups received training items that were difficult, moderate, and easy (as judged by the number of subjects solving them in preliminary studies). The test items were of moderate difficulty and identical for all groups. Subjects were told that they could expect to solve about 50% of the anagrams, although this was an overestimate for those with difficult training items and an underestimate for those with easy training items. The outcome was that the number of test items solved was greatest after easy train-ing items and least after difficult training items.

The problems used in all these studies were ones that could con-ceivably give rise to more or less blind trial and error, but there can be little doubt that subjects relied heavily on directed thinking in their attempts to cope with them.

It seems that difficulty, which we have tentatively equated with conflict, works in two opposite directions. The more difficult a task, the greater the satisfaction (in conflict reduction, in heightened self-esteem, and in social acclaim) to be gained from success, which fa-vors undertaking it. At the same time, the more difficult a task, the more stress and frustration it is apt to generate and the greater the chances of failure, which militates against undertaking it. The subtle interaction between these two factors must determine where the preferred level of difficulty lies. Earl (1957) asked 10- to 15-year-old children to solve some block-design puzzles and then asked for judgments that enabled him to scale the puzzles on a dimension of "amount of figuring" (that is, difficulty). It was found that naive subjects tended first to take up the puzzle judged simplest and then to proceed through the others in order of increasing difficulty. As experience with the task was prolonged, some subjects shifted their points of maximum preference (calculated from judgments of "amount of fun") from simpler to more difficult items.

Certainly, one of the skills that an ideal educational system would impart is that of judging which problems are and are not worth thinking about. Many people are, it is true, inordinately ready to give up in face of a little puzzlement and apt to underestimate gravely what their own intellectual powers can accomplish if used efficiently and with persistence. We want schoolchildren to be immunized against this error, but it is equally important for them not to waste their time trying to think out solutions to problems that are beyond their capacities or their present knowledge. One mark of a master chess player is knowing when to resign!

Competition with Other Forms of Epistemic Behavior

Finally, we must bear in mind that directed thinking is only one form of epistemic behavior, even though it is an indispensable accompaniment of other forms when they are used. Considering the costs and risks of thinking and how often thinking fails to attain its goals, there must be constant competition between it and alternative epistemic activities, namely, consultation and observation. The problem of when to think and when to interrupt thinking in order to obtain further empirical data is perennial and ubiquitous in all branches of intellectual work. Personalities and cultures obviously vary in their readiness to do the one or the other. The rationalist and empiricist epistemologists of the 17th and 18th centuries held hotly defended opposing positions on the relative merits of thinking and of observation, and most of the schisms that divide psychologists to this day are traceable to their disputes. In recent centuries, the most advanced societies have certainly grown progressively less inclined to rely on thinking alone or combined with consultation of authorities and progressively more prone to use thinking as an adjunct to experimental and observational techniques.

Chapter 11

The dynamics of directed thinking

Once a directed thought process is in full swing, other motivational functions of conceptual conflict must come into play. These will be at least three in number. First, fluctuations in degree of conflict will underlie fluctuations in the level of arousal or drive, which will be reflected in the intensity, degree of exertion, and possibly persistence, with which the thought process is conducted, as well as in the usual psychophysiological indices. Second, the content of conceptual conflict will play some part in guiding the course of thinking and biasing selection at the various choice points through which the thinker passes. Third, relief of conceptual conflict will mark the point at which the thought process has reached a solution and can appropriately end; its reinforcing power will cause the products of the thought process to be retained and held in reserve for the treatment of future problems.

Thinking and Indices of Arousal

Several experimenters have compared indices of arousal when a subject is engaged in mental arithmetic and when the same subject is sitting or lying in a relaxed condition. Although a few of them (for example, Toman, 1943; Mundy-Castle, 1951) have failed to find reliable differences, most have reported that a transition from relaxation to intellectual activity brings on changes characteristic of heightened arousal. Alpha waves are likely to disappear from the EEG tracing (Berger, 1930; Tyler, Goodman, and Rothman, 1947), and mean EEG frequencies are likely to increase (Hadley, 1941). Muscle tension recorded from EMG electrodes placed on the neck (Davis, 1938) or on the forearm (Davis, 1938; Hadley, 1941; and Shaw and Kline, 1947) rises. Heart rate and integrated cardiac bioelectric potential go up (Hadley, 1941; Ford, 1953). Skin resistance falls (White, 1930), and perspiration on palms and soles increases (Kuno, 1930).

There are further studies indicating that these signs of heightened arousal are more marked when problems are more "difficult." We have already reviewed reasons for believing that greater "difficulty" means greater conceptual conflict. Davis (1938) and Shaw and Kline (1947) have shown that the rise in muscular tension in the forearm is greater the smaller the percentage of subjects (in the experimental population or in a test population) who solve the problem that the subject is attempting. Hadley (1941) manipulated problem difficulty by varying the number of digits in the numbers that his subjects had to multiply. He found the extent of the rise in muscle tension to increase with difficulty judged by this criterion. Hess and Polt (1964) found, likewise, that, when subjects were given mental multiplication problems, pupil size (known to be an index of arousal—see Berlyne, 1960a) varied directly with difficulty judged by the same criterion as Hadley used.

Abel (1930) used problems of a different sort. Subjects were exposed for 5 sec. to statements, or to verbal formulas equivalent to statements, and had to decide whether each was true or false. Afterward, they were interrogated about their subjective reactions. Some items elicited "predicamentive reports," indicative of "clear or strong attitudes of the 'difficulty-met' or 'predicament-encountered' type (e.g., 'surprise,' 'gee whiz!', 'got stuck,' 'searched around') and indications of somaesthetic experiences characteristic of a predicamentive situation (e.g., 'reacted with my whole organism, upset' or 'heavy dull pressure in my chest which meant that I was stuck')." Such items produced GSR deflections 75% of the time. On the other hand, items that the subjects found easy, making such remarks as "Nothing to it!" and "Saw it right away!", elicited GSR deflections about once in five times.

Blatt (1961) studied heart rate in connection with the kind of directed thinking required by the John-Rimoldi Problem-Solving and Information (PSI) Apparatus. This apparatus consists of a panel bearing a number of buttons and lights arranged in a circle. The subject has to discover a sequence of buttons that, when pressed, will cause a light in the center to be illuminated. Various logical relations—facilitation, combinatory facilitation and inhibition—obtain between the effects of pressing the various buttons, and these can be discovered by observing which of the lights in the circle light up. It was found that, in inefficient subjects, heart rate reached peaks at three crucial points in the problem-solving process. These were (1) the point at which the subject had secured access to the information (about the effects of the button presses) that was necessary and sufficient to find the solution to the problem, (2) the point at which he shifted from a preponderance of "analytic" questions (questions about the action of one button or about the causes of the illumination of one light) to a preponderance of "synthetic" questions (questions about the effects of combinations of button presses), and (3) the discovery of a solution. We must exercise caution in relating these findings to motivating effects of conflict. Blatt himself interprets them rather differently. He points out that different portions of the problem-solving process are likely to require differing degrees of arousal for optimal performance, and that an efficient subject may be one who is capable of boosting his own arousal level when required. We may, however, note that Blatt's data show a sharp drop in arousal (if heart rate is regarded as an index of arousal) immediately after the crucial points that he lists. These are points at which we should expect an abrupt drop in conceptual conflict. It is true that these points are preceded by sharp rises, which together with the subsequent drops produce the peaks. These may, however, be due to rises in drive level as the subject senses that these subgoals are coming into view, perhaps akin to Hull's (1932) "goal gradient" or Miller's (1944) "approach gradient."

These peaks in heart rate did not appear with inefficient subjects, who failed either to gather the necessary information economically or to make adequate use of it once they had it. Over-all levels of heart rate were, moreover, lower in these subjects. Beckman and Stein (1961), using the same apparatus, found likewise that less efficient subjects had more frequent alpha activity in their EEG tracings. These data seem to imply that more efficient subjects owe their superior performance in part to their higher level of motivation. Nevertheless, Shaw and Kline (1947) found that more intelligent children, who solved a higher proportion of mental-arithmetic problems than others, had lower muscle tension.

This apparent discrepancy may be resolved by recognizing that the PSI apparatus requires subjects to discover techniques that are new to them. In such a situation, subjects with more arousal or alertness or determination to work things out may well be more effective. Mental arithmetic, on the other hand, makes use of familiar, established procedures, and it may be that, with these, proficient subjects can proceed smoothly without disturbance, whereas less able ones are balked and subject to conflict.

EMG Recording of Subvocal Speech

We noted in Chapter 6 that thinking is commonly accompanied by action currents in the muscles that participate in speech and that these action currents can be detected with sufficiently sensitive apparatus even though no vocalization occurs. We have found grounds for doubting that thinking can be identified with these peripheral motor processes. What their significance is remains, however, an open question. Various answers have been proposed: they may represent some kind of overflow of energy from the central nervous system to the skeletal musculature, or they may represent responses whose kinesthetic feedback exerts a dynamogenic facilitatory influence on the thought process, so that the subject has learned to utilize them whenever such an influence is required.

A. N. Sokolov (1960) has carried out a series of experiments in which potentials indicative of "inner speech" were recorded from EMG electrodes placed on the lower lip, under the tongue, and on the throat. Recordings made with subjects engaged in a variety of tasks show that the tracing is sometimes relatively flat and regular but that, at other times, high-amplitude oscillations appear, usually in bursts. There is commonly rather close synchronization between the oscillations that are recorded from different parts of the organs of speech, with exceptions that appear to correspond to the different roles that the organs would have played if a word had been pronounced aloud. The activity is often found to spread to other parts of the body, such as the forehead or the hand.

High-amplitude oscillations are especially likely in conditions where covert verbal responses would be expected. They are prominent when a subject is told to write down numbers, but they are absent when he is to form visual images of objects with his eyes closed. Instructions to recall drawings that have just been seen or to attempt a maze problem elicit high-amplitude oscillations from subjects prone to verbalization but not from those identifiable as visualizers.

In general, however, Sokolov's findings suggest that the intensity of bioelectric potentials in the speech muscles reflects level of arousal. Subvocal speech must be a consequence of interaction between excitatory and inhibitory processes, in which the inhibitory processes are sufficiently powerful to preclude audibility. But the motor facilitation due to increased arousal may well strengthen the excitatory processes to a degree productive of conspicuous EMG potentials. At times of exceptional stress, there is, as everybody knows, a tendency for thoughts that are normally kept to oneself to be uttered out loud.

Amplitude is particularly apt to increase at times of difficulty, especially of a kind clearly conducive to conflict. It increases when a subject has to count silently to himself while tapping his finger in a prescribed rhythm, when he is reading or listening to material in a foreign language, when he has to count to himself backward. Amplitude is high in face of the kind of difficulty that can be expected to elicit thinking, for example, listening to verbal material that is hard to understand, answering questions such as "On which floor of the building is the laboratory?" or "What day of the week is September 1st?" Significantly enough, amplitude does not rise when subjects are asked these questions a second time or when they are asked any question to which the answer is readily available. Mental arithmetic gives rise to an increase in amplitude that is commensurate with the subject's proficiency, as judged by the speed with which he arrives at solutions. In less able subjects, the activity is especially intense whenever there is a change from one kind of arithmetical operation to another, for example, from addition to multiplication.

Hesitation Phenomena During Speech

In experiments using various techniques, Goldman-Eisler (1958, 1961) has shown that the length of the pause between two consecutive words of a spoken sentence varies inversely with transitional probability. The pause is relatively short when the word that follows is one that is highly likely to appear in that context. It is, however, relatively long when the probability is low, which means that the word had to be selected from a number of alternative words of comparable likelihood. This implies, of course, that hesitation increases with uncertainty and conflict, thus indicating, as Goldman-Eisler puts it, "the subjective activity of producing information."

Interword pauses are also lengthened by conditions that would seem to require thinking, that is, those in which conflict can be resolved only by finding words with a low initial probability of occurrence. In one study, subjects were shown humorous cartoons without captions and required, in turn, to describe their content and to formulate "the general point, meaning or moral of the story in as concise a form as you can." The activity of summarizing gave rise to longer pauses than that of description. Furthermore, subjects who summarized in fewer words tended to pause longer between words than those who were more long-winded. Finally, hesitancy decreased steadily as subjects were asked to repeat their descriptions or summaries up to five or six times.

A long pause before a word about which there is considerable uncertainty might simply reflect the weakness of the associative bond between this word and its predecessor. Alternatively, it could conceivably mean that a long succession of information-producing or alternative-eliminating processes has to be completed before a higher quantity of uncertainty can be removed. Experiments concerned with other kinds of behavior (Berlyne, 1957b, 1960a) suggest, however, that a lengthened reaction time is, in some circumstances, a sensitive index of disturbance or heightened arousal due to conflict. This phenomenon may well be related to the "arrest reaction" or suspension of motor activity that has been found to result from stimulation of the thalamic reticular nuclei and to the external inhibition that, as Pavlov pointed out, accompanies the orientation reaction. Goldman-Eisler's claim that the formation of a simple sentence is an example of thinking is justified in the light of our definitions (Chapter 1). Our definitions imply, moreover, that it is reasoning, and therefore directed thinking, of a simple order. Every point of transition between two successive words in an uttered sentence is a point of greater or lesser conflict, which must presumably have a motivational role not unlike that imputed to conflict in covert directed thinking.

Conceptual Conflict and Symbolic Tree Hierarchies

The ultimate objective of a directed thought process is the construction of a solution chain. This is a symbolic transformational behavior chain, leading from the initial problem situation to a represented terminal situation, which is capable of relieving the epistemic curiosity that actuated the thinking in the first place. When the solution chain has been completed, the subject may engage in an overt behavior chain, mirroring the symbolic solution chain, if the problem is a practical one and the subject's motivational condition has a prominent extrinsic component.

As we have noted, the process of solving a problem can be depicted with reference to a compound symbolic habit-family hierarchy corresponding to a tree graph. The solution chain corresponds to a path, or sequence of branches, leading from the root of the tree to one of the terminal nodes belonging to its final level or "crown." In the course of constructing or identifying a solution chain, the subject has to go through a sequence of intermediate nodes, each of which represents a choice-point from which a number of alternate branches diverge.

If the subject is reconstructing a highly familiar chain of transformations, for example, rehearsing to himself the route by which he goes home from work every evening or carrying out a routine piece of computation, the appropriate response will come to the fore without delay at each choice-point. Previous reinforcements will have given it a far greater strength than any of its competitors. But if the subject is solving a particular problem for the first time and finds the going a little rough, the alternative responses that offer themselves at each choice-point are bound to be more even in strength, which means that there will be appreciable conflict.

The psychological process represented by a node of the tree can be characterized from a number of different points of view. From the point of view of symbolic response structure, when the subject arrives at a particular node, he has just committed himself to a hierarchy of a particular level, that is, the hierarchy branching out from that node. This hierarchy must, however, consist of a number of alternative subhierarchies belonging to the next level (or of a number of specific transformational chains if the lowest level of all has been reached), and the subject has to make a selection among these.

From the point of view of information theory, the subject has determined some of the properties (for example, some of the components) that the solution chain will have, but he still has some uncertainty to resolve with respect to its remaining properties. This brings us close to the aspect of thinking on which Thurstone (1924) was focusing when he wrote that "to think is to add new attributes to that which we are thinking about" and recognized that this addition of attributes must occur step by step until the attributes have been identified sufficiently to "point towards specified adjustments."

Then, we must not neglect the motivational point of view. Duncker (1945) concluded, after his intensive studies of human problem solving, that "the final form of a solution is typically attained by way of mediating phases of the process, of which each one, in retrospect, possesses the character of a solution, and, in prospect, that of a problem." In other words, before a problem can be solved, it must generally be broken down into subproblems, each of which may in its turn be broken down into sub-subproblems, and so on. At each node, the subject has made progress toward solving a subproblem of one level, but this means confronting himself with a subproblem of the next lowest level. As we have seen, a problem is a conflict situation that gives rise to epistemic curiosity. The decomposition of an over-all problem into a series of constituent problems, each of which must be solved in its turn, implies therefore that the initiating curiosity must generate a succession of "subcuriosities" or more specific forms of curiosity. Each of these lower-level curiosities must be relieved before the more general initial curiosity, induced by the over-all problem, can be eliminated. This is part of our justification for suggesting that, even when a thought process is prompted by the crassest extrinsic motives, epistemic curiosity, akin to that which prompts the most disinterested search for knowledge, must be playing a part.

Last, there is the point of view of an observer concerned with a population of subjects. Since most symbolic responses are culturally determined, diminishing conflict within an individual can be expected to go together with diminishing variability among individuals. Bartlett (1958) has, in fact, noted that, as the successive steps toward the solution of a problem unfold, subsequent steps become more and more predictable. There is, he states (p. 77), "a minimum amount of evidence at or below which any extension of that evidence is a matter of individual idiosyncrasy." When "more than that minimum of evidence is available, still the ways in which gaps are filled are very much smaller in number than the way in which they might theoretically be filled." In a later passage (p. 190), he writes:

. . . as the number of steps taken towards filling up a gap increases, the number of probable next steps decreases, until a stage in the sequence is reached beyond which all thinking must proceed through the same number and order of steps to the same terminus.

Special Forms of Problem Decomposition

There are many variants of the process of breaking down a problem into subproblems as a means to solving it, but three are of sufficient importance to be worth specifying:

1. RETROGRESSION. One of the many advantages of reasoning over overt trial-and-error behavior is that the components of the solution chain need not be discovered in the order in which they will occur in the chain. Symbolic responses representing later stages can certainly occur anticipatorily and, as analyses of animal reasoning show, representation of the final goal situation from the outset is usually an essential condition for the discovery of an adaptive response by reasoning. So a thinker often proceeds by selecting a subgoal, or situation intermediate between his present position and the ultimate goal, and seeks a chain of transformations that will lead him to it.

This is partly because he will often already have at his disposal a chain of transformations leading from the subgoal to the ultimate goal, so that the problem is solved as soon as he has a way of getting to the subgoal. Somebody trying to prove that A implies B may be able to demonstrate without difficulty that B implies C, and so he will try to establish that A implies B. A chess player may recognize that, if he can arrive at a certain position, checkmate is inevitable within three moves, and so he will concentrate on finding a way of attaining that position.

Second, there are inherent advantages in solving a problem backward. Newell, Shaw, and Simon (1957) make abundant use of the successive adoption of subgoals in their problem-solving computer programs. They write, with special reference to their program for proving theorems in logic:

Since there is only one theorem to be proved, but a number of known true theorems, the efficiency of working backward may be analogous to the ease with which a needle can find its way out of a haystack, compared with the difficulty of someone finding the lone needle in the haystack.

2. VERTICAL DECOMPOSITION OF TRANSFORMATIONS. Transformational symbolic responses can exist with varying degrees of generality. Thinking must therefore often proceed by commitment to a more general transformation, which may be regarded as a class of more specific transformations.

Once a general transformation has been selected, it is often necessary to replace it with a more specific transformation before the problem can be deemed to have been solved and before overt action can be embarked on. For example, a subject may decide that a certain objective can be gained by traveling from Toronto to New York. But once this has been decided, there is the problem of making a selection among alternative means of transportation. So, once the higher-level problem has been solved by incorporation of the journey between the two cities into the solution chain, the next step is to solve a lower-order problem that will add attributes to the journey.

3. HORIZONTAL DECOMPOSITION OF TRANSFORMATIONS. Often, a subject will have identified a general transformation that will lead him from one situation to another situation, such as going from Toronto to New York, but, before he can resolve his conceptual conflict fully, he must break down that transformation into a sequence of transformations of smaller range, which will lead him in turn through a series of intermediate situations. For example, a subject who has decided that he must travel from Toronto to New York by car will subsequently, unless he has driven between the two cities repeatedly in the past, have to work out the sequence of intermediate cities—Buffalo, Syracuse, Albany, etc.—through which he must pass. Having done this, he must apply transformation-selecting habits to decide on transformations (that is, itineraries) that will take him from Toronto to Buffalo, from Buffalo to Syracuse, and so on.

Conflict Reduction and Transitive-Group Hierarchies

In Chapter 8, we considered some reasons why transitive-group habit-family hierarchies may be particularly valuable and some senses in which they may be said to represent a peak of equilibrium. As we turn our attention to motivational factors dependent on conceptual conflict, some further points relevant to these questions come into view and may be worthy of examination, even though they may at the present stage be flagrantly speculative.

When we speak of the "structure" of a system of symbolic responses (such as a transformational habit-family hierarchy), we may be referring either to its *bare structure* or to its *stochastic structure*. Bare structure is defined by specifying the responses that are associated, as alternative next steps, with each represented stimulus situation at which a subject might arrive. In the case of a transformational hierarchy, this means specifying the alternative transformational responses that can branch out from each situational thought and specifying the new situational thought to which each would lead. Stochastic structure, on the other hand, is defined by specifying the bare structure together with the probability of each response that can lead away from a given represented situation. A bare structure may thus be represented by a nonevaluated graph, which consists simply of a set of nodes and branches. Stochastic structure must be represented by a stochastic evaluated graph, that is, a graph with a number, denoting a probability, labeling each branch. The numbers attached to branches that issue from one node must, of course, add up to 1.

Now, bare structure must depend on the forms of learning and generalization that build up habit-family hierarchies. It must be available for application to a wide variety of problems with a wide variety of specific contents, and yet it must preserve itself intact whatever the subject matter for which it is used, so that conflict due to inconsistency can be avoided. Bare structure is exemplified by the most basic and most widely utilizable systems of mathematics and logic.

The probabilities that define stochastic structure must, in contrast, vary with the particular problem to which the hierarchy in question is applied. Furthermore, these probabilities must undergo continual changes as thought processes using the hierarchy succeed one another. First, these probabilities change in the course of one and the same thought process: the initial probability of certain responses will diminish through extinction as they turn out to be sterile, while other responses will become correspondingly more probable. Second, once the problem has been solved, the responses constituting the solution chain will be evoked with a probability approaching certainty when the same problem is encountered anew, although these probabilities must have been relatively low at the outset, especially if the problem was initially a difficult one. Third, repeated success with a certain general line or strategy of thought must make this line or strategy one of the first to be taken up when the subject meets problems of a comparable sort. Devices for ensuring that methods with a high likelihood of proving successful will be tried earlier than others form the "heuristics" that are indispensable to computer programs for problem solution (Newell, Shaw, and Simon, 1958). There has, in fact, been a great deal of work on methods of programming that will enable computers to develop their own heuristics, by benefiting from accumulating experience and gradually raising the priority of routines that have led quickly to solutions.

It is true that the bare structure of a hierarchy may be modified under the influence of new learning, but such modifications are more likely with a hierarchy that reflects a particular sector of the physical world, in which facts can change or can be discovered little by little, than with the indefinitely generalizable hierarchies of mathematics or logic. Furthermore, such modifications usually entail additions of new component chains to the hierarchy rather than alterations of those that are already established. One can always find new short-cuts in a well-known stretch of country or new calculating procedures without having to give up more familiar routes or procedures.

Turning to motivational aspects, we can see that, at each choice-point in a thought process, that is, each represented stimulus situation at which a number of competing transformational responses are instigated, there will be a certain degree of uncertainty and therefore of conflict. The degree of conflict will depend on the number of competing responses, their probabilities and their absolute strengths. Of these three factors, the last two will vary with the content of the thought process and the nature of the problem. The first factor, the number of competing responses, will, on the other hand, be represented in the bare structure. Suppose that a bare structure were to contain a chain of responses leading to choice-points that have progressively fewer alternative responses branching out from them. This chain would invariably lead to progressive reduction of uncertainty and hence of conflict. This means, if our assumption is correct, that the responses making up this chain would be reinforced by conflict reduction, which would bias the thinker toward this particular chain whenever he made use of this hierarchy.

It is of considerable interest that van de Geer (1957), starting out with a very different kind of theoretical orientation, has outlined a hypothesis, which he calls the "substitute-goal rule," that is essentially the same as the conclusion that we have just drawn. He conceives of a thought process as a succession of "moves," each of which selects from a set of alternatives made available by the last move. The thinker is assumed to be able to see ahead a certain number of moves. At each choice-point, he considers the sequences open to him and identifies the sequence that will leave him with the smallest number of elements to be selected from. The move he chooses to make will then be the move that initiates this sequence.

Similarly, Bartlett (1958, p. 107) writes, in connection with his own experiments on thinking, "The indication in the case of closed systems was that the strongly preferred move is one that reduces the number of probable next moves." What he calls "thinking within closed systems" is "extrapolative" or "interpolative" thinking, for which, in our terminology, existing symbolic habit-family hierarchies suffice. It is contrasted with "adventurous" thinking, which evidently requires reorganization and extension of existing hierarchies.*

Now, adaptation requires that a subject be biased toward a particular chain of responses, namely the solution chain, when attacking a particular problem. But it is highly undesirable for him to be biased toward certain of the chains belonging to a bare structure that is to be useful for a vast array of problems. Apostel (1957) has developed a concept of "equilibrium" applicable to graphs, based on an analogue of the concept of a "derivative" used in differential calculus. He asks himself what kinds of graph will be in "neutral equilibrium" throughout. These will be graphs that possess no "point of stability," that is, no point such that, as one approaches it, the number of points accessible in one move becomes progressively smaller. Apostel deduces that the only graphs that satisfy this criterion will be so-called *trivial* or *complete graphs*, that is, graphs in which there is a branch leading from every node to every other node. These are, of course, precisely the graphs that can be used to represent transformational habit-family hierarchies with transitive-group structure. The lack of a point of stability means that they will contain no chains that lead to a progressive reduction in the number of alternative responses, with consequent bias in their favor due to the reinforcing effect of conflict reduction.

So we have a glimpse of one more way in which hierarchies of this sort can be said to surpass others in "equilibrium" and to have wider adaptive potentialities as a result. The term "neutral equilibrium,"

---

* There is also some evidence that expert chess players first consider those moves that leave their opponents the fewest replies. See H. A. Simon and A. Newell, "Information processing in computer and man," *Amer. Scientist*, 1964, **52**, 281–300.

although given a precise technical meaning by Apostel, suggests an apt metaphor for the character of the highest symbolic structures. Neutral equilibrium is exemplified by the state of a ball on a horizontal plane. The ball can remain indefinitely where it is, but, as soon as a force is exerted on it, it can move freely to any other point, remaining in place as soon as the force ceases to act. This state is contrasted with unstable equilibrium, in which the slightest displacement from the present location of an object causes it to overbalance at an accelerating rate in that direction, and stable equilibrium, in which the slightest displacement is followed by a prompt return to the initial location. Both of these kinds of equilibrium have their counterparts in behavior. Unstable equilibrium corresponds to "vicious circles," or explosive processes, which are virtually always maladaptive. Stable equilibrium corresponds to the homeostatic, self-corrective, or negative-feedback processes that are necessary for the maintenance of life, but other forms of stable equilibrium can be strongly inimical to functions like learning and thinking that are responsible for adaptive change.

Recursive Anchoring

In the foregoing discussion, we have seen how selection of a transformational symbolic response resolves the specific conflict, representing a specific subproblem, that corresponds to the immediately prior choice-point. But this is only one part of the motivational function of transformational responses that we must unravel. We must now take a broader view and recall that the piecing together of a sequence of "legitimate steps" or acceptable transformations is necessary before the over-all conflict, corresponding to the problem that initiated the thought process, can be resolved. We noted in Chapter 5 that a represented goal situation will furnish terminal reinforcement only if it appears at the end of a chain of transformations that connect it with the initial situation. Only when this is achieved can the inhibition that prevents belief and action be removed.

There thus results a process that we may call *recursive anchoring*. It invites comparison with the technique that is used to rescue somebody who has fallen through a hole in the ice covering a pond. A chain of rescuers is built out from the shore by having each person grasp the legs of the next until the last one can secure a firm grip on the victim. As long as the first member of the chain has a solid foothold on land, his security is transmitted throughout the chain until it ultimately reaches the victim, who is thereby prevented from sinking.

Processes that fit this analogy are ubiquitous in practical problem solving as well as in logical, mathematical, and scientific thinking. The subject begins with a represented stimulus situation that he recognizes as real (for example, his present predicament) or some proposition that he accepts as true. In sophisticated hypothetico-deductive reasoning, the starting point may be an axiom, postulate, or hypothesis that is not actually known to be true but is temporarily taken as true "for the sake of argument." The subject then establishes a transformation, and the represented situation that results from this transformation is thereby invested with the same status of truth or reality that belongs to the initial situation. Any inhibition that accompanied its previous contemplation is thereby suspended. This same status of truth or reality is then transmitted to yet another represented situation by the next transformation, and so on.

So, when we think of a state of affairs existing in the past, present, or future, and we develop a sequence of physical processes that are known to be capable of starting out from that state of affairs, all the stages through which the sequence passes acquire the same standing in relation to our belief as the initial state of affairs. In logic, if A is taken to be true and it is acknowledged that A implies B, then B becomes equally true; if B is then acknowledged to imply C, C becomes true, etc. In mathematics, there is the widely used method of proof by "mathematical induction" or "recursion," discussed in Chapter 7. A proposition is established as true when $x = 0$. It is then established that, if the proposition is true with $x = n$, it must be true also when $x = n + 1$. At this point, it can be deduced that the proposition must be true with x equal to any integer.

We are still far from the time when we shall understand the exact psychological mechanism, let alone the physiological mechanism, of recursive anchoring, which conveys the sanction of validity from the starting point to the end point of a solution chain and relieves conceptual conflict by neutralizing the inhibitory factor from which doubt and suspended belief derive. As with all complex forms of behavior, a helpful way to begin the search for understanding is to relate the behavior in question to its nearest analogues in simple animal behavior. A promising clue that is surely worth following up is provided by some experiments carried out by Napalkov (1961).

This experimenter, working with dogs, rabbits, and rats, has set up complex systems of motor responses, which he explicitly relates to human behavior using intellectual capacities. In one kind of experiment, he first established a chain of conditioned responses, which was terminally reinforced with food. The performance of each response in the chain was followed by the appearance of an external signal that marked the occasion for the next response. During certain trials, a conditioned inhibitor (a blue light, a bell, etc.) was presented for 30 sec. or longer. While this stimulus was on, the food-seeking sequence was never reinforced with food. Consequently, "the animal began, after ten to fifteen combinations, to respond to the conditioned stimuli (the food chain of reflexes) only when the conditioned inhibitor was turned off." Napalkov continues:

> . . . the conditioned inhibitor was capable of serving as reinforcement for the elaboration of new conditioned reflex reactions. If we turned the conditioned inhibitor off several times after the dog performed a specific motion (without reinforcement by food), the animal subsequently began to carry out this motion.

Similar results were obtained by a positive-patterning procedure. Food was forthcoming only when the food-seeking responses were performed in the presence of a combination of two stimuli (a light and a gurgling sound). When only one of these two stimuli was present, food reinforcement was withheld. The animals then learned to perform a new sequence of responses on receiving one element of the combination, the sequence being reinforced at its termination by the appearance of the second member.

We thus find a number of phenomena here that are akin to essential aspects of the recursive-anchoring process in directed thinking:

(1) The elimination of a condition that is productive of inhibition (the presence of a conditioned inhibitor or the incompleteness of a combination of conditioned stimuli) acts as a reward.

(2) The conditioned inhibitor or incomplete pattern thus acts as an aversive condition. We may surmise this is due to conflict resulting from the simultaneous action of an inhibiting agent and conditions that would otherwise evoke motor behavior.

(3) The conditioned inhibitor or incomplete pattern acts as a discriminative cue, evoking the responses that will be reinforced by the removal of inhibition. In this respect, their mode of functioning is similar to that of other aversive agents, for example, stimuli paired with pain. Napalkov refers to them as "switch-on stimuli" (cf. the "switching mediators" discussed in Chapter 7).

(4) A motor pattern that is instigated by certain features of the external situation is withheld while the inhibiting agent is present but allowed to run off as soon as the conditioned inhibitor is turned off or the missing element of the pattern is turned on.

The patterning case seems particularly apposite to directed thinking, since the inhibition and resulting conflict that beset the thinker are due to an incomplete combination of symbolic stimulus elements. He has the initial situation and, in addition, he may represent to himself the goal situation or some intermediate portions of the solution chain.   But as long as he does not have a complete solution chain leading from the initial situation to the goal situation, he is subject to inhibition and conflict.   Once, however, this chain has been completed, he experiences the rewarding effect of conflict reduction, and a course of overt action that was held in check may then be given its head.

Further Complications

The way our discussion has gone so far might encourage the impression that directed thinking is a matter of sailing through one choice-point after another, with an occasional holdup at an exceptionally troublesome one.   This may sometimes be the case, for example, when a subject is carrying out a standard computing procedure or when he is recalling the way he solved a comparable problem in the past.   Directed thinking aimed at the solution of a new problem, especially a recalcitrant one, is, of course, generally not of this form.   There are a number of additional phenomena that must be taken into account and that make the picture considerably more complicated.   Three in particular must receive some attention.

1. Implicit Trial and Error

It is clear that, in most thought processes, a great deal of time is spent on false starts and symbolic equivalents of blind alleys.   Thinking, in fact, often takes the form of "implicit trial and error" (Dewey, 1910; Claparède, 1933).   Yet the analogies with animal behavior that these terms suggest must be treated with caution.   Even the behavior of the cat in a new puzzle box or the rat in a new maze cannot rightly be described as "blind" or "random" trial and error; it consists mostly of responses, whether learned or unlearned, that have an above-average chance of being helpful.   In human reasoning, the number of alternative combinations of symbolic responses must be immeasurably higher than the number of motor responses open to a baffled animal.   As Newell, Shaw, and Simon have repeatedly pointed out (for example, 1958), anything in the way of random selection of thought elements must have a negligible probability of solving a problem within a reasonable time.   Human thinking must inevitably make use of "heuristics" or procedures whereby lines of thought with the greatest chances of success are tried out first and more remote possibilities are left until later.

How a human being recognizes that the line of thought he is pursuing is not going to lead him to a solution and should therefore be given up is a great problem, presumably akin to the problem of what makes the thinker decide whether to abandon a problem altogether after a certain period of unavailing effort.   Computers loaded with problem-solving programs are likewise instructed to explore the fruitfulness of a number of approaches, corresponding to coordinate branches of a tree structure, in a prescribed order, giving each one up in favor of the next as it proves inapplicable.   A computer recognizes inapplicability by finding that the formula with which it is dealing does not satisfy some necessary condition or by coming to the end of a list of items without finding one with the required property.   The cues that lead a human thinker to give up a certain direction of thought can hardly be so clear-cut.   For one thing, he cannot usually tell that he has exhausted his stock of relevant ideas.   In fact, a tendency to give up a line of thought too soon has often been cited as a common source of inefficiency in thinking.   Presumably, what distinguishes a blind alley from genuine progress toward the goal is some kind of exacerbation of conflict.

Many writers have pointed to the possibility of making errors with impunity as one of the unique advantages of thinking over overt trial and error.   Piaget has insisted that the ability to reverse an error and return to the last point reached on the correct line of thought requires the use of the operations that are inverses of the ones that turned out to be erroneous.   Otherwise, thought would be inconsistent and chaotic, and the thinker would not find himself at a represented situation equivalent to where he would have been if he had never embarked on the mistaken sequence.   Since the state of a thinker depends on the situational thought that he is at present entertaining and this, in its turn, is defined in terms of a series of transformations leading up to it, there must be some truth in what Piaget says.   A rat that goes down a blind alley could recognize where he is and start afresh without prejudice if an experimenter were to whisk him from the end of the blind alley to the choice-point where he went wrong. But normally, a rat has to retrace his steps.   A thinker has no alternative to retracing his steps, since he has otherwise no way of telling when and where he is back on the right track.

2. Divergent and Convergent Thinking

Guilford (1956, 1959), having used factor analysis to map out the structure of intellectual abilities, has distinguished two groups of "production factors," which he associates with "divergent" and "convergent" thinking respectively. Convergent thinking, he writes (1956), "has to do with the production of some end-result. After one has comprehended the situation, or the significant aspect of it at the moment, usually something needs to be done to it or about it . . . Having understood the problem, we must take further steps to solve it." Among the factors associated with it are ones named "eduction of correlates," "ordering," and "symbol substitution." Abilities dependent on possession and use of transformation-selecting and transformation-applying habits are therefore clearly included. "The unique feature of divergent production," Guilford states (1959), "is that a variety of responses is produced." Among the pertinent factors are "word fluency," "associational fluency," "ideational fluency," and "spontaneous flexibility" (measured by a test that requires the subject to enumerate unusual uses of a specified object).

Although Guilford has been concerned with identifying abilities that contribute to the efficiency of thinking and with which individuals are endowed to differing extents, it is clear that processes corresponding to these two groups of factors must participate in any piece of directed thinking, so that the terms "divergent thinking" and "convergent thinking" have come into general use.

The selection of items to be formed into a solution chain evidently belongs to the convergent aspect of thinking. This work must, however, often be preceded by processes that make available an assortment of items on which convergent thinking can draw. These constitute divergent thinking. Processes partaking of the free-associative nature of autistic thinking must figure prominently in divergent episodes. This means that, although we have been at pains to stress the dependence of directed thinking on transformational chains, transformational and free-associative thinking must usually interact and collaborate in practice.

McKellar (1957) aptly describes the interaction between autistic and directed thinking as an "authorship-editorship" relation. Autistic thinking often supplies thought material, from which directed thinking selects items to be fashioned into a solution chain. This will, of course, not always be the case. Sometimes, transformation-applying and transformation-selecting habits will bring up the elements that are needed without much strain. But at other times, when a problem is especially new or difficult, the thinker will occasionally be "stuck," and he will resort to free-associative processes to remedy the dearth of elements to work on. Manuals of advice on how to improve thinking often recommend that the process of finding ideas and the process of critically assaying them should be separated from one another. They sometimes recommend such devices as exposing oneself to a varied assortment of external objects, preferably in unusual combinations, in the hope they will give rise to unexpected lines of thought.

Problem-solving computers using "list-processing languages" (Green, 1963) must similarly alternate between times when they are applying operations to formulas and times when they are running through lists to find operations to apply or to find formulas on which to operate. When they run through a list, they make use of an arrangement reminiscent of autistic thinking rather than of directed thinking: as each item comes up, it is coupled with the address of the location where the next item on the list is to be found, so that the computer finds its way down the list by a series of associations connecting each item with its immediate successor.

Symbolic structures must, in other words, store information in at least three forms which are at the disposal of directed thinking: transformational chains, free-associative chains of situational thoughts, and free-associative chains of transformational thoughts.

Divergent phases of thinking may not only fail to fit the pattern of progressive conflict reduction. They may even run counter to it. A search for new thoughts, a drastic extension of the boundaries within which material for the solution chain may be gleaned, is apt to land the thinker in deeper and deeper morasses of complexity, doubt, overloading of information-processing channels, and frustration. The hope is, of course, that this aggravation of conflict will be transient and will hasten the discovery of a thought sequence that can effectively quench conflict.

Some relevant experimental findings were made by Bartlett (1958) in connection with what he called "adventurous thinking." He first presented subjects with a simplified sectional road map and explained that the task was to find a route to a point off this map to the northwest. When one of the roads leading off the first section had been chosen, a map of the adjoining region was presented and so on, until the whole route had been worked out. Subjects faced with this task were a little more likely to opt for roads that branched out into three directions in preference to those that branched out into two. Bartlett comments:

. . . if a generalization is legitimate from these map-section results it would seem that, when a thinker is working in an open, or relatively open, system (roads, for example, may proceed in any direction) he inclines to prefer the evidence which releases the greater rather than the smaller number of possibilities . . . The working, though not the formulated, rule seems to be that it is better to explore along the line of the greater number of possibilities, because it is more likely that the one sought will be found when there are a lot of chances than when there are only a few.

The risk of suffering intensified stress before relief is secured bedevils virtually all recourses to exploratory or epistemic behavior (Berlyne, 1960a, 1963). There is usually a choice between seeking further information (which generally means postponing relief but giving oneself a chance to dispose of a problem definitively and rendering it innocuous for the future), and other reactions, for example, turning away from a conflict-inducing situation or suppressing thoughts about it (which may afford immediate comfort but lays one open to recurrent disturbance from the same source). This kind of choice is, needless to say, by no means confined to curiosity-arousing situations. It is, for example, equally typical of situations that arouse fear. Evidently, certain temperaments are more partial to behavior that maximizes long-term remedies at the cost of short-term stress, while others are less willing or able to pay the price (see Berlyne, 1960a, 1963).

3. Phases of Analysis and Synthesis

A number of writers on directed thinking have distinguished an initial phase of analysis and a subsequent phase of synthesis. Russian writers (for example, Rubinshtein, 1958, 1960; Ponomarev, 1960) have been particularly fond of this dichotomy, apparently because Pavlov often named analysis and synthesis as the two main functions of the cerebral cortex. American writers, however, have also made use of it (for example, Heidbreder, 1924; Blatt and Stein, 1959).

Processes that contribute directly to the composition of a solution chain clearly belong to the synthetic phase. The analytic phase includes processes with auxiliary and preliminary functions to perform. The precise activities denoted by the term "analysis" have, however, varied from one writer to another. Blatt and Stein (1959) have used it in connection with the kind of thinking that is elicited by the John-Rimoldi PSI Apparatus. This apparatus, it will be recalled, requires the subject to find out how to turn on a light in the center of a panel by pressing a combination of buttons. What Blatt and Stein call the "analysis" phase is the necessary preliminary period of ascertaining the effects of pressing the various buttons separately. Only after this has been done can there be an "analysis-to-synthesis shift," following which the subject makes use of the information he has obtained in this way to construct a sequence that will fulfill his objective.

Rubinshtein, on the other hand, thinks of "analysis," in a Pavlovian spirit, as a term covering processes whereby the subject apprehends, distinguishes, and abstracts properties of stimulus patterns. He, like Duncker (1945), lays preponderant stress on the "analysis of the problem." This means such things as determining the essential features of the material and the problem, locating specific difficulties that will have to be overcome, and setting up subgoals whose attainment seems likely to facilitate the attainment of the terminal goal.

The American writers appear, therefore, to be discussing a phase of exploratory and epistemic behavior which secures information without which the problem cannot be solved. The processes that the European writers have in mind appear to be ones that expose the subject to specific conflicts which motivate and guide the subsequent search.

Russian specialists in thinking (Rubinshtein, 1958; Ponamarev, 1960) have, in fact, had some controversy regarding the best time to give the subject help in the form of an easier subsidiary problem drawing attention to a principle that can be used in the solution of the main problem. The experimental data that are cited are superficially at variance, some suggesting that the subsidiary problem should be presented first and others that it should be presented after the subject has been wrestling with the main problem for a while. It clearly makes a great deal of difference when the subsidiary problem is presented, even though the optimal times will vary with the content of the main problem.

The upshot seems to be that the subject cannot profit from the subsidiary problem if the way in which he has analyzed the main problem prevents him from recognizing its relevance. The subsidiary problem will be helpful only if it can direct him toward an appropriate way of analyzing the main problem or if it comes at a time when he has spontaneously analyzed the main problem appropriately. This can easily be understood in the light of our hypotheses: the information latent in the subsidiary problem can hardly contribute to conflict reduction unless the subject has confronted himself with a conflict that this information is capable of resolving.

Chapter 12

Productive thinking

SELZ (1913) used the terms *reproductive thinking* and *productive thinking* to refer, respectively, to the kind of thinking that simply reproduces previous experience and the kind that generates new mental content. Later authors have found the same distinction, or one approximating it, helpful. For example, Maier (1945) writes of solutions that depend solely on "equivalence reactions" as products of reproductive thinking; he mentions as an illustration the use of a pair of pliers as a pendulum bob when one has in the past "reacted to its weight aspect." Productive thinking takes place when "past learning is subject to modification and reorganization," for example, when an individual who has never "reacted to the weight aspect" of a pair of pliers conceives of its possible use as a pendulum bob "during the stress of the problem situation."

It is not hard to see what such a dichotomy means in terms of our conceptualization. Reproductive thinking is what happens when responses suitable for the solution chain are already high up in the hierarchies that confront the thinker at the choice-points through which he passes. These responses are thus readily recognized and adopted. Such is the case when someone represents to himself a habitual sequence of events or when he makes use of a familiar computational procedure. It may also occur in other standardized forms of reasoning, such as the "trouble-shooting" procedure by which an electronic technician ascertains what is wrong with a piece of equipment. Productive thinking, on the other hand, occurs when the sought-after responses are low in their respective hierarchies and overshadowed by stronger but less adaptive competitors. They will thus be reached only after some delay, conflict, and effort.

In Chapter 1, we introduced a distinction between "S-thinking" and "R-thinking." S-thinking, which results in the performance of a familiar response pattern in a new stimulus situation, will often be reproductive. Primary or secondary stimulus generalization will often be enough to bring the correct response to the fore without serious competition. But much S-thinking is evidently productive, giving rise, for example, to the use of an object in a highly unfamiliar and unlikely way. According to a recent newspaper story, an airline pilot discovered a fault in his landing gear and required a piece of wire to make a short circuit. Having no wire within reach, he caught sight of a hairpin in a stewardess's hair and borrowed it for that purpose. Köhler's ape, being accustomed to pulling in a banana with a stick, found no stick within reach and instead pulled off the branch of a tree to use as a substitute that could serve instead. Other feats of productive S-thinking were achieved by Boole, when he recognized that notations and operations that had long been used in algebra could be applied to logical problems, and by Shakespeare when the thought of "human kindness" elicited from him the verbal response "milk," which had previously been associated with the thought or sight of the fluids with which infant mammals are nourished.

R-thinking, we must suppose, will almost always be productive, as a response pattern that the subject has never before performed will normally be low in his habit-family hierarchies. It might be thought that, if a response has never been performed before, the subject does not yet possess it and we should not speak of it as existing in his hierarchies at all. But as long as a subject is physically capable of a response pattern and may sooner or later come up with it as a solution to a problem, it must be considered to have some finite probability of occurrence, however small. It would therefore seem a more helpful usage to regard it as present within the subject, even though the conditions for its evocation have never yet been fulfilled. Moreover, since it is more likely to come out in some stimulus conditions than in others, it must be deemed to possess associations with certain stimulus conditions. This usage is in line with Skinner's (1957) practice of describing a response as "existing in some strength" although it has not been emitted.

There could, however, be forms of stimulus-response generalization that bring an unprecedented response pattern to the top of the hierarchy immediately, making for reproductive R-thinking. Maier's example of the use of pliers as a pendulum bob by a subject who has had occasion in the past to react to the weight of a pair of pliers may be a case in point if, as is likely, the subject has never before gone through the sequence of attaching an object to the end of a length of string, hanging up the string, and setting it swinging.

Productive Thinking and Intelligent Learning

A close connection is readily detected between productive thinking and the intelligent learning that is promoted by discovery methods of instruction. Productive thinking is typically a product of stimulus-response generalization, and it invariably permits of wide extension to future problem situations through further stimulus-response generalization. Susceptibility to stimulus-response generalization is, as we have seen, one of the paramount attributes of transformational thinking, and this is the kind that arises in the course of intelligent learning, in contrast with the rote serial recall or rigid motor patterns that are apt to come from mechanical learning.

It has already been inferred (in Chapter 9) that the peculiarities of intelligent learning are bound up with the reinforcing effects of relief of conceptual conflict. Productive thinking must entail considerable conflict as it causes initially weak responses to rise above their initially strong competitors, and such an exacting process could hardly be undertaken unless there were strong conflict from some other source to set it in motion. Discovery methods in education deliberately precipitate such conflicts and train a child to endure a temporary worsening of conflict for the sake of the eventual assuagement that he can be confident will follow. The reinforcing effect of this assuagement may, in its turn, build up a general willingness to resort to productive thinking, despite its rigors, and facilitate the retention of the solutions that are arrived at.

Productive Thinking and Creativity

The word "creativity" is commonly applied to productive thinking, although the meanings given to it are not always uniform. Not infrequently, the term "creative thinking" is used as a synonym for "productive thinking." More usually, however, social influence and social value are taken into account in assessing how "creative" a piece of thinking is.

To be deemed creative, a product of a thought process must be initially improbable and hence unpredictable. The great accomplishments in the history of science and literature are hailed as creative, at least partly because no one—not even their creators—could have specified these combinations of verbal symbols beforehand as ones that might prove adequate to the purposes they were designed to fulfill. The selection of the one correct answer out of four in a multiple-choice examination is not usually considered creative, although a student might give an extremely unexpected and creative reason for selecting it. The recognition of one answer out of four as correct might, however, be considered creative if it is one that the vast majority of students would have rejected.

There are many reasons why a particular thought product should be improbable, but two possible reasons stand out. There may be one dominant response pattern so firmly established in a social group that any alternative has a minute chance of acquiring enough strength to challenge it. The creative individual is thus often the courageous nonconformist, who finds fault with long entrenched practices, which have rarely or never been called in question, and proposes advantageous innovations. Alternatively, there may be so many possible lines of thought or action that the chances of fortuitously lighting on a fruitful one are initially low. A special case is a situation in which the community as a whole is baffled, so that the numerous courses of thought and action that suggest themselves to most of its members are impracticable, dangerous, or irrelevant.

The second requirement for a piece of thinking to be adjudged creative is that it be socially valuable. The "word salad" or "flight of ideas" of the psychotic are, for this reason, not held to deserve the epithet, even though the combinations to which they give rise may be exceedingly improbable.

Since a high proportion of an individual's stock of symbolic responses is derived from social interaction and culturally determined, a response pattern that has a low probability of occurring in the social group as a whole will, in all likelihood, be relatively weak and occupy low hierarchical positions within any individual. And although a happy constellation of circumstances may occasionally toss up a new and valuable response pattern without any struggle, the generation of a creative thought product will generally climax a conflict-ridden period of gestation. The socially dominant pattern of behavior or belief will correspond to a strong habit, and any fresh form of overt or symbolic behavior that is destined to overthrow it must generally pass through a painful phase of collision with its rival before it can prevail. Likewise, when the group is faced with a multitude of divergent and not very promising leads, a corresponding multitude of mutually discrepant response-tendencies must generally fight it out within the individual. So greater creativity tends to issue from greater conflict which, in view of our identification of degree of conflict with degree of problematicity, fits the fact that greater creativity, on the whole, comes from willingness to attack greater or more difficult problems.

What was a great problem for the creative individual may well have been, for sometime, a great problem for his group. The first flying machines were devised after centuries of perplexity and frustration growing out of the human desire to emulate the birds. Einstein's special theory of relativity came when physicists had been confused and mystified for 24 years by the results of the Michelson-Morley experiment.

At other times, the creative individual must supply the problem and induce the corresponding conflict in others before he communicates the solution that he has devised. The scientist reports an observation that raises questions: Rumford finds that heat is generated when a cannon barrel is bored and is eventually led to conclude that heat consists of motion rather than of a special kind of substance; Pavlov notices that dogs whose stomach secretions he is studying salivate anticipatorily on seeing food and is drawn into the study of conditioned reflexes. A philosopher raises questions concerning matters that are familiar enough but whose problematic aspects most men have failed to experience through lack of reflection. A mathematician invents a new function whose properties and behavior immediately raise questions, and he then reports research by which some of these questions are disposed of.

Skinner (1957) writes:

We are especially reinforced by speakers and writers who say what we are almost ready to say ourselves—who take the words "off the tip of our tongue." Significantly enough, we call such writers or speakers "stimulating." . . . they . . . make us think, in the sense of making us behave verbally with respect to some state of affairs.

He does not explain why we find it particularly satisfying to listen to or hear something that we came near to saying or thinking ourselves. Presumably, it is because the thoughts or utterances in question or the elements out of which they are built existed within us in conflict with antagonistic responses. The authoritative pronouncements or convincing arguments of a speaker or writer relieve our conflict by selectively strengthening some of the competing processes and weakening others. We are, it may be supposed, rewarded by conflict reduction, but this will generally be effected only if we have first undergone a conflict resembling the one that motivated the speaker or writer.

In order to undergo such a conflict, we must have the makings of the conflict—habits from which conflicting response can spring—inside us. We must, in other words, know something about the subject matter. Symbolic material that is completely beyond our ken we simply do not "understand" or find "interesting." To quote Skinner further:

> Intraverbal sequences which do not follow from the contiguous usages of our own experience . . . are both worthless and dull . . . we say that we do not "get it" or do not "see what the writer is driving at" or why he says what he says. . . . (it) does not supplement verbal behavior in us which exists in any considerable strength.

Going beyond Skinner's view, we may suppose the main point to be that such material does not relieve conflict by strengthening a symbolic response pattern that is competing with others.

Creative thinking often receives special treatment as a phenomenon apart, but this practice seems unjustified and will not be followed here. For one thing, the distinguishing marks of creative thinking, in so far as they depend on social evaluation, do not imply that it depends on unique psychological processes. Second, creative thinking is productive thinking and must surely be investigated in conjunction with noncreative forms of productive thinking, which, in their turn, cannot be fully understood until we know more about reproductive thinking. Many worthwhile findings about the personality traits that characterize creative individuals have been collected (Golann, 1963), but the elucidation of interindividual differences in creativity can hardly advance very far until we understand the mechanisms of directed thinking in general.

Ways of Strengthening Submerged Responses

It will be evident from the foregoing discussion that creative thinking raises, in a particularly acute form, the question that is basic to any analysis of productive thinking in general: how do response patterns that are low in existing symbolic habit-family hierarchies, and thus initially improbable, become strong enough to supplant the dominant response patterns under which they are submerged? They can clearly do so only if the dominant responses can be weakened or if they themselves can be strengthened or, of course, both. To find ways in which such changes could come about, we must turn to some of the general principles of behavior theory.

Maltzman (1955) has, in fact, laid the foundations for such an inquiry, and we may extend his suggestions to arrive at a list of relevant mechanisms. But we must first recall the main substance of Maltzman's contribution, which is to point out that thinking is not simply a matter of selectively strengthening and weakening specific responses or response sequences. When, in everyday parlance, we speak of "ideas" emerging or disappearing, being accepted or rejected, we may be referring to specific responses, to specific response sequences, or to classes of response sequences, that is, subhierarchies corresponding to general ways of approaching the problem. When Hull introduced the notion of a habit-family hierarchy, he spotlighted as one of its principal properties the fact that, when the performance of a particular chain is followed by reward or frustration, the hierarchy as a whole is strengthened or weakened. Maltzman emphasizes that, in thinking that makes use of compound habit-family hierarchies, a given subhierarchy may similarly be strengthened or weakened without the necessity of going through every component of the subhierarchy in turn.

The mechanisms that could accomplish what we are after thus fall into three classes:

1. EXTINCTION. The uppermost member of a hierarchy is the one most likely to be tried out first. If it proves unavailing, the subject will sooner or later discard it and take up another member of the hierarchy, most probably the one occupying the second position. This process continues until a member that leads to success is found.

This is, of course, the familiar process of "implicit trial and error," which must be a feature of all productive thought processes except for those blessed with extraordinary luck. It is also an invariable feature of computer programs designed to simulate productive thinking. These programs have, in fact, been found so valuable largely because they are able to run through and reject many more unsuccessful processes than a human thinker could in an acceptable period of time. The resemblance between the implicit trial and error of thinking and the overt trial and error that characterizes an animal's first moments in a novel environment (for example, a puzzle box or a maze) has long been recognized. Hull (1930) ascribed the abandonment of incorrect responses in such situations to extinction due to "failure of reinforcement."

There are, however, some important differences between the crudest kinds of overt trial and error and what happens in thinking. First, the rejection of a thought sequence or a line of attack (subhierarchy) does not result solely from lack of reinforcement. How soon rejection takes place is not simply a matter of how long the subject has persisted with it and how much effort he has given it. There are evidently cues that enable a subject to recognize that his present train of thought is unlikely to bring him nearer to a solution and that he must start off on a new tack. We have already speculated that exacerbation of conflict is an important constituent of such cues. Second, we have already seen why transformational responses must lead the subject back, from the point to which the mistaken line of thought has brought him, to a situational thought from which he can advance in a different direction. These returning transformations will be especially vital when he does not have to go back to the starting point of his inquiry but can resume at some partial result that he has achieved or at some intermediate point that can confidently be taken to be on the route to the goal. Third, we must remember that, with symbolic subhierarchies as with the kinds of overt habit-family hierarchy that Hull described, a whole area of inquiry may be given up after a few sorties within it have proved unpromising. The ability to judge when an approach should be repudiated, even though all the possibilities within it have not been fully explored, is, in fact, one of the most important ingredients of skill at thinking, and both failure to follow up one direction long enough and excessive obstinacy in pursuing inauspicious leads have often been mentioned as causes of inefficiency.

Köhler (1921, p. 123) remarks, for example:

It occasionally happens that one will start working on a mathematical or a physical problem with perfectly correct premises, and calculate or think up to a point where one gets lost. The whole proceeding is then rejected, and only later will one discover that the method was quite right, and that the difficulty was only a superficial one and could easily have been overcome.

He compares this to the reaction of one of his apes that was attempting to reach an objective by stacking boxes when one box happened to slip sideways:

. . . then Grande lets it fall altogether, and shows distinctly by her behavior that, for her, the whole method is now completely spoiled.

Despite these peculiarities, it seems justifiable to include the weakening of dominant response patterns in the course of implicit trial and error under the rubric of "extinction," since the relegation to a lower position in the hierarchy is usually lasting but reversible: the subject is much less likely to resort to them, and correspondingly more likely to begin with the more successful ones that were initially weaker, when he next finds himself at the choice-point in question.

The analogy with extinction of simple learned responses is substantiated further by evidence that futile initial responses persist longer, and the appearance of the correct response is correspondingly delayed, when motivation is inordinately strong. Apes studied by Birch (1945a) took less time to solve string-pulling and stick problems when they had been deprived of food for 24 hours than after longer or shorter durations of deprivation. "When motivation is very low," he writes, "the animals are easily diverted from the problem by extraneous factors and behavior tends to deteriorate into a series of nongoal-directed acts. Under conditions of very intense motivation, the animals concentrate upon the goal to the relative exclusion of other features of the situation which are essential to the solution of the problem" and waste time with behavior expressive of frustration. Likewise, Lewin (1935) reports that, when a child sees a goal object behind a barrier, an excessive increase in the attractiveness of the goal object will make it "doubly difficult" for the child to move away from it and walk round the barrier. "Instead, the child will execute, with all its energy, effective meaningless actions" in the direction of the goal object.

2. REINFORCEMENT. A response pattern that is low in a hierarchy may be brought higher, and thus made more accessible, if it, or some other response pattern belonging to the same subhierarchy, is subjected to reinforcement before the subject applies himself to the problem of interest. This can happen, for example, if the subject is first exposed to a preliminary problem situation in which a response pattern of the subhierarchy is likely to be tried out early and to be followed by success.

An experiment by Rees and Israel (1935) illustrates such selective strengthening of one class of responses over others that are in competition with it. One group of subjects was first given a training series of 20 simple five-letter anagrams whose solutions consisted of words having to do with eating, for example, *aeksc* (cakes). They then went through 20 test anagrams that were each amenable to two solutions, only one of which had to do with eating, for example, *aephc* (peach, cheap). Another group underwent the same procedure, except that solutions concerned with natural phenomena were substituted for solutions concerned with eating. Control groups received the test anagrams scattered among unrelated items. The results showed a marked tendency for the experimental groups to find the "eating" and "nature" solutions to the test anagrams respectively.

In another experiment, an experimental group was put through a training series of 15 anagrams that could all be solved by permuting the letters in the order 34521, for example, *lecam* (camel). A control group received instead 15 anagrams with randomly chosen permutations. When both groups were given test anagrams that were capable of two solutions, one of which was produced by the 34521 permutation, for example, *raspe* (spear, pears), "the Experimental Group solved 94.6 per cent of the critical anagrams according to the prescribed order whereas the percentage for the Control Group was 47.3."

Other experimenters have used problems whose solutions were less readily come by. Saugstad (1957) turned his attention to Maier's (1930) celebrated problem situation in which two pendulums with chalks at the ends of them must be set up in such a way as to mark specified spots on the floor. One of Saugstad's groups was first given three preliminary problems that resembled the three constituent operations of the solution to the pendulum problem (making a plumb line by attaching a clamp to the end of a string and inserting a pencil in the clamp, making a long pole by clamping two short poles together, wedging a T-shaped arrangement of poles in a doorway). Subjects who tackled these preliminary problems successfully were significantly more likely to solve the pendulum problem than those who tried them but failed or than members of another group who simply had the three operations demonstrated to them. There seems, therefore, to have been some reinforcement coming from a successful encounter with the preliminary problems that was absent when their solutions were merely witnessed. Our earlier discussions favor the conjecture that it derived from conflict reduction. Comparisons with discovery methods in education suggest themselves.

Ponomarev (1960) reports an extensive series of studies in which the effects of various preliminary treatments on the probability of solving the four-dot problem (mentioned in Chapter 11) were examined. He found a number that were capable of leading some subjects to the correct solution, provided that they were presented after the initial confrontation with the problem. The most successful of all, which caused ten out of ten subjects to discover how four dots can be joined with three connected lines, consisted of practice at drawing triangles circumscribing a square. After comparing the effects of introducing subsidiary tasks at different stages, Ponomarev names "competing factors" as the chief obstacles to benefiting from these tasks. The most favorable moment to introduce them, he states, is "when the subject has exhausted inadequate methods but has not yet lost the desire to carry out the task, i.e. the searching dominant has not extinguished." What this means in our language is that the reinforcing effects of a subsidiary task can best help the correct response pattern to emerge when the dominant subhierarchies corresponding to incorrect methods of approach are extinguished but the supraordinate hierarchy itself is not yet extinguished, that is, the drive to solve the problem has not yet been neutralized by the inhibitory effects of frustration to the point at which the subject is ready to quit.

The aforementioned studies have focused on the influence of auxiliary tasks in bringing optimal responses to the fore. Other studies have dealt with essentially the same phenomenon while focusing on the power of auxiliary tasks to delay the appearance of the optimal response by causing wrong responses to be reinforced. Research of this kind is generally conducted under such headings as "rigidity," "functional fixedness," and "*Einstellung.*"

The most active exponent of this particular line of investigation has been Luchins (1942, 1954, etc.), who has used problems in which a certain quantity of water has to be measured out with the help of three jars of stated capacities. He first presents a number of "set-inducing" tasks, for example, 100 pints has to be obtained with the help of jars A, B, and C, whose capacities are 21, 127, and 3 pints, respectively. The set-induced problems can all be solved by an indirect method, which may be denoted by B-A-2C. Then follow the crucial tasks, which can be solved either by the same indirect method as proved applicable to the set-inducing tasks or by a more direct method. For example, 20 pints can be measured out with jars holding 23, 49, and 3 pints respectively, either by B-A-2C or by A-C. The preliminary experience with the set-inducing problems usually inclines subjects toward the less efficient indirect method and makes them less likely to discover the more economical direct method when they face the crucial problems. Luchins found this effect to be more pronounced when eight set-inducing problems were used than when there were only five of them. It was, on the other hand, reduced when "extinction" problems, that is, problems that were not amenable to the A-B-2C solution, were interspersed among the set-inducing problems.

These last findings of Luchins underline the obvious analogies between the phenomena under discussion and the kinds of reinforcement that govern simple forms of learning. Strictly speaking, however, the term "reinforcement" is appropriate only if the auxiliary problems can be shown to induce learning, which means that their response-strengthening effects must last for at least a day. Whether this is, in fact, the case seems not to have been ascertained. If it is not the case, we shall have to speak of them as productive of temporary sets rather than of reinforcement.

3. SUPPLEMENTARY STIMULATION. The remaining way in which a desirable response can be elevated from a depressed position in a hierarchy to a position of prepotency is by the occurrence of a supplementary stimulus.

In Chapter 5, we reviewed arguments opposing the constellation theory, according to which a thought element is evoked because two stimuli (for example, a cue stimulus and a motivational stimulus) are both associated with it. Instead, we favored the view that a symbolic response is evoked by a combination of stimuli through patterning. These arguments applied, however, to phases of thought in which the thought that is to come up is already dominant. What we are now concerned with is the divergent phase of thinking, in which the subject is "looking for ideas" because the dominant responses leave him in the lurch. In this case, patterning may play its part: the original situational stimulus and the supplementary stimulus might happen to be associated, as a combination, with a response that meets the thinker's requirements. But it is more likely that the kind of mechanism envisaged by the constellation theory here comes into its own and that the two stimuli will collaborate in evoking a response that possesses relatively weak associations with both of them (see Figure 12-1).

Here, the responses that branch out from each stimulus may be ones that have at different times acquired associations with that stimulus, or they may be responses representing some kind of response generalization continuum. In the latter case, the response that is brought forth is likely to be qualitatively or quantitatively intermediate between the dominant responses associated with the two stimuli. If the emerging response (or combination of responses) is not evoked through positive patterning by the combination consisting of the preceding thought and the supplementary stimulus, it may have become associated with either of these stimuli as the result of primary stimulus generalization, or it may be elicited by a mediator possessing associations with both of the stimuli. These three cases correspond to the "serendipity," "similarity," and "mediation" mechanisms that Mednick (1962) lists as "ways of attaining creative solutions" by "bringing the requisite associative elements together."

The supplementary stimulus pattern may take the form of verbal instructions. Maltzman and Morrisett (1953) performed an experi-

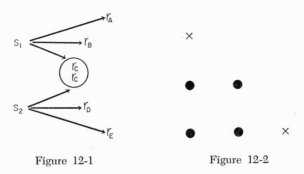

Figure 12-1   Figure 12-2

ment using the anagram tasks devised by Rees and Israel. One group had a training series of anagrams whose solutions were connected with eating and a test series of anagrams possessing both an "eating" solution and another solution. A second group differed from this one in being instructed at the outset to look for words connected with eating. The group that had had the instruction discovered more "eating" solutions than the other group in the test phase. A similar but greater difference showed up between two groups that received corresponding treatments except that the training anagrams could be solved by means of the 34521 permutation and the instructions drew attention to the order of the letters.

Verbal supplementary stimulation need not, however, take the form of explicit instructions, and it may be self-administered. In an experiment by Judson, Cofer, and Gelfand (1956), subjects had to learn lists of words and were then given Maier's (1931) string problem, in which two strings hanging from the ceiling must be tied together. To achieve this, one of the strings must be set swinging. Male subjects for whom "rope, swing, pendulum, time, clock" was one of the lists to be learned solved the problem more frequently than other groups that did not have the three crucial words together in one list.

An effective supplementary stimulus can also be nonverbal. Maier (1931) made subjects more likely to solve this same string problem by having the experimenter brush against one of the strings so as to start it swinging.

In one of his series of experiments, Ponomarev (1960) introduced subjects to the four-dot problem by showing four spots of light, forming a square on a panel. After the subjects had been wrestling with this problem for differing lengths of time, supplementary stimulation was presented in the form of spots of light at the two remaining corners (represented by crosses in Figure 12-2) of the triangle whose delineation constituted the solution. These spots were presented below the absolute threshold at first and then gradually increased in intensity. Six subjects out of 40 solved the problem, but, although the supplementary stimulation began at intervals varying from 15 sec. to 10 min. after the initial presentation of the problem, there were no successful subjects when the interval was less than 2 min. 45 sec. or greater than 6 min. 30 sec. Once again, there appears to be an optimal intermediate lapse of time between starting on the problem and receiving help. The presumption is that, when the time is too short, dominant wrong responses are still too strong to be overcome by the weaker correct response even when the latter is boosted by the supplementary stimulus, and that, when the time is too long, motivation to exert oneself at the problem has grown too weak—the compound hierarchy as a whole is succumbing to extinction.

Motivational conditions are, of course, major sources of supplementary stimulation. In earlier chapters, we noted the role of motivational stimuli in selectively facilitating responses that bid fair to contribute to the solution of the problem on hand. Postman and Crutchfield (1952) found, however, that a motivational condition may not exert a selective influence over symbolic responses if these are not capable of leading to its alleviation. Their test items consisted of incomplete five-letter words, with two letters to be supplied, having two possible solutions of which one had to do with food. An example is "GRA—," its possible solutions being "GRAVY" and "GRADE." Subjects who had been deprived of food for four to six hours were not significantly more likely to choose "food" solutions than those who were less hungry, except when a set had been induced beforehand by means of five preliminary items that admitted only of "food" solutions. So the ways in which drive-conditions and other factors interact have complications that remain to be unraveled.

The kinds of diffuse and pervasive motivational conditions that are commonly labeled with terms like "anxiety" are apt to have little in the way of selective associations. Their influence over thought must thus depend principally on their general energizing function, and the form this takes will vary with circumstances. Since the energizing effect of drive seems to work by increasing the strength of all instigated responses multiplicatively (Hull, 1943; Spence, 1956), a high level of anxiety can be expected to decrease the probability that a relatively weak correct response will occur when incorrect responses are stronger. This is because the difference in strength between the two will be augmented, thus giving the correct response more leeway to make up. When, on the other hand, a correct response is at least as strong as its competitors, high anxiety should accelerate its appearance.

These inferences have been confirmed in two experiments by Maltzman, Fox, and Morrisett (1953). They first found, using Luchins's water-jar-problem procedure, that subjects with high scores on the Taylor Manifest Anxiety Scale gave fewer direct solutions to test problems, just as Luchins (1954) found subjects to be particularly prone to the *"Einstellung* effect" in "autocratic, nonpermissive, and emotionally stressful atmospheres." In the second experiment, Maltzman and his collaborators used the anagram technique. Subjects first went through a training series including equal numbers of "eating" and "nature" items, which presumably made the two classes of response (the two subhierarchies) about equally strong. They were then given test items that consisted entirely of either "eating" or "nature" items. High-anxiety subjects performed better in this situation.

Evidence for Importance of Preavailability

Before we conclude this section, it is worth citing an experiment that supports the crucial assumption that the probability of solving a problem increases with what has been called (Duncan, 1959) the "preavailability" of elements of the solution, that is, how high these responses are initially placed in the relevant hierarchies or subhierarchies and how readily they are evoked. Saugstad (1955) used Maier's (1933) candle problem, in which subjects have to find a way of blowing out a candle flame at a distance of 70 inches with the help of various objects put at their disposal. The objects must actually be assembled to form a tube through which breath can be directed at the flame. Subjects in an experimental group were first shown the objects and then required to list and explain all the "functions" that they could think of for them. It turned out that all 13 subjects who gave the functions of "make tight," for the putty that had to be used to join the components of the tube, and "could hang," for the rod from which the tubing had to be hung, solved the problem. Of the 43 who failed to give both of these "functions," only 25 were successful with the problem.

Insight

The concepts of "implicit trial and error" and "insight" have long served as rallying points around which contending theories of productive thinking have deployed themselves. Implicit trial-and-error processes are clearly ones that rely heavily on the mechanism of extinction to eliminate dominant wrong response patterns one by one, so that a correct pattern that is relatively low in the hierarchy can emerge. The concept of "insight," which is bound up with some of the most crucial problems connected with reasoning, calls for a somewhat more extended examination.

The term "insight" was introduced more or less simultaneously in its present usage by Yerkes (1916) and by Köhler (1921). Both of these men were reporting experiments with apes for which they had been using techniques originated by Hobhouse (1915). The apes were tested for their ability to use a stick to draw toward them an objective that was beyond their reach in a horizontal direction, to move a box to a position where they could stand on it in order to obtain an objective that was high out of reach, etc. Yerkes (1916, p. 87) seems to have treated the word "insight" as synonymous with "idea-tion," while Köhler used it interchangeably with "understanding" and "intelligence." Both of these authors, like many of their contemporaries, appear to have assumed that everybody would know what these various words mean.

Of the two, Köhler developed the concept of "insightful" problem solving more extensively and more influentially. His views on the behavior that he had studied in apes were eventually merged with the general theoretical position of the Gestalt school. Since they were put forward, there have, especially in English-speaking countries, been many criticisms of Köhler's theoretical treatment of reasoning, and a number of alternative treatments have been proposed as improvements on it. There have also been a few attempts to collect further experimental data on the kinds of behavior that Köhler investigated. It is not generally known in Western countries that a team led by Pavlov was particularly active in taking up the challenges embodied in Köhler's work. Pavlov devoted some of his famous Wednesday seminars to rather captious strictures on Köhler's view, and, having received two chimpanzees as a gift a few years before his death, he organized an ambitious series of experiments in which they were exposed to situations resembling those used by Köhler (Roginski, 1948; Vatsuro, 1948).

Points Made by Köhler

In expounding what seemed to him the salient characteristics of the behavior he observed in his ape subjects, Köhler (1921) puts forward four main points, which are worth taking up in turn:

1. IMPORTANCE OF PAUSES. Köhler makes much of the fact that an ape would typically spend some time in relative immobility after making some unsuccessful attempts to reach the objective and before first performing the correct response pattern. He writes:

Chimpanzees . . . show by their careful looking around that they really begin with something very like an inventory of the situation. And this survey then gives rise to the behavior required for the solution.

He mentions a demonstration he once arranged for a visitor in which the ape Sultan took part. Sultan "made one attempt at solution, then a second and a third; but nothing made so great an impression on the visitor as the pause after that, during which Sultan slowly stretched his head and moved nothing but his eyes and his head gently, while he most carefully eyed the whole situation."

Köhler thus draws the conclusion that, during these pauses, the ape is bringing himself nearer to a solution by examining the external situation and perhaps doing something analogous to thinking about it.

There are, however, alternative explanations for these pauses, and there is certainly a danger of misinterpreting animal behavior through misleading analogies with human behavior. Pavlov (Vatsuro, 1955) attributed the same pauses to fatigue due to "mental work." Our earlier discussions suggest a related explanation: the lack of success attendant upon performing the dominant responses in the hierarchy is likely to have led, in accordance with the fundamental properties of habit-family hierarchies, to inhibition of the hierarchy as a whole. The animal would become active again when spontaneous recovery had dissipated the inhibition sufficiently or when a combination of stimulus factors, external or internal, instigated the correct, and so far untried, response pattern with sufficient strength.

Köhler's interpretation of the ape's behavior during the pauses is reminiscent of the role frequently ascribed to the "vicarious trial-and-error (VTE)" behavior of the rat (Muenzinger, 1938; Tolman, 1939). A rat faced with a choice-point in a maze or with two discriminative stimulus objects will commonly remain stationary for a while, turning his head from side to side. It looks as if he is "weighing up" the situation and extracting useful information about the cues that are available to him. Yet there seems so far to be no evidence showing that the rat's VTE behavior actually improves his chances of making an adaptive choice. So quite different explanations, which indicate no such useful role for it, are open, for example, that it is a maladaptive by-product of conflict (Goss and Wischner, 1956; Taylor and Reichlin, 1951).

2. RESPONSE TO RELATIONS. Köhler stresses that insightful behavior depends on "the grasp of the material inner relation of two things to each other . . . (more universally: the grasp of the structure of a situation)." He takes pains to point out that the word "relation" here means "an interconnection based on the properties of these things themselves." It does not mean "a frequent following each other" or "occurring together," he writes, evidently thinking of the relation of contiguity on which 19th-century associationist theories depended so heavily.

When Köhler speaks of a "relation" or of the "structure" of a situation (thought of as a system of relations), what he says fits very closely the notion of a relation as a class of spatially or temporally ordered pairs of stimulus objects (see Chapter 3). And as we have seen, the association of a response with such a relation or pattern of relations is not only perfectly congenial to neoassociationist psychological theory but well authenticated by experimental data.

If insightful solutions appear in response to stimulus relations, this means that their constituent repsonse patterns are evoked by combinations of stimuli. "Insight" is thus closely related to the third of our mechanisms by which an initially weak response pattern can be brought to the fore, namely, the combined action of a choice-point situational stimulus with a supplementary stimulus. However, while Köhler confines his attention to configurations of stimulus elements in the external stimulus field, we recognize that the elaborating combination may consist of an external and an internal stimulus pattern. The latter is likely to take the form of a motivational stimulus, for example, a representation of a desired goal situation.

3. EXCLUSION OF CHANCE. The point that Köhler develops at greatest length is that the correct response sequence could not be occurring by chance at the time that it is observed; nor can it be ascribed to previous learning of the sort described by Thorndike's famous formula of "trial and error and accidental success." In many instances, he asserts, the apes could never have performed that response sequence in the past and could never have witnessed its performance by another ape or a human being.

As an argument against the hypothesis of chance performance, he mentions the way in which "suddenly the smooth and unchecked movement occurs along the corresponding curve of solution. We are forced to the impression that this curve appears as an adequate whole from the beginning, the product of a complete survey of the whole situation." He ridicules the view that chance could have produced the required series of component actions—grasping the stick, pushing it forward so that its end is placed on the ground just behind the objective, moving it forward so that it drags the objective with it, etc.— in the right order.

The absence of trial-and-error behavior before the initial appearance of the correct response sequence is often taken as a defining characteristic of insight (cf. Newell, Shaw, and Simon, 1958). This would seem to be a mistake. Köhler makes it clear that the solution would often be arrived at after a whole succession of errors. The commonest error is attempting to reach the objective by stretching out the arm alone although the objective is out of reach. An ape may stack boxes in such a way that the "tower" is unstable and bound to fall down. He may commit "crude stupidities," such as dragging a box to the bars of the cage when the objective is lying outside (a kind of error reported also by Pavlov).

Hull (1935) suggested an experiment in which an ape would be presented with two short sticks that could be fitted together either in such a way as to form a T or in such a way as to form a long stick by which an objective could be reached. The existence of insight would, he held, be demonstrated if the ape realized the second possibility significantly more often than the first. Pavlov, interestingly enough, performed precisely such an experiment, and it was found that an ape might well make a T-shaped contrivance and thrust it unavailingly between the bars before trying out the more fruitful response of inserting the first stick into the hollow at the end of the other.

The main point about an insightful solution is not that it appears immediately without being preceded by errors but that it is a kind of response sequence that would be extremely unlikely to occur by chance at all, with or without a succession of prior errors. Simpler or more direct response patterns that are inappropriate to the present situation must inevitably have been strongly reinforced in the past, so that they will become dominant at one stage or another. It is therefore necessary that these responses be inhibited through nonreinforcement before the correct response sequence can come out. Sometimes the erroneous responses have to be eliminated by extinction in the problem situation. Sometimes, they will already have been eliminated by prior discrimination training. An ape, like a human child, must go through a stage in which stimulus generalization makes him stretch out his arm toward objects that are too far away to be grasped. At a later stage, the ape, like the older child, will have learned to distinguish an object that is within reach from an object that is out of reach and to withhold reaching responses toward something that is recognizably out of reach. How long vain reaching out with the bare arm will delay the discovery of the use of the stick will thus depend on the stage that this discriminative learning has reached.

Köhler makes much of the fact that the errors committed by an ape are generally "good errors." They are responses that, while they are maladaptive in the present situation, might well have led to success if the situation had been somewhat different. "They are the after-effects of former genuine solutions, which were often repeated, and so developed a tendency to appear secondarily in later experiments, without much consideration for the special situation." Yet the errors that precede performance of the correct response in the simplest selective-learning situations are likewise almost invariably "good errors."

For example, Thorndike (1898) describes the behavior of a cat when first put into a puzzle box:

It tries to squeeze through any opening; it claws and bites at the bars or wire; it thrusts its paws out through any opening and claws at everything it reaches; it continues its efforts when it strikes anything loose and shaky; it may claw at things within the box.

It is obvious, although Thorndike does not say so explicitly, that these responses are not a random sample of the behavior of which the cat is capable but are ones that, in the light of the cat's prior experience, have an above-average chance of being useful in a situation of this kind.

For these reasons, despite the sometimes acrimonious disputes that have divided the partisans of implicit trial and error and insight, it is now becoming generally accepted (for example, Newell, Shaw, and Simon, 1958; Ponomarev, 1960) that the two processes are not absolutely distinct and that they both have some part to play in all but a few exceptional kinds of productive thinking. It is clear that cases occupying every possible intermediate position between the two exist and that the extremes of blind groping on the one hand and instantaneous illumination on the other are rare. Trial and error may narrow things down to a limited "region of search" (Ponomarev, 1960), within which a review of stimulus conditions may abruptly bring out a precise solution. Alternatively, the "region of search" may be delimited right from the start by the stimulus situation. Computer-simulation studies have, as was mentioned earlier, revealed the indispensable role of "heuristics," that is, mechanisms that regulate the search for a solution in such a way that lines of thought with the greatest chances of success are tried out first. Newell, Shaw, and Simon (1958) argue that this kind of mechanism is midway between insight and implicit trial and error. Random sampling with or without replacement would, they show, have a negligible probability of arriving at a solution within a reasonable time, even when computers capable of many hundreds of thousands of elementary operations per second are used. On the other hand, with any really creative piece of thinking, the chances that the solution will be recognized immediately *in toto* are likewise negligible.

4. KÖHLER'S PERCEPTUAL THEORY OF REASONING. In the final chapter of his book *The Mentality of Apes*, Köhler (1921) concludes:

In the field of the experiments carried out here the insight of the chimpanzee shows itself to be principally determined by his optical apprehension of the situation . . .

This emphasis on visual perception was vehemently attacked by Pavlov, who organized a number of experiments showing that the chimpanzee Raphael relied on tactual and kinaesthetic cues much more than on visual cues in his discriminative behavior. As the work of the Gestalt school proceeded, the notion of "insight" was elaborated further (for example, Köhler, 1929, Ch. X). "Insight" was defined as "the direct awareness of determination," using the word "determination" in the sense of causal influence, etc. Reasoning, whether in the ape or in man (cf. Wertheimer, 1945), was believed to depend on a restructuring of perception, and perceptual structure was regarded as something common to all sensory modalities, and in fact to virtually all psychological processes, being by no means confined to vision.

This Gestalt theory of reasoning has often come under attack on a number of grounds. For example, it has sometimes been held to constitute a mere description rather than an explanation of the behavior with which it is concerned. It does not, for example, enable one to predict when insightful discovery will occur. The charge that it is only a description is, however, not in itself fatally damaging. Many of the alternative conceptions of reasoning that have been proposed, including perhaps the one worked out in this book, are also open to the criticism that they are inadequate as explanations and constitute little more than descriptions. Descriptions, as we have been arguing, form a necessary preliminary to the kind of research that will eventually satisfy the desire to explain and predict. The essential question is whether the Gestalt theory represents a good or a bad kind of description. And there are several reasons for supposing it to be a bad kind of description.

First, while no description can be complete, the Gestalt theory leaves us entirely in the lurch with respect to one vital phase of the problem. It may point to some conditions in which insightful perceptual restructuring is more likely than otherwise to occur, but it does not tell us how the restructuring produces a change in behavior. It does not even tell us how the subject recognizes that he has arrived at a fruitful restructuring, except to tell us that he becomes aware that he has.

A good description should bring into prominence the variables that are of most moment and that are therefore likely to repay experimental study most bountifully. The Gestalt theory draws attention to structural properties of the perceptual field: it suggests that the ape might, for example, solve the stick problem more readily if the stick is placed near the bars so that it is more likely to be included with the objective in a single glance, if the stick is placed pointing towards the objective, etc. One of the most decisive factors, namely the status of the objective as a goal object, is not represented in the stimulus field at all. It is true that the Gestalt psychologists came to draw a distinction between the "geographical world," consisting of the physical stimulus situation, and the "behavioral world" or perceived world, and that they would have held the motivational role of the objective to be represented in the "behavioral world" in the form of a "force" or "stress" or "valence," impelling the subject toward it. The "behavioral world" is, however, a joint product of stimuli exciting sense organs and variables (including motivational conditions) within the organism. To speak about internal processes in terms of their putative perceptual correlates must surely deflect one from studies aimed at ascertaining their nature and origin.

Furthermore, Gestalt terminology leads one to underestimate the influence of past experience. Köhler (1921) concedes that "every chimpanzee above a certain very low age" must have had a stick in his hands before the experiment; "he will have seized a branch in play, scratched on the ground with it, and so on." Later experiments by Jackson (1942) and Birch (1945b) indicate that he was wrong to attach little importance to such prior experiences. Both of these experimenters took apes that failed to pull in an objective with a stick and then gave them opportunities to play with a stick in their normal surroundings. Jackson gave one such subject access to the stick for two hours on each of seven consecutive days, while Birch gave four of them access to the stick for three consecutive days. In all cases, this relatively short experience of handling the stick led to rapid discovery of the solution when the problem was again presented.

Ladygina-Kots (1959) has described in particularly rich detail the exploratory and manipulatory activity that the chimpanzee directs toward any new object that comes within his reach and that forms the necessary basis for the later use of implements to solve practical problems. The ape first exposes his various sense organs in turn to the stimuli that can be extracted from the object. He then "plays" with the object, sampling the assortment of motor activities that it makes possible. He spends an especially long time "elaborating" it, that is, subjecting it to as many changes in appearance as it will sustain: he attaches it to other objects, pulls it to pieces, deforms it.

In short, therefore, the most important determinants of the probability that an ape will solve problems of this kind seem to be (a) his motivational condition, (b) the nature and quantity of previous learning experiences with objects resembling the implement and the objective, and (c) the number and nature of the resemblances between the problem situation and the situation in which relevant learning experiences have taken place. None of these is allotted a conspicuous role by the perceptual theory that the Gestalt psychologists have championed.

Conclusions

The crux of the phenomena with which the concept of "insight" was meant to deal is that the goal can be reached only by performing a certain sequence of responses in the right order and that, in animals high enough in the phyletic scale, such sequences appear so frequently that their fortuitous occurrence can be excluded. The crucial problem is thus what makes these sequences occur. This can be broken down into two questions, namely what makes the first element of the sequence occur, and what makes each later element occur at the right time after its immediate predecessor has occurred.

The second question, being slightly less recalcitrant, may be taken up first. The most promising answer would seem to be that a later response element is evoked by stimuli that present themselves once the earlier elements have been completed but not before. Hull (1952) provides some plausible examples with reference to the stick problem. He points out that, once an ape has grasped the stick and is poking it at the ground, his hand receives tactual stimuli resembling those that occur when the hand is touching the ground. When he pushes the stick forward, the kinaesthetic and visual sensations consequent on the movement of the end of the stick toward the objective and on the decrease in the distance between the end of the stick and the objective resemble those that occur when the bare hand moves toward a reachable target. Stimulus generalization could thus explain why the ape continues to push the stick forward until the end lies beyond the objective and then reverses the direction of movement, just as it could explain how movements deviating from the right direction are corrected. In other cases of reasoning, the operative stimuli cannot be identified so readily. In much human directed thinking, the steering function may be exercised by some kind of conflict reduction.

With regard to the first question, concerning the initiation of the sequence, Pavlov's work (Vatsuro, 1955) suggests that Köhler may well have overlooked a number of possibilities.

One piece of behavior that Köhler discusses at length is the fitting together of two rods that are individually too short to reach the objective so that a long enough stick is formed. He stresses that apes do not try to fit two rods together if the end of one does not have a hollow into which the other can be inserted. He mentions also that an ape will chew at the end of a board that is too wide to fit into the hollow, until it is shaved down sufficiently.

Pavlov's group (Vatsuro, 1955) claimed that behavior of this sort might very well appear in the course of exploratory behavior or play. The contention was supported by a number of their findings. An ape will insert the end of one rod into a hollow that is in the middle of the second rod rather than at its end. He is prone to chew at the end of any rod and pull away flaps of wood, even when the end is already thin enough to fit into the hollow. He will pull away flaps of wood that are in the middle of a rod, so that they do not affect his ability to connect it with another rod. Pavlov even suggested that the behavior of removing superficial layers of wood results from an unlearned response pattern enabling apes to peel the fruits and vegetables that they eat.

Despite the cautionary value of these observations, the graphic descriptions provided by Köhler, as well as by other writers performing similar experiments (for example, Yerkes, 1916; Birch, 1945b; and Ladygina-Kots, 1959), convince one that these explanations do not always hold. In at least some cases, the ape definitely seems to be performing the first response in the sequence *because* it is the first link in a chain of responses that can bring him into contact with the objective. Be that as it may in the case of the ape, there are certainly plenty of instances of human reasoning in which a response is embarked on solely because it is the opening step of a sequence that can lead to a goal.

We must therefore consider what mechanisms could cause the initial component of an adaptive response sequence attributable to reasoning to be performed. And apart from the Gestalt concept of perceptual reorganization, whose shortcomings we have already considered, there appear to be three kinds of mechanism that, in the present state of knowledge, call for consideration:

1. HULL'S THEORY OF REASONING. Hull (1935) developed a theory that was primarily designed to handle the kinds of reasoning that Maier (1929) claimed to have demonstrated in the rat, even though later work (Wolfe and Spragg, 1934) had cast doubt on the validity of this demonstration. The theory was, however, extended to the kind of insightful problem solution in primates exemplified by Köhler's experiments (Hull, 1952).

In order to outline Hull's theory of reasoning, let us represent the situation in a simplified form as a chain of two segments (see Figure 12-3). S_0 represents the initial stimulus situation, including the sight of the distant objective and the sight of the stick. R_A is the response sequence of grasping the stick and drawing in the objective. This leads to S_{G1}, which is the stimulus situation in which the objective lies close to the subject. It is assumed to be a subgoal situation: it has some reward value, whether of the intrinsic kind that governs exploratory behavior and play or secondary reward value due to its frequent closeness to the enjoyment of the objective. S_{G1} then evokes R_B, the response of picking up the objective and putting it in the mouth. The ultimate goal situation, having the objective in the mouth (S_{G2}), is thereby attained, and eating (R_{G2}) concludes the sequence.

It is assumed that the second segment, S_{G1}-R_B-S_{G2}, is learned first (see Figure 12-4). Using the line of deduction that we discussed in Chapter 4, Hull concludes that r_{G2}, an implicit response that represents S_{G2} and corresponds to an "expectation of" and "desire for" S_{G2}, will occur anticipatorily and be evoked immediately by S_{G1}. When

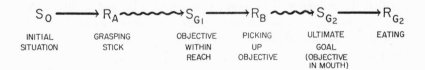

$$S_0 \longrightarrow R_A \rightsquigarrow S_{G1} \longrightarrow R_B \rightsquigarrow S_{G2} \longrightarrow R_{G2}$$

| INITIAL SITUATION | GRASPING STICK | OBJECTIVE WITHIN REACH | PICKING UP OBJECTIVE | ULTIMATE GOAL (OBJECTIVE IN MOUTH) | EATING |

Figure 12-3

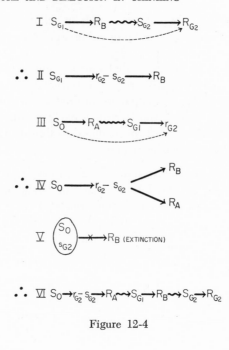

Figure 12-4

the sequence S_0-R_A-S_{G1} is acquired independently on a later occasion, r_{G2} will come forward from S_{G1} to S_0. Consequently, s_{G2}, the feedback stimulus produced by r_{G2}, will become associated with R_A. Later, when the animal finds itself in the problem situation and its motivational condition is such as to include r_{G2} (that is, the desire for S_{G2}) and the direct response of reaching with the arm alone has been extinguished, s_{G2} will evoke R_A, thus initiating the solution sequence.

A serious flaw in Hull's theory has been pinpointed by Deutsch (1956, 1960) and by Ritchie (1959). Either one must assume that expectations like r_{G2} are reinforced only by the occurrence of the goal situation to which they correspond (in this case, S_{G2}), or one must assume that they are reinforced by any situation that has a reward value. If the first, then there is no reason why r_{G2} should become associated with S_0. If the second, then various anomalies arise, implying that the animal will in some circumstances be just as likely to engage in a bootless and erroneous response sequence as in the solution sequence. Some inkling of this argument can be gathered from Deutsch's analogy:

Suppose the child expects some ice cream but instead is rewarded by being given a shilling; then if his expectation functions as a response, the next time in the same situation the child should expect ice cream even more strongly.

The close affinity between this criticism of Hull's theory and Selz's criticism of the constellation theory (see Chapter 5) is worthy of note.

The point is well taken when directed against Hull's earlier (1935, 1952, pp. 309–317) argument, in which he attempted to deduce that the responses constituting the solution chain would be more likely to occur from the outset than erroneous lines of behavior. In his latest discussion (1952, pp. 317–324) of insightful tool-using behavior in apes, exemplified by Köhler's experiments, he attributed the abandonment of incorrect responses (for example, extending the arm without the stick) to extinction and deduced that the correct response sequence would come to the fore only after this extinction had taken place. As we have seen, chimpanzees often spend some time on mistaken responses, which are of no avail, before embarking on the solution chain, and the crucial question with respect to insightful behavior in apes is why the solution chain occurs at all. This question is answered by the relevant portions of Hull's theory which, unlike his account of putative reasoning in the rat, are not marred by the dilemma to which Deutsch and Ritchie have drawn attention.

There are, however, certainly times when a solution chain due to reasoning is, especially in human beings, executed without being preceded by overt errors. In such cases, the mechanism envisaged by Hull will not suffice, so that additional mechanisms must be sought.

2. EVOCATION OF SUBGOAL REPRESENTATIONS. There is one further piece of evidence against Hull's theory. It requires the assumption that the second segment of the chain is acquired before the first. Now, it is extremely probable that an ape will have had experience of picking up a nearby fruit and eating it before he had experience of moving objects about with the end of a stick. It was, however, found by Kendler and Kendler (1961) that a child's ability to solve analogous problems (in which one of two switches must be operated to gain access to a box that can be pulled to secure a toy chain) is not affected by the order in which the segments constituting the solution are acquired.

In the theory depicted in Fig. 12-4, the second segment must have been experienced first, in order that (a) S_0 can come to evoke r_{G2} and (b) s_{G2} can come to evoke R_A. This requirement can, however, be circumvented with the help of a modified version of Hull's theory, depicted in Fig. 12-5.

342 STRUCTURE AND DIRECTION IN THINKING

We assume, first, that the subject has learned to use response R_A as a means of getting from the initial situation, S_0, to the subgoal situation, S_{G1} (I). He has, for example, learned to bring a distant object within reach with the help of a stick. Once again, we assume that S_{G1} will have some reward value, extrinsic or intrinsic (perhaps due to a rapid rise and fall in arousal). The fractional anticipatory goal response, r_{G1}, thus becomes associated with S_0, and the combination of S_0 and s_{G1} becomes associated with R_A, an instance of a transformation-applying habit (II). Next (III), we assume that, although the sequence constituting the solution chain has never occurred before, other behavior chains have included the segment S_{G1}-R_B-S_{G2}. For example, the subject may have found food at his feet and thus been able to pick it up and eat it, as a consequence of performing response R_C in stimulus situation S_X. S_X will then evoke both r_{G1} and r_{G2}. Since S_{G2} is more powerfully rewarding than S_{G1}, r_{G2} will be evoked first, so that s_{G2} acquires the power to evoke r_{G1} (IV). Finally, in the problem situation, S_0 is accompanied by s_{G2}, symbolizing S_{G2}, and the subject is motivated to bring about S_{G2}. For example, the sight of food in the distance is accompanied by an internal representation of food in the mouth as a terminal goal situation. In other words, r_{G2} is evoked jointly by the subject's motivational condition and S_0 through stimulus generalization. But in the absence of a prepotent transformational response leading directly from S_0 to S_{G2}, evoked through positive patterning by the combination of S_0 and s_{G2}, responses associated with the components of the combination can be expected to occur. Responses associated with S_0 alone (for example, reaching for the distant lure with the bare arm) will soon extinguish or will already have extinguished. The other component, s_{G2}, will evoke r_{G1} (by IV). The combination of S_0 with s_{G1}, which is associated (by II) with R_A, will thus be produced, accounting for the occurrence of R_A (V).

A salient element in this account is the deduction that the representation of a terminal goal situation will evoke a representation of a subgoal, that is, a situation that the subject has habitually gone through before reaching a terminal goal of that sort. For example, a representation of the ultimate goal of fruit in the mouth is followed by a representation of the sight of the fruit lying within reach. The operation of a transformation-selecting habit could then explain how the first action belonging to the solution chain occurs: the initial stimulus situation, coupled with the situational stimulus representing the food close at hand, evokes a transformational response capable of changing

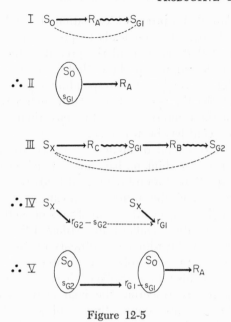

Figure 12-5

the one into the other, namely, the response of pulling in the fruit with a stick.

Ladygina-Kots (1959) describes the behavior of an ape that has to thrust a wire implement into a pipe, in order to obtain a lure, but has found that the implement is too wide. He then manipulates the wire so as to decrease the width of the implement and tries again. This author concludes that the ape is guided by a "generalized visual image of a suitable implement," that is, one that will fit into the pipe, and acts in such a way as to bring the actual object in front of him nearer to this image. We can see here a clear instance of a transformation-selecting habit at work. The response is determined jointly by the sight of the implement as it is and a representation of the shape that the implement will have to possess if it is to be serviceable. This anticipated shape is a subgoal whose achievement will carry the animal nearer to the terminal goal of grasping the lure, and the transformational response that results is one that changes the shape of the implement into an approximation of the anticipated and desired shape. If the combination of the present shape and the imagined shape acts as the cue stimulus, the motivation must come from conflict due to the discrepancy between the two.

Of recent behavior theories, Deutsch's (1953, 1960) makes unique

use of the postulate that a process ("excitation of a link") corresponding to a terminal goal situation leads to processes corresponding to
stimulus situations that have regularly preceded the terminal goal
situation. The order in which these "links" are excited is the reverse of the order in which the corresponding situations are encountered. Subsequently, the subject first acts in such a way as to bring
about the first of these intermediate situations, then the second, etc.,
until the terminal goal has been realized.

Whether or not this kind of analysis is suited to all behavior, as
Deutsch feels, writers on thinking have made much of the mechanism
by which contemplation of an ultimate goal leads to contemplation of
a way station from which the ultimate goal can be reached with relative ease, so that the subject first concentrates on getting to the way
station (cf. Duncker, 1945; Dollard and Miller, 1950). Routines following this pattern are cardinal constituents of Newell, Shaw, and
Simon's (1958, 1960) problem-solving computer programs.

If a mechanism of this type is invoked, there is the question of how
a symbolic response representing the final goal situation comes to
evoke a symbolic response representing a subgoal. The process depicted in Figure 12-5 illustrates one way in which this question might
be answered. Apart from that, something like backward conditioning
or backward association might be invoked. There is evidence that
these retrogressive kinds of learning can occur (particularly in connection with verbal responses, which might well represent goals and
subgoals in human subjects), but they have, on the whole, been found
to be relatively weak. Finally, the possession of inverse transformational responses, supported by stimulus-response generalization, should
stand human beings in good stead when they need to trace a route
to a goal by working backward.

3. EXTRAPOLATIVE REPRESENTATION. The third kind of mechanism
is close to the spirit of Köhler's views and those of later theorists of a
cognitivist persuasion (for example, Tolman, 1932). Referring to the
behavior of Köhler's star chimpanzee subject in a problem situation,
Tolman voices two assumptions: (a) "that Sultan in struggling to
get food . . . was continually ideating . . . the portions of the
means-end-field involved in such actions," and (b) "that after, or
during, these trials and errors, there occurred suddenly the new idea-
tion or the ideational extrapolation of the field, which was necessary
for the solution." In other words, Sultan was representing to himself various possible sequences of events starting out from the present
stimulus situation. In our terminology, he was going through a num-

ber of symbolic transformational chains, and, at one point, he hit upon a representation of the goal situation.

However, Tolman does not dispose adequately of two essential questions, namely what makes the animal perform the corresponding motor chain once he has constructed an implicit symbolic solution chain, and why only the solution chain is translated into action and not one of the other transformational sequences that must have occurred in the course of his "ideation." To recognize that it is adaptive for the ape to behave as he does is, of course, not to explain how it comes about.

This is, of course, a special form of the difficulty that has always dogged cognitivist theorists. The cognitivists (see Hilgard, 1948) have been inclined to believe that even the simplest forms of learning consist in acquiring expectations or representations relating to impending sequences of events. They seem commonly to have felt that there is no need to explain why an animal acts as he does once he has acquired relevant "cognitions." There has been a tendency to suppose that if, for example, it can be inferred that a hungry rat has learned that food will come into view after he has run down a certain alley, his behavior has been adequately explained because, as N. E. Miller has put it, "any fool would run down an alley if he were hungry and knew that food was to be found at the end of it." Arguments of this sort are, needless to say, insufficient for the purposes of science.

In later formulations of cognitive theory (MacCorquodale and Meehl, 1953; Tolman, 1955, 1959), a principle governing performance was added to rescue the animal that had previously, as Guthrie (1952) put it, been left "buried in thought." The principle stated that, when an action is expected to lead to a certain state of affairs, the strength of the tendency to perform the action increases with the strength of the expectation and the net "positive valence" (that is, attractiveness) of the object.

In the present state of knowledge, it is not possible to do much more than posit such a principle for cases where behavior cannot be accounted for without concepts like "expectation." It seems possible, and therefore advisable, to dispense with such concepts when one considers some of the simplest kinds of learning, for example, classical conditioning, in which case the present problem does not arise.

Much human overt behavior, however, must unavoidably be attributed to preceding thought processes culminating in an implicit symbolic solution chain. Here, as with reasoning in the ape, if we use this kind of interpretation, there is no escaping the interconnected questions of how a solution is recognized once arrived at and how it eventuates in action. We have adopted the widespread view that covert representational processes, such as expectations, consist of sensorimotor processes that are prevented by inhibition from involving the musculature except in an extremely attenuated way. We have further hypothesized that, as soon as a transformational chain leading from the initial situation to the goal situation has been constituted, the sensorimotor processes are released from inhibition, with consequent conflict reduction and motor expression. This hypothesis certainly falls far short of a complete elucidation, but it may possibly take us a slight step nearer.

It is worth pointing out that this interpretation of insightful problem solution, which is in some ways close to Köhler's, makes particularly clear the affinity, rather than the opposition, between insightful processes and implicit trial and error. Internal representational processes bear the onus of the inevitable phase of going through abortive attempts at solution, with the result that the cost of overt trial and error in danger, effort, and time can be avoided.

Future years may well add to this list of possible mechanisms. From our present vantage point, it would seem that all the mechanisms that we have just considered must have their parts to play. Research aimed at filling in their details is clearly called for.

Be that as it may, anything more than a fragmentary understanding of the most impressive accomplishments of the human, or even the anthropoid, intellect can hardly be expected for some time. Their inner workings must remain beyond our ken until we are more fully acquainted with the structural and motivational principles that extend through the whole gamut of reasoning and thinking. These principles may be most easily coaxed into view if we first pay a great deal of attention to the more humdrum forms of reproductive S-thinking, with continual glances at the simplest forms of learned and unlearned behavior for purposes of comparison and perspective.

Bibliography

Abel, T. M. Attitudes and the galvanic skin reflex. *J. exp. Psychol.,* 1930, **13,** 47–60.

Abelson, R. P. Modes of resolution of belief dilemmas. *Conflict Resolution,* 1959, 3, 343–352.

Abelson, R. P., and Rosenberg, M. J. Symbolic psycho-logic: a model of attitudinal cognition. *Behav. Sci.,* 1958, 3, 1–13.

Ach, N. *Über die Willensthätigkeit und das Denken,* Göttingen: Vandenhoeck & Ruprecht, 1905.

Ades, H. W. Effects of extirpation of parastriate cortex on learned visual discrimination in monkeys. *J. Neuropath. exp. Neurol.,* 1946, **5,** 60–65.

Andrew, R. J. The origin and evolution of the calls and facial expressions of the primates. *Behaviour,* 1963, **20,** 1–109.

Andrew, R. J. The concept of stimulus contrast, *Anim. Behav.* (in press).

Anokhin, P. K. [Peculiarities of the afferent apparatus of the conditioned reflex and its significance in psychology.] *Vop. Psikhol.,* 1955, 1(6), 16–38.

Anokhin, P. K. [New data on the functional heterogeneity of the reticular formation of the brain stem.] *Zh. Vys. Nerv. Deiat.,* 1959, **9,** 489–499.

Apostel, L. Equilibre, logique et théorie des graphs. In L. Apostel, B. Mandelbrot and J. Piaget. *Logique et équilibre.* (*Etudes d'Epistém. Génét.,* II). Paris: Presses Universitaires de France, 1957.

Apostel, L. Logique et apprentissage. In L. Apostel, A. R. Jonckheere and B. Matalon. *Logique, apprentissage et probabilité.* (*Etudes d'Epistém. Génét.,* VIII). Paris: Presses Universitaires de France, 1959.

Apostel, L., Jonckheere, A. R., and Matalon, B. *Logique, apprentissage et probabilité.* (*Etudes d'Epistém. Génét.,* VIII). Paris: Presses Universitaires de France, 1959.

Arnold, W. J. An exploratory investigation of primary response generalization. *J. comp. Psychol.,* 1945, 38, 87–102.

Ashby, W. R. *Design for a brain.* London: Chapman & Hall, 1952.

Ashby, W. R. *An introduction to cybernetics.* London: Chapman & Hall, 1956.

Atkinson, J. W. Motivational determinants of risk-taking behavior. *Psychol. Rev.,* 1957, **64,** 359–372.

Attneave, F. *Applications of information theory to psychology.* New York: Holt, Rinehart & Winston, 1959.

Ausubel, D. P. Learning by discovery: rationale and mystique. *Bull. Nat. Assoc. Sec. School Princ.,* 1961, **45,** 18–58.

Bain, A. *The senses and the intellect.* London: Longmans Green (1st ed.), 1855; (3rd ed.) 1868.

Bain, A. *The emotions and the will.* London: Longmans Green (3rd ed.), 1880.

Bartlett, F. C. Feeling, imaging and thinking. *Brit. J. Psychol.,* 1925, **16,** 16–28.

347

Bartlett, F. C. *Remembering*, Cambridge: Cambridge University Press, 1932.

Bartlett, F. C. *Thinking*. London: Methuen, 1958.

Becker, G. M. Sequential decision-making: Wald's model and estimates of parameters. *J. exp. Psychol.*, 1958, **55**, 628–636.

Beckman, F. H., and Stein, M. I. A note on the relationship between per cent alpha time and efficiency in problem solving. *J. Psychol.*, 1961, **51**, 169–177.

Berger, H. Über das Elektrenkephalogramm des Menschen. II. *J. Psychol. Neurol., Lpg.*, 1930, **40**, 160–179.

Beritov (Beritashvili), I. S. *O nervnykh mekhanizmakh prostranstvennoi orientatsii vysshikh pozvonochnykh zhivotnykh* (*On the neural mechanism of spatial orientation in higher vertebrates*). Tbilisi: Acad. Sci. Georgian SSR, 1959.

Beritov, I. S. *Nervnye mekhanizmi povedeniia vysshikh pozvonochnykh zhivotnykh* (*Neural mechanisms of behavior in the higher vertebrate animals*). Moscow: Acad. Sci. USSR, 1961.

Beritov (Beritashvili), I. S. [On the role of different regions of the brain in conditioned behavioral activity.] *Trudy Inst. Fiziol. Beritashvili*, 1963, **13**, 3–14.

Berlyne, D. E. Knowledge and stimulus-response psychology. *Psychol. Rev.*, 1954, **61**, 245–254(a).

Berlyne, D. E. A theory of human curiosity. *Brit. J. Psychol.*, 1954, **45**, 180–191(b).

Berlyne, D. E. An experimental study of human curiosity. *Brit. J. Psychol.*, 1954, **45**, 256–265(c).

Berlyne, D. E. Uncertainty and conflict: A point of contact between information-theory and behavior-theory concepts. *Psychol. Rev.*, 1957, **64**, 329–339(a).

Berlyne, D. E. Conflict and choice time. *Brit. J. Psychol.*, 1957, **48**, 106–118(b).

Berlyne, D. E. *Conflict, Arousal, and Curiosity*. New York: McGraw-Hill, 1960(a).

Berlyne, D. E. Les équivalences psychologiques et les notions quantitatives. In D. E. Berlyne and J. Piaget, *Théorie du comportement et opérations*. (*Etudes d'Epistém. Génét.*, XII). Paris: Presses Universitaires de France, 1960(b).

Berlyne, D. E. L'apprentissage sériel et les relations d'ordre. In D. E. Berlyne and J. Piaget, *Théorie du comportement et opérations*. (*Etudes d'Epistém. Génét.*, XII). Paris: Presses Universitaires de France, 1960(c).

Berlyne, D. E. Conflict and the orientation reaction. *J. exp. Psychol.*, 1961, **62**, 476–483.

Berlyne, D. E. Note on food deprivation and extrinsic exploratory responses. *Psychol. Rep.*, 1962, **11**, 162(a).

Berlyne, D. E. Uncertainty and epistemic curiosity. *Brit. J. Psychol.*, 1962, **53**, 27–34(b).

Berlyne, D. E. Motivational problems raised by exploratory and epistemic behavior. In S. Koch (ed.), *Psychology: a study of a science*. Vol. 5. New York: McGraw-Hill, 1963.

Berlyne, D. E. Emotional aspects of learning. *Ann. rev. Psychol.*, 1964, **15**, 115–142.

Berlyne, D. E., Craw, M. A., Salapatek, P. H., and Lewis, J. L. Novelty, complexity, incongruity, extrinsic motivation, and the GSR. *J. exp. Psychol.*, 1963, **66**, 560–567.

Berlyne, D. E., and McDonnell, P. Effects of stimulus complexity and incongruity on the duration of EEG desynchronization. *Electroencephal. Clin. Neurophysiol.*, 1965 (in press).

Binet, A. *L'étude expérimentale de l'intelligence.* Paris: Schleicher, 1903.
Birch, H. G. The relation of previous experience to insightful problem-solving. *J. comp. Psychol.,* 1945, **38**, 367–383(a).
Birch, H. G. The role of motivational factors in insightful problem-solving. *J. comp. Psychol.,* 1945, **38**, 295–317(b).
Birkhoff, G., and MacLane, S. *A survey of modern algebra.* New York: Macmillan, 1953.
Black, A. H., and Lang, W. M. Cardiac conditioning and skeletal responding in curarized dogs. *Psychol. Rev.,* 1964, **71**, 80–85.
Blatt, S. J. Patterns of cardiac arousal during complex neural activity. *J. abn. soc. Psychol.,* 1961, **63**, 272–282.
Blatt, S. J., and Stein, M. Efficiency in problem solving. *J. Psychol.,* 1959, **48**, 193–213.
Bloch, B., and Trager, G. L. *Outline of linguistic analysis.* Baltimore: Linguistic Society of America, 1942.
Boiko, E. I. [The problem of conditioned-reflex mechanisms of higher mental processes.] In B. G. Anan'ev et al. (eds.), *Psikhologicheskaia nauka v SSSR* (*Psychological science in the USSR*), Vol. I. Moscow: Acad. Pedag. Sci., 1959. (Translation published by U.S. Joint Publications Research Service.)
Boiko, E. I. (ed.) *Pogranichnye problemy psikhologii i fiziologii* (*Borderline problems of psychology and physiology*). Moscow: Acad. Pedag. Sci., 1961.
Bourbaki, N. *Les structures fondamentales de l'analyse. Livre II: Algèbre. Chap. I: Structures algebriques.* Paris: Hermann, 1940.
Brain, W. R. The semantic aspect of aphasia. *Arch. Ling.,* 1956, **8**(2), 20–27.
Brehm, J. W., and Cohen, A. R. *Explorations in cognitive dissonance.* New York: Wiley, 1962.
Bresson, F. Perception et indices perceptifs. In J. S. Bruner, F. Bresson, A. Morf, and J. Piaget. *Logique et perception.* (*Etudes d'Epistém. Génét., VI*). Paris: Presses Universitaires de France, 1958.
Britton, K. *John Stuart Mill.* London: Penguin Books, 1953.
Broadbent, D. E. *Perception and communication.* London and New York: Pergamon, 1958.
Brown, J. S. *Motivation of behavior.* New York: McGraw-Hill, 1961.
Brown, J. S., and Farber, I. E. Emotions conceptualized as intervening variables —with suggestions toward a theory of frustration. *Psychol. Bull.,* 1951, **48**, 465–495.
Brown, R. W., and Fraser, C. The acquisition of syntax. In C. F. Cofer and B. S. Musgrave (eds.), *Verbal behavior and learning.* New York: McGraw-Hill, 1963.
Brown, J. S., and Jacobs, A. The role of fear in the motivation and acquisition of responses. *J. exp. Psychol.,* 1949, **39**, 747–759.
Brown, Thomas. *Lectures on the philosophy of the human mind.* Edinburgh: Tait, 1820.
Bruner, J. S. *The process of education.* Cambridge, Mass.: Harvard University Press, 1960.
Bruner, J. S. The course of cognitive growth. *Amer. Psychol.,* 1964, **19**, 1–15.
Bruner, J. S., Goodnow, J. S., and Austin, G. A. *A study of thinking.* New York: Wiley, 1956.
Bruner, J. S., Mandler, J. M., O'Dowd, D., and Wallach, M. A. The role of overlearning and drive level in reversal learning. *J. comp. physiol. Psychol.,* 1958, **51**, 607–613.

Brunswik, E. Distal focussing of perception: size-constancy in a representative sample of situations. *Psychol. Monogr.*, 1944, **56**, No. 1 (Whole No. 254).

Brushlinski, A. V. [The role of analysis and abstraction in knowledge of quantitative relations.] In S. L. Rubinshtein (ed.), *Protsess myshleniia i zakonomernosti analiza, sinteza i obobshcheniia* (*The process of thought and the laws governing analysis, synthesis and generalization*). Moscow: Acad. Sci. USSR, 1960.

Bühler, C. Zwei Grundtypen von Lebensprozessen. *Z. Psychol., Abt. 1*, 1928, **108**, 222–239.

Bunch, M. E., and Lund, W. R. An experiment on backward association in animal learning. *J. comp. Psychol.*, 1932, **13**, 143–156.

Cannon, W. B. *The wisdom of the body.* New York: Norton, 1932.

Carnap, R. Testability and meaning. *Phil. Sci.*, 1936, **3**, 419–471; 1937, **4**, 1–40.

Caron, A. J. Curiosity, achievement, and avoidant motivation as determinants of epistemic behavior. *J. abn. soc. Psychol.*, 1963, **67**, 535–549.

Cartwright, D., and Harary, F. Structural balance: a generalization of Heider's theory. *Psychol. Rev.*, 1956, **63**, 277–293.

Cattell, J. McK. Psychometrische Untersuchungen. III. Die Association unter willkürlich begrenzten Bedingungen. *Phil. St.*, 1888, **4**, 241–250.

Chang, H. T., Ruch, T. C., and Ward, A. A. Topographical representation of muscles in motor cortex of monkeys. *J. Neurophysiol.*, 1947, **10**, 39–56.

Chapanis, N. P., and Chapanis, A. Cognitive dissonance: five years later. *Psychol. Bull.*, 1964, **61**, 1–22.

Chomsky, N. *Syntactic structures.* The Hague: Mouton, 1957.

Chorazyna, H. Investigation of recent memory of acoustic stimuli in normal dogs. *Bull. Acad. Polon. Sci.*, 1959, **7**, 119–121.

Claparède, E. La genèse de l'hypothèse. *Arch. Psychol., Genève*, 1933, **24**, 1–54.

Cofer, C. N. (ed.), *Verbal Behavior and Learning.* New York: McGraw-Hill, 1961.

Cofer, C. N., and Musgrave, B. S. (eds.), *Verbal learning and verbal behavior.* New York: McGraw-Hill, 1963.

Coombs, C. H. Psychological scaling without a unit of measurement. *Psychol. Rev.*, 1950, **57**, 145–158.

Coombs, C. H., Raiffa, H., and Thrall, R. M. Some views on mathematical models and measurement theory. *Psychol. Rev.*, 1954, **61**, 132–144.

Dashiell, J. F. A quantitative demonstration of animal drive. *J. comp. Psychol.*, 1925, **5**, 205–208.

Dashiell, J. F. Direction orientation in maze running by the white rat. *Comp. Psychol. Monogr.*, 1930, **7**, No. 2.

Davis, R. C. Relation of muscular action potentials to difficulty and frustration. *J. exp. Psychol.*, 1938, **23**, 141–158.

Dember, W. N., and Earl, R. W. Analysis of exploratory, manipulatory and curiosity behaviors. *Psychol. Rev.*, 1957, **64**, 91–96.

Dember, W. N., and Fowler, H. Spontaneous alternation behavior. *Psychol. Bull.*, 1958, **55**, 412–428.

Descoeudres, A. Couleur, forme et nombre. *Arch. Psychol., Genève*, 1914, **14**, 205–241.

Deutsch, J. A. A new type of behaviour theory. *Brit. J. Psychol.*, 1953, **44**, 304–317.

Deutsch, J. A. The inadequacy of the Hullian derivations of reasoning and latent learning. *Psychol. Rev.*, 1956, **63**, 389–399.

Deutsch, J. A.   *The structural basis of behavior.*   Chicago: University of Chicago Press, 1960.

Deutsch, J. A., and Clarkson, J. R.   Reasoning in the hooded rat.   *Quart. J. exp. Psychol.,* 1959, 11, 150–154.

Dewey, J.   *How we think.*   Boston: Heath, 1910.

Diven, K.   Certain determinants in the conditioning of anxiety reactions.   *J. Psychol.,* 1937, 3, 291–308.

Dodge, R.   *Elementary conditions of human variability.*   New York: Columbia University Press, 1927.

Dollard, J., and Miller, N. E.   *Personality and psychotherapy.*   New York: McGraw-Hill, 1950.

Dorcus, M. D.   The establishing of backward associations in forward learning of the maze by albino rats.   *J. comp. Psychol.,* 1932, 8, 11–17.

Dove, C. C., and Thompson, M. E.   Some studies on "insight" in white rats.   *J. genet. Psychol.,* 1943, 63, 235–245.

Duffy, E.   *Activation and behavior.*   New York: Wiley, 1962.

Duhem, P.   *Introduction à la mécanique chimique.*   Paris: Grasse, 1893.

Duncan, C. P.   Recent research on human problem solving.   *Psychol. Bull.,* 1959, 56, 6, 397–429.

Duncker, K.   On problem solving.   *Psychol. Monogr.,* 1945, 58, No. 5, Whole No. 270.

Earl, R. W.   Problem solving and motor skill behaviors under conditions of free choice.   Unpublished Ph.D. thesis, University of Michigan, 1957.

Earl, R. W.   *A theory of stimulus selection.*   Fullerton, Calif.: Human Factors Section, Hughes Ground Systems, Special Document SD61-132, 1961.

Eritsian, M. S.   [Materials on the psychology of deductive inference.]   *Izvestiia Akad. Pedag. Nauk,* 1962, 120, 131–187.

Feather, N. T.   The relationship of persistence at a task to expectation of success and achievement related motives.   *J. abn. soc. Psychol.,* 1961, 63, 552–556.

Festinger, L.   *A theory of cognitive dissonance.*   Stanford: Stanford University Press, 1957.

Festinger, L., and Bramel, D.   The reactions of humans to cognitive dissonance.   In A. Y. Bachrach (ed.), *Experimental foundations of clinical psychology.*   New York: Basic Books, 1962.

Ford, A.   Bioelectrical potentials and mental effort: I. Cardiac effects.   *J. comp. physiol. Psychol.,* 1953, 46, 347–351.

Fraisse, P., Ehrlich, S., and Vurpillot, E.   Etudes de la centration perceptive par la méthode tachistoscopique.   *Arch. Psychol., Genève,* 1956, 35, 193–214.

Frege, G.   *Begriffschrift.*   Halle: Nebert, 1879.

Freud, S.   *Die Traumdeutung.*   Leipzig and Vienna: Deuticke, 1900.   [*The interpretation of dreams.*   In A. A. Brill (ed.), *Selected works of Sigmund Freud.*   New York: Modern Library, 1938.]

Freud, S.   *Der Witz und seine Beziehung zum Unbewussten.*   Leipzig and Vienna: Deuticke, 1905   [*Wit and its relation to the unconscious.*   In A. A. Brill (ed.), *Selected works of Sigmund Freud.*   New York: Modern Library, 1938.]

Freud, S.   Triebe und Triebsschicksale.   *Intern. Z. ärztl. Psychoanal.,* 1915, 3, 84–100.   [Instincts and their vicissitudes.   In S. Freud, *Collected Papers,* Vol. 4.   London: Hogarth, 1925.]

Galton, F. Psychometric experiments. *Brain,* 1879–1880, **2**, 149–162.

Ganz, L., and Riesen, A. H. Stimulus generalization to hue in the dark-reared macaque. *J. comp. physiol. Psychol.,* 1962, **55**, 92–99.

Garner, W. R. *Uncertainty and structure as psychological concepts.* New York: Wiley, 1962.

Garner, W. R., and McGill, W. J. Relation between information and variance analyses. *Psychometrika,* 1956, **21**, 219–228.

Gast, H. Der Umgang mit Zahlen und Zahlgebilden in der frühen Kindheit. *Z. Psychol.,* 1957, **161**, 1–90.

Geer, J. P. van de. *A psychological study of problem solving.* Haarlem: de Toorts, 1957.

Golann, S. E. Psychological study of creativity. *Psychol. Bull.,* 1963, **60**, 548–565.

Goldman-Eisler, F. Speech production and the predictability of words in context. *Quart. J. exp. Psychol.,* 1958, **10**, 96–106.

Goldman-Eisler, F. The predictability of words in context and the length of pauses in speech. *J. Commun.,* 1961, **11**, 95–99.

Goss, A. E., and Wischner, G. J. Vicarious trial and error and related behavior. *Psychol. Bull.,* 1956, **53**, No. 1, 35–54.

Goustard, M., Gréco, P., Matalon, B., and Piaget, J. *La logique des apprentissages.* (*Etudes d'Epistém. Génét.,* X). Paris: Presses Universitaires de France, 1959.

Gréco, P. L'apprentissage dans une situation à structure opératoire concrète. In Gréco, P., and Piaget, J., *Apprentissage et connaissance.* (*Etudes d'Epistém. Génét.,* VII). Paris: Presses Universitaires de France, 1959.

Gréco, P. Recherches sur quelques formes d'inférences arithmétiques et sur la compréhension de l'itération numérique chez l'enfant. In P. Gréco, J. B. Grize, S. Papert, and J. Piaget, *Problèmes de la construction du nombre.* (*Etudes d'Epistém. Génét.,* XI). Paris: Presses Universitaires de France, 1960.

Gréco, P. Quantité et quotité. In Gréco, P., and Morf, A. *Structures numériques élémentaires* (*Etudes d'Epistém. Génét.,* XIII). Paris: Presses Universitaires de France, 1962.

Gréco, P. Le progrès des inférences itératives et des notions arithmétiques chez l'enfant et l'adolescent. In P. Gréco, B. Inhelder, B. Matalon, and J. Piaget. *La formation des raisonnements récurrentials* (*Etudes d'Epistém. Génét.,* XVII) Paris: Presses Universitaires de France, 1963.

Gréco, P., and Piaget, J. *Apprentissage et connaissance* (*Etudes d'Epistém. Génét.,* VII). Paris: Presses Universitaires de France, 1959.

Green, B. F. *Digital computers in research.* New York: McGraw-Hill, 1963.

Grize, J. B. Du groupement au nombre. In P. Gréco, J. B. Grize, S. Papert, and J. Piaget, *Problèmes de la construction du nombre.* (*Etudes d'Epistém. Génét.,* XI). Paris: Presses Universitaires de France, 1960.

Guilford, J. P. The structure of intellect. *Psychol. Bull.,* 1956, No. 4, 267–293.

Guilford, J. P. Three faces of intellect. *Amer. Psychol.,* 1959, **14**, 469–479.

Guthrie, E. R. *The psychology of learning.* New York: Harper, 1st ed., 1935, 2nd ed., 1952.

Guttman, N., and Kalish, H. I. Discriminability and stimulus generalization. *J. exp. Psychol.,* 1956, **51**, 79–88.

Hadley, J. M. Some relationships between electrical signs of central and peripheral activity. II. During mental work. *J. exp. Psychol.,* 1941, **28**, 53–62.

Hamilton, R. V. Psycholinguistic analysis. *J. soc. Psychol.*, 1955, **41**, 271–286.

Harary, F., and Norman, R. Z. *Graph theory as a mathematical model in social science.* Ann Arbor: University of Michigan Institute for Social Research, 1953.

Harlow, H. F. The formation of learning sets. *Psychol. Rev.*, 1949, **56**, 51–65.

Harlow, H. F. Learning set and error factor theory. In S. Koch (ed.), *Psychology: A study of a science*, Vol. 2. New York: McGraw-Hill, 1959.

Harris, J. D. Habituatory response decrement in the intact organism. *Psychol. Bull.*, 1943, **40**, 385–422.

Head, H. *Aphasia and kindred disorders of speech* (2 vols.). New York: Macmillan, 1926.

Hebb, D. O. *The organization of behavior.* New York: Wiley, 1949.

Hebb, D. O. Drives and the C.N.S. (conceptual nervous system). *Psychol. Rev.*, 1955, **62**, 243–254.

Heider, F. Attitudes and cognitive organization. *J. Psychol.*, 1946, **21**, 107–112.

Heidbreder, E. An experimental study of thinking. *Arch. Psychol.*, N.Y., 1924, No. 73.

Herbart, J. F. *Umriss pädagogischer Vorlesungen.* Göttingen: Dieterich, 1835.

Hess, E. H., and Polt, J. M. Pupil size in relation to mental activity during simple problem solving. *Science*, 1964, **143**, 1190–1192.

Hess, W. R. *Diencephalon: autonomic and extrapyramidal functions.* New York: Grune & Stratton, 1954.

Hilgard, E. R. *Theories of learning.* New York: Appleton-Century-Crofts, 1948.

Hobhouse, L. T. *Mind in evolution* (2nd ed.). London: Macmillan, 1915.

Hoijer, H. The relation of language to culture. In A. L. Krober (ed.), *Anthropology today.* Chicago: University of Chicago Press, 1953.

Holst, E. von, and Saint Paul, U. von. Vom Wirkungsgefüge der Triebe. *Naturwissenschaften*, 1960, **47**, 409–422.

Holst, E. von, and Saint Paul, U. von. Electrically controlled behavior. *Scient. Amer.*, 1962, **206**, 50–59.

Hoppe, F. Erfolg und Misserfolg. *Psychol. Forsch.*, 1930, **14**, 1–62.

Horton, D. L., and Kjeldergaard, P. M. An experimental analysis of associative factors in mediated generalization. *Psychol. Monogr.*, 1961, **75**, 11 (Whole No. 515).

Hubel, D. H., and Wiesel, T. N. Receptive fields, binocular interaction and functional architecture in the cat's visual cortex. *J. Physiol.*, 1962, **160**, 106–154.

Hughlings Jackson, J. On the nature of the duality of the brain. *Med. Pr. & Circ.*, 1874, **17**, 19–21.

Hull, C. L. Knowledge and purpose as habit mechanisms. *Psychol. Rev.*, 1930, **37**, 511–525.

Hull, C. L. Goal attraction and directing ideas conceived as habit phenomena. *Psychol. Rev.*, 1931, **38**, 487–506.

Hull, C. L. The goal gradient hypothesis and maze learning. *Psychol. Rev.*, 1932, **39**, 25–43.

Hull, C. L. *Hypnosis and suggestibility, an experimental approach.* New York: Appleton-Century-Crofts, 1933.

Hull, C. L. The concept of the habit-family hierarchy and maze learning. *Psychol. Rev.*, 1934, **41**, 33–52; 134–152.

Hull, C. L. The mechanism of the assembly of behavior segments in novel combinations suitable for problem solution. *Psychol. Rev.*, 1935, **42**, 219–245.

Hull, C. L. The goal-gradient hypothesis applied to some "field-force" problems in the behavior of young children. *Psychol. Rev.*, 1938, **45**, 271–299.

Hull, C. L. *Principles of behavior.* New York: Appleton-Century-Crofts, 1943.

Hull, C. L. *A behavior system.* New Haven: Yale University Press, 1952.

Hunt, J. M. Motivation inherent in information processing and action. In O. J. Harvey (ed.), *Cognitive factors in motivation and social organization.* New York: Ronald Press, 1963.

Inhelder, B., and Piaget, J. *De la logique de l'enfant à la logique de l'adolescent.* Paris: Presses Universitaires de France, 1955. [*The growth of logical thinking from childhood to adolescence.* New York: Basic Books, 1958.]

Inhelder, B., and Piaget, J. De l'itération des actions à la récurrence élémentaire. In P. Gréco, B. Inhelder, B. Matalon, and J. Piaget, *La formation des raisonnements récurrentiels. (Etudes d'Epistém. Génét.,* XVII). Paris: Presses Universitaires de France, 1963.

Irwin, F., and Smith, W. A. S. Value cost and information as determinants of decision. *J. exp. Psychol.*, 1957, **54**, 229–232.

Isaacs, N. Children's "why" questions. In S. Isaacs, *Intellectual growth in young children.* London: Routledge, 1930.

Ivanov-Smolenski, A. G. (ed.), *Na puti k izucheniia vysshikh form neirodinamiki rebenka. (On the way to the investigation of the higher forms of neurodynamics in the child.)* Moscow: Medgiz, 1934.

Ivanov-Smolenski, A. G. [On the study of the collaboration of the first and second signal systems of the cerebral cortex.] *Zh. Vys. Nerv. Deiat.*, 1951, **I(1)**, 55–66.

Ivanov-Smolenski, A. G. (ed.) *Ob'ektivnoe issledovanie vysshei nervnoi deiatel'nosti, osobenno vzaimodeistviia pervoi i vtoroi signal'nykh sistem pri fiziologicheskikh i patologicheskikh usloviiakh u detei (The objective investigation of higher nervous activity, especially of the interaction of the first and second signal systems in physiological and pathological conditions in children).* (*Trudy Inst. Vys. Nerv. Deiat.,* Pathophysiological Series, II.) Moscow: Acad. Sci. USSR, 1956.

Ivanov-Smolenski, A. G. *Opyt ob'ektivnogo izucheniia raboty i vzaimodeistviia signal'nykh sistem golovnogo mozga (An attempt at objective study of the work and interaction of the signal systems of the brain).* Moscow: State Publishing House for Medical Literature, 1963.

Jackson, T. A. Use of the stick as a tool by young chimpanzees. *J. comp. Psychol.*, 1942, **34**, 223–235.

Jacobson, E. Electrical measurements of neuromuscular states during mental activities. I. Imagination of movement involving skeletal muscle. *Amer. J. Physiol.*, 1929, **91**, 567–608.

Jacobson, E. Electrical measurements of neuromuscular states during mental activities. II. Imagination and recollection of various muscular acts. *Amer. J. Physiol.*, 1930, **94**, 22–34.

Jacobson, E. The electrophysiology of mental activities. *Amer. J. Psychol.*, 1932, **44**, 677–694.

James, William. *Principles of Psychology.* New York: Holt, 1890.

Jeffrey, W. E. The effects of verbal and nonverbal responses in mediating an instrumental act. *J. exp. Psychol.*, 1953, **45**, 327–333.

Jenkins, J. J. Mediated associations: paradigms and situations. In C. N. Cofer, and B. S. Musgrave (eds.), *Verbal behavior and learning.* New York: McGraw-Hill, 1963.

Jennings, H. S. *The behavior of lower organisms.* New York: Columbia University Press, 1906.

Johnson, D. M. *The psychology of thought and judgement.* New York: Harper, 1955.

Judson, A. J., Cofer, C. N., and Gelfand, S. Reasoning as an associative process: II. "Direction" in problem solving as a function of prior reinforcement of relevant responses. *Psychol. Rep.,* 1956, **2**, 501–507.

Jung, C. G. *Diagnostische Assoziationsstudien.* Leipzig: Barth, Vol. I, 1906; Vol. II, 1910. [*Studies in word association.* London: Heinemann, 1918.]

Kendler, T. S., and Kendler, H. H. Inferential behavior in children: II. The influence of order of presentation *J. exp. Psychol.,* 1961, **61**, 442–448.

Kersh, B. Y. The adequacy of "meaning" as an explanation for the superiority of learning by independent discovery. *J. educ. Psychol.,* 1958, **49**, 282–292.

Kersh, B. Y. The motivating effect of learning by directed discovery. *J. educ. Psychol.,* 1962, **53**, 65–71.

Kessen, W., and Mandler, G. Anxiety, pain and the inhibition of distress. *Psychol. Rev.,* 1961, **68**, 396–404.

Kimble, G. A. *Hilgard and Marquis' conditioning and learning,* 2nd ed. New York: Appleton-Century-Crofts, 1961.

Koffka, K. *Zur Analyse der Vorstellungen und ihrer Gesetze.* Leipzig: Quelle, 1912.

Koffka, K. *Principles of Gestalt psychology.* New York: Harcourt, Brace, 1935.

Köhler, W. *Intelligenzprüfungen an Menschenaffen.* Berlin: Springer, 1921. [*The mentality of apes,* New York: Harcourt, Brace, 1925.]

Köhler, W. *Gestalt psychology.* New York: Liveright, 1929.

Krasnogorski, I. N. [An attempt to obtain conditioned reflexes in children.] *Russk. Vrach.* No. 36, 1907.

Kuno, Y. The significance of sweating in man. *Lancet,* 1930, **218**, 912–915.

Lacey, J. I., and Smith, R. L. Conditioning and generalization of unconscious anxiety. *Science,* 1954, **120**, 1045–1052.

Ladygina-Kots, N. N. *Konstruktivnaia i orudiinaia deiatel'nost' vysshikh obezian.* (*The constructive and tool-using activity of apes.*) Moscow: Acad. Sci., 1959.

Lanzetta, J. T. Predecisional information processes: some determinants of information acquisition prior to decision-making. Paper read to Symposium on "Predecisional processes in decision-making," Wright-Patterson Air Force Base, 1962.

Lanzetta, J. T., and Kanareff, V. T. Information cost, amount of payoff, and level of aspiration as determinants of information seeking in decision making. *Behav. Sci.,* 1962, **7**, 459–473.

Lashley, K. S. The problem of serial order in behavior. In L. A. Jeffress (ed.), *Cerebral mechanisms in behavior.* New York: Wiley, 1951.

Lawrence, D. H., and De Rivera, J. Evidence for relational transposition. *J. comp. physiol. Psychol.,* 1954, **47**, 465–471.

Lawrence, D. M., and Festinger, L. *Deterrents and reinforcement—the psychology of insufficient reward.* Stanford: Stanford University Press, 1962.

Leeper, R. Cognitive processes. In S. S. Stevens (ed.), *Handbook of experimental psychology.* New York: Wiley, 1951.

Lehr, P. E., Burnett, R. W., and Zim, H. S. *Weather.* New York: Golden Press, 1957.

Lewin, K. *A dynamic theory of personality.* New York: McGraw-Hill, 1935.

Lewin, K., Dembo, T., Festinger, L., and Sears, P. S. Level of aspiration. In J. McV. Hunt (ed.), *Personality and the behavior disorders.* Vol. I. New York: Ronald Press, 1944.

Lipps, T. *Ästhetik.* Hamburg and Leipzig: Franz, 1903–1906.

Logan, F. A. *Incentive: how the conditions of reinforcement affect the performance of rats.* New Haven: Yale University Press, 1960.

Lovaas, O. I. Interaction between verbal and nonverbal behavior. *Child Develp.*, 1961, **32**, 329–336.

Lovaas, O. I. The control of food-intake in children by reinforcement of relevant verbal behavior. *J. abn. soc. Psychol.*, 1964 (in press).

Luce, R. D. *Developments in mathematical psychology.* Glencoe, Ill.: The Free Press, 1960.

Luchins, A. S. Mechanization in problem solving: The effect of Einstellung. *Psychol. Monogr.*, 1942, **54**, No. 248.

Luchins, A. S. A variational approach to the role of set in problem solving. *Proc. XIV Int. Con. Psychol.*, Montreal, 1954, 215–217.

Lukaszewska, I. A study of returning behaviour of white rat on elevated maze. *Acta Biol. Exp.*, 1961, **21**, 253–265.

MacCorquodale, K., and Meehl, P. E. Preliminary suggestions as to a formalization of expectancy theory. *Psychol. Rev.*, 1953, **60**, 55–63.

Maier, N. R. F. Reasoning in white rats. *Comp. Psychol. Monogr.*, 1929, **6**, 93.

Maier, N. R. F. Reasoning in humans. I. On direction. *J. comp. Psychol.*, 1930, **10**, 115–143.

Maier, N. R. F. Reasoning in humans. II. The solution of a problem and its appearance in consciousness. *J. comp. Psychol.*, 1931, **12**, 181–194.

Maier, N. R. F. An aspect of human reasoning. *Brit. J. Psychol.*, 1933, **24**, 144–155.

Maier, N. R. F. Reasoning in humans. III. The mechanisms of equivalent stimuli and of reasoning. *J. exp. Psychol.*, 1945, **35**, 349–360.

Maier, N. R. F., and Schneirla, T. C. *Principles of animal psychology.* New York: McGraw-Hill, 1935.

Malinowski, B. *Sex and repression in savage society.* New York: Harcourt, Brace, 1927.

Malmo, R. B. Anxiety and behavioral arousal. *Psychol. Rev.*, 1957, **64**, 276–287.

Malmo, R. B. Activation: a neuropsychological dimension. *Psychol. Rev.*, 1959, **66**, 367–386.

Maltzman, I. Thinking: from a behavioristic point of view. *Psychol. Rev.*, 1955, **62**, 275–286.

Maltzman, I. Motivation and the direction of thinking. *Psychol. Bull.*, 1962, **59**, 457–467.

Maltzman, I., Fox, J., and Morrisett, L. Some effects of manifest anxiety on mental set. *J. exp. Psychol.*, 1953, **46**, 50–54.

Maltzman, I., and Morrisett, L. Effects of task instruction on solution of different classes of anagrams. *J. exp. Psychol.*, 1953, **45**, 351–354.

Mandelbrot, B. Sur la définition abstraite de quelques degrés d'équilibre. In L. Apostel, B. Mandelbrot, and J. Piaget, *Logique et équilibre.* (*Etudes d'Epistém. Génét.*, II). Paris: Presses Universitaires de France, 1956.

Mandler, G. Response factors in human learning. *Psychol. Rev.*, 1954, **61**, 235–244.

Mandler, G. Comments on Professor Russell's paper. In C. N. Cofer (ed.), *Verbal learning and verbal behavior.* New York: McGraw-Hill, 1961.

Matalon, B. Etude du raisonnement par récurrence sur un modèle physique. In P. Gréco, B. Inhelder, B. Matalon, and J. Piaget, *La formation des raisonnements récurrentiels.* (*Etudes d'Epistém. Génét.*, XVII). Paris: Presses Universitaires de France, 1963.

Max, L. W. An experimental study of the motor theory of consciousness. I. Critique of earlier studies. *J. gen. Psychol.*, 1934, **11**, 112–125.

McClelland, D. C., Atkinson, J. W., Clark, R. A., and Lowell, E. L. *The achievement motive.* New York: Appleton-Century-Crofts, 1953.

McConnell, T. R. Discovery versus authoritative identification in the learning of children. *Univer. of Iowa Studies in Education*, 1934, **9**, No. 5.

McGill, W. J. Multivariate information transmission. *Psychometrika*, 1954, **19**, 97–116.

McKellar, P. *Imagination and thinking: a psychological analysis.* New York: Basic Books, 1957.

McReynolds, P. A restricted conceptualization of human anxiety and motivation. *Psychol. Rep.*, 1956, **2**, 293–312.

Mednick, S. A. The associative basis of the creative process. *Psychol. Rev.*, 1962, **69**, 220–232.

Milerian, E. A. [Psychological characteristics of the transfer of technical skills in older school children.] *Vop. Psikhol.*, 1960, **11**(2), 51–59. [English translation in B. Simon, and J. Simon. *Educational Psychology in the USSR.* Stanford, Calif.: Stanford University Press, 1963.]

Mill, J. *Analysis of the phenomena of the human mind.* London: Baldwin and Cradock, 1829.

Miller, G. A. What is information measurement? *Amer. Psychologist*, 1953, **8**, 3–11.

Miller, G. A. Some psychological studies of grammar. *Amer. Psychologist*, 1962, **17**, 748–762.

Miller, G. A., Galanter, E. H., and Pribram, H. H. *Plans and the structure of behavior.* New York: Holt, 1960.

Miller, N. E. Experimental studies of conflict. In J. McV. Hunt (ed.), *Personality and the behavior disorders.* Vol. 1. New York: Ronald, 1944.

Miller, N. E. Learnable drives and rewards. In S. S. Stevens (ed.), *Handbook of experimental psychology.* New York: Wiley, 1951.

Miller, N. E. Some reflections on the law of effect produce a new alternative to drive reduction. In M. R. Jones (ed.), *Nebraska symposium on motivation 1963.* Lincoln, Neb.: University of Nebraska Press, 1963.

Miller, N. E., and Dollard, J. *Social learning and imitation.* New Haven: Yale University Press, 1941.

Milner, P. M. The cell assembly: Mark II. *Psychol. Rev.*, 1957, **64**, 242–252.

Mittman, L. R., and Terrell, G. An experimental study of curiosity in children. Paper read to Soc. Res. Child Dev., Berkeley, Calif., 1963.

Morel, G., Burgermeister, J. J., and Dick, P. Mémoire dite visuelle et activité cérébrale. *Mschr. Psychiatr. Neurol.*, 1955, **130**, 193–208.

Morf, A., Smedslund, J., Vinh-Bang, and Wohlwill, J. F. *L'apprentissage des structures logiques.* (*Etudes d'Epistém. Génét.*, IX). Paris: Presses Universitaires de France, 1959.

Morgan, C. L. *Introduction to comparative psychology.* London: Walter Scott, 1894.

Morgan, C. T., and Stellar, E. *Physiological psychology* (2nd ed.). New York: McGraw-Hill, 1950.

Morozova, N. G. [The psychological conditions for the arousal and modification of interest in children in the process of reading popular scientific literature.] *Izvestiia Akad. Pedag. Nauk,* 1955, **73,** 100–149.

Morris, C. R. *Signs, language and behavior.* New York: Prentice-Hall, 1946.

Morris, C. R. Prospects for a new synthesis: science and the humanities as complementary activities. *Daedalus,* 1958, **87,** 94–101.

Mowrer, O. H. On the dual nature of learning: a re-interpretation of "conditioning" and "problem-solving." *Harvard Educ. Rev.,* 1947, **17,** 102–148.

Mowrer, O. H. The psychologist looks at language. *Amer. Psychol.,* 1954, **9,** 660–694.

Muenzinger, K. F. Vicarious trial and error at a point of choice: I. The general survey of its relation to learning efficiency. *J. genet. Psychol.,* 1938, **53,** 75–86.

Müller, F. M. *The science of thought* (2 vols.). New York: Scribner, 1887.

Müller, G. E. Zur Analyse der Gedächtnistätigkeit und des Vorstellungsverlaufs. III. Teil. *Z. Psychol.,* 1913, Ergbd. 8.

Müller, G. E. Zur Analyse der Gedächtnistätigkeit und des Vorstellungsverlaufs. II. Teil. *Z. Psychol.,* 1917, Ergbd. 9.

Mundy-Castle, A. C. Theta and beta rhythm in the electroencephalogram of normal adults. *EEG clin. Neurophysiol.,* 1951, **3,** 477–486.

Musselman, D. R. Free choice behavior as a function of stimulus changes along three dimensions of complexity. Unpublished Ph.D. thesis, Claremont Graduate School, 1963.

Nagel, E. *The structure of science.* New York: Harcourt, Brace, 1961.

Napalkov, A. V. [Physiological characteristics of some complex forms of behavior.] *Vop. Psikhol.,* 1961, **7**(6), 136–146. [English translation in *Sov. Psychol. Psychiatr.,* 1963, **1,** 3–9.]

Naroditskaia, G. D. [The formation in childhood of new conditioned connections without prior elaboration.] In A. G. Ivanov-Smolenski (ed.), *Na puti k izucheniia vysshikh form neirodinamiki rebenka.* (*On the way to studying the higher forms of neurodynamics in the child.*) Moscow: Medgiz, 1934.

Neilson, J. M. *Agnosia, apraxia, aphasia. Their value in cerebral localization.* New York: Hoeber, 1946 (2nd ed.).

Newell, A., Shaw, J. C., and Simon, H. A. Empirical explorations of the logic theory machine: a case study of heuristic. *Proc. Western Joint Comput. Conf.,* 1957, **11,** 218–230.

Newell, A., Shaw, J. C., and Simon, H. A. Elements of a theory of human problem solving. *Psychol. Rev.,* 1958, **65,** 151–166.

Newell, A., Shaw, J. C., and Simon, H. A. A variety of intelligent behavior in a general problem solver. In M. C. Yovits and S. Cameron (eds.), *Self-organizing systems.* London and New York: Pergamon, 1960.

Newell, A., and Simon, H. A. The simulation of human thought. In W. Dennis (ed.), *Current trends in psychological theory.* Pittsburgh: University of Pittsburgh Press, 1961.

Ogden, C. K., and Richards, I. A. *The meaning of meaning.* New York: Harcourt, Brace, 1923.

Oléron, P. *Recherches sur le développement mental des sourds-muets.* Paris: Centre National de la Recherche Scientifique, 1957.

Ore, O. *Graphs and their uses.* New York: Random House, 1963.

Osgood, C. E. The nature and measurement of meaning. *Psychol. Bull.,* 1952, **49,** 197–237.

Osgood, C. E. *Method and theory in experimental psychology.* New York: Oxford University Press, 1953.

Osgood, C. E. Motivational dynamics of language behavior. In M. R. Jones (ed.), *Nebraska Symposium on Motivation 1957.* Lincoln, Neb.: University of Nebraska Press, 1957.

Osgood, C. E. On understanding and creating sentences. *Amer. Psychologist,* 1963, **18,** 735–751.

Osgood, C. E., Suci, G. J., and Tannenbaum, P. H. *The measurement of meaning.* Urbana, Ill.: University of Illinois Press, 1957.

Osgood, C. E., and Tannenbaum, P. H. The principle of congruity in the prediction of attitude change. *Psychol. Rev.,* 1955, **62,** 42–55.

Parsons, C. Inhelder and Piaget's, "The growth of logical thinking." II. A logician's viewpoint. *Brit. J. Psychol.,* 1960, **51,** 75–84.

Pavlov, I. P. *Conditioned reflexes.* Oxford: Oxford University Press, 1927.

Pavlov, I. P. *Lectures on conditioned reflexes.* New York: Liveright, 1928.

Peel, E. A. Curiosity and interest in motivating school learning. *Proc. 14th. Int. Cong. Appl. Psychol.,* 1961, Vol. 3, 153–160.

Penfield, W., and Jasper, H. *Epilepsy and the functional anatomy of the human brain.* Boston: Little, Brown, 1954.

Perky, C. W. An experimental study of imagination. *Amer. J. Psychol.,* 1910, **21,** 422–452.

Phillips, L. W. Mediated verbal similarity as a determinant of the generalization of a conditioned GSR. *J. exp. Psychol.,* 1958, **55,** 56–62.

Piaget, J. *Le langage et la pensée chez l'enfant.* Neuchâtel: Delachaux & Niestlé, 1923. [*The language and thought of the child.* New York: Harcourt, Brace, 1926.]

Piaget, J. *Le jugement et le raisonnement chez l'enfant.* Neuchâtel: Delachaux & Niestlé, 1925. [*Judgement and reasoning in the child.* New York: Harcourt, Brace, 1928.]

Piaget, J. *La naissance de l'intelligence chez l'enfant.* Neuchâtel: Delachaux & Niestlé, 1936. [*The origins of intelligence in children.* New York: International Universities Press, 1952.]

Piaget, J. *La construction du réel chez l'enfant.* Neuchâtel: Delachaux & Niestlé, 1937. [*The construction of reality in the child.* New York: Basic Books, 1954.]

Piaget, J. Le mécanisme du développement mental et les lois du groupement des opérations. *Arch. Psychol., Genève,* 1941, **28,** 215–285.

Piaget, J. *La formation du symbole chez l'enfant.* Neuchâtel: Delachaux & Niestlé, 1945. [*Play, dreams and imitation in childhood.* New York: Norton, 1951.]

Piaget, J. *La psychologie de l'intelligence.* Paris: Colin, 1947. [*The psychology of intelligence.* London: Routledge & Kegan Paul, 1950.]

Piaget, J. *Traité de logique.* Paris: Colin, 1949(a).

Piaget, J. Le problème neurologique de l'intériorisation des actions en opérations réversibles. *Arch. Psychol., Genève,* 1949, **32,** 241–258(b).

Piaget, J. Les relations entre l'intelligence et l'affectivité dans le développement de l'enfant. *Bull. Psychol., Paris,* 1953–1954, **7**, 143–150; 346–361; 522–535; 699–701.

Piaget, J. Logique et équilibre dans les comportements du sujet. In L. Apostel, B. Mandelbrot, and J. Piaget, *Logique et équilibre.* (*Etudes d'Epistém. Génét.,* II). Paris: Presses Universitaires de France, 1957.

Piaget, J. Apprentissage et connaissance. First part in P. Gréco and J. Piaget. *Apprentissage et connaissance.* (*Etudes d'Epistém. Génét.,* VII). Second part in M. Goustard, P. Gréco, B. Matalon, and J. Piaget. *La logique des apprentissages.* (*Etudes d'Epistém. Génét.,* X.) Paris: Presses Universitaires de France, 1959.

Piaget, J. *Les mécanismes perceptifs: modèles probabilistes, analyse génétique, relations avec l'intelligence.* Paris: Presses Universitaires de France, 1961.

Piaget, J. *Comments on L. S. Vygotsky's "Thought and language."* Cambridge, Mass.: M.I.T. Press; New York: Wiley, 1962.

Piaget, J., and Inhelder, B. *Le développement des quantités chez l'enfant.* Neuchâtel: Delachaux & Niestlé, 1941.

Piaget, J., and Inhelder, B. *La représentation de l'espace chez l'enfant.* Paris: Presses Universitaires de France, 1948. [*The child's conception of space.* London: Routledge and Kegan Paul, 1960.]

Piaget, J., and Inhelder, B. *La genèse des structures logiques élémentaires: classifications et sériations.* Neuchâtel: Delachaux & Niestlé, 1959. [*The early growth of logic in the child.* New York: Harper & Row, 1964.]

Piaget, J., and Inhelder, B. Le développement des images mentales chez l'enfant. *J. Psychol. norm. path.,* 1962, **59**, 75–108.

Piaget, J., and Lambercier, M. Recherches sur le développement des perceptions. II. Le problème de la comparaison visuelle des hauteurs à distances variables dans le plan fronto-parallèle. *Arch. Psychol., Genève,* 1942–1943, **79**, 173–254.

Piaget, J., and Szeminska, A. *La genèse du nombre chez l'enfant.* Neuchâtel: Delachaux & Niestlé, 1941. [*The child's conception of number.* New York: Humanities Press, 1952.]

Pitts, W., and McCulloch, W. S. How we know universals; the perception of auditory and visual forms. *Bull. math. Biophys.,* 1947, **9**, 127–147.

Poincaré, H. *La science et l'hypothèse.* Paris: Flammarion, 1902. [*Science and hypothesis.* New York: Dover, 1952.]

Poincaré, H. *La valeur de la science.* Paris: Flammarion, 1914.

Ponomarev, I. A. *Psikhologiia tvorcheskogo myshleniia.* [*The psychology of creative thinking.*] Moscow: Acad. Pedag. Sci., 1960.

Posner, M. I. An informational approach to thinking. Unpublished Ph.D. thesis, University of Michigan, 1962.

Postman, L., and Crutchfield, R. S. The interaction of need, set, and stimulus-structure in a cognitive task. *Amer. J. Psychol.,* 1952, **65**, 196–217.

Prokasy, W. F. The acquisition of observing responses in the absence of differential external reinforcement. *J. comp. physiol. Psychol.,* 1956, **49**, 131–134.

Razran, G. H. S. Semantic, syntactic, and phonetographic generalization of verbal conditioning. *Psychol. Bull.,* 1939, **36**, 578(a).

Razran, G. H. S. Studies in configural conditioning: I. Historical and preliminary experimentation. *J. gen. Psychol.,* 1939, **21**, 307–330(b).

Razran, G. Semantic and phonetographic generalizations of salivary conditioning to verbal stimuli. *J. exp. Psychol.*, 1949, **39**, 642–652.

Rees, H. J., and Israel., H. E. An investigation of the establishment and operation of mental sets. *Psychol. Monogr.*, 1935, **46**, No. 6 (Whole No. 210, 1–26).

Rey, A. L'évolution du comportement interne dans la représentation du mouvement. *Arch. Psychol.*, *Genève*, 1948, **32**, 209–234.

Rey, A. Les images mentales en psychophysiologie. *Dialectica*, 1958, **12**, 130–145.

Reynolds, G. S. Attention in the pigeon. *J. exp. Anal. Behav.*, 1961, **4**, 203–208.

Rhine, R. J. The effect on problem solving of success or failure as a function of cue specificity. *J. exp. Psychol.*, 1957, **53**, 121–125.

Ritchie, B. F. Explanatory powers of the fractional antedating response mechanism. *Brit. J. Psychol.*, 1959, **50**, 1–15.

Roginski, G. Z. *Navyki i zachatki intellektual'nykh deistvii u antropoidov (shimpanze)*. (*Habits and beginnings of intellectual activity in apes (chimpanzees)*.) Leningrad: Leningrad University Press, 1948.

Rosenberg, M. J. An analysis of affective-cognitive consistency. In M. J. Rosenberg, C. I. Hovland, et al., *Attitude organization and change*. New Haven: Yale University Press, 1960.

Rosenblatt, F. The perceptron: a probabilistic model for information storage and organization in the brain. *Psychol. Rev.*, 1958, **65**, 386–408.

Rubinshtein, S. L. *O myshlenii i putiakh ego issledovaniia* [*On thinking and the ways of investigating it*]. Moscow: Acad. Sci. USSR, 1958.

Rubinshtein, S. L. (ed.). *Protsess myshleniia i zakonomernosti analiza, sinteza i obobshcheniia (The process of thinking and the laws governing analysis, synthesis and generalization)*. Moscow: Acad. Sci. USSR, 1960.

Ruch, T. C. Motor systems. In S. S. Stevens (ed.), *Handbook of experimental psychology*. New York: Wiley, 1951.

Russell, B. *Introduction to mathematical philosophy*. London: Allen and Unwin, 1919.

Russell, B. *Inquiry into meaning and truth*. New York: Norton, 1940.

Samson, E. *Information theory: questions and uncertainties* (AFCRC Technical Report 54-1). Cambridge, Mass.: Air Force Cambridge Research Center, 1954.

Saugstad, P. Problem-solving as dependent on availability of functions. *Brit. J. Psychol.*, 1955, **46**, 191–198.

Saugstad, P. An analysis of Maier's pendulum problem. *J. exp. Psychol.*, 1957, **54**, 168–179.

Schifferli, P. Etude par enregistrement photographique de la motricité oculaire dans l'exploration, dans la reconnaissance, et dans la représentation visuelles. *Mschr. Psychiatr. Neurol.*, 1953, **126**, 65–118.

Sechenov, I. M. [Elements of thought.] *Vestnik Evropy.*, 1878, **3**, 39–107. [English translation in I. Sechenov, *Collected works*. Moscow and Leningrad: Medgiz, 1935.]

Selz, O. *Über die Gesetze des geordneten Denkverlaufs*. Stuttgart: Spemann, 1913.

Selz, O. *Zur Psychologie des produktiven Denkens und des Irrtums*. Bonn: Cohen, 1922.

Seward, J. P. The sign of a symbol: a reply to Professor Allport. *Psychol. Rev.*, 1948, **55**, 277–296.

Seward, J. P. An experimental analysis of latent learning. *J. exp. Psychol.*, 1949, **39**, 177–186.

Seward, J. P., and Levy, N. Sign learning as a factor in extinction. *J. exp. Psychol.*, 1949, **39**, 660–668.

Shannon, C. E., and Weaver, W. *Mathematical theory of communication.* Urbana, Ill.: University of Illinois Press, 1949.

Shaw, W. A., and Kline, L. H. A study of muscle action potentials during the attempted solution by children of problems of increasing difficulty. *J. exp. Psychol.*, 1947, **37**, 146–158.

Sherrington, C. S. *Integrative action of the nervous system.* Cambridge: Cambridge University Press; New Haven: Yale University Press, 1906.

Shepard, R. N., Hovland, C. I., and Jenkins, H. M. Learning and memorization of classifications. *Psychol. Monogr.*, 1961, **75** (13, Whole No. 517).

Shevarev, P. A. [Generalized associations.] *Vop. Psikhol.*, 1958, 4(1), 16–23.

Simon, B., and Simon, J. *Educational psychology in the USSR.* Stanford, Calif.: Stanford University Press, 1963.

Skinner, B. F. The concept of the reflex in the description of behavior. *J. gen. Psychol.*, 1931, **5**, 427–458.

Skinner, B. F. *The behavior of organisms.* New York: Appleton-Century-Crofts, 1938.

Skinner, B. F. Are theories of learning necessary? *Psychol. Rev.*, 1950, **57**, 193–216.

Skinner, B. F. *Science and human behavior.* New York: Macmillan, 1953.

Skinner, B. F. *Verbal behavior.* New York: Appleton-Century-Crofts, 1957.

Smedslund, J. Apprentissage de la notion de la conservation et de la transitivité du poids. In A. Morf, J. Smedslund, Vinh-Bang, and J. F. Wohlwill. *L'apprentissage des structures logiques.* [*Etudes d'Epistém. Génét.*, IX]. Paris: Presses Universitaires de France, 1959.

Smedslund, J. The acquisition of conservation of substance and weight in children. II. External reinforcement of conservation of weight and of the operations of addition and subtraction. *Scand. J. Psychol.*, 1961, **2**, 71–84(a).

Smedslund, J. The acquisition of conservation of substance and weight in children. III. Extinction of conservation of weight acquired "normally" and by means of empirical controls on a balance. *Scand. J. Psychol.*, 1961, **2**, 85–87(b).

Smedslund, J. The acquisition of conservation of substance and weight in children. V. Practice in conflict situations without external reinforcement. *Scand. J. Psychol.*, 1961, **2**, 156–160(c).

Smedslund, J. The acquisition of conservation of substance and weight in children. VI. Practice on continuous versus discontinuous material in problem situations without external reinforcement. *Scand. J. Psychol.*, 1961, **2**, 203–210(d).

Smedslund, J. Development of concrete transitivity of length in children. *Child Develpm.*, 1963, **34**, 389–405.

Smith, K. Curare drugs and total paralysis. *Psychol. Rev.*, 1964, **71**, 77–79.

Smith, S. M., Brown, H. O., Toman, J. E. P., and Goodman, L. S. The lack of cerebral effects of d-tubocurarine. *Anesthesiology*, 1947, **8**, 1–14.

Sokolov, A. N. [On the speech mechanisms of intellectual activity.] *Izvestiia Akad. Pedag. Nauk*, 1956, **81**, 65–98.

Sokolov, A. N. [The dynamics and functions of internal speech (latent articulation) in the thought process.] *Izvestiia Akad. Pedag. Nauk*, 1960, **113**, 149–182.

Sokolov, E. N.   [Modeling processes in the central nervous system of animals and man.]   In I. S. Beritashvili (ed.), *Gagrskie Besedy [Gagra Symposia]*, IV. Tbilisi: Acad. Sci. Georgian SSR, 1963.

Spearman, C.   *The nature of "intelligence" and the principles of cognition.*   London: Macmillan, 1923.

Spence, K. W.   *Behavior theory and conditioning.*   New Haven: Yale University Press, 1956.

Sperry, R. W.   Neurology and the mind-brain problem.   *Amer. Scientist*, 1952, 40, 291–312.

Staats, C. K., and Staats, A. W.   Meaning established by classical conditioning. *J. exp. Psychol.*, 1957, 54, 74–80.

Staats, A. W., Staats, C. K., and Heard, W. G.   Denotative meaning established by classical conditioning.   *J. exp. Psychol.*, 1961, 61, 300–303.

Stevens, S. S.   On the theory of scales of measurement.   *Science*, 1946, 103, 677–680.

Suchman, J. R.   Training children in scientific inquiry.   Paper read to Soc. Res. Child Dev., Bethesda, Md., 1959.

Suchman, J. R.   Inquiry training: building skills for autonomous discovery. *Merrill-Palmer Quart.*, 1961, 147–169.

Suchman, J. R.   The inquiry process and the elementary school child.   Paper read to Amer. Educ. Res. Assoc., Atlantic City, N.J., 1962.

Suppes, P., and Zinnes, J. L.   Basic measurement theory.   In R. D. Luce, R. R. Bush, and E. Galanter (eds.), *Handbook of mathematical psychology.*   Vol. 1. New York: Wiley, 1963.

Tannenbaum, P. H.   Attitudes toward source and concepts as factors in attitude change through communications.   Unpublished Ph.D. thesis, University of Illinois, 1953.

Taylor, J. G.   *The behavioral basis of perception.*   New Haven: Yale University Press, 1962.

Taylor, J. G., and Reichlin, B.   Vicarious trial and error.   *Psychol. Rev.*, 1951, 58, 389–402.

Thorndike, E. L.   *Animal intelligence.*   New York: Macmillan, 1898.

Thorpe, W. H.   *Learning and instinct in animals.*   London: Methuen, 1956.

Thorson, A. M.   The relation of tongue movements to internal speech.   *J. exp. Psychol.*, 1925, 8, 1–32.

Thurstone, L. L.   *The nature of intelligence.*   New York: Humanities Press, 1924.

Tinbergen, N.   *The study of instinct.*   Oxford: Oxford University Press, 1951.

Tinbergen, N., and Perdeck, A. C.   On the stimulus situation releasing the begging response in the newly hatched Herring Gill chick (*Larus A. Argentatus Pont.*).   *Behaviour*, 1950, 3, 1–38.

Tolman, E. C.   *Purposive behavior in animals and men.*   New York: Appleton-Century, 1932.

Tolman, E. C.   Prediction of vicarious trial and error by means of the schematic sowbug.   *Psychol. Rev.*, 1939, 46, 318–336.

Tolman, E. C.   Principles of performance.   *Psychol. Rev.*, 1955, 62, 315–324.

Tolman, E. C.   Principles of purposive behavior.   In S. Koch (ed.), *Psychology: a study of science.*   Vol. 2.   New York: McGraw-Hill, 1959.

Tolman, E. C., and Honzik, C. H.   Insight in rats.   *Univ. Calif. Publ. Psychol.*, 1930, 4, 215–232.

Toman, J. E. P.   The electroencephalogram during mental effort.   *Fed. Proc.*, 1943, 2, 49.

Trautscholdt, M. Experimentelle Untersuchungen über die Association der Vor-stellungen. *Phil. St.*, 1883, **1**, 213–250.

Triger, R. D. [The conditions for the coming to the fore of the scientific con-tent of an educational story in older pre-school children.] *Izvestiia Akad. Pedag. Nauk*, 1955, **73**, 165–185.

Tyler, D. B., Goodman, J., and Rothman, T. The effects of experimental insom-nia on the rate of potential changes in the brain. *Amer. J. Physiol.*, 1947, **149**, 185–193.

Usnadze, D. Zum Problem der Relationserfassung beim Tier. *Arch. ges. Psy-chol.*, 1927, **60**, 361–390.

Uttley, A. M. A theory of the mechanism of learning based on the computation of conditioned probabilities. *Proc. I. Int. Cong. Cybernet.*, 1956, 830–856.

Valentine, W. Visual perception in the white rat. *J. comp. Psychol.*, 1928, **8**, 369–375.

Vatsuro, E. G. *Issledovanie vysshei nervnoi deiatel'nosti antropoida (shimpanze).* (*An investigation of the higher nervous activity of the ape (chimpanzee).*) Moscow: Acad. Med. Sci., 1948.

Vatsuro, E. G. *Uchenie I.P. Pavlova o vysshei nervnoi deiatel'nosti (The teach-ing of I.P. Pavlov on higher nervous activity).* Moscow: Uchpedgiz, 1955.

Vincent, M. Rôle des données perceptives dans l'abstraction. *Enfance*, 1956, **9**, 1–20.

Vincent, M. Sur le rôle du langage à un niveau élémentaire de pensée abstraite. *Enfance*, 1957, **10**, 443–464.

Vincent, M. Les classifications d'objets et leur formulation verbale chez l'enfant. *Psychol. Franç.*, 1959, **4**, 190–204.

Volkova, V. D. [On some peculiarities of the formation of conditioned reflexes to speech stimuli in children.] *Fiziol. Zh. SSSR*, 1953, **39**(5), 540–548.

Volkova, V. D. [On the corrective influence of the environment in the formation of conditioned reflexes to certain speech stimuli.] *Zh. Vys. Nerv. Deiat.*, 1957, **7**, 525–533.

Vygotski, L. S. *Myshlenie i rech'.*, Moscow: Acad. Pedag. Sci., 1956. [*Thought and speech*, Cambridge, Mass.: MIT Press; New York: Wiley, 1962.]

Washburn, M. F. *The animal mind.* New York: Macmillan, 1926 (3rd ed.).

Watson, J. B. *Behaviorism.* Chicago: University of Chicago Press, 1924.

Wehling, H. E., and Prokasy, W. F. Role of food deprivation in the acquisition of the observing response. *Psychol. Rep.*, 1962, **10**, 399–407.

Weiss, P. Self-differentiation of the basic patterns of coordination. *Comp. Psy-chol. Monogr.*, 1941, **17**, 1–96.

Wertheimer, M. *Productive thinking.* New York: Harper, 1945.

White, M. M. The relation of bodily tension to electrical resistance. *J. exp. Psychol.*, 1930, **13**, 267–277.

Whitehead, A. N., and Russell, B. *Principia mathematica.* Cambridge: Cam-bridge University Press, Vol. I, 1910. Vols. II and III, 1912.

Whorf, B. L. Science and linguistics. *Tech. Rev.*, 1940, **42**, 3–7.

Whorf, B. L. Language and logic. *Tech. Rev.*, 1941, **43**, 18–23(a).

Whorf, B. L. The relation of habitual thought and behavior to language. In L. Spier (ed.), *Language, culture and personality.* Menasha, Wis.: Sapir Mem. Pub. Fund, 1941(b).

Wickens, D. D. Voluntary and involuntary finger conditioning. *Psychol. Bull.*, 1938, **35**, 716.

Wiener, N. *Cybernetics.* New York: Wiley, 1958.

Wolfe, J. B., and Spragg, S. D. S. Some experimental tests of reasoning in white rats. *J. comp. Psychol.,* 1934, **18,** 455–469.

Wolpe, J. *Psychotherapy by reciprocal inhibition.* Stanford, Calif.: Stanford University Press, 1958.

Woodworth, R. S. *Experimental psychology.* New York: Holt, 1938.

Yerkes, R. M. The mental life of monkeys and apes: a study of ideational behavior. *Behav. Monogr.,* 1916, **3,** 1–145.

Yule, G. U., and Kendall, M. G. *An introduction to the theory of statistics.* London: Griffin, 1947.

Zankov, L. V. [Combination of the verbal and the visual in teaching.] *Vop. Psikhol.,* 1957, **3**(6), 40–57. [English translation in B. Simon and J. Simon (eds.), *Educational psychology in the USSR.* Stanford, Calif.: Stanford University Press, 1963.]

Zaporozhets, A. V. Development of voluntary movements. *Proc. XIV Int. Cong. Psychol., Montreal,* 1954, 187–188.

Zaporozhets, A. V. [The role of orienting activity and the image in the formation and persistence of voluntary movements.] In L. G. Voronin et al. (eds.), *Orientirovochny refleks i orientirovochno-issledovatel'skaia deiatel'nost'.* (*The orienting reflex and exploratory behavior.*) Moscow: Acad. Pedag. Sci., 1958.

Zaporozhets, A. V. *Razvitie proizvol'nykh dvizhenii* (*The development of voluntary movements*). Moscow: Acad. Pedag. Sci., 1960.

Zinchenko, V. P. [On the formation of a conditioned image.] In L. G. Voronin et al. (eds.), *Orientirovochny refleks i orientirovochno-issledovatel'skaia deiatel'nost'.* (*The orienting reflex and exploratory behavior.*) Moscow: Acad. Pedag. Sci., 1958.

Zipf, G. K. *Human behavior and the principle of least effort.* Reading, Mass.: Addison-Wesley, 1949.

Name index

Subject index